DAUGHTERS
OF THE NORTH

By the same author

Josephine Tey: A Life

DAUGHTERS
OF THE NORTH

Jean Gordon and Mary, Queen of Scots

Jennifer Morag Henderson

SANDSTONE PRESS

First published in Great Britain in 2022 by
Sandstone Press Ltd
PO Box 41
Muir of Ord
IV6 7YX
Scotland

www.sandstonepress.com

ISBN: 978-1-913207-75-5
ISBNe: 978-1-913207-76-2

Sandstone Press is committed to a sustainable future.
This book is made from Forest Stewardship Council ® certified paper.

The publisher acknowledges support from Creative Scotland
towards the publication of this title.

Cover design by Daniel Benneworth-Gray
Typeset by Iolaire, Newtonmore
Printed and bound by TJ Books Limited, Padstow, Cornwall

Contents

Contents

Acknowledgements

Researching and writing this book is a project that has taken me many years. One unintended consequence of this is that I have lost touch with several people who helped me in the early stages. I would like to extend a general 'thank you' to everyone who encouraged me in my interest in Jean Gordon, Bothwell and Mary, Queen of Scots: help and enthusiasm is not as common as you might think and I am grateful to everyone who took the time to answer my many questions, talk about Scottish history and recommend where and how I might continue my research.

I would like to acknowledge the grant I received from the Society of Authors' Authors' Foundation, which helped me during the final stages of research and writing, particularly with attendance at a course on palaeography. The grant was a huge boost, not only for the financial help but also because of the Foundation's belief in the project and in my abilities.

I would like to acknowledge the institutions where I carried out research, including the National Library of Scotland, the Highland Archive Centre, Inverness Library and the Museum of Edinburgh. Other important places I visited for research included Spynie Palace and Darnaway Castle; thank you to the staff and owners there. Thank you to Scott Morrison, manager at Dunrobin Castle, and to the Sutherland Dunrobin Castle Trust, especially for help with photographs. Thank you to the Altyre Estate for permission to use and reproduce manuscripts. I would also like to thank the Marie Stuart Society for their support.

I would particularly like to thank Rosalind Marshall for her help in transcribing and translating original documents relating to Jean, and for her interest and encouragement. I would like to thank Fred Bothwell and Alastair Buchan-Hepburn for permission to quote from their private emails to me, and Paul Macdonald for permission to use information from his work at Macdonald Armouries. Special thanks to Pól Arni Holm for discussion of the song "Sinklar's Vísa", and to him and his band Hamradun for inspiration. Thank you also to Sarah Fraser.

Thank you to S.G. MacLean for reading a draft of the book and making several helpful suggestions, some of which I even listened to. Thank you to Professor David Worthington of the University of the Highlands and Islands for sharing his wide knowledge of Highland history, and for his patience with my many questions. And thank you both, Shona and David, for our walks and discussions of Scottish history.

Many thanks to my publishers Sandstone Press and all their dedicated staff, including Robert Davidson, Moira Forsyth, Kay Farrell and Ceris Jones.

Thank you to my sister Kathryn, who gave me important help in identifying 16th and 17th century artists. Thank you to Stuart Wildig, who is not only a supportive friend but has also been a one-man IT department with infinite patience even when I suggested going back to a typewriter.

Finally, thank you to my family, who have been there the whole time, especially my mum Christine, my husband Andrew and our perfect sons Alec and Neal. After two children and a worldwide pandemic I am very glad that I have finally achieved what I set out to do, and only my family really know what that has been like. Thank you for spending all your holidays climbing round ruined castles.

List of Illustrations

HUNTLY CASTLE
Huntly Castle, Aberdeenshire. Jean's childhood home was substantially remodelled in her lifetime by her nephew. Photo by Jennifer Morag Henderson

FINDLATER CASTLE
Findlater castle, near Portsoy, Banff. The former Ogilvie stronghold was held by Jean's brother against Mary, Queen of Scots. Photo by Jennifer Morag Henderson.

BOTHWELL AND JEAN PORTRAITS
The marriage miniatures of Lady Jean Gordon, Countess of Bothwell and James Hepburn, 4th Earl of Bothwell. Scottish National Portrait Gallery.

MARY QUEEN OF SCOTS
Portrait of Mary, Queen of Scots, from Dunrobin Castle. This painting is known as the 'Orkney portrait': several versions of this image exist, which appear to be based on an earlier miniature. Sutherland Dunrobin Castle Trust.

JOHN KNOX
Stained glass window showing preacher John Knox. From the John Knox House in Edinburgh.

ALEXANDER
Alexander Gordon, 12th Earl of Sutherland: Jean's second husband. Sutherland Dunrobin Castle Trust.

SPYNIE PALACE
Spynie Palace, near Elgin. Bothwell's childhood home, to which he later fled after his defeat at Carberry. Also the site of imprisonment for Jean's brother-in-law the Master of Forbes, and the English spy Rokesby. Photo by Jennifer Morag Henderson.

ALEX OGILVIE FRONTISPIECE
The first page of 'A collection of the names of herbes...' written by Alex Ogilvie, dated 1587. The initials 'R' and 'K' have been added in different ink. National Library of Scotland / Altyre Estates.

SINCLAIR GIRNIGOE
Sinclair-Girnigoe Castle, the home of the Earls of Caithness. The impressive ruin shows the remains of the new castle remodelled by Wicked Earl George. Photo by Jennifer Morag Henderson.

ALEXANDER OF NAVIDALE
Sir Alexander Gordon, Knight of Navidale. Jean's youngest son. Painting attributed to Adam de Colone, 1631. Sutherland Dunrobin Castle Trust.

ROBERT GORDON
Sir Robert Gordon, the Tutor of Sutherland, c1621. Jean's middle son, the family historian. Sutherland Dunrobin Castle Trust.

LETTER FROM JEAN TO ROBERT
Letter from Jean Gordon to her son Robert, discussing servants, Caithness and estate business. 'Loving son, I have written these few lines...' Showing her handwriting and spelling in the old Scots style. National Library of Scotland / Altyre Estates.

JEAN GORDON
Lady Jean Gordon, Countess of Sutherland. Attributed to George Jameson, c1620. Sutherland Dunrobin Castle Trust.

MACKAY'S REGIMENT
Mackay's regiment, landing on the continent, 1630. The regiment of Jean's grandson, Donald Mackay, shown wearing their distinctive plaids. Image based on an old German print.

BOYNE CASTLE PANORAMA
The author at the romantic ruins of Alex Ogilvie's Boyne Castle. Photo by Andrew Thomson.

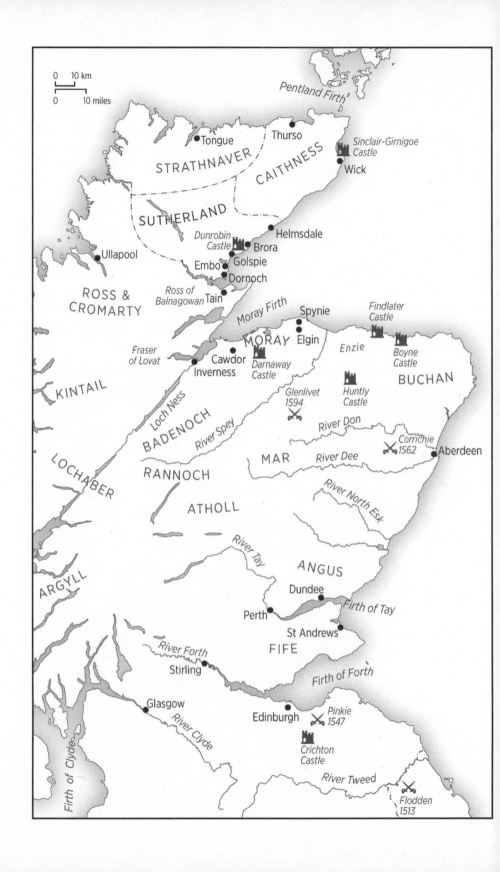

Jean Gordon

This is the story of Jean Gordon, her family and the land they lived in.

Jean Gordon was one of Mary, Queen of Scots' ladies. Her long life is a unique love story, full of action from regicide to clan warfare. Jean's biography covers a period of great change in Scottish history from the time of the Reformation to the opening up of the New World, ranging across the whole of Scotland from the Borders to the Highlands, from the royal court to the wild Mackay clan lands. Jean's story is both grand, in her and her family's involvement in politics; and personal, with her story of husbands, children and romance.

Jean was one woman caught up in the events around Mary, Queen of Scots; one tiny piece of the religious struggles that tore Europe apart; a still centre around which history raged. She navigated the storm of history with unfailing loyalty to her own Gordon family – and managed to carve out her own luck. It is sometimes said that everyone at the court of Mary, Queen of Scots became cursed: Mary's servants were murdered, her supporters died in battle, even those opposed to her were struck down. Mary herself was imprisoned for years and beheaded on the orders of her own cousin. Jean Gordon, and the man she loved, Alex Ogilvie, crawled out of the wreckage of Mary's court to finally find happiness together – but only at the end of long lives full of adventure.

Jean is best remembered today as the first wife of the notorious James Hepburn, Earl of Bothwell. She was Bothwell's alibi for the night of the murder of Darnley, Mary, Queen of Scots' second husband. Jean then agreed to divorce her husband so that Bothwell could pursue and marry Mary herself and become King of Scots. This makes Jean Gordon often a footnote in histories of Mary, Queen of Scots, and it was the idea of Jean's unlikely love story and happy ending with Alex Ogilvie that first attracted me to the idea of writing her biography. But this would not have been enough to hold my interest for the many years that I have researched and written about her. As I learnt more, I became fascinated by Jean herself, by her extraordinary Gordon family, by the life that women could lead in the sixteenth century, and by her hold over my home, the north of Scotland.

Jean's life was entwined with the Gordon downfall and struggle back to power and their fight for control over northern and north-eastern Scotland. Jean and her brothers, the tightly-knit Gordon siblings, still inhabit the imagination of the north-east. Echoes of their stories shifted into song, both bothy ballads of Jean's love for Alex Ogilvie, and darker tales of her closest brother Adam and how he gained the nickname 'Herod of the North'.

In her lifetime, Jean had three husbands and more than one title: she was not just Countess of Bothwell, but, before she was able to marry the man she loved, she was also Countess of Sutherland. Jean met her second husband Alexander Gordon, Earl of Sutherland, as a result of a blood feud, a botched poisoning plot and kidnapping, but against all the odds they had a happy marriage. After her second husband's death, Jean continued to run the Sutherland estate for her eldest son and through the minority of her grandson, providing a continuity of control that has been ignored in analysis focused on the male line of heirs. Her second marriage made Jean the most powerful woman in the north of Scotland, and her decisions had implications which fed into the complex relationships between the Earls, the Clan Chiefs and their clans; into much later events such as the Highland Clearances; and on into contemporary debates over land ownership and reform. Jean's lifetime corresponded with a change in the position of the clans, as they began to be seen more and more as the 'Other' to the earls.

This book is not a re-telling of stories from the time of Mary, Queen of Scots so much as a reframing: by shifting the focus to the north of Scotland, and by looking more closely at Jean and her family links, different things become important and different things become clear. For example, Jean's relationship with Bothwell's sister, Janet Hepburn, did not end with Jean's divorce from Bothwell. If historians think of Janet Hepburn at all, it is in relation to the parties and dancing that Mary's court was known for. But Janet and Jean were part of a wider Highland-Border alliance at a crucial point in Mary, Queen of Scots' life: an alliance that took the edges of Scotland and brought them into the heart of the court. Janet Hepburn's second marriage kept her and Jean in contact for years after Bothwell's death. Women's roles and relationships to each other changed power dynamics. Jean's decisions as a businesswoman with interests in salt pans and coal mining, and her relationship and conflict with her daughter-in-law over these businesses, had a huge impact on the north of Scotland. Meanwhile, other major events, such as the scandalous poisoning of Jean's father- and mother-in-law, happened in the north while the nobles in Scotland were distracted by the events at Mary's court – and historians have continued to be distracted. The 'Far North', where Jean latterly lived, is not just a geographical description but a specific area which had particular characteristics – particular relations between Earls and clans, for example – that set it apart from other areas of the country.

Jean's story is a series of vivid tales that are sometimes unfamiliar, but as memorable as anything that happened with Mary, Queen of Scots and Darnley: the trial of the corpse of Jean's father in the Scottish Parliament; Jean appearing after her wedding day to Bothwell dressed in mourning for her lost love; Wicked Earl George bursting onto the scene as he shot his father's jailor dead at a football match. The characters are hugely memorable, from Jean's eldest daughter Jane, married to the Chief of Mackay as part of the great battle for power between the earls and the clans; to Jean's clever son Robert, the intelligent and urbane courtier; or Robert's brother, playmate and polar opposite, Alexander, Knight of Navidale – or their enemy Wicked Earl George. The stories and the characters held my interest; the reframing changed the way I see the history of my home.

Jean's story is simultaneously long ago and within touching distance: the sixteenth century is the early modern period, recognisable to us. Jean's time saw the increase in the use of weaponry such as guns and gunpowder, and the questioning of religion. As I wrote about the Battle of Glenlivet, a friend told me that he was refurbishing a sword which had been used to fight at that battle: he could touch history with his hands and see the marks on the blade where it was used to hack at the armour Jean's enemies were wearing. Having absorbed the prevailing wisdom about Jean's first husband Bothwell's guilt, reading the partisan biography of Bothwell by Robert Gore-Browne was a jolt: a lesson in reframing history. It was a reminder that history is written by the victors and that truth, the daughter of time, can be searched for.[1] We can only view history from our present time: I am interested in why people still care about whether or not Jean's first husband Bothwell was guilty, and the fight for the repatriation of his mummified corpse to Scotland. I am curious about why the singer in a Faroese heavy metal band today cares about the mercenaries who went to Europe from Jean's home in Sutherland and nearby Caithness: these stories are all in my narrative as well as the story of Jean and her family.

It was important to me, however, to try to find the truth as well as the stories: there are, of course, many valuable and informative secondary sources available that mention Jean, especially her time with Mary, Queen of Scots, but there are also several letters written in her own hand still in existence. Transcriptions of these letters are easy to find; in the National Library of Scotland I also looked at the originals and read Jean's own words in her own handwriting. Going deeper into the archives, I found more letters, both from and to her, as well as many more documents from her family. Learning to read the old Scottish handwriting, Scots and French languages, I transcribed and translated letters and papers, gaining insights into family relationships and reading about the momentous events of Scottish history in real time, by people who lived through it: 'Huntly is dead', one woman wrote to her husband, 'I am sad, not just at the death of this man, but because it means you will have to stay to sort things out, and won't be able to come straight home to me and the children, and we miss you so.'[2] Some of the letters had only been read a handful of times since they were first written in the 1600s, and I was particularly pleased to discover invaluable information about Alex Ogilvie, the man Jean loved but was separated from when he was married to one of the Queen's Four Maries. This turned Alex Ogilvie from a footnote of love to a living, breathing man who I could finally picture, working in his orchard and herb garden.

Portraits were hugely important when imagining Jean and her family. In her home, Dunrobin Castle, I saw original, contemporary pictures of Jean and her family, and their many descendants. Visiting the impressive ruins of other castles and sites associated with Jean gave me an idea of the scale of her life. And the internet enabled me to access huge amounts of information from my desk in my own house: books that were out of copyright, as is the case with many transcriptions of historical documents and old history books, are now digitised and freely available, meaning I could easily find and read a first-hand description of Rizzio's murder, from which Jean's mother, husband and brother helped Mary, Queen of Scots escape; or read about the sudden and mysterious death of Jean's brother George. The internet meant I could use quality sources to study the north, while still living in the north; something that was not so easy to do only a few dozen years ago. Primary sources, too, are more easily accessible now that digital scanning and print-on-demand services are available. This meant that from my first gloved handling of the incredible family history written by Jean's son Robert in the special collections department at the University of Glasgow, I could move to reading a facsimile paperback at home giving unparalleled details of many of the events of Jean's life, from her legal battles with the Earl of Caithness to descriptions of the home of the wet-nurse who looked after her children. I am not a historian, I am a writer, and I have used my imagination to reconstruct what Jean and her contemporaries thought and felt: but at every point I have referred to as many primary sources and respected historians as possible, and have provided these references in endnotes for anyone wishing to follow up and read the originals themselves.

Why does it matter to me to know the history of the people and places of the north? Why do I think people should question their history? In my life, people have told me what being a Highlander means: they have told me that everyone from my home town is lazy, they have told me what it means to be a wife and mother in the north, they have come to my home and explained to me how the legacy of the clans has shaped me. Some of these things have not been true, and others have had a piece of truth in them. Sometimes I could not recognise my home or myself in what people said. In between the tourist trails and the fictions, everything about clan and family in the north started to sound made up. Eventually I wanted to find out for myself, to look for and find as much of the truth as I could, and then I wanted to tell the story myself, instead of having it told to me. Some of Jean's story was how I imagined it when I began to research. Some of her life, like everyone's, was complicated. From what I have learnt, I feel I understand my home better, and I think that sharing the story is important: this is our history, our community. The 'north' – the clans, the Highlands, all the rest – is often a symbol for many people, who live in many different places. By searching to understand the real north, it is possible to see things differently. Instead of a symbol, there are real people, who had real choices: by understanding them better, we can make more informed choices now. By following the thread of Jean's life, the facts of history become more than facts: they become a story in which we can see people's situations and decisions and try to understand them and understand what they left to us.

When Jean's son Robert came to write his family genealogy and the stories of the Gordons, he explained that he wanted to 'bring to light that which had been long obscured and too much neglected'.[3] He had read many histories 'for my private delight', and wanted to share the information he had found there, collecting together and ordering everything relevant that he had found. Although he claimed to want to be authentic, relating the history 'without passion ... prejudice or partiality', his real aim was to glorify the House of Gordon – but he realised that 'posterity ... will give to everyone his due': Robert knew that truth should be the ultimate aim of a historian. Robert wished that "these dead papers" of his history would be taken in the spirit of love and enquiry in which he had written them.[4]

In her lifetime, Jean saw the throne pass through the regency of Mary of Guise to Mary, Queen of Scots,[5] to Moray and the other Regents, to James VI and finally to Charles I. Scotland and England were united, Scotland changed from Catholic to Protestant, relations within Europe shifted dramatically and the New World began to open up. Jean was born into a rich family who came close to losing everything; she married for the first time on the orders of her queen, and divorced for the same queen; she married again for her family and had children and land to care for; and she married a third time for herself. Family was the main organising principle of the sixteenth century, and – with the one possible exception of her enduring love for Alex Ogilvie – Jean dedicated her life to the Gordons, who influenced so much of what happened in sixteenth-century Scotland. This is not just Jean's story; it is also the story of her family, and the story of the north – history seen through one person's life. Jean was a fascinating woman, and a rich woman who had great power. She and her family affected the people around her, and shaped the history – and the future – of the north of Scotland.

PART ONE

The Marian Years

CHAPTER ONE

The King of the North's Daughter: 1545–1561[1]

When she was born in 1545, Jean was the youngest daughter of the most powerful man in Scotland: 'the Cock o' the North', George Gordon the 4th Earl of Huntly. The House of Huntly controlled much of the north-east, but their powerbase extended around the blue and white coast, across the fertile Aberdeenshire and Moray farmland, and up to the peat browns and windswept skies of Sutherland and the Far North.

Huntly Castle was where Jean Gordon grew up.[2] It was only one of several dwelling-places owned by her father Huntly, but it was his main base, and he had spent the last few years developing and re-decorating the castle. Huntly had accompanied Mary of Guise when she had visited France in 1550 to see her daughter, and he had been inspired by the richness of the French court. Huntly Castle was an outpost of French design and opulence in the middle of rural Aberdeenshire. Jean was living in luxury.

When Jean Gordon was about ten years old, she and her family were visited by Mary of Guise, the mother of Mary, Queen of Scots. Mary of Guise and her retinue rode up from the south of Scotland through striking scenery, the close mountains made even more dramatic by the constantly changing weather. As they came ever further north, the Frenchmen and women who accompanied Mary of Guise felt like they were riding backwards into the past, on into a savage, foreign wilderness: after the splendour of the French court or of

Paris, with its half a million inhabitants, even Edinburgh, the capital of Scotland, was tiny, with a population of only about 15,000.[3] Now in the north of Scotland they really were in the middle of nowhere.

They were truly astonished, then, to see Huntly Castle looming up before them.

The castle was really a collection of buildings: the original tower house was opposite the newly remodelled three-storey tall palace, with other domestic buildings such as a bakehouse and brewery making up a square around a central courtyard with stabling. It was a well-established stronghold, and the mound of an old motte from 400 years before rose off to one side of the palace.

After their long journey through farmland, woods, scrubland and mud-tracks, Mary of Guise and her retinue now came onto a cobbled path leading up to the castle entrance,[4] where they were met by a guard of honour of 1,000 Gordon men. Jean lived at Huntly Castle with her family, surrounded as well by their kinsmen and women, cousins and 'cadet' Gordon families, i.e. the huge clan-like grouping of the House of Huntly. The Earl could call on large numbers of followers and supporters from the surrounding countryside, as he was landlord and chief of a vast swathe of territory in the north and north-east. There were between 52 and 150 families with the name Gordon in the area over time, linked to Jean's family by blood or allegiance.[5] It was as if Mary of Guise was being welcomed into another royal household.

Jean's father, the Earl of Huntly, was an enormous mountain of a man, whose large powerbase was matched with a large physical presence. He held various titles at different times in addition to his Earldom, and was at this time Lord Lieutenant of the North, and had been or was to be the Sheriff of Inverness, Sheriff of Aberdeen, Privy Councillor, Lieutenant of the Borders, Provost of Aberdeen and recipient of the French order of St Michel.[6] In addition to his official titles Huntly had the unofficial nickname 'Cock o' the North'. He was the unquestionably the most powerful man in the north of Scotland, and the most powerful Catholic nobleman in the country. In England he was described as 'King of the North' – and later the 'Terror of the English'.[7]

By his side was Jean's mother, Elizabeth Keith, Countess of Huntly. She was from another powerful north-east family, but although their marriage was certainly a sensible one in terms of local politics, the Earl and Countess of Huntly were also well-matched in personality. Elizabeth was a strong, resourceful woman who was equally capable of bringing up her large family and running the estate, and she never wavered in her loyalty to her husband and the promotion of Gordon-Huntly interests. Literate and well-educated, she handled the Huntly business correspondence, and had frequently written to their guest Mary of Guise.

Huntly and Elizabeth Keith had 11 living children. Their heir and eldest son Alexander had recently died, leaving the well-thought-of George, now around 20 years old, ten years older than his sister Jean, as the successor to the title. Jean had seven other tough Gordon brothers as well as two older sisters, Margaret and Elizabeth, to make up the close-knit family.

Welcomed into the heart of the Huntly Castle complex, Mary of Guise could see the surroundings where Jean and her siblings had grown up. Huntly was delighted to show off the improvements he had made to the palace. There was plenty of room for the lowlier members of Mary of Guise's retinue, who would have been sent either to the stables, domestic rooms such as the kitchen, or the basement rooms (next to the castle's prison). The male and female members of the house were separated, as was common at the time, and the Earl and Countess each had one floor of the palace set aside for their use. These had been arranged by Huntly in the fashionable 'piano nobile' (principal or noble floor) style which he would have seen used by James V at Stirling Castle, with public rooms in descending order of size and privacy.[8] Both the Earl and Countess had a Hall where general followers were settled, and where the company ate. The leading members of Mary of Guise's retinue could then be brought into the smaller Great Chambers, where more private discussions could take place. The most important visitors of all were admitted into the bedrooms. Sixteenth-century bedrooms were also used as public rooms, with the great four-poster beds covered with wooden velvet-covered tabletops during the daytime, and they were not private rooms for an individual, but a place where many people slept: the Countess in the four-poster would be joined in the room by her daughters or trusted servants, or younger members of their entourage on smaller truckle beds.[9] The sense of everyone living together as family or clan was very strong.

When Jean saw Mary of Guise in her mother's apartments she saw a striking tall Frenchwoman with pale skin and auburn hair of around 40 years of age, dressed in mourning black for her two lost husbands and three lost sons – but she would not have been overawed, because Jean also saw a distant relative by marriage. The Huntlys were related to the Scottish royal family, and Jean was secure in her place as daughter of a rich household.

Each of the public rooms in Huntly Castle were fantastically decorated. To keep the warmth in, the stone walls of the castle were lined: on one wall of the public rooms was a huge tapestry in five panels, depicting birds and "greit leiffis of treis" – great leaves of trees – and there was another stunning panel of gilt leather in what become known as the 'Leather Chamber'.[10] In Huntly's Hall there was a crimson satin cloth of state embroidered with gold fixed to the wall behind Huntly's seat, which was, as later events would show, literally fit for royalty.[11] There were velvet cushions to sit on, and in the bedrooms there were yellow, violet, blue, green and red velvet and silk coverings and curtains for the beds. It was common to paint intricate decorations on wooden panelling on the walls, or have a painted ceiling. Lit by candlelight, the colours could be richer than the pale walls of a modern house lit with blank electricity, and at a time when sumptuary laws limited the use of certain materials and colours to nobility, Huntly Castle was a vividly colourful home designed to make an impression.

Dinner was served in the Hall, where Huntly and his wife feasted their guests, serving elaborate meals every day for a week. Mary of Guise was astonished at their lavishness: she knew that entertaining a royal party was an expensive affair, and, after a few days, she offered to move on. Huntly replied that it was not a problem. The royal party could stay as long as they liked, he said expansively, and, to prove it, he took them on a tour of his store-rooms: they were absolutely crammed with supplies of food and drink. This demonstration did not have quite the effect that he had hoped for. Mary of Guise's French followers began to mutter among themselves, and, once they had finally left the castle, the mood began to turn against Huntly. The "wings of the 'Cock of the North'," they said, "should be clipped".[12]

Huntly had really wanted to impress Mary of Guise, as she was taking control of the Regency of Scotland for her baby daughter. Huntly had been at the centre of power since his childhood, when he was brought up at the Scottish court alongside the future King James V. He had remained one of James V's closest companions and had effectively been in control of the whole country of Scotland twice already: he himself had been trusted as Regent when James V went to France to collect his first bride, and he had been appointed Governor of the Realm after King James V died. James V had turned his face to the wall and died shortly after the disastrous Scottish defeat at the Battle of Solway Moss in 1542, while his second wife Mary of Guise lay recovering from childbirth. The baby Mary, Queen of Scots, succeeded to the throne when she was only six days old. As Mary of Guise regained her strength, the Earl of Arran had stepped in and taken over as Regent. Arran's alliances fluctuated, and he switched allegiances more than once, moving in his 'godly fit' from Catholic to Protestant, from French-supporting to English-supporting, and back again. His actions were always tempered by his knowledge that should the baby Mary, Queen of Scots die, Arran himself was next in line to the Scottish throne. Jean's father Huntly had maintained close ties with Arran, and his eldest son Alexander was married to Arran's daughter – and, after Alexander's unexpected early death, the Huntly-Arran link was later maintained when Jean's brother George was married to Arran's third daughter.[13]

With Scotland undergoing another royal minority and religious upheaval upsetting the balance of power, the English king, Henry VIII, had pursued his own interest in the Scottish throne, and battered the south of the country in an attempt to force an alliance between his son and the infant queen. 'We like not the manner of the wooing,' said Jean's father Huntly, 'and we could not stoop to being bullied into love' – giving rise, much later, to Walter Scott's coining of the phrase 'Rough Wooing' to describe this period.[14] The Scots resisted the English attacks, turning to the French for help – but at the same time many Scots were drawn to the new Protestant religion that had taken hold in England and mistrusted the Catholic French who wished to use Scotland as a tool in their own battles with the English and Spanish. People changed sides and allegiances, and the political and religious landscape was constantly shifting.

The accession of Edward VI to the English throne and Scotland's disastrous defeat at the Battle of Pinkie Cleugh in 1547 marked another punctuation in developments. Jean's father Huntly, fighting on foot and wearing a fantastic massive suit of gilded and enamelled armour, was taken prisoner at Pinkie. The Scots tried to negotiate a ransom for him, but the English refused, saying he was such a deadly foe he must stay prisoner until there was peace. The Scots then suggested that Huntly should be allowed the comfort of his family, and that Lady Huntly, Jean and her siblings should be allowed to travel to see him. This too was refused, but it was agreed that Huntly might be moved to the north of England so his wife could visit him occasionally. The English pressed Huntly to support them, returning him his hawks and greyhounds in exchange for his professed support, but Huntly was secretly laying plans for escape. After his move to the north of England, he gained some of the trust of his captors, engaging them in a card game. After a brief moment of danger when Huntly inadvertently spoke his thoughts aloud, he tricked the friendly captors by sneaking out to the toilet while they were busy. Bypassing the facilities, Huntly and his servant ran to a pre-arranged meeting-point and their friends, and rode hard north to Edinburgh where Huntly was 'joyfullie and honorablie received' by his wife and friends.[15] Jean's father did not keep any of his promises to the English, but had returned instead to help Mary of Guise. Huntly wanted Mary of Guise to know that he was one of her allies – and he expected that he and his family would be rewarded for being her ally.

Mary of Guise's policy was to keep the throne safe for her daughter at all costs, and to do this she wanted to maintain and strengthen the links between her home country and Scotland. She saw Scotland as a minor player on the European stage, which would do well to ally with Catholic France against England and against Protestantism. She took advice from her brothers, the powerful Ducs de Guise, who were busy working their family's own way closer to the French throne. Mary of Guise spent years charming the noblemen of Scotland while aiming towards her goal of taking over the reins of power to hold the kingdom for her daughter, Mary, Queen of Scots. After more than a decade of political manoeuvring, Mary of Guise was finally made Regent in 1554. Along the way she had made many promises, and now Huntly and others were waiting for her to deliver.

Jean Gordon's family were effective rulers over a huge part of north-east Scotland. The Huntly area of influence spread over the north-eastern coast, down to Aberdeen and along to Elgin. They had interests in Inverness-shire as well, and family links in Sutherland: their world centred around the coastline of the Moray Firth. This territorial link was to be a key and recurring theme throughout Jean Gordon's life; it was an idea central to her thinking from an early age, and she spent much of her life travelling back and forth around this coast. Some of this area was not fixed on the Earl of Huntly though: the Earldom of Moray was officially a crown title, one not solely hereditary, as the Earldom of Huntly was, but which could be given as a favour by the King or Queen. Huntly wanted ultimate control of Moray. If he ruled Moray, that would link his territory in the east with Inverness, where he held the sheriffship, and enable him to strengthen Gordon links with the Far North as well. Moray was also particularly covetable as it was good, fertile land.

Mary of Guise had indicated to Huntly that Moray would be the reward for helping her. However, she had said the same thing to the Earl of Sutherland. Huntly was briefly given control of the Earldom of Moray in 1549, but it was taken from him only five years later.

Now, Huntly was feeling hunted: he wrote to Mary of Guise explaining that there had been an attempt on his life by some of the clansmen of the north. The letter does not say exactly who these clansmen were, but there were several it could have been: there were still the remnants of two competing systems of government in Scotland. The system of Earls and Earldoms, in a hierarchical structure headed by the King, was only one way of understanding the organisation of Scottish society. In the Highlands, particularly to the west but also in the Far North, there were still many Gaelic speakers, clansmen and women who dressed in plaids and paid direct allegiance not to their Queen Regent and her Earls, but to their Clan Chief. This was no minor fringe: clan lands covered up to half the land-mass of Scotland and up to half of all the Scottish people.[16] The clans had originally operated a different form of land ownership,[17] and there were still clashes as the king or queen and their earls imposed feudal systems over land which had traditionally been clan-owned and used, forcing Clan Chiefs to formally and legally become the vassals or subordinates to the earls and the king.[18] The year of Jean's birth, 1545, also saw the death of the last claimant to the Lordship of the Isles, which had given united clans a power to rival the Scottish throne. Now, leaderless and fractured, feuding among the clans reached unprecedented levels and Jean's family sought to take advantage of this. The clan system may have already started its inexorable decline, but it died a slow and violent death.[19]

The House of Huntly itself looked almost like a clan from the outside – a group of people bound by family ties – but the Huntly Gordons formally paid allegiance to the crown and saw themselves as almost a different race to the clansmen. The tension between loyalty to kinsmen and loyalty to the throne was a constant in many countries, but in Scotland the kin loyalty of the clans still clung onto its formalised structure, and the Clan Chiefs were often in direct competition with the Earls.

Huntly's messages to Mary of Guise took on a pleading tone: "treuylly, madam, I newyr offendit your grace nor newyr thynkis do" – 'truly, madame, I never meant to offend you' – a surviving letter states, continuing, 'I shall justify this before your grace my lord governor and, if need requires, before the king of France or any other prince. Whatever be said . . . I shall be found a true servant to your grace, and surely I will be no longer in any doubt . . . you shall never have a truer man in this realm of my degree, nor readier to obey your grace's command . . . I dare not be so bold as to write further on this matter for fear of offending your grace, but shall, with God's help, be shortly with your grace myself in order to declare my part . . .' [20]

Mary of Guise was not sympathetic. Soon after she became Regent in 1554, one of the first things she did was not to reward her supporter Huntly, but to put him in prison.[21] Mary of Guise's stated reason for imprisoning the Cock o' the North and depriving him of the Earldom of Moray was his failure to adequately go against the northern clans:[22] but it also solved the problem of how to control such a powerful man, how to deal with someone whose loyalty was suspect, how to settle the competing claims for the Earldom of Moray – and, furthermore, it showed her detractors that she was not going to work with Huntly to force Catholicism on Scotland. If the Clans and the Earls were two competing structures and ways of understanding links in Scotland, there was also a third and very important structure: the Church. The Nobility, Clans and Church are an alternative 'Three Estates', or three divisions of society.[23] Like royalty and the Earls, and the Clan Chiefs, the Church and bishops in Scotland were another hierarchical structure that provided a different way of looking at and understanding the country, the land and finances. As the ideas of the Protestant reformation were taking hold across Europe, the noblemen in Scotland were taking their positions on each side of the struggle between Catholicism and Protestantism. Huntly was very definitely ranged on the side of Catholicism, and his dislike of England and support for Mary of Guise was partly fuelled by this. There was constant interaction between people's religious ties, nationalistic feeling and family relationships, all contributing to the continually shifting allegiances.

The year before Mary of Guise was finally made Regent, Mary Tudor ascended the throne of England. Bloody Mary Tudor was a

Catholic, and was already starting to reverse the religious changes that had been set in motion in England after Henry VIII's break with Rome and the Pope. She was set to marry the Catholic Prince Philip of Spain, a union not well received in England. Mary of Guise, a Catholic and a foreigner in Scotland, wanted to send a message to the Scottish nobles and people that she was going to try and be tolerant: she was not going to impose Catholicism on them using the combined forces of Huntly and France.

For Jean Gordon in Huntly Castle, the imprisonment of her father by Mary of Guise did not immediately alter her day-to-day life. This was the second time in Jean's short life that her father had been jailed, and she knew that prison, for noblemen, was not necessarily a harsh place. A nobleman would be treated with the respect due to his position of birth even in jail, and Huntly was housed in reasonable comfort in Edinburgh Castle – he certainly wouldn't be languishing in a tiny, damp stone cellar as a common criminal imprisoned in Huntly Castle might be. Huntly's power in the north was sufficient that there would be no immediate danger of an attack on his property while he was away either, particularly when the Countess of Huntly was surrounded by loyal retainers and had eight fine sons and one son-in-law, three or four of whom at least were by now of an age where they could fight, and all of whom were being trained to be ready to defend their land and title. Jean's training and upbringing would be continuing as normal.

As the youngest daughter, Jean spent a considerable amount of time with her brothers and was always very close to them. Both her older sisters were already married,[24] so Jean, like many noblewomen in the Renaissance period, learnt alongside her brothers. The key to education was literacy. Around half the population of Scotland could probably read to some extent – at least enough to follow basic religious writings such as popular prayers[25] – and, as the daughter of a nobleman, Jean also learnt to write. Writing required a certain amount of specialised equipment such as pens and ink, preparation and time, and was regarded as a dangerous skill because it carried the potential power of influence and so it was reserved to people of high status. Jean learnt to read and write in Scots, but one of the first lessons that educated children learnt in the sixteenth century were language lessons. It was expected that an educated person would have a working knowledge of more than their own native tongue not least because languages were essential for Bible study, the most important part of a person's education. Jean's brothers, two of whom become priests, were taught Latin, the language of the Church, and Jean herself owned annotated books in this language.[26] In a country where the Dowager Queen and many of the court attendants were French, and where the heir to the throne was currently based at the French court and engaged to the Dauphin, the French language was naturally an asset, and there is some evidence that Jean and her family may have had a working knowledge of Gaelic, which was widely spoken in the north and west of Scotland.[27] Other European countries traded with Scots and so their languages were heard both in ports and across the country.[28] There was a high tolerance for different dialects and different ways of speaking, and although Jean's native Scots tongue had many different words to the English spoken in England, a slightly different grammar, and some French influence, there were still people who argued that the whole of Britain spoke the one tongue.[29] Jean's Scots is still readable (with some effort) for a modern Scot today.[30]

Linguistics were not the only lessons, as subjects such as mathematics were considered just as important for girls as boys, with practical arithmetic an essential skill for someone who would be expected to help run an estate. Girls' education also had a large element of practical housekeeping, as well as skills that were both useful and artistic, such as embroidery. Jean's contemporaries Mary, Queen of Scots, and Elizabeth of England were notably well-educated, and their peers followed their examples.

The Countess of Huntly, as well as supervising her children's education, continued to agitate for her husband's release. She seems to have been in correspondence with both her husband and others at court, as Huntly wrote to the French ambassador in Scotland from prison that 'my wife has told me that the queen's grace [Mary of Guise] has an evil opinion of my service towards her grace'.[31] Although Mary of Guise threatened to send Huntly into exile in France, in the end Jean's father returned north to Huntly Castle after around eight months of imprisonment. Some of his land had been taken away, he had been fined a large sum of money and his influence at court was greatly reduced. His letters to Mary of Guise and her advisors betray a certain amount of bewilderment – Huntly just cannot seem to understand why the Queen Regent would not trust him and his allegiance to the Scottish crown, and pleads for understanding – but he and his family felt certain that his fortunes would rise again. He thought these were just the normal ups and downs of the volatile Scottish court. His powerbase in the north of Scotland was as strong as ever, and Mary of Guise was starting to run into problems: she would soon need the help of the House of Huntly again.

The Scottish nobles and the Scottish people were not happy with the French influence at court. Mary of Guise had put her trusted French advisors into many of the top roles in government. Mary, Queen of Scots had been sent to France, where she was engaged to the Dauphin Francis, the heir to the French throne – but she was not married yet. What sort of country was Scotland going to be if its queen was living abroad? What sort of power would the Scottish nobles have in that situation, they asked themselves – and, crucially, what religion would they have to follow? Catholic France was currently Scotland's friend, while Protestant England was the Scots' enemy – but the new religion was gaining force in Scotland. Mary of Guise had chosen not to ally with Catholic Huntly, but her policy of religious toleration was not working and her grasp on power was slipping.

Mary of Guise tried hard to enforce her rule, travelling to the far south and then the far north of the country to hold justice ayres. In 1556 she arrived in Inverness, where she ran into problems with the clans. The powerful Chief of Mackay, Aodh, was ordered to come to court in Inverness to stand trial, accused of spoiling and molesting Sutherland territory, but he refused to appear, flouting royal command and authority with contempt.[32] The Clan Mackay's relationship with the Scottish crown was fraught. Aodh had fought for James V at Solway Moss, where he had been captured. Aodh had then spent time as a 'guest' at the court of Henry VIII; interestingly this experience had led to a tolerance for both England and Protestantism. Aodh had argued against Scotland allying with France, and followed his words with actions by joining in an attempt on Regent Arran's life, then taking his men to fight the Scottish army for the English during the 'Rough Wooing' of baby Mary, Queen of Scots. There was some feeling among the Gaels and clans that rule by England might even be preferable to rule by southern Scotland.[33]

Jean's father the Earl of Huntly had supposedly been imprisoned for his failure to control the clans and enforce the law and, even if this had been partly an excuse, the clans did need to be managed. After Aodh's failure to turn up in Inverness, Mary of Guise instructed Earl John of Sutherland to go against the Clan Mackay. Mary, Queen of Scots wrote to the Earl John at her mother's instruction, giving him permission under her name and authority to pursue the Mackays north in Sutherland and then over into their own territory of Strathnaver, 'if need be to besiege houses wherein they shall happen to be', and to "rais fyre, committ slauchter and mutilatioun vpoun thame".[34] Desperate measures were needed to show that the Queen Regent and her Earls were the ones in control of the north, not the clansmen.

Back south in Edinburgh Mary of Guise's troubles were not over: true sectarian civil war was breaking out in Scotland. Many leading noblemen, the ones who had been so concerned about French influence at court, banded together to form the association known as the Lords of the Congregation. They were opposed to the marriage of Mary, Queen of Scots and the Dauphin Francis, and actively promoted the new Protestant religion. Mary of Guise needed any allies she could get, and by 1557 Aodh, Chief of Mackay, was forgiven so that he could be counted among her allies. Huntly, too, was restored to favour. She also brought in soldiers from France, who were stationed in Leith. The Scots began to see this French army as an army of occupation, and their presence was resented so much that even today in Edinburgh there is a faint but persistent memory of Mary of Guise's French troops. There was a great personal respect for Mary of Guise herself, but Scotland did not want to become part of France. Mary of Guise consistently underestimated the desire for independence in Scotland: it might have been a small country, insignificant by French standards and overshadowed by its more powerful neighbour, but it had a long and proud history as a nation and a distinct culture. There were also distinct differences in the way the ruler of Scotland was viewed: they were not leader of a country but leader of a people – Queen of Scots, not of Scotland. After years of royal minorities, the Scots saw their leader as first among equals, ruling through negotiation rather than imposition of will – while preacher John Knox promoted the radical Protestant idea that even the Queen or King was not above God's judgement.

Mary, Queen of Scots was finally married to the Dauphin Francis in 1558, becoming the wife of the heir to the French throne. Francis was offered the crown matrimonial, which would make him King of Scots in his own right.[35] In England in the same year, Bloody Mary died after naming the Protestant Elizabeth Tudor as her successor. Encouraged by the French king, Mary, Queen of Scots declared her claim to the English throne, arguing that she was the real successor rather than Elizabeth. In France, where the claim was a matter of drawing new arms for Mary, this seemed a reasonable statement, particularly in view of the European political game that France was playing with Spain and England. To a Scot in the Border region, who had lived through the Rough Wooing, the battles of Solway Moss and Pinkie Cleugh and the numerous skirmishes in between, antagonising the English this way with no military backup must have seemed little short of lunacy. The Scots did not want to become part of England, but nor did they want to become part of France or a pawn in French politics. Scots would have been horrified to learn that when Mary, Queen of Scots got married, she had signed secret documents that stated that, if she died childless, Scotland would essentially become a French dominion.[36]

In Scotland, there was reaction to this string of world-changing events, and a growing strain of Protestantism. There were religious riots in Edinburgh, and John Knox returned from exile on the continent to preach again. The Lords of the Congregation made the decision to ask Elizabeth of England for her help and support. Despite Jean's family being Catholic, her father Huntly reluctantly and somewhat half-heartedly supported the Lords of the Congregation– a Protestant independent Scotland was better than a Catholic Scotland that was merely a French satellite.

Huntly was not an old man – he was in his forties – but in an era when, due to illness and war, the average life expectancy has been estimated as being as low as 35,[37] he had seen many of his contemporaries die; James V at Solway Moss, others at Pinkie Cleugh, while a new generation were coming up. Huntly's own eldest son George might have only attracted attention for his sober, sensible behaviour, but his next son John was an altogether wilder prospect. There were plenty of other men of that generation who Huntly needed to consider, not least James Stewart. By now in his late twenties, James Stewart was the bastard son of James V, making him the elder half-brother of Mary, Queen of Scots.[38] James Stewart was almost exactly what Scotland wanted: the son of King James V, strong and of age and ready to rule, but his illegitimacy prevented him from being the heir to the throne – and he had a little too much abrasiveness and not enough of the Stewart charm. He had an understandable grievance about his illegitimacy, and even his supporters agreed that he was a difficult personality to get on with, with a huge sense of his own importance, rough and ready habits and argumentative speaking style. He had become a Protestant after hearing John Knox speak, but his devotion to the cause of the new religion was sometimes secondary to his devotion to the established rule of the noblemen and the Scottish crown – or rather his devotion to the cause of one James Stewart. Although he could negotiate with a little more finesse than some of his contemporaries, the English ambassador Thomas Randolph summed him up as dealing "according to his nature, rudely, homely and bluntly".[39] James

Stewart worked well when he was treated with respect and things were going his way, but reacted badly when his personal power was questioned. He was one of the acknowledged leaders of the Lords of the Congregation, but he began to antagonise Huntly.

Huntly's main concern when he belatedly joined the Lords of the Congregation was that his powerbase in the north should not become unstable. There were significant potential gains for the Lords as land and money was taken away from the Church, and Huntly made a special request of the Lords that any confiscated church lands in the north-east should only be given to Huntly supporters. Although John Knox's inflammatory sermons in places like Perth encouraged people to smash up churches and attack friars, indicating the popular opinion pushing through the Reformation, the new preaching had not yet had quite so much influence on ordinary people in the north of Scotland. Jean watched as some of the treasures were removed from the northern churches – gold and silver vessels, statues and candlesticks, rich textiles such as altar cloths and vestments, and other items such as a silk tent captured by Robert the Bruce from the English king, which had been in a cathedral in Aberdeen – but they were carefully removed for safekeeping into her own home of Huntly Castle.[40] Huntly knew that if his support for Protestantism grew too strong that he would run into problems with his own followers in the lands round about Huntly Castle. His own personal Catholicism remained constant. Huntly worked as a negotiator, going between Mary of Guise and the Lords to try and work out a solution of religious tolerance that might be acceptable to both sides. He hoped to keep the balance of power in Scotland, but Mary of Guise never fully trusted him while James Stewart was to become his implacable enemy.

Huntly's hopes of maintaining stability were overtaken by events. The French king Henri II, a man of good health who was in his prime, was fatally injured in a freak jousting accident, when a lance splintered, sending one shard of wood into his right eye and a second into his throat. For nine days his life hung in the balance and the French court was in a state of suspended animation. Henri's put-upon Italian wife, Catherine de Medici, talked of dire prophecies and omens. When the news finally came of Henri's death, Mary, Queen of Scots and her husband Francis fell to their knees and asked God for guidance. The Queen of Scots was now the wife of the King of France. To the Guise family, this seemed to be what they had been working towards for years: a member of their family was now in charge in both Scotland and in France, and, taking advantage of Francis II's personal weaknesses, the Guise brothers started work behind the French throne.[41] However, their sister Mary of Guise had become unwell.

Mary of Guise's urgent appeals for French help, and the French troops she had already brought in, were not enough to maintain her power in Scotland. She agreed to the Scots' demands for freedom of worship, but the Lords of the Congregation wanted more. Supported by Elizabeth of England, they began to march on Edinburgh. Mary of Guise retreated to Leith, where her French troops were based, but she was suffering from severe financial problems, as well as increasing ill health. 'I am still lame and have a leg that assuages not from swelling. If any lay his finger upon it, it goes in as with butter,' Mary of Guise lamented, and, as Leith struggled under siege, she struggled to even move. An English observer said that the only reason the fluid in her body and her swelling reduced at all was that she cried so many tears. Realising that she was dying, Mary of Guise sent for James Stewart and other representatives of the Lords of the Congregation and, weeping, entreated them to remain friends with France, begging their forgiveness if she had ever offended them. These strong Scottish men, her enemies, were in tears themselves as they parted from this dignified woman.[42]

Mary of Guise died on 11th June 1560. The following month, Scotland, France and England signed a treaty agreeing that all foreign soldiers – French and English – would leave Scotland.[43] A month later Scotland was declared a Protestant country. It was not a nominal change introduced from the top-down by nobles, but a profound shift in the fabric of society, driven by popular feeling and altering the landscape of Scotland: "The monasteries are nearly all in ruins," a Catholic observer described, "some completely destroyed; churches, altars, sanctuaries are overthrown and profaned, the images of Christ and of the Saints broken and lying in the dust. No religious rite is celebrated in any part of the kingdom, no Mass ever said in public..."[44] Mary of Guise was not allowed a Catholic burial and, afraid of riots, the Scottish Lords refused permission for her body to be buried beside her husband James V and their sons. Seven months after Scotland became officially Protestant, Mary of Guise's body was finally released from where it lay in state in Edinburgh Castle, and in the dead of night put on board a boat and sent to be laid to rest in France.[45]

France, however, was already in the grip of more instability. Mary, Queen of Scots' husband, Francis II, was not a strong man. Just months before Mary of Guise's body was finally sent home to be buried, Francis had succumbed to a serious ear infection, which turned into meningitis. He died aged only 16, after being king for just over a year, leaving his ten-year-old brother Charles IX and his mother, Catherine de Medici, to take over the rule of France. Francis' widow, Mary, Queen of Scots, eventually rejected the idea of remaining in the new French court with her difficult mother-in-law, and made the first of her fateful choices, deciding to return to Scotland. Nineteen-year-old Mary, Queen of Scots, only three years older than Jean, set sail from France. Her ships were driven before the wind to arrive in Scotland earlier than expected, and she landed at Leith at nine o'clock on an August morning in 1561, in thick fog, to a hastily assembled welcome party. Huntly had privately asked Mary, Queen of Scots to land in the north, imagining that they might lead a Catholic army together to take back control of Scotland. When he heard instead of her arrival in the south, Huntly "came post with sixteen horses", travelling as fast as could down from Huntly Castle to find out what the arrival of the Queen of Scots would mean for him and his family.[46]

CHAPTER TWO

They Would Go to Aberdeen: 1562

While Huntly was in the south of Scotland dealing with the new reality of a present Queen and a Protestant country, his daughter Jean in the north was facing the future with the optimism and confidence of youth. Aged 17, Jean was looking beyond Huntly Castle and family out to wider society: nearby Aberdeen. A university town and trading port, Aberdeen was one of the major centres in Scotland. The Gordons' status in Aberdeen was high, but there were many merchants, students and other landowners based there who did not owe them automatic loyalty, and the hierarchy in the town and university was undergoing changes as Scotland became officially Protestant.

As a young girl in a noble family Jean would expect to be married soon, for the benefit of her House. Jean had two older sisters to show her paths forward in life: Elizabeth, Jean's eldest sister and some years removed from her, had been married to the Earl of Atholl. She had died relatively young, though she left behind children, who were being brought up as loyal Gordon family supporters.[1] Then, while Jean's father had been in prison in England, Jean's mother, protecting her family, had arranged a marriage with the Forbes, in the hope of calming a long-standing Forbes-Gordon enmity.[2] In this way, a sometimes bloody feud would be halted – or, as the marriage contract optimistically put it, there would be a 'renewing of the old amity, love and kindness that has aye been betwixt the houses of Huntly and Forbes... [leading to] a perfect amity kindness to continue in all times coming.' The plan was for one of the remaining unmarried Gordon daughters, Margaret or Jean, to marry John, Master of Forbes, when they came of age.[3] If anything had happened to her middle sister, Jean's future would have been as a Forbes wife. As it was, Jean's second sister Margaret, who was two years older than Jean, had been married to John, Master of Forbes. Margaret was 14 and John, Master of Forbes was 17. However, this marriage had not gone well from the start: the Forbes were Protestant, and Margaret, coming from a Catholic family, did not find this easy to settle into and may have preferred to return to spend time with her family – or to socialise in Aberdeen.[4] Margaret and Jean seem to have been close: although there was a five-year wait before Margaret's marriage produced any children, when she did have a daughter Margaret named her 'Jean' after her sister.[5]

Young noblewomen like Jean and her sisters attracted a good deal of attention: their planned weddings could affect the future of whole families and there was a good deal of interest in who Jean might marry. The ballads or story-songs of the north-east of Scotland are a long tradition, sometimes printed on cheap sheets of paper but more often sung in Jean's day, passed on through people hearing and repeating them: they were a way of sharing stories and gossip. The surviving versions of the ballads sometimes distort the known facts, and sometimes change them to fit a traditional story-pattern, but their history can often be traced back very accurately, and the kernels of truth picked out. "The Duke o' Gordon's Daughter" begins:

"The Duke of Gordon has three daughters,
Elizabeth, Margaret and Jean,
They wou'd not stay in bonnie Castle Gordon,
But they wou'd go to bonnie Aberdeen.[6]

"They had not been in Aberdeen," the song continues,
"A twelvemonth and a day,
Till Lady Jean fell in love with Captain Ogilvie,
And away with him she wou'd gae."[7]

Jean's parents would be expected to have a say over her choice of partner but, as the youngest girl in a large family, the last daughter at home protected by a loving mother and all those brothers, Jean thought that she had a good chance of doing something a little different, and marrying for love – unlike her sister Margaret's example of an unhappy arranged marriage. Jean had met and fallen in love with a young man, slightly older than her, called Alexander Ogilvie.[8] We know little about their early courtship, but the story can be pieced together from the glimpses in song and the details which came out later in Jean's life. Alex Ogilvie came from a high-ranking family of minor nobility in the north-east, who lived at Craig o' Boyne, not far from Huntly Castle. Although not a well-known name on the national stage, the Ogilvies of Boyne had a great influence on what happened in Portsoy and the surrounding area, and Alex Ogilvie's family were distantly linked to the Gordons already by marriage.[9] Alex Ogilvie's father died around 1561, meaning his son acceded to the title and became Alex Ogilvie, 4th of Boyne, a young head of household.[10] However, although Alex Ogilvie himself may have been personally unexceptional as husband material, there was a growing obstacle to a new Gordon link with the Ogilvies. Despite the real attachment between Alex and Jean, there was no immediate family approval for their relationship:

> "Word came to the Duke of Gordon,
> In the chamber where he lay –
> 'Lady Jean has fell in love with Captain Ogilvie,
> And away with him she wou'd gae.'
>
> 'Go saddle me the black horse,
> And you'll ride on the grey;
> And I will ride to bonnie Aberdeen,
> Where I have been many a day.'
>
> They were not a mile from Aberdeen,
> A mile but only three,

Till he met with his two daughters walking,
But away was Lady Jeanie ..."[11]

In the song, Jean's father forbids the marriage but he is too late:
Jean runs away with Alex Ogilvie. In real life, Jean was persuaded to
wait. The Huntlys' position in the new Marian Scotland was far from
secure, and marriage alliances were an important way for nobility to
cement friendships – Jean could make a marriage that was better for
the Gordons. And, although Alex was from a respectable family that
did not seem to attract much attention to themselves, another branch
of the same family, the Ogilvies of Findlater, had become entangled
with Jean's family in a scandalous way, through her brother John.[12]

John Gordon was Huntly's third son, Jean's very dashing and
handsome older brother. A wild young man, he had a loyal following in the north, where his good looks and sweeping ways made him
very attractive to men and women of his own age. As the third son,
he could have expected to inherit less than his older brothers and so
have less standing in the community, but he seemed to have made
his own luck when he was formally adopted as heir by family friend
Ogilvie of Deskford and Findlater.[13] This adoption had happened
in very unusual circumstances. A few years earlier, the matter had
been brought to the attention of Mary of Guise: 'Madame, as to the
lord of Findlater's business,' wrote Jean's uncle, 'I have brought
it to a good end in that my lord my brother [Huntly] has encouraged me to work with him and his returning heir, which truly,
madame, is a meritable [good] thing to do, and to the greater good
of our House, and to take control of the scandal ...'[14] A scandal it
certainly was, and it was to get more scandalous still: the Ogilvie
connection was to be the spark that triggered the beginning of the
fall of the House of Huntly. Jean had not been lucky when she first
fell in love with an Ogilvie.

Ogilvie of Findlater had married, as his second wife, a woman
called Elizabeth Gordon, who was a distant kinswoman of Huntly
and Jean.[15] However, shortly after they were married, Elizabeth
Gordon told her new husband that his son from his first marriage,

James Ogilvie,[16] had tried to seduce her. Not only that, Elizabeth continued, but this was part of a plot by James Ogilvie to get control of his father's estates: James had been going to imprison his father 'and put him in a dark house and there keep him awake until such time as he became stark mad, and that being done ... enter himself into possession of the house and lands.'[17] Ogilvie of Findlater believed his new wife, and disinherited his son. On his death in 1554, Ogilvie of Findlater left Findlater Castle and all his lands, except some which were reserved to his wife, to Jean's brother John. If John died, the lands were to go to Jean's other brothers, and provision had been made for the event of their deaths for lands to go to other Ogilvies, including the branch of the family that Jean was involved with.[18] The son and original heir James Ogilvie was to get nothing.

Jean's brother John adopted the name Ogilvie – and then got together with the widow, Elizabeth Gordon. It was alleged that this was the plan all along, and that the whole story about James Ogilvie had been made up by Elizabeth Gordon and John so that John could take over Ogilvie of Findlater's estates and castle.

However, something went wrong for Elizabeth Gordon. Just a few months later John realised that he could not get all the land he wanted from her so disowned her as either mistress or wife and locked her up in a room in Findlater Castle.[19] Nobody seemed to be able or willing to do very much to help her, and her former stepson James Ogilvie was still trying very hard to recover his lost inheritance. John Gordon and James Ogilvie had been locked in this battle for several years and by 1562, as Jean was falling in love with Alex Ogilvie, they had reached the stage of taking their quarrel to Edinburgh to be settled at court.[20]

By the spring of 1562, Jean's father had returned north to his family and Huntly Castle. He said that he had pains in his leg that prevented him from attending any more of the regular meetings of the Privy Council, the group of noblemen who advised the queen – which wasn't unlikely given his enormous bulk – but his real reason was that he was unhappy with Mary, Queen of Scots' tolerance for Protestantism and, particularly, her interest in protecting her claim to the English line of succession. Mary, Queen of Scots had not accepted Huntly as one of her close confidantes, and instead chose to rely on her half-brother Lord James Stewart.[21] Huntly and James Stewart had publicly clashed, arguing about religion in front of the young queen in an incident gleefully reported on by the English ambassador.[22] However, although he chose to withdraw from court, Huntly had left two of his sons in the Central Belt: his heir, George, was staying with his in-laws the Hamiltons, while John was in Edinburgh to take care of the court case against James Ogilvie.

James Ogilvie had been a loyal supporter of the Scottish crown for many years: he had served Mary of Guise and even travelled to France in her retinue when she had visited in 1550[23] and was more hopeful of getting his inheritance and Findlater Castle back through the courts in Edinburgh than in the north of Scotland where Huntly was in control of the justice system. However, the case was instead brought out onto the streets. Mary, Queen of Scots was ensconced in Holyrood Palace at the bottom of the Royal Mile, while the tall stone houses ran up the hill towards the castle. The wynds and narrow closes of Edinburgh's Old Town are still there today, and we can picture the scene: on the night of 27th June 1562, between nine and ten at night, when in the long Scottish summer evening it was still light enough to see clearly, James Ogilvie and his supporters met John Gordon and his entourage coming the other way. There was a brawl, with 'many blows given and taken'.[24] James Ogilvie, seeing that he was in trouble, tried to run, but was chased and several of his men hurt – then, in the melee, John Gordon badly wounded Lord Ogilvie of Airlie's right arm.[25] Some reports said Ogilvie of Airlie's arm was completely severed; he was 'evil hurt' and mutilated.[26] People in the houses nearby heard the noise and came running out, understandably shocked and angry at this large group of people bringing their northern brawls onto their streets and disturbing their rest. John Gordon was "apprehended by the citizens" of Edinburgh, and thrown into the Tolbooth.[27] The unlucky Ogilvie of Airlie was taken to a surgeon, along with the other injured from both sides. The surgeon declared that the great artery in Ogilvie of Airlie's arm was cut, and that "gyf he bledis agane the samyn wilbe his deid".[28]

Mary, Queen of Scots' half-brother Lord James Stewart saw immediately that this was a situation he could take advantage of. He was pleased at his own raised status at his half-sister's court, and did not like Huntly: anything that decreased Huntly's power while increasing his own power was a good thing, in his opinion. John Gordon was in prison for a little while, but, since prison for people of noble rank was generally fairly lenient, when John learnt that he would not get bail, he escaped and returned north to his family.[29] Lord James then persuaded his half-sister Mary, Queen of Scots that what she needed to do was support her loyal retainer James Ogilvie, follow John Gordon to the north and deal with both John Gordon and his father Huntly decisively.

Lord James Stewart had another motivation behind this as well. Just four months previously he had been wed to Agnes Keith. For Jean's family, there had initially been two main interests in this wedding ceremony: the first was that the errant John Gordon had been returned to favour enough to be knighted there,[30] while the second was their family links to the bride, Agnes Keith. Agnes was Jean's cousin on her mother's side. Jean's mother was close to her family, and Jean was to keep up her links with Agnes for many years. In existing portraits of Jean and Agnes, there is a strong family resemblance; the same oval face and direct gaze. Agnes' portrait shows a haughty woman, dressed in the very finest black and white clothes full of detail and embroidery, with a high collar and small ruff, and a long, knotted double string of pearls. The matching wedding portrait of James Stewart shows him also dressed in black: at first glance it is a sober, austere costume, but in rich, dark clothes with fine embroidered detail Lord James could look wealthy yet restrained in a suitably Protestant way. The Lord James Stewart has something of the look of his father King James V, but his features are less regular, his countenance less appealing. Both Agnes and James stare out of their portraits in a challenging and commanding way, a well-matched couple. In some ways there was potential here for

Jean's family and Lord James Stewart to move closer, particularly as it was a love match: Lord James had actually rejected his mother's choice of bride for him – uncharacteristically giving up land and power – and had waited a long time to marry Agnes.[31] However, what Jean and her family did not know was that at the wedding Mary, Queen of Scots had secretly made Lord James Stewart the Earl of Moray – taking that land away from Huntly, who had been its administrator.[32] Lord James had been given the title to those covetable lands right next to Huntly's own area in the north-east. The new Earl of Moray had several motivations, now, to see Huntly's power reduced even further.

Mary, Queen of Scots was keen to travel north and see more of her kingdom – particularly as plans to meet Elizabeth of England had fallen through – and she treated the journey as something of a pleasure trip. The list of places that Mary visited in Scotland is a gift to the tourist industry and, in some ways, that is exactly what Mary was: a tourist in a country she barely knew. It seemed she sometimes treated her early days in Scotland as a little holiday: she had been brought up to believe that France was the superior country, and her place was in French or European politics, and she behaved accordingly. She did not take seriously the idea that she should be fully immersed in learning the intricacies of Scottish politics, as her mind was firmly focused on the bigger picture of relations with England and within Europe. After the French court, Edinburgh seemed like a small place of little significance, while the north of Scotland was an exotic, wild territory where she could see interesting subjects in Highland dress, rather than a vital piece of her kingdom that she would do well to learn how to manage properly. Moray did not disillusion her: a Lowland Scot himself, for him the north was a place where he could obtain land and titles, and the more his half-sister relied on his interpretation of Scottish politics the more he could influence things the way he wanted.

In August 1562, Mary, Queen of Scots set out from Edinburgh, accompanied by a large armed guard, including Huntly-haters Moray and James Ogilvie, who wrote a diary of their journey.[33]

Mary, Queen of Scots made a slow progress towards the north-east, stopping on the way at Stirling and various other smaller places. By the time they reached Aberdeen, the English ambassador Randolph, who had accompanied Mary, Queen of Scots all the way, was fed up. He had found the whole experience particularly dreadful: 'Her grace's journey is cumbersome, painful and marvellously long, the weather extremely foul and cold, all victuals marvellously dear, and the corn is not likely to come to ripeness...'[34]

As Mary, Queen of Scots finally rode up to Aberdeen, she was greeted at the city gates by Jean's mother, Elizabeth Lady Huntly. As usual, Lady Huntly was surrounded by her Gordon retinue, including Jean herself,[35] and the effect on Mary, Queen of Scots was similar to the effect Huntly Castle had had on Mary of Guise. Mary, Queen of Scots and her followers were tired and travel-stained; Elizabeth, Countess of Huntly, and her family and followers were magnificent. Lady Huntly bore off the young queen and pressed her to show leniency to her son John. Mary replied that John would have to come to Aberdeen and be tried there. He could bring up to 100 men with him, she stated. John promptly showed up in town – but brought with him about a thousand of his own men. Mary, on Moray's advice, said that John should take himself to Stirling Castle, to await the outcome of judgement on his actions. John replied that he was ready to agree to this – until he found out that he would be guarded there by one of Moray's kinsmen: he considered this to be far too dangerous, and refused to go to Stirling, leaving Aberdeen instead, with his men, for the safety of his castle of Findlater.[36]

Thinking to try and salvage something from the situation, the Earl and Countess of Huntly invited Mary, Queen of Scots to Huntly Castle, and Jean and her family began to make elaborate preparations for a royal visit to their house. Huntly suggested that Mary, Queen of Scots could even hear a private Mass in his family chapel. However, as Scotland was now officially Protestant, this welcoming gesture was in fact illegal: only Mary and her household were allowed to hold Mass. Huntly's offer could be interpreted as an attempt to entice Mary away from her line of religious tolerance, and into openly celebrating her Catholic faith – and it made him seem as though he were over-stepping his authority. To Mary, Queen of Scots, it seemed like Huntly was acting as though he were the royalty in the north, instead of him and his family submitting to her authority. Even though Huntly Castle was relatively close to her base in Aberdeen, Mary, Queen of Scots refused to visit – though she did allow the English ambassador Randolph and the Earl of Argyll to take up the offer of hospitality. The visit to the comforts of Huntly Castle cheered Randolph up a bit after his moans about the journey north, and he reported to Elizabeth of England that not only was Huntly Castle fairer furnished than any other nobleman's home he had seen in Scotland, but also, in his opinion, Huntly was a fairly good subject, on the whole, and certainly not a major threat to Mary, even if he did dislike Moray.[37] Jean and her family had done a good job in offering hospitality to their guests – it was just unfortunate that they had not persuaded Mary, Queen of Scots to visit.

Mary, however, continued to rely on her half-brother Lord James' assessment of the situation, and avoided Huntly Castle as she travelled back towards Inverness, making various stops along the way. One important stop was Darnaway Castle, the official residence of the Earl of Moray, where, under the great medieval hammerbeam roof of the banqueting hall, she held a meeting of her Privy Council and publicly proclaimed that her half-brother now held the Earldom of Moray.[38] She added that the land in dispute between John Gordon and James Ogilvie should be forfeit to the crown, and that no one should assist John Gordon in any way.[39]

The following day Mary travelled the short distance to Inverness, where she was incensed to be refused entry to the castle. There were only 12 men inside the castle, but their commander refused to open up to the man he was informed was the new Earl of Moray, and said that he only took orders from the Earl of Huntly, or from Huntly's son George, as Sheriff of Inverness. The castle commander may have already had orders from John Gordon to wait for reinforcements, or he may have been acting from a misplaced sense of duty – George was still in the south of Scotland with his in-laws, and had assumed that Mary, if she visited Inverness, would be accompanied by his father, so had not given any orders to Inverness Castle to welcome the Queen of Scots.[40] Mary had to stay the night in a private house opposite the castle.[41]

Mary was outraged at what she saw as a personal affront to her dignity and position, always one of her first considerations, and Moray was easily able to turn those feelings of anger towards Huntly and his family, and to emphasise the personal threat to Mary herself. However, Mary was distracted and charmed by the arrival the following morning of the northern clans to pay homage to their queen. Aodh Mackay, no lover of Huntly, brought his men down to show his support for the Queen of Scots, and he was joined by the Munros, Mackintoshes and others.[42] The young Lord Lovat brought 400 of the Fraser men, 'truly prime, expert men, most of them gentlemen's children, the flower of the clan', as well as some of the women of the family, and made a particular impression: neither Mary nor many of her retinue had ever seen a mustering of the clans before, and they were delighted by the colourful plaids, the handsome dark-haired men, the picturesque Gaelic speakers ready to pledge loyalty, and the flattering reminiscences of the Dowager of Lovat, who remembered meeting Mary's mother. The feeling was mutual: Lord Lovat was only 17 and this was his first public outing; his head was completely turned by the beautiful young queen and he engaged to escort Mary in safety to wherever she needed to go.[43]

Later that day, Mary was finally allowed into Inverness Castle – but only after orders from Huntly had been hastily delivered. At Huntly Castle, where Huntly and the rest of his family were still waiting and hoping that Mary would visit them, there was confusion over what was happening, as rumours reached them by messenger. Jean's brother John was playing his own game at Findlater Castle, and now there were problems in Inverness as well – and it was suddenly getting more brutal. As retaliation for the previous day's events and what Mary and Moray saw as his insolence, the commander of Inverness Castle was hanged over the battlements. After some time his head was severed from his body and displayed on the castle walls.[44] The other men in the garrison had their hands bound and were condemned to death or 'perpetual prison'; five more were hanged though some were given mercy.[45] Having disposed of them, Mary and some of her attendants found time to do some shopping, ordering from Inverness some of the Highland dress and plaids they were so taken with.[46]

Mary set out again for Aberdeen after about five days, followed now by around three thousand men. The young Lord Lovat chivalrously escorted her part of the way, but was sent home as Mary very prettily said that she did not want to be the cause of more clan warfare: she did add to Lovat though, that perhaps he would soon hear of the downfall of his clan's enemies, the Huntlys.[47] On the way back to Aberdeen, Mary and her force stopped at various places, including receiving hospitality from Bishop Patrick Hepburn at Spynie Palace,[48] and also at Boyne, the family home of Alex Ogilvie, the young man that Jean was in love with. At Boyne, Mary 'dined and supped'[49], and, in the course of the evening, took an interest in her young host. Alex Ogilvie's father had only recently died, and Alex was a young and inexperienced head of his House. Now he was not only being asked to entertain royalty, but he was also being asked to entertain a royal queen who was in pursuit of the most powerful man in the area: Huntly. Although Alex was an Ogilvie, on the side of a family Mary was supporting, she must have known that local gossip was strongly linking Alex Ogilvie with Jean Gordon, the daughter of her enemy. Alex Ogilvie was only a minor nobleman, and he was in a difficult position, while Mary held all the cards. Mary, Queen of Scots decided her play would be to grant to Lord Mar the gift of marriage of Alex Ogilvie.[50] This meant Mar had a say in who Alex Ogilvie could marry. A gift of marriage was not a wholly unusual arrangement; it gave the recipient a certain measure of power and possible financial gain, and it could have been given without any knowledge of Jean's attachment to Alex Ogilvie. It wasn't a power that Mar exercised, and Mary, Queen of Scots herself later set little store by it. But it looked very like Mary, Queen of Scots was deliberately attacking Huntly through his daughter

Jean: Mary was showing that she could block any marriage that any member of the House of Huntly wanted and that she had ultimate control not only over Alex Ogilvie but over all the Scottish nobles. For Jean, this would have felt like another piece of the battle she and her family were fighting.

Meanwhile, Mary, Queen of Scots moved on towards Banff, stopping at Findlater Castle, the former Ogilvie stronghold now in the possession of Jean's brother John Gordon. Mary sent a trumpeter forward to summon the commander of the castle but, as in Inverness, she was refused entry. Findlater Castle is situated on a rocky promontory jutting out into the water, in a supremely defensible position, and Mary, frustrated, had no option but to carry on, though she left behind a small party of men in the hope that they could contain the castle's inhabitants.

The situation was somewhere in an uncomfortable position between a war footing and a tourist trip, and when Mary arrived back in the city of Aberdeen, she was welcomed with 'entertainments', 'spectacles, plays interludes' and 'many great tokens of her welcome', including presents such as a valuable double gilt silver cup with 500 crowns in it.[51] While she enjoyed these and rested, she sent for more arms and men, and dispatched a further messenger to Huntly Castle demanding that Huntly give up the two impressive cannon that sat intimidatingly in the castle courtyard. The messenger was received at Jean's family home with courtesy, as Huntly told him that the cannon did not need to be moved, as obviously both the cannon and Huntly himself were at Mary's disposal, ready to work for her. Jean's father, in the demonstrative emotional fashion of the time, added that he was not responsible for his son John's actions or feud with the Ogilvies: 'These and other like words, mingled with many tears and sobs, he desired to be reported to his dear mistress from her most obedient subject'.[52] After Jean's father had thus prostrated himself to show willing to Mary, Jean's mother Elizabeth Lady Huntly added her piece, and took Mary's messenger to the chapel at Huntly Castle, which still lay waiting its royal visitor, where she emphasised the fact that the Gordons were some of the few loyal Catholic supporters left to Mary: "The lady his wife with heavy cheer leadeth the messenger into her holy chapel, fair and trimly hanged, all ornaments and mass-robes ready lying upon the altar, with cross and candles standing upon it, and said unto him: Good friend, you see here the envy that is borne unto my husband; would he have forsaken God and his religion, as those who are now about the Queen's grace and have the whole guiding of her have done, my husband had never been put at as now he is. God, saith she, and He that is upon this holy altar, whom I believe in, will, I am sure, save us, and let our true-meaning hearts be known; and as I have said unto you, so I pray you let it be said unto your mistress. My husband was ever obedient unto her, and so will die her faithful subject."[53]

The Countess of Huntly's words were reported to Mary, Queen of Scots in secret, but Mary soon broadcast to everyone the fact that she did not believe Huntly and his wife at all. She did not trust the entire family.

Moray's aim was to keep Huntly away from Mary: he wanted to encourage a sense of unreality, to keep Mary thinking that it was all a sort of game where she would continue to receive presents and entertainments wherever she went, while troops and handsome Highland clansmen flocked to protect her as the sinister looming figure of Huntly was dealt with in the background. If Huntly spoke to Mary directly, presenting himself in the flesh as a portly, avuncular friend of Mary's mother, the spell might be broken.

In Huntly Castle, the atmosphere was entirely different. There were no entertainments here, and Jean and her family realised that the situation was grave. The news of Mary's attempts to gain entry to Inverness and Findlater Castles, and her subsequent actions on refusal, made Huntly realise that both he and his son John's lives were truly in danger. Only a few months ago, Jean had been secure in her family's position. It would have been inconceivable that their power in the north could be threatened, no matter what happened in the south. Now, Huntly took to spending his nights sleeping in different places, returning to Huntly Castle to see his wife, Jean and her siblings only during the day. Jean and her family were busy putting Huntly Castle on a war footing, packing away tapestries, and hiding Catholic decorations. Learning how Huntly spent his days and nights, 14 of Mary, Queen of Scots' men, including the tenacious Kirkcaldy of Grange,[54] rode up to Huntly Castle in the daytime, hoping to catch Huntly as he ate his meal – but as they were spotted, Jean's brother John and his followers were also sighted riding nearby, and, in the confusion, Huntly escaped over a back wall – without even his boots or sword – and rode away.[55]

The pursuers were unable to catch up with Huntly, who was on a fresh horse and was a notable horseman like all the Gordons, and so they returned to Huntly Castle. Lady Huntly was forced to welcome them in, and Jean had the opportunity once again to see her formidable mother's command and control of even the most unwelcome situation. Lady Huntly 'made such cheer as she could' but showed her uninvited guests a changed Huntly Castle: she and her family had stripped the castle of many of its riches, turning it from a palace in readiness for a royal visit into a defensive fortress ready to withstand attack.[56] The only place they had left untouched was the chapel, which was still ready and waiting for Mary, Queen of Scots. Jean and her family were trying to emphasise their shared Catholic faith to their new young Queen, but Mary, encouraged by her half-brother Moray, refused to agree that the Huntlys could be her biggest allies.

Meanwhile, at Findlater Castle, the small party besieging Jean's brother John had a spectacularly unsuccessful time as the castle inhabitants received reinforcements then sneaked out during the night to attack the Queen's party while they slept, stealing all their arms and money, capturing their leader and forcing the rest of the men to leave the neighbourhood.[57] Mary, Queen of Scots was furious at this humiliation of her troops, and now officially put all the Gordons to the horn, meaning that no one should aid them, and demanded the surrender of not only Findlater Castle but now also Huntly Castle.[58] Mary went on to pardon everyone who was at feud with Huntly, including the Forbes and Mackintosh families, on the condition that they supported Mary against Huntly.[59]

As this was all taking place in the north of Scotland, Mary was also avidly reading the reports she was receiving from elsewhere, about the Earl of Bothwell escaping from his prison in Edinburgh Castle, and the news from France, where her beloved uncles, the Ducs de Guise, were celebrating victory over Protestants. Mary was so busy thinking about Catholics in France that she did not seem to realise that what she was doing in Scotland was taking down her biggest Catholic supporter. Not only that, but the Protestants in France had been supported by England, and the English queen was unhappy about Scotland's support of France. Queen Elizabeth of England was sickening for smallpox, but she was already writing in a "hot fever" to Mary, talking of tragedy: "Whilst the ravens croaked," Elizabeth wrote dramatically, she "kept her ears stopped, like Ulysses; but when her counsellors thought her too improvident she woke from her slumber . . . it will not be her fault if peace is not maintained between England and Scotland".[60] The Queen of Scots was acting like a Frenchwoman who could only see the French side of a victory. She might have been in the Highlands, but she was not thinking about the different areas of Scotland, or even about Scottish power politics. Her focus was disappointingly elsewhere; Jean's family were being brought down without thought on Mary's part, as Moray stage-managed events for his own advancement.

Jean's family made two more desperate attempts at reconciliation with Mary. As Mary waited in Aberdeen, a boy came to her with what he said were the keys to Findlater Castle, where Jean's brother John was holding out. The castle door was open to Mary, the boy said. Mary refused to accept the keys, saying that a boy was not the right person to deliver them and that the whole thing seemed suspicious.[61] She had other means to open these doors, she stated.

When the keys were rejected, Lady Huntly herself then set off for Aberdeen, with her usual entourage of family, serving men and women. Before Lady Huntly even got to the gates of Aberdeen city, a messenger arrived to say that Lady Huntly would not be welcome and that she should return to Huntly Castle. The messenger spoke for Mary, but may have come from Moray. Lady Huntly turned around and went home.

Back in Huntly Castle, with its sumptuous furnishings packed away and the cannons in the courtyard as the place was prepared for war, a furious Lady Huntly searched for a way forward. It was popularly said that she consulted with witches, who prophesised that by nightfall Huntly would be in Aberdeen without a wound on his body.[62] Encouraged by this, Lady Huntly urged her husband and son John to stop their game of hiding and instead to take their armed men and meet with Queen Mary.

Huntly had boasted that he could raise thousands of men for Mary, Queen of Scots, but it was another thing to raise men to march against her. The whole situation was hopelessly confused: Huntly saw Mary as standing against Catholicism by rejecting him, but Mary had many prominent Catholics on her side, including Huntly's own son-in-law, the Earl of Atholl (husband of Jean's late sister Elizabeth). Huntly's ally and kinsman the Earl of Sutherland had been supporting Mary in Aberdeen – but Sutherland was also quietly passing on information to Huntly. The current situation had been triggered by John's conflict with the Ogilvies, but rumours were growing in the strange atmosphere of war and entertainment and it was now being said that John wanted to kidnap and marry Mary, Queen of Scots and bring back Catholic rule in Scotland. The conflict cut across family and religious lines – it was not, in fact, a northern conflict at all, but had been engineered by Moray. It made no sense in the interests of the north of Scotland, and little sense in terms of Mary's own interests, but perfect sense if the aim was for Moray to oust a powerful man and take over.

Jean and her mother were left in Huntly Castle, while Huntly and two of his sons, John and 17-year-old Adam, gathered what forces they could – around seven hundred men – and marched towards Aberdeen. Moray, with around two thousand followers, met them about 12 miles away from the city at Corrichie. A sympathetic Catholic report written after the event stated that Moray tried to tempt Huntly's troops away by sending over a herald who said that everyone could leave unmolested except Huntly himself, but other reports said that Huntly surprised a small body of Moray's men and gained the first advantage before Moray rushed up with the rest of his troops. The same Catholic report has the text of a long speech supposedly made by Huntly who rallied his troops by saying that if they did not stand and fight for Catholicism now, there would be nothing left in Scotland worth fighting for. Encouraged by this, the two sides started to fight. Huntly charged first, and "came with such resolution that he beat Moray back with some slaughter of his men; but being too hote in the chase, engaged himselfe so farr that before he was aware, he was surrounded and oppressed with number, and totalie routed".[63] Huntly was outnumbered and retreated to high ground, where he might have had a commanding position, but Moray had superior weapons, and guns were fired on Huntly's troops.[64] Huntly led his men forward again and soon he was fighting hand-to-hand with men he recognised, who had once counted as his friends. Local men like the Forbes broke and ran, but Moray's experienced Lowland troops stood firm, with pikes outstretched. The Gordon charge broke on the pikes. Around 220 of Huntly's men were killed. He was surrounded on all sides by the enemy. Huntly and his sons John and Adam were forced to surrender and Moray's men prepared to take them, along with 120 of their followers, as prisoners to Aberdeen.[65]

The entire fight had taken place between 3 and 4pm in the afternoon of 28th October. That hour's work not only affected Jean's family, but also changed the power balance in the north of Scotland and arguably brought any possibility of a Counter-Reformation in Scotland to an end.

As the massive defeat of the Huntlys became apparent, rumours and symbolism swirled around descriptions of the event. Lady Huntly's consultation with witches before the battle was talked about, and, as Huntly was led away a prisoner, another case of prophetic witchcraft was invoked: Huntly asked the name of the place where they were – "Corrichie", he was told. "Corrichie!" he cried – long ago, a witch had prophesised that he would die at Corrichie. He had always thought this meant Crichie, a stop on the route from Huntly Castle to Aberdeen, which he had deliberately avoided for years. "Corrichie!" he cried again. Then, in the memorable words of the *Diurnal of Remarkable Occurrents that have passed within the country of Scotland*, Jean's father Huntly suddenly 'swelled and burst': speaking not one word, he "suddenly fell from his horse stark dead".[66] Overweight, overtired after weeks of being under stress and on the run, the corpulent Huntly's health finally gave up. He probably died of a heart attack or stroke. There was confusion as his sons saw their father fall in front of them, but Moray's troops managed to convey John and Adam, and the body of their father, to Aberdeen.

CHAPTER THREE

The Downfall of the House of Huntly:
1562–1564

The prophecy of Lady Huntly's tame witches had been fulfilled: Huntly was in Aberdeen without a scratch on him as they had promised – but he was dead. John Knox said that Lady Huntly blamed her chief witch for the defeat, but the witch defended herself by saying that her prophecy had come true to the letter.[1] Huntly's body had been carried from the battlefield with some difficulty; eventually thrown over two creels, or fish-baskets, and transported that way, and taken, along with Jean's brothers John and Adam and the other prisoners, to Aberdeen Tolbooth. Huntly's body lay there overnight, and was an object of curiosity for many, who came to see the extraordinary downfall of the Earl, as he lay dressed only in a canvas doublet, grey hose, and hastily covered by one of the fine wool tapestries more usually found hanging on the walls.[2] One of Huntly's children may have been able to come to him: Jean's middle sister, Margaret, wife of the Master of Forbes. There had been Forbes on both sides of the conflict at Corrichie, but Margaret's husband and parents-in-law were resolutely Protestant and had opposed Huntly. Margaret's mother-in-law was in Aberdeen, and the morning after Corrichie she joined the groups of people who wished to view Huntly's body: "What stability shall we judge to be in this world?" Margaret's mother-in-law asked when she saw him. "There lieth he that yesterday in the morning was held the wisest, the richest, and a man of greatest power that was in Scotland."[3] "In man's opinion," said John Knox, other than the royal family, "there was not such a one these three hundred years in this realm produced" as Huntly.[4] He was the very greatest in the land, brought to the very worst end. His sons, Jean's brothers the dashing John and the young Adam, were in prison. Moray's triumph was almost complete.

As news of Huntly's defeat was brought to Mary, Queen of Scots in Aberdeen, there was a scramble to decide what to do next. Moray at least had a plan and a vision. Meanwhile, Mary, Queen of Scots dined, passing her supper 'in mirth', and was distracted only by the fact that the English ambassador Randolph had just received a letter from Queen Elizabeth. Mary told Randolph that she hoped to now travel as far south as she had travelled north – since she was now 'assured of good quietness at home',[5] but Randolph reported to Elizabeth that no one quite knew what to do with Huntly's body, with some arguing that he should be buried and the matter thus laid to rest, while others advanced the competing idea of beheading the corpse.[6]

The first thing to do was to try Huntly's sons. It was decided that Adam should be freed on account of his young age,[7] but John must finally be brought to trial. The original feud with the Ogilvies was forgotten in the new fault of taking arms against the Queen. Compromising letters from the Earl of Sutherland had been discovered in Huntly's possession, which were shown to Mary, Queen of Scots to prove that not only Huntly but also Sutherland and others had treasonable thoughts. John, once again in a comfortable prison, was as confident and arrogant as ever, and declared that any fault must lie with his father, avowing his love and support for Mary, Queen of Scots.

However, faced with the implacable Moray, John had no chance this time of escaping or persuading Mary, Queen of Scots that he could be redeemed. He was sentenced to death, and the execution was to be carried out immediately.

Huntly Castle had become forfeit, to be handed over to Mary,

Queen of Scots' men, so Jean and her mother had to leave their home and travel to Aberdeen. Jean's mother tried her best to speak to Mary, Queen of Scots, but once again she was refused an audience.[8] Jean and her mother were left to watch events unfold without hope of influencing them.

John's execution was designed to be a public event to show the crowds in Aberdeen what would happen to those who stood against royal authority, a public declaration that bands of young Gordon men were not in control of the north-east and that the new Earl of Moray was taking charge, under the lead, of course, of his half-sister, Mary, Queen of Scots. Mary herself, and her ladies-in-waiting, all came out to watch the execution as though it was another entertainment laid on for them.

His hands bound by ropes, Jean's brother John was led to the Castlegate, the main marketplace where public executions often took place, followed by four of his closest friends.[9] They were to be beheaded. John was young and handsome, and the crowd was moved by his strength and resolution in the face of death. When John saw the queen, it was said that he cried out that her presence gave him solace. He needed that solace, because the executioner, "a butcherlie fellow", made a botch job of the killing.[10] It was a truly horrendous scene, as a blunt blade meant several strokes were needed before John was dead. Mary, Queen of Scots was so appalled that she broke down completely, weeping uncontrollably, and had to be carried away by her waiting-women before spending the rest of the day, and much of the following day as well, resting in her chamber.[11] The unseen killing of unknown soldiers at Inverness Castle was one thing but witnessing the horrendous death of a young nobleman who was known to her was another. It was only a few months earlier that John had been knighted at Moray's wedding. The tourism aspect of Mary's trip north was emphatically over.

Mary's reaction was noted by the crowd, but it only increased the rumours about her and John: people whispered that she had considered marrying the handsome young Gordon man, and their shared religion was noted. If Mary had hoped by subduing Huntly to prove that she would not re-impose Catholicism on Scotland, she had not succeeded. The only real winner was Moray.

Mary left Aberdeen after John's execution to return to Edinburgh; the journey from the north was not a happy one. John's fate had finally made Mary uneasy about her treatment of the Huntlys, while the weather continued to be poor, and illness followed the Queen's party. The cost of food and drink continued to be prohibitive. Randolph, the English ambassador, who had been miserable enough on the way there, reached new depths on the way back as he endured the new disease of flu – he had "buried the best servant he had, and left another sick behind him, his horses are marred, and his charges so unreasonable that less pleasure he never took of journey, nor worse country he never came into".[12]

Mary was not the only one on her way south. It was decided that the body of Huntly was to be taken to Edinburgh as well: he was charged with the most serious offences, high treason against the monarch and threatening the security of the kingdom, and the law stated that an offender in this case could be brought before Parliament – living or dead. The body of Jean's father was disembowelled, filled with spices by a French physician and embalmed, before being transported by boat to Edinburgh. There it was taken to the Abbey of Holyrood, where the corpse was treated again to make sure it did not putrefy before its trial could finally take place.

Jean and her mother were also on their way to Edinburgh. They could not return to Huntly Castle, as that had been forfeit to the queen – the reason we know so much about the way that Huntly Castle was furnished is that the Queen of Scots had the castle stripped and its contents itemised before they too were sent down to Edinburgh. Jean's family's belongings continued to turn up, reused over the next few years – ecclesiastical items from Aberdeen Cathedral taken by the crown as spoils of war, items spirited away by Moray for his new property of Darnaway Castle, their hangings placed over a royal bed, clothes re-fashioned into a doublet for someone else.[13] Jean and her mother had to find somewhere new to stay.

Others were also leaving: the Earl of Sutherland went into exile in

France after Corrichie, as he was considered to have aided Huntly by passing on information and letters from Aberdeen when Mary was staying there. The Scottish crown was creating a power vacuum and the conditions for a lawless north: where Huntly had been in control, now there was only the new Earl of Moray, who would not be resident in the north and had no prior connections there, while the clans and the troublesome Earl of Caithness in the Far North were to be left to their own devices. The Chief of Mackay, Aodh (who was linked to the Earl of Caithness by marriage) had not only been given remission for his treason in the minority of Mary, Queen of Scots, but it was now even being proposed that he accompany Mary when she visited Queen Elizabeth of England: it was remembered that Aodh had spent time at the court of Elizabeth's father, Henry VIII.[14]

It was one thing to revoke the title of the Earl of Huntly, but this did not mean that Jean and her family were left destitute. Lady Huntly was from a wealthy family background, and Mary, Queen of Scots would have believed, like all her contemporaries, that to be noble was to be born differently: nobles would not ever be expected to live like peasants, and the women in particular needed to be provided for as dependents. Mary was in some ways responsible for Jean and her mother – who were, of course, also related to her – and she was ready to receive them at court. The wife of the exiled Earl of Sutherland was also shown compassion.[15]

Jean was one of a family of 12. Since Mary, Queen of Scots had based herself in Edinburgh, several of her siblings had already made journeys down to the capital of Scotland, and had taken part in events there, making sure from the moment of Mary's arrival that the family had a presence in the royal orbit. Of Jean's brothers and sisters, two of the eldest were already deceased before Corrichie. Huntly's heir, George,[16] had made a base in Edinburgh, living with his wife and his in-laws, the family of the former Regent Arran. Jean's older sister Margaret, married to Lord Forbes, had her married home in the north of Scotland. John had been killed, and Adam was now in prison. That left the five middle sons: William, James, Patrick, Robert and Thomas.

William and James both pursued careers in the church, and James in particular was notably well-educated. To receive an education, men travelled: James started as a student at St Andrews in the early 1550s.[17] Time spent at court, or travelling on the continent, was also considered part of the education of a Scottish noble. William may in fact have already left Scotland to study abroad.

Jean was definitely the youngest daughter of the large Gordon family, and it is generally said that she was the youngest child as well – but this is probably not right. Her date of birth is known to be some time in 1545, making her 17 around the time of Corrichie, but there is little information about some of her brothers. Patrick, Robert and Thomas were not mentioned as fighting at Corrichie, but if they were younger than Jean, that would explain why.[18] It was usual for the sons of nobility to be fostered out with appropriate families as one way of teaching them the importance of family bonds and the skills needed to operate within noble households – with Patrick, Robert and Thomas making homes, for example, within the wider network of the House of Huntly. Their later careers show their strong roots within the Huntly network in the north of Scotland.

Adam, captured after the battle, is described as being Huntly's younger son, which most people assume means the youngest: as he was 17 years old, that makes him very close in age to Jean herself. There is never any hint that Jean and Adam were twins, but two children being born in the same year was certainly not unusual for a noble family, where one aim was to ensure succession by having many children. The violent, warlike Adam seems to have been Jean's closest brother, in age at least. So, Jean had one brother just out of prison (Adam), one sister (Margaret) and three younger brothers (Patrick, Robert and Thomas) probably remaining in the north of Scotland, one older brother (William) studying abroad, and at least two older brothers (James, and the oldest George) waiting for her in Edinburgh.

George was in a bad position. He had been living in Edinburgh with the former Regent, who was now known by his French title of the Duke of Chatelherault, gained when he helped Mary of Guise.

Chatelherault's son Arran was next in line to the throne if Mary, Queen of Scots died childless, so Chatelherault's position at court was undoubtedly high, but his son Arran, who had been traded as a hostage twice in his youth[19] and was already known to be unstable, was in the grip of mental illness, "drowned in dreams",[20] and personally out of favour with Mary, Queen of Scots. Meanwhile Chatelherault's vacillating when he was Regent, the way he had switched allegiance from France to England, Catholic to Protestant, meant that he was often regarded with suspicion by all parties, and he could not offer protection to George. When Mary, Queen of Scots returned to Edinburgh at the end of November after her trip north, Chatelherault was ordered to hand George over. At two o'clock on 28th November, Jean's brother George was seized in Kirk o' Field wynd, at his father-in-law's lodging. He was taken to Edinburgh Castle and imprisoned there awaiting trial.[21] He spent about two months in Edinburgh Castle, before being convicted of treason. The punishment, as for his brother John, was death. However, the sentence was to be carried out at the Queen's pleasure. This meant, for the time being, that he had a stay of execution. George was ordered to go to the castle of Dunbar, where he was put in free ward, meaning he couldn't leave the castle but that his captivity was not too arduous. Dunbar Castle was crown property, and was one of the strongest fortresses in Scotland.

While George was in Dunbar Castle, Moray continually reminded Mary, Queen of Scots of the dangers he perceived in leaving the Huntly heir alive. When Mary refused to have George immediately executed, it is said that Moray tried to have Jean's brother killed by stealth: stealing a secret warrant from the queen, Moray rode to Dunbar and ordered the captain of the castle to execute George. The captain, suspicious about the legality of the warrant, refused to perform the execution and delayed until it could be checked again with Mary herself. When Mary heard of this, she forbade the execution and took George under her protection.[22] Whatever the exact chain of events, it seems that Mary, Queen of Scots was beginning to realise the extent of Moray's ambition, and that she needed the

Gordons as counterweight to Moray's power. The Gordon influence in the north of Scotland had been diminished but not totally destroyed by the Earl of Huntly's death, and Mary began to see that by keeping George alive she had different options.

The winter after the death of the Earl of Huntly, Mary, Queen of Scots remained for the most part at Edinburgh, where her court became more established. It was the first time in a long time that Scotland had had a young, single ruler, enjoying a period of relative stability, and the nobles came to her court to see what the Queen was like. John Knox was not impressed at all by the "all manner of vice which then began to abound; and specially avarice, oppression of the poor, excess, riotous cheer, banqueting, immoderate dancing, and whoredom."[23] Used to the social whirl of the French court, Mary encouraged gaiety, feasting, music and especially dancing. Like many others at the court and in Edinburgh, Knox was particularly concerned with who Mary might marry: Knox told the English ambassador that he was worried about strangers or foreigners being brought into the realm – particularly Catholic ones.[24]

Jean and her mother were in Edinburgh. It is sometimes said that they became ladies-in-waiting to Mary, Queen of Scots, but their names do not appear on the list of people dining as part of the royal household. It seems likely instead that the Countess of Huntly set up her own establishment, with her own domestic arrangements, very close to the Queen's palace. There is a Huntly House on the Royal Mile which is strongly associated with the Gordon family: my research shows this Huntly association is of a later date, but this is exactly the sort of establishment, close to the Palace of Holyrood, that Jean and her mother would have looked for.[25] They were in regular attendance on Mary, Queen of Scots, who encouraged them to be near to demonstrate that she did not hold a grudge against the Gordons.[26] Jean's mother tried her best to pursue the Gordon family interest, not only by showing Mary her willingness to work alongside her, but also by engaging legal help to work on the treason trials that her son, and her deceased husband, were facing.[27]

All this time, the corpse of Jean's father, the Earl of Huntly, had lain in Holyrood Abbey. In May 1563, seven months after Corrichie, Parliament was finally called. On 26th May Parliament opened with Mary, Queen of Scots, "her robes upon her back and a rich crown upon her head", leading all her noblemen and 30 of her ladies to Parliament house, where she made a speech. The speech was written in French but Mary translated it into Scots and spoke in that language, which she was becoming more accustomed to. The following Friday, the deceased Huntly was officially brought to Parliament to answer for his treason.[28] His body was carried through the streets of Edinburgh in a coffin, and displayed for the curious at the Tolbooth, before being brought into the council chamber, where the coffin was propped up to stand before the noblemen of Parliament. Following orders to attend, George had travelled from Dunbar and was there as well. As a woman, Jean was less likely to have attended – though John Knox, in his description of the events, mentions her mother, and draws attention to the number of ladies at the Parliament, so Jean could also have been there.[29] Jean and her sister Margaret were specifically mentioned in the lists of Gordons during the proceedings.[30] Mary, Queen of Scots overlooked proceedings from her throne, with less hysterics than she had watched the execution of Jean's brother John, though the scene in front of her was no less macabre, with the dead body of Huntly propped up his coffin in front of her.[31] A report from an eyewitness was preserved, describing 'the coffin set upright, as if the Earl stood upon his feet'. A piece of 'good black cloth' was put on the coffin, with a picture of the arms or insignia of the House of Huntly pinned to it. The charges and accusations against Huntly were read out to the corpse, and a spokesman was allowed to answer, as if speaking for Huntly. After the charges were discussed, Huntly was found guilty. Immediately, the good black cloth above his coffin was symbolically taken down and replaced by 'a worse' piece of cloth. The arms or insignia of the House of Huntly, which had been pinned on that good cloth, was then torn to pieces 'in sight of the people', and 'likewise struck out of the herald's book'.[32]

The symbolic destruction of the arms of the House of Huntly was hugely significant. In a time when literacy was not universal, signs and symbols took on more importance: the arms would have been a recognisable sign of the power of the House of Huntly – their destruction carried some of the same power as the public burning of a country's flag might today. The Parliament continued, and the Earl of Sutherland was also condemned to remain in exile, despite the protests of his wife, and 11 other Gordon earls and barons were forfeited.[33] Meanwhile, Moray's position as Earl was confirmed, and he received the sheriffdoms of Elgin, Forres and Inverness, as well as the keys to Inverness Castle.[34]

"The parliament ended with great solemnity as it began," the English ambassador Randolph wrote.[35] Before they left, the nobles were treated to a sermon from John Knox: Knox was spectacularly unimpressed with the Parliament, from the overly rich clothes that people wore, the vanity of the nobles, the "stinking pride of women",[36] to the attitude of the Earl of Moray himself. Knox had seen Moray as a Protestant ally who would promote the new religion over everything else at Parliament, but now Knox was offended to see what he thought was Moray putting his own advancement first; focusing on the downfall of the House of Huntly in order to promote Moray's status. Knox wanted Parliament to focus on laws to punish adultery, to seek the restitution of the glebes and manses to the ministers of the kirk, and for the kirk to receive reparation. It was more than a year and a half before Knox and Moray made up to their former friendliness. "There is not one of you against whom was death and destruction threatened, perished in that danger; and how many of your enemies has God plagued before your eyes," thundered Knox, reminding the nobles of the fight they had had to establish Protestantism. "Shall this be the thankfulness that ye shall render unto your God, to betray his cause, when ye have it your own hands to establish it as you please?" Knox saw this as an important Parliament after the establishment of the reformed religion in Scotland: Huntly and other Catholics had been defeated but instead of offering thanks to God and forging on with the establishment of the new religion, the nobles had made a show of taking away Huntly's arms then focused on redistributing honours among themselves. "I can see nothing but such a recoiling from Christ Jesus …" continued Knox. For him, the downfall of the House of Huntly was not enough to prove Mary's commitment to Protestantism. Mary was so offended by Knox's words, particularly his pronouncements on who she should marry, that she held a face-to-face interview with him. As at their previous meetings, Knox was undaunted; Mary cried.[37]

Elizabeth of England was anxious to know what was going to happen now the Parliament was over, but her ambassador Randolph was keen to get leave to come home on private business. Everyone was preparing for a holiday, Randolph wrote, Mary, Queen of Scots finding the chance to wear the Highland clothes she had bought on her shopping trip in Inverness after hanging the castle defenders there: "As many take their journey into Argyll are preparing their Highland apparel, which the Queen has ready, marvellously fair … The writer [Randolph] framed himself as near as he could in outer shape to have been like unto the rest, but received some comfort from him to return into England, which does him more good than any pleasure he should have taken either in a saffron shirt or an Highland plaid."[38] Many of the nobles in Edinburgh might have been preparing for a holiday, but it was a different world for Jean, the remainder of the House of Huntly, and especially for those in the Gordon lands in the north. The bad weather and problems obtaining food which Randolph had complained about so bitterly on his journey north with Mary, Queen of Scots had continued, and the crops had failed again. Ordinary people in Scotland were facing famine conditions, and the problem was especially acute in the north. Many people died from hunger. Knox, when he railed against the Parliament for excess in their dress, was aware of the problems faced by the ordinary people, the subjects of Mary, Queen of Scots. He saw the famine as divine punishment for Mary's religion and actions: "And so did God, according to the threatening of his law, punish the idolatry of our wicked queen … For the riotous feasting, and excessive banqueting, used in court and country, wheresoever that wicked woman repaired, provoked God to strike the staff of bread, and to give his malediction upon the fruits of the earth."[39]

For Jean and her family, their whole world had changed. The trauma of watching the macabre sight of Huntly's corpse put on trial was followed by a period when the Huntlys did not know if they were safe, or what other punishments would be taken against them.[40] George, Jean's brother and Huntly's heir, had just recently become a father himself, to a baby son also called George, but he was not allowed to return to his family. Sent back to captivity in Dunbar Castle, his future was uncertain. At some point in this captivity, George seems to have turned to the Protestant religion.[41] George had been living with Chatelherault, who had worshipped as both a Protestant and Catholic. John Knox was an incredibly powerful speaker, and so many of the things he said made sense to his listeners as he talked about corruption in the old church. Many of the noblemen in Scotland, like the ordinary people, became true converts. Others found it politic to follow the status quo.

Of Jean's other brothers, James took a different path. He made the choice to leave Scotland and become a Jesuit. Before Corrichie, James had seen the visit of Jesuit Nicolas de Gouda, who had come as an emissary from the Pope to speak with Mary, Queen of Scots about the state of Catholicism in Scotland. De Gouda's visit was met with rage from John Knox, who called him a Nuncio of Baal and Beelzebub sent by the Antichrist (the Pope), and de Gouda's success with Mary was limited. De Gouda eventually experienced some difficulty in leaving Scotland safely, but his visit did result in convincing several young Scotsmen, including Jean's brother James, that the best thing they could do would be to join the Jesuit mission. James travelled to Cologne, where he entered the Society of Jesus at the end of September 1563, going on to study theology in Rome.[42] Younger brother Thomas may also have briefly followed James, before returning to the north-east.[43]

The religious status of Jean and some of her brothers and sisters at this time is vague, or at least changeable. Jean was living in a new Scotland now, one that was officially Protestant: where the most powerful Catholic nobleman, her father, had been unable to raise a strong army and therefore comprehensively beaten; where a

Catholic queen worshipped in private but did nothing to allow her subjects to hear Mass. Everything Jean knew and thought settled had been turned upside down – not just her family, but the whole society around her was changing. The old religion seemed doomed, while the new religion spoke directly to ordinary people and their everyday concerns. Jean and her mother continued to live in Edinburgh, attending Mary, Queen of Scots as part of the court but not fully part of the royal household; and under the influence of John Knox, trying to make their way in this new order in which they now found themselves.

CHAPTER FOUR

The Royal Court: 1565–1566

By 1565, Jean Gordon was in Edinburgh, where the nobility flocked to see Mary, Queen of Scots and join the dancing and entertainment she liked to surround herself with. As a young girl in Huntly Castle, Jean had been eager to go out to see the world, but now not only was her family in disgrace, but in order for Jean to fully participate in the social life of the court she had to personally become in some way reconciled to the woman who had ordered the killing of her father and brother.[1]

Mary, Queen of Scots was a young, beautiful, rich woman, and by all accounts she possessed the indefinable quality of charm: people liked her and wanted to be near her. Jean was Mary's relative, a cousin, even if the connection was not close. The nobility was a small group in Scotland, with many complicated layers of intermarriage and Jean would have found it inconceivable to step outside this circle. It is still difficult to imagine Jean and her mother becoming Mary's confidantes, yet Mary was attended by not only Jean and the Countess of Huntly, but also by Jean's sister-in-law, even as Jean's brother George remained in prison.[2] Over time, as the tumultuous events of Mary's reign continued, Jean's Gordon family would become some of Mary's staunchest supporters.

Jean and her mother were companions to Mary, Queen of Scots: they were at court as friends, ready to carry out her orders and help her if need be – for example, they might make up the numbers for a card game or a dance, or, more seriously, give advice on people's backgrounds and whether or not they could be trusted. Mary liked to have people around her, and, after her upbringing in France, she needed trusted Scotswomen who could fill her in on the background of Scottish politics and advise her about the people who came to court and their complicated family relationships. Most of Mary's official royal household had come with her from France, but, as with her half-brother Moray, Mary felt she had a special connection to people in Scotland that she was related to by blood. She welcomed Jean and the other Gordon women, and they responded – at first thinking to encourage her to see the Gordons in a positive light, but slowly helping Mary more and more. Jean's mother seems to have particularly taken this route, and her name begins to crop up when Mary's companions are listed at important events.

Jean was more in the background, but she was now part of Mary's inner circle, regularly spending time in the royal quarters. It was a background familiar to Jean from her youth at Huntly Castle, as Mary lived in luxurious surroundings, surrounded by the finest things, from clothes to music to food – Mary and her court sat on cushioned chairs of gilded leather, carved on the back with the royal crown; they ate at massive, elaborately carved oak tables; they walked on floors of polished oak covered with Turkish carpets;[3] the walls around them were covered with tapestries of gilded leather, velvet or cloth of gold showing images of the Judgement of Paris, the Triumph of Virtue, pictures of armorial shields, great trees and holly branches. In the evenings they listened to fine musicians, danced or read in the library of theology, romance, poetry and music books.[4] Jean knew how to operate in this world and made a good impression on people who met her in Edinburgh. She was a "good, modest and virtuous woman", according to one burgess of Edinburgh who kept a diary mentioning events and people at Mary's court.[5] She was "an excellent noble lady", according to a bishop, and a "proper and virtuous gentlewoman".[6] All these assessments were made by Protestants, so Jean was outwardly conforming to the new religion, and not drawing attention to herself. It would not have been politic for the Gordons to draw any negative attention, and it fits with the pattern of Jean's life: she was generally quiet and contained in outward appearance, however strongly her internal feelings raged.

One of the main topics at court continued to be who Mary would choose as her husband, and love and romance were the main concerns of Mary's court at this time. Alex Ogilvie had also come from the north of Scotland to Edinburgh, and Jean was able to continue seeing him. However, unless the status of the Gordon family was in some way restored, Jean and Alex Ogilvie had no chance of getting married: even without taking into account the Gordons' relationship with the Ogilvies, an unmarried daughter was an important bargaining tool for a family who wanted to raise their status. Without their title, Jean's family also had limited income, as money from the Gordon lands was diverted elsewhere, and, for the moment, Jean was dependent partly on the charity of Mary, Queen of Scots, both financially and socially. Jean received no encouragement from her family to believe a union with Alex Ogilvie was possible. In fact, the Forbes, Jean's sister Margaret's in-laws, made a new marriage arrangement that seemed designed to disrupt Jean's romance. Margaret's sister-in-law Elizabeth, who was the same age as Jean, was offered in marriage to Alex Ogilvie. A contract was drawn up, and a date set: Alex Ogilvie was supposed to marry the daughter of Lord Forbes by 1st November 1565. Even the venue was chosen.[7]

Mary, Queen of Scots loved to matchmake, and had promoted marriage between one of her half-brothers, John Stewart, and Janet Hepburn, the sister of the Earl of Bothwell, when she first arrived in Scotland, as well as encouraging her attendants, the Four Maries, to look for love. The first of the Four Maries, Mary Livingstone, was married in 1565, while the Queen's Secretary, the intelligent and sincere William Maitland of Lethington, was causing much hilarity with his determined pursuit of Mary Fleming. Lethington, a widower 18 years older than Fleming, was thought to be a most unsuitable husband for her, but he was besotted with the "flower" of the Four Maries who was described "as contending with Venus in beauty, with Minerva in wit".[8] Preacher John Knox despaired as the court went on in a whirl of dancing and romance.

However, no matter how romantic she was, Mary, Queen of Scots did not think that she herself would be marrying only for love. She, like Jean, was well aware that noblewomen entered into marriage alliances suitable for their families and their status, and that this particularly applied to queens. One reason that Mary took such vicarious interest in the romantic lives of her ladies-in-waiting was that the shortlist of eligible husbands for the Queen of Scots was somewhat problematic, and her search for a husband was stalling.

Mary, Queen of Scots, the widow of the King of France, wanted to marry someone of equal status to herself, which ideally meant someone from a royal family. However, if her husband was already king of another country, Scotland would be forced into an alliance which might be as unpopular as Bloody Mary of England's union with Spain. As in that case, the religion of the Queen of Scots' intended husband was a particular question point. It was unthinkable to Mary's Parliament that she marry a Catholic, while she herself would have preferred not to marry a Protestant. Marrying a Scottish nobleman could cause problems, as it might raise one family above another and upset the delicate balance of power in the country. Mary was also anxious to marry someone of whom Elizabeth of England approved, as she continued her long-term policy of looking towards the English succession and maintaining peace with England. This raised its own questions: there were no royal Englishmen available, and marrying an English nobleman was something Elizabeth could perceive as problematic, as it would mean that one of Elizabeth's subjects was potentially raised to equal his queen in status. Despite this, Elizabeth of England put forward some startling suggestions, including her own favourite, Robert Dudley. One entertaining biography of Mary, which is actually written by a descendant of the family of one of her potential suitors, draws up a helpful table of the relative merits and drawbacks of each of the men it was proposed that she marry.[9] Merits included being the ruler of large parts of Europe.[10] Drawbacks ranged from indolence of character,[11] to being married already,[12] to being homicidally mad,[13] or being a hunch-backed gluttonous sadistic megalomaniac (Don

Carlos, Crown Prince of Spain – probably Mary's own favoured candidate to begin with).

Into this unimpressive list of suitors walked a man who would change everything. When Henry Stuart, Lord Darnley first travelled to Scotland from England, Mary, Queen of Scots was on progress in Fife.[14] Since they were not officially part of her household, Jean and her mother may have remained in Edinburgh, so they missed the appearance of this tall, handsome, fair young man.[15] Darnley presented himself to Mary, as was proper for any arriving nobleman in Scotland, but went on to the house of his father, the Earl of Lennox. Mary noted Darnley's appearance, and was quite taken with him, but she was busy with her work.[16] When she was on progress, Mary, Queen of Scots was making sure that her subjects got a chance to see her, and to see her dispensing justice, as she sat in court over any disputes.

Darnley was back at Mary's side days after visiting his father though, and from that moment remained with her court, in high favour. When he became ill a few months later, Mary helped to nurse this new and interesting acquaintance back to health. Her mothering instincts roused, Mary fell in love – or in lust – with Darnley. It did seem like it could be the perfect match of personal and public interest. Darnley was closely related to the royal families of both England and Scotland, with a strong claim to the English throne through his mother and rights to the Scottish succession through his father.[17] It seemed that Elizabeth of England favoured his suit, as she had allowed him to travel to Scotland. Even though he was a Scottish nobleman, the fact that he had grown up in England meant that he was not too personally involved in the feuds and friendships that made up the tangled dealings of the Scottish nobility. He was nominally a Catholic and attended Mass with Mary in her private chapel, but he had also gone publicly to hear John Knox preach and seemed able to balance the two religions. He was tall and striking – particularly appealing for Mary, Queen of Scots, a tall woman who dwarfed many of the Scottish noblemen around her at her court. Charming and good-looking, Darnley was very personally attractive to Mary. Mary was a young widow, whose first marriage had been an arranged match of two children, and at 23 she felt that she deserved happiness in marriage. This seemed to be a union that would suit everyone.

The only barrier to the logical correctness of Darnley as a husband was the young man himself. Darnley was a lightweight: his main interests were dancing, drinking and generally living the high life, and, although he looked good and was charming on the surface, he had very little depth.[18] His overwhelming characteristic, partly instilled in him by his strong-minded parents, seemed to be his belief that he was going to be king one day. Darnley lived as though this would be true without actually doing very much to make himself fit for leadership, relying solely on the status conferred upon him by his birth. It is worth noting that the bout of illness, said to be measles, which brought him and Mary together was later thought to actually be the first stage of the STI syphilis.[19]

Darnley was treated warily by the members of Mary's court, who saw from the start that he had the potential to be their king. For Jean and her family, there seemed to be no initial advantage to Mary choosing Darnley. Darnley had been officially welcomed by the main party at court, led by Moray, dining with Moray and the English ambassador Randolph. However, when one of Mary's other half-brothers[20] showed Darnley a map of Scotland with the extent of the new Earl of Moray's lands marked out, Darnley showed his lack of grasp of statecraft by artlessly remarking that it seemed like Moray had an awful lot of land: too much, in fact. Mary made Darnley apologise to Moray, but the damage to Moray and Darnley's relationship had been done.[21] Now, any enemy of Moray could be a friend of Jean Gordon's family – though it was hard to be friends with Darnley.

Darnley had arrived in Scotland in February 1565, and by April of that year it was made official that he and Mary, Queen of Scots were to be married. As Mary rushed headlong into the union with Darnley, it became apparent that this marriage was not going to be welcomed by Moray. Moray signed a bond with several other noblemen saying that they would oppose the marriage, including among the signatories Chatelherault, the father-in-law of Jean's brother George. Chatelherault, of course, had his own claim to the Scottish throne, and would move further down the line of succession if Mary married and had children.[22] According to one Catholic bishop, Moray even spoke to his half-sister Mary personally, making the bold request that she should pass a law making him and his children the next in succession to the crown. As he was a bastard, Moray did not officially register in the line of succession at all, despite the fact that he was the previous King's son. His request, according to Bishop Leslie, was too much for Mary: one of her reasons for marriage was to have children and ensure the succession that way, and she was "shocked at such arrogance and presumption" and the "storm of ambitious hope that seemed to rage in her brother's breast".[23]

Elizabeth of England announced her disapproval of the match, and Mary also received furious opposition from her ambassador to England, Maitland of Lethington. Her Guise relatives and European connections counselled against the union. The effect was to make Mary more resolute. Darnley, meanwhile, became more obnoxious, puffed up with pride, ostentatiously displaying the gifts and clothing he received from Mary, and threatening violence to anyone who stood in his way.

Moray's opposition to Darnley was not just verbal. Moray knew that his time of influence at the Scottish court would wane and disappear once Mary married, and this was his last chance. He and his supporters approached Elizabeth of England for financial backing. Moray was prepared to go against his sovereign.

Mary and Darnley were married on 29th July 1565. On 1st August, Mary and Darnley summoned Moray to explain his conduct: if he did not, he would be pronounced a rebel and put to the horn. On 3rd August, Mary ordered the release of Jean's brother George from prison.[24] At 11 in the morning, it was openly proclaimed at the market cross in Edinburgh by the Queen's Herald that George was received in peace and free to travel anywhere he pleased in Scotland.[25] Mary needed strong support to counterbalance the threat from her half-brother, and Jean's family were to be restored to favour on condition that they supported their queen against Moray. Jean's problem on arriving at court was how to be reconciled to the woman who had ordered the killing of her father and brother: the answer Mary finally gave her was that these killings had been carried out at the order of Moray. Moray had always been the villain and now that Mary's eyes were opened to her half-brother's ambitious designs on the throne, Mary wished to ally herself with her loyal Gordon supporters. Jean's brothers, starting with George, accepted this interpretation of events wholeheartedly. On his release from prison George went straight to the palace of Holyroodhouse, where he was 'gently entertained' by Mary and Darnley.[26]

Moray was declared a rebel on 6th August, three days after George's release,[27] and another proclamation was made at Edinburgh's Mercat Cross, ordering all earls, lords, barons, freeholders, gentlemen and others of substance, as well as all inhabitants of the burgh of Edinburgh aged between 16 and 60 to come, with enough food for 15 days, to escort the new King and Queen to Fife.[28] Mary wanted an army.

What became known as 'The Chaseabout Raid' began. Mary and Moray chased each other around about the country, their armies and supporters never quite meeting in battle. For Jean's family, the most gratifying thing was how George was received: not only was he now in favour at court, but his return to power in the north was greeted with fervour. George sent the fiery cross round in the traditional summons to battle, and over 6,000 men answered his call. Randolph described how: "There comes a great sort out of the north with Lord Gordon . . ."[29] and "the whole force of the north is come to her [Mary]".[30] After the poor show at Corrichie it was clear that this time, the Gordon summons was answered. The people of the north were happy to fight again under the leadership of the Gordons when working for the Queen of Scots and were happy to see George back in control. Jean's family were now irrevocably committed to Mary, Queen of Scots, and were to become her most loyal supporters. In return Mary belatedly began to recognise the importance of their backing. By 25th August, George was 'restored by open proclamation at the Mercat Cross of Edinburgh, to his fame, honour and dignity, and to the lordship of Gordon.'[31]

Mary and Darnley entered into the Chaseabout Raid with gusto. Mary led her troops personally, wearing a helmet, chainmail under a cloak, and carrying a 'pistolet' in her hand. Darnley wore a decorated armour, a 'gilt corslet'.[32] Moray fled to England, his army never meeting Mary's in battle, the countryside in chaos as large groups of men moved around. Mary's force was far greater, not only because she was supported by many of the noblemen but also because she had superior weaponry[33] and the support of the common people in Scotland, who chose a rightful Catholic queen over her Protestant bastard half-brother. When Moray tried to take Edinburgh, he was driven out not only by cannon fire from Edinburgh Castle but also by the citizenry, whose support for Mary he had underestimated.[34] Although Moray appealed to Elizabeth of England to support him as a Protestant, ultimately Elizabeth would not fully support Moray because she could not openly support the overthrow of an anointed queen by one of her subjects – even though she agreed with Moray that Darnley was an unsuitable king who might promote Catholicism. Moray and his followers eventually admitted defeat and exiled themselves to England, but Elizabeth, threatened by warnings from France that Mary, Queen of Scots had French support, took no further action against Darnley.[35]

Mary began to change the people around her at court. After his support and the numbers of men he had been able to summon from the north, George was fully restored to his title of Earl of Huntly in October of 1565.[36] The people Moray had advised her to listen to were now out of favour, while Moray's enemies were promoted. The Gordon Earl of Sutherland, exiled after Corrichie, was allowed to return home from France, and Mary, Queen of Scots personally intervened when he was detained in England on his way back.[37]

Another major new returnee from exile was the Earl of Bothwell, who slipped past the English ships that were trying to intercept him and returned to Scotland from the continent. "It is told that Earl

Bothwell is arrived," said Randolph, "whose power is to do more mischief than ever he was minded to do good in his life; a fit man to be a minister to any shameful act, be it either against God or man."[38] The English loathed him, as Randolph's vitriolic descriptions show. He "takes great things upon him, and promises much. A fit captain for so loose a company as now hangs upon him!"[39] Bothwell was one of the few Scottish noblemen who refused to take English bribes and had alienated Moray and his followers when he had intercepted a shipment of English gold that was heading for the Lords of the Congregation, and handed it over to Mary of Guise. As a Borderer, Bothwell lived on the dividing line between the two countries and had seen first-hand and on a regular basis the effects of animosity between Scotland and England, and he was a steadfast Scottish patriot at a time when many of the noblemen were happy to make alliances based on religious, rather than national, affiliation. However, Bothwell followed the same religion as the Lords of the Congregation and as a devout Protestant regularly attended John Knox's sermons, never wavering in his choice of religion. For this reason, although he was not allied with the Lords of the Congregation, nor had he been a trusted ally of Mary, Queen of Scots. Like Huntly, Bothwell had been a supporter of Mary, Queen of Scots' mother, but Mary of Guise's advice to trust him had been discarded in favour of Moray's advice to cut him off. If Moray hated Huntly, he hated Bothwell even more.

Jean and her family were naturally drawn to this enemy of their enemy. Jean's brother George had met Bothwell before: during the period before Corrichie, George had canvassed for support for his father in the south of Scotland, and had spoken then to Bothwell, who, characteristically, had refused to countenance any action against his queen.[40] Bothwell also had a particularly difficult relationship with George's brother-in-law, the mentally unstable Arran, which had started with the seizure of that English money and continued with various retaliations including an unedifying argument over Arran's mistress, which had exacerbated Arran's fragile mental state.[41] The Gordon defeat, however, had put Bothwell in a bad position, as his enemies like Moray were in the ascendant, and it was shortly after Corrichie that he had temporarily removed himself from Scotland. George and Bothwell now saw that they had common cause: they may not have worked together before, but they both wanted, now, to support their queen and make sure that Moray did not return to favour.

Bothwell, a committed Protestant, also supported George as he explored his faith. John Knox's family traditionally paid allegiance to Bothwell's Hepburn family, and their connection was an old habit that seemed hard to break.[42] Knox continued to preach in St Giles Cathedral, and young noblemen attended the sermons with their entourages. It must have been an extraordinary spectacle and it is easy to imagine Bothwell and George carried away with the rest of the Edinburgh folk who thronged to St Giles every week to hear the great orator Knox raging for their souls with never less than total commitment and conviction. As Knox preached, he asked rhetorical questions of his audience, counting them off on his fingers, then thundering out the decisive responses which he, as a prophet directly inspired by God, knew with certainty.[43] Knox could move a congregation of thousands to tears – or violence. His loud voice proclaimed a central populist and dangerous idea: that Knox believed people had to be what God wanted them to be, even if it was against what the queen said – so disagreement and even open rebellion against monarchs was possible.[44] Moray, Bothwell and George all heard this, and each interpreted it in their own way.

The drawn-out Chaseabout Raid, with Mary pitched against her half-brother Moray, was over by the autumn. Randolph's dispatches to England, always full of colour, were by now extremely partisan: he had wholly committed himself to Moray and his Protestant supporters, was afraid for his own safety after being attacked, having trouble with safe-conduct passes, and generally disgusted with Mary, Queen of Scots and Darnley: "A wilfuller woman, and one more wedded to her own opinion, without order, reason, or discretion, he never knew or heard of than this Queen. Her husband, in all these conditions, and many worse, far passes herself. Her Council, such men as never were esteemed for wisdom or honesty . . ."[45] Mary was wholly reorganising the things Randolph had come to know in Scotland. For Jean, this meant a momentous change in circumstance. Mary, Queen of Scots decided that Jean was to be married to the Earl of Bothwell.

Events had moved extremely quickly. From almost three years out of favour, since Mary's marriage to Darnley the Huntlys had been restored to power in less than a year. Bothwell had become a force to be reckoned with in the six months since he had returned to Scotland.[46] Mary, Queen of Scots saw it as imperative that she shored up her power immediately, since her rebel noblemen, led by her half-brother, were communicating with the royal households in other countries. She needed powerful, allied nobles around her, all working together in her cause – and she particularly wanted strong noblemen to advise her, as Darnley's weakness and inability to lead was becoming obvious.

The union between Bothwell and Jean also made sense in another way: with Bothwell the main power in the Borders, and Jean's family the main power in the north of Scotland, it was a union of two parts of the country that were sometimes marginalised in favour of the power of nobles from the area around Edinburgh. For such a small country, Scotland was amazingly diverse, with different cultures and communities in areas like the north-east (seat of Huntly power), Galloway or the north Highlands. Focusing on the small area around the court and the official seat of power ignored huge swathes of the country, and by learning about Bothwell and Huntly's home territories Mary was potentially opening up new areas of support for herself: as shown by the large numbers of men that George had been able to bring south to help her. The Mary who had treated her trip to the Highlands as a holiday in a quaint land was finally realising that the land and people there were an essential part of the country she ruled. Uniting the Borders and the Highlands in active favour of the crown was a genuinely far-sighted policy that could have changed the way that Scotland was seen and governed.[47] Bothwell already had some links to the north as he had been partly brought up in the north-east, at the home of his great-uncle Bishop Patrick Hepburn, Spynie Palace. Near Elgin, this was very close to Huntly territory. Bothwell had further northern links on his mother's side of the family, and through his sister Janet's second marriage.

Janet Hepburn had originally been one-half of a youthful, energetic marriage to Lord John Stewart, one of Mary, Queen of Scots' half-brothers. Janet had as strong, wild and outrageous a personality as her brother Bothwell, and Lord John, an active man memorably described as 'leaping and dancing',[48] had fallen in love with her from the moment he had met the feisty young woman. Janet had been in attendance on Mary since the young queen's arrival in Scotland, and was well known at court: Randolph the English ambassador had written to England, alluding to a 'merry' scandal not long before Janet's first marriage[49] – 'merry' in Elizabethan language having sexual connotations, though we never learn any details. However, Janet had been widowed before her marriage was even two years old, when Lord John had suddenly sickened and died. Since then she had returned to court. At some point around 1566 she had become engaged and married to John the Stout,[50] Master of Caithness, either because he fell for Janet's charms or because Mary wanted to augment the links she was building up between those from the far south of Scotland, like Janet, and those from the Far North, like the Master of Caithness. Bothwell's marriage to Jean would build on this.

Mary was finally trying to learn about and understand the country that she had moved to, rather than relying on the men around her, her half-brother or her husband, to make her choices for her. Mary started to make decisive choices on her own and push them through quickly. Mary, Queen of Scots had always thought, as she had been taught to do by her mother and those who had raised her, that Scotland was essentially a backwater that had to be brought into the modern world by France. This was the first glimmer that Mary was starting to look at the country in its own right.[51]

Jean's commitment to her Gordon family was being tested: she always wanted to do what was best for the House of Huntly, but now she was being asked to give up Alex Ogilvie for good and marry

someone not of her choice, who was a particularly complex character. Since the arrival of Mary, Queen of Scots in Scotland, Bothwell's
fortunes had fluctuated: he had been imprisoned in Edinburgh
Castle, escaped, imprisoned in the Tower of London, and travelled
on the continent. Compared with the fate of Jean's own father and
brothers, it was not so different, but Bothwell did seem to attract a
particular level of personal vitriol. Ultimately, Bothwell was a loose
cannon who operated on his own terms. Much like Huntly in the
north, he wielded huge power and influence in his own territory in
the Borders. An intelligent, well-educated man, Bothwell had spent
time studying on the continent. He spoke fluent French and was one
of the few Scottish nobles of the sixteenth century to write in the
neat, new and fashionable 'italic' hand. The spread of italic script
throughout Europe was "intimately linked with the Renaissance.
Those Scots who learned and employed this Italian script were
aware that they were using something new and fashionable...
italic... can be used as an indicator of the diffusion of Renaissance
ideas... it was a mark of an education which had included distinct
continental influences".[52] He was also a romantic, drawn to tales of
chivalry – but without forgetting that streak of violence necessary
to be a successful warrior knight. Attention had been caught, too,
by Bothwell's unconventional romantic entanglements. He had been
in love with the handsome, strong-minded and much older Janet
Beaton, the thrice-widowed 'Wizard Lady of Branxholm', more formally known as Lady of Buccleuch. Later, in his European travels,
Bothwell had contracted some sort of handfasting, if not marriage,
to the dramatically Spanish-looking daughter of a Norwegian nobleman and admiral, Anna Throndsen, who is still known in Norway
today as 'Skottefruen', or 'The Scottish Lady'.

In the same way that people are divided about whether Bothwell
was a hero or a villain, they are divided over whether he was handsome or ugly, attractive to women or not: "an ape", "simian", or
"the most ungraceful and the ugliest man you could see" were some
of the comments thrown at him, but others contradicted this with
descriptions of "a handsome presence" and "pre-eminent gifts of

body and mind".[53] A sympathetic biographer summed Bothwell up as a man with "a sleepless glance that seeks to unmask the stratagems of enemies and the treacheries of friends . . . an adventurer with an imagination who lived on his nerves and was never sure what the next moment would bring."[54] A miniature portrait of Bothwell shows a wary-looking, richly dressed man with short dark hair, who is vivid and alive. He looks like the kind of man whose interest comes in his movements.

By 9th February, Jean, her mother, her brother George, and Bothwell, overseen by Mary, Queen of Scots, had drawn up the financial arrangements that would accompany Jean's marriage. The Huntlys were far more well-off than Bothwell now they were restored to their lands, and Bothwell was keen to pay off his creditors – mainly Edinburgh merchants – and have access to some ready cash. Jean's brother, as head of the House of Huntly, agreed to pay a dowry for Jean, and, in return, Bothwell agreed that some land, and his main castle of Crichton, would be in Jean's legal possession during her lifetime.[55] It was a marriage contract that benefitted both bride and groom financially, though Bothwell's immediate gain of paying off his debts was not such a good long-term investment as Jean's land holdings were to be.

Bothwell insisted that the marriage ceremony should be conducted according to Protestant rites, solemnised by the 'holy kirk',[56] but someone took the trouble to apply to the Pope for a Special Dispensation, which Bothwell and Jean needed according to Catholic law, as their families had previously been linked by marriage and so they were actually distantly related to each other.[57] This sort of dispensation was very common in Scotland because of the many intermarriages among the ruling class, but the fact that it was applied for even though the marriage was to be nominally Protestant shows that Jean and her family, despite appearances, had not totally abandoned their Catholic faith – and neither, of course, had the promoter of Jean and Bothwell's match, Mary, Queen of Scots. This dispensation was to be important later on as well, but meanwhile Jean kept it safely and privately among her papers.

Jean had continued to see Alex Ogilvie after her move to Edinburgh, and their attachment was openly known at court. Even the planned Forbes marriage had not dissuaded Jean and Alex Ogilvie, and when the arranged date for the Forbes wedding had passed with no union taking place – perhaps understandably, given the chaotic events of the Chaseabout Raid – they could hold out hope. Now, however, Jean had no option but to agree to marriage with Bothwell: her sovereign had ordered the match, and her family supported it. George aimed for the best legal settlement possible for his sister, which would be to both her advantage and the advantage of the Gordons and Bothwell too, while Mary, Queen of Scots, so recently ready to risk her kingdom to marry for love, was determined that this practical union should go ahead for the good of the country.

Jean seems, however, to have had at least one supporter in her family who was dubious about the marriage with Bothwell. The financial documents and marriage contract were prepared at the beginning of February, and signed by Mary, Queen of Scots, by George and by other witnesses. Jean's mother Elizabeth Keith also signed – but beside her signature she wrote the caveat 'with my hand led on the pen by the lord bishop of Galloway'. The bishop was her brother-in-law, Huntly's brother who had converted to Protestantism and who was to perform the marriage ceremony.[58] Historical commentators on Jean's wedding have consistently assumed that Jean's mother was illiterate, and this was why she needed help signing her name: this was not true. There was absolutely no need for Elizabeth Keith, Lady Huntly, to have her hand guided to sign her name. She was a literate woman who had for years managed correspondence for her husband and their estates, and several holograph letters – that is, letters in her handwriting – are transcribed and published among the correspondence of Mary of Guise.[59] When her husband had been imprisoned by the English, Elizabeth had organised her eldest daughter Margaret's marriage contract with the Forbes family.[60] Why would Elizabeth now need help to sign Jean's marriage contract? As her actions over the next few months show, Jean's mother was in good health. The conclusion is that she was reluctant to sign: she, like Jean, was not happy about the marriage, but there was nothing she could do about it except register her unwillingness to sign in this small way. As a committed Catholic, the Protestant ceremony was likely one of her sticking points: John Knox was a stern critic of Jean's mother, and did not believe, despite George's interest in the reformed church and the family's outward conformance with the reformed religion, that Lady Huntly had converted from Catholicism. He said, "the devil, the mass, and witches, have as great credit of her this day . . . as they had [at the time of Corrichie]."[61] It is possible that Lady Huntly disapproved of the bridegroom on the grounds of his religion, and disapproved also of her children George and Jean's acceptance of that new religion. Jean herself, despite her wish to be with Alex Ogilvie, defiantly signed the marriage contract below her mother's statement, writing her name and subscribing it: "Jean Gordon: With my hand."[62]

Jean and Bothwell sat for miniature portraits to commemorate the wedding: expensive trinkets that showed just how lavish an affair it was going to be. Bothwell's portrait shows that wary face full of personality discussed earlier. Jean's portrait, although acclaimed by art historians as the superior in terms of technicality, is far less revealing.[63] She is shown as a beauty by the accepted standards of the day, with a fashionably high forehead and pale, clear skin. Her hair is drawn tightly back from her face, but what can be seen of it seems to be a fair colour, somewhere between light brown and reddish-brown. There is enough of a resemblance to the portrait of her cousin Agnes, and a later portrait of Jean herself, to be sure that the painter was not taking too much licence when he made her look like a beauty, but, compared to Bothwell, Jean is giving nothing away. She may have been wishing that the wedding would not take place, but it was this mask of self-possessed coolness and calm she chose to present to the world. Jean was 21 when she married, ten years younger than her bridegroom, and this is a portrait of a young woman, still with rounded features in an oval face, a full lower lip, fashionably arched eyebrows, and a long, straight nose. Her head-dress and high collar, and what can be seen of her necklace-chain and clothes are richly decorated and obviously expensive. For the wedding itself, Mary, Queen of Scots supplied Jean with the material for her wedding dress: 12 yards of cloth of silver, a heavy material with the precious metal literally woven through it in thin strands, and six yards of white taffeta for wide sleeves and a train. Royalty was the only person allowed to outshine the bride, and the queen wore a crimson dress lined with Lyons taffeta for the ceremony, fringed with gold thread, and covered in black and gold tracery, then changed into a white dress (her favourite colour, as it flattered her the most) for the celebrations afterwards.[64]

The marriage of Jean Gordon and James Patrick Hepburn, Earl of Bothwell, took place on 24th February 1566 at the Abbey Kirk of Holyrood, next to Mary's royal residence of Holyroodhouse.[65] Mary, Queen of Scots had wished the wedding to take place in the chapel royal, during Mass, but the Protestant bridegroom – and his bride – refused. The Abbey had seen better days, having been damaged during both the Rough Wooing and again in the Reformation, but part of it was still in use, and it welcomed a large crowd to witness Jean's marriage, including not just her family and other nobles but other, less wealthy, guests and onlookers. Bothwell and Jean stood hand in hand in front of Jean's uncle, Alexander Gordon, the Bishop of Galloway,[66] who chose to stand on the same level as the couple rather than ascend into the pulpit. This made it difficult for the large congregation to see clearly what was going on, but the occasion was celebrated with "greit nobilitie and magnificence".[67]

After the ceremony was complete, Jean, Bothwell and their guests streamed out of the church and walked up the Royal Mile to have the wedding breakfast at Kinloch House, the home of a rich Edinburgh townsman who was in favour with the crown.[68] It was an honour to host a royal-approved marriage like this, and it also defrayed the expenses for the cash-strapped Mary, Queen of Scots. Bothwell, like Huntly, did not maintain a house in town. Constant need for ready money was one of the reasons that, at this time, the middle classes in Edinburgh were rising in power and influence and involved in events like this. The celebration did not end that night, but continued for another five days, including not only elaborate meals but also 'jousting and tournaments'. Mary gave out favours, making five men into 'knights of Fife'.[69]

When the celebrations were over, Jean departed with Bothwell for Seton Castle. Lord Seton was master of Mary's household, a loyal Catholic friend to the crown and the half-brother of one of the queen's attendants, the Four Maries: his castle was easily accessible from Edinburgh and Mary, Queen of Scots had been a frequent happy visitor there. However, Jean and Bothwell's honeymoon was a disaster. Judging by his previous relationships with Skottefruen Anna and Janet Beaton, Jean was not the type of woman that Bothwell found attractive: his taste ran to dark-haired, passionate women who were prepared to risk all for dangerous love affairs. Jean was a cool, fair beauty, whose life ran on ordered lines and whose marriage of convenience she had accepted because of its importance to her family. However, it was one thing to commit to a marriage that would suit the Gordons, which Jean likely imagined as being run on similar lines to her parents' established marriage, with separate suites of rooms for the husband and wife; it was another thing to go through with the emotionally charged closeness of a wedding night and honeymoon. Left alone, Bothwell and Jean found that they had some way to go before they could work out how to live together. Whatever happened between them in private spilled out into public view, enough to give rise to some gossip. The story goes that Jean openly voiced her attachment to Alex Ogilvie, before going as far as the outrageous action of appearing before her new husband wearing mourning for her lost love.[70] Jean made it abundantly clear to Bothwell that, as far as she was concerned, theirs was not the marriage she had originally wanted.[71] Less than a week after their honeymoon began, Jean and Bothwell returned, separately, to Edinburgh, and Bothwell threw his interest into affairs of state.

Mary, Queen of Scots kept her side of the bargain for the Gordons though: in return for supporting her, Jean and her family were now decisively back in favour after the disaster of Corrichie.

CHAPTER FIVE

Jean and Bothwell: 1566

Following their bad start, Jean and Bothwell's marriage faced other, outside challenges. Just over two weeks after their wedding, Rizzio, the Queen's Secretary, was murdered in a brutal attack that wholly compromised the queen's husband, threatened the safety of the queen and her unborn child and was the next step in the unravelling of the queen's power in Scotland. Bothwell, Jean's brother George and Jean's mother all played crucial roles in the aftermath of Rizzio's death.

Moray and his immediate supporters were still banished from court, but they had plenty of sympathisers who remained near Mary. Jean's husband's speedy return to the capital after only one week of honeymoon was perhaps evidence of the disastrous relations between him and Jean, but Bothwell was also needed in Edinburgh to serve and protect his queen. Jean may have been left behind at the honeymoon destination of Seton initially,[1] but she was now officially part of Bothwell's household rather than the Gordon household run by her mother, so she was to return to new living arrangements. Both Bothwell and Jean were to stay in quarters at Holyrood Palace with the queen. At least George Gordon, if not also Jean's mother and Bothwell's sister Janet, were all there too.[2] Jean's social circle of family and friends had not radically changed, but her status as a Hepburn wife rather than a Gordon daughter did make things different. Edinburgh was intended to be a staging point before Jean went south to take over the running of Bothwell's household and affairs – but events were overtaking the married couple's plans.

Mary, Queen of Scots was now in about the sixth month of pregnancy, and having trouble sleeping. In the evening of Saturday 9th March 1566 in Holyrood Palace, she, her half-brother Robert, her half-sister Jane, Countess of Argyll, and her secretary David Rizzio were getting ready for a meal, playing cards in her chamber, attended by other courtiers and servants. Despite the recent coolness between them, Mary's husband Darnley unexpectedly joined the party. The whole room was lit by a blaze of candles. In March, daylight started to fade around six, and it would be dark not long after 8pm. It was the height of decadence to stay up late in this way – most peoples' lives were regulated by natural light, and only royalty and the very rich could afford the candles necessary to light a scene like this. Mary thought nothing of it – this was how she often spent her time, with her trusted companions around her. Many of her household were still French, but she had augmented her social group with others as her time in Scotland passed, including her half-siblings and Jean's mother. Another newer friend was Rizzio, an Italian who had first come to court in 1561 in the train of the ambassador of Savoy.[3] Rizzio had first attracted Mary's attention through his musical talent – she loved to have musicians around to entertain her – and he had stayed at the Scottish court. A swarthy, ugly little man, something in his clever personality struck a chord with Mary, and she found him intelligent, entertaining company. He spoke several languages, and when she was in need of a secretary, he was well-placed to take over. Keen to advance his social position, Rizzio was cordially disliked by many, who saw him as an over-ambitious Catholic foreigner usurping their place at court. Rizzio had made a friend of Darnley and was one of the few who had supported Mary in her choice of husband. As Mary had become more estranged from Darnley, however, Rizzio had supported his queen. Mary's enemies saw how they could take advantage of this.

Darnley, stumbling around the intrigues of the Scottish court like a stupid child, was easily persuaded that Mary's friendship with her secretary was something more sinister: Rizzio had undue influence, people whispered – how strange for such an ugly foreigner. Perhaps he was a secret envoy from the Pope? Perhaps he was even Mary's lover? Mary was not spending much time with Darnley, she did not want to go hunting or hawking or to spend money on him or give him the crown matrimonial: perhaps this had nothing to do with the fact that she was pregnant or the Scottish crown had little cash or that Darnley had not shown any sign of taking on any responsibility. Perhaps it was rather because she liked Rizzio more than Darnley. Darnley was complaining that his pregnant wife was no longer sharing her bed with him on a regular basis – perhaps this had less to do with her pregnancy – or to do with the fact that Darnley made no allowances for either her condition or anything other than his own enjoyment – and more to do with the fact that someone had replaced him?

It did not take long for Darnley to be convinced that the only way for him to get full power at court, to gain the purse-strings and the crown matrimonial and be King of Scots in his own right instead of Mary's husband, even to regain Mary's full attention – was to get rid of Rizzio.

Darnley was kin of the Douglas family, one of the four families that circled the Scottish throne.[4] The Douglases were the only one of the major families to have never fully gained control of Scotland, and in Darnley they saw a route to power. Anti-Catholics, supporters of Moray, and the Douglas faction worked together, and a bond was signed with Darnley saying that his interests as King would be promoted. There were several different motivations for nobles to plot with Darnley, but their common idea was that Darnley would be much easier to control on the throne than Mary. Lord Ruthven and the Earl of Morton were two notable conspirators, but they were supported by many others, including Moray from afar.[5] Their plot was widely known: John Knox had preached an ominous sermon not long beforehand, while Elizabeth of England's secretary Cecil was able to tell Darnley's mother about it the day before it happened, but Mary and her new support team of Bothwell and Jean's brother George were let down by their communications networks and were completely unprepared. Darnley had spent the Saturday afternoon playing tennis with Rizzio to lull him into a false sense of security. He now joined Mary for her evening meal, leaving the door open behind him.[6]

Into that brightly candlelit room burst several men, led by the unsavoury Lord Ruthven, an unpleasant man popularly thought to be some sort of warlock. "I know him to use enchantment," Knox reports Mary as saying.[7] Ruthven was clad in full armour, a heavy contrast to the brightly coloured evening robes, velvet hose, satin doublets and soft hats that the seated men at the table wore. He was a sick man, and his deathly pallor was obvious as he stood in the doorway and demanded that Rizzio was handed over to him. Mary, Queen of Scots, always at her best in a crisis situation, rose and put herself between Ruthven and Rizzio, and demanded to know just what was happening and why.

"Let yonder man Davie come forth of your presence," demanded Ruthven, "for he hath been over-long here." "What offence hath he made?" asked Mary. "Great offence to her Majesty's honour; the King her husband, the nobility and commonweal of the realm . . . he hath offended your Majesty's honour; which I dare not be so bold to speak of: As to the King your husband's honour; he hath hindered him of the crown matrimonial, which your grace promised him, besides many other things which are not necessary to be expressed. And as to the nobility, he hath caused your Majesty to banish a great part, and most chief thereof, and fore-fault them at this present Parliament, that he might be made a lord . . ." [8]

Ruthven ordered Darnley to take hold of Mary, and as he did so, the people around Mary came out of their stunned silence and began to approach Ruthven. Ruthven began to shout, and more of his Douglas accomplices came into the room, knocking over the table, all the food and the candlesticks as they charged in. One of Mary's ladies, her half-sister Jane, Countess of Argyll, had the presence of mind to grab the candlesticks as they fell, preventing the tragedy from taking a fiery turn, but that left the deadly scene lit only by one candle and the flickering flames from the fireplace. Rizzio crouched behind his queen, clinging to Mary's skirts, but his fingers were prised off one by one and the queen was pushed away from him and towards her waiting husband. Rizzio, unable to defend himself, was swarmed upon by the group of men, and stabbed with a dagger taken from Darnley. Meanwhile, a loaded pistol was held at Mary's pregnant belly by one of the conspirators, Kerr of Fawdonside.[9] Rizzio was then dragged from the room, and stabbed 56 times in total before his lifeless body was thrown down a flight of stairs. Darnley's dagger was left ostentatiously sticking out of his chest. As Mary remonstrated with Darnley, Lord Ruthven sat down – an insult in itself, as he should have remained standing in the queen's presence – and demanded a drink. Mary turned on Ruthven, but he was implacable in his conviction that he was doing the right thing.

Jean's husband and brother were in their own quarters in Holyrood Palace, waiting for their meal. Like Huntly Castle, Holyrood Palace was divided along gender lines, with separate quarters for men and women. The queen chose her companions, the men dined together, and Jean would have been in a separate room, with her mother and others. George and Bothwell were dining with several people, including the Earl of Sutherland (newly returned from exile), the Earl of Caithness and John the Stout, the Master of Caithness (i.e. the Earl of Caithness' son). It was a family gathering: not only was Bothwell happy to spend time with his new brother-in-law George, the Master of Caithness was also his brother-in-law, as he was married around this time to Bothwell's sister Janet.

Others in attendance at Bothwell's meal included the Earl of Atholl and the Laird of Grant. Bothwell was surrounded by northern lords. This was the new Highland-Border alliance that Mary, Queen of Scots had been promoting, about to be seen in action. Bothwell and his companions soon heard the commotion coming from the queen's quarters. Those of Mary's servants who were not in her room were already rushing to her aid, and the war-cry "A Douglas! A Douglas!" could be heard. Bothwell and George shouted to their servants to follow them and took up what weapons were to hand. Their cooks grabbed the sharp spits the meat was roasting on. Rushing towards the noises of shouting and screaming, Bothwell and George found doors barred against them. The conspirators in Mary's room began to send out word that all was under control, and that the King was in charge. Ruthven lumbered out of Mary's chamber to shake hands with Bothwell and George and share a drink with them: everything was fine, Ruthven assured them, but no, they couldn't see the queen. The whole evening was a strange mixture of extreme courtesy expressed, according to the participants, in reasoned language, mixed with ruthless and barbaric violence. Ruthven left Bothwell and George to their own devices and continued to speak to the Earls of Caithness and Sutherland.[10] Hearing rumours of Moray's imminent return from England, and finding doors in the palace barred to them, Jean's husband and her brother seized the moment and decided to escape: their only way out was through a small window that gave onto the lion pit, but lions were not going to stop them, and, using "some cords" (ropes) out they went.[11]

Out in the city, the movements of men around the palace were noticed, and rumours of an attempt on the queen's life were already spreading. Alarm bells were rung, and the Provost of Edinburgh led a band of around 35 armed citizens carrying torches up to Holyrood Palace where they demanded to see the queen. They were shown instead the queen's husband Darnley, who assured them that everything was under control. With the gates locked and large numbers of the nobility inside, there was little else the people of Edinburgh could do. Mary remained in her quarters, guarded by 80 men.

Now that Bothwell and George were outside the palace, however, they were able to start planning. The key player in their plans was Lady Huntly, Jean's mother. There is some confusion over where exactly Lady Huntly was and whether she was able to meet with Bothwell and George beforehand or whether she acted on her own initiative, but she seems to have spent the evening after Rizzio's murder comforting Mary, Queen of Scots. "The queen passed the night in tears and lamentations, in the company only of the elder

Lady Huntly, and some other of her female attendants, who did their best to comfort her."[12] After Mary had passed the rest of the night under strict guard, with no midwife to check on her condition, Lady Huntly, mother of 12, insisted the following day that she must not only see Mary again to ascertain that she was okay, but that this must be done in private. Mary herself certainly always believed that one of the aims of the conspirators was to deliberately attack her unborn child and even to make her miscarry. The two women withdrew so that Mary could use the 'chaise percée' (which was an early type of portable toilet) and had time for a brief chat. Jean's mother seems to have had a chance to speak with Bothwell or George during the night, and "Lady Huntly (right glad to have her revenge upon Moray) gave [Mary] a message from the Earl of Huntly, her son, and some other noblemen who had escaped, to the effect that they had raised some troops, and that if [Mary] could manage to descend from a window, which they would point out to her, by means of a rope ladder, they all would be in waiting to receive her. Lady Huntly undertook to bring this ladder to the queen, between two dishes, as if it had been some meat."[13] Mary was generally an active young woman, but for someone going into the third trimester of pregnancy this was perhaps asking a bit much: instead Mary had her own, ultimately more effective, plan: Bothwell and George were ordered to be ready to meet her the following night near Seton, where Bothwell and Jean had so recently spent their honeymoon. There was just time for Mary to write a short letter with instructions before one of her more suspicious captors burst into the room.

Lady Huntly hid Mary's letter of instructions in her underwear, next to her skin, and, although the suspicious guards were wary and gave her dress a cursory pat-down, they did not dare to ask Jean's formidable mother to be strip-searched before leaving Mary's chambers. Elizabeth Lady Huntly walked out of the palace unchecked.

Mary, soon to undergo the dangerous and life-threatening experience of childbirth, finally saw that the only way to effectively rule Scotland was compromise and reconciliation. As the lords – their number now augmented by Moray, who had arrived from

England – came and spoke to her reasonably, the contrast between their words and actions seemed stronger than ever. It was clear to Mary, though, that her party would never be strong enough to wholly overcome the Protestant Lords of the Congregation, and that the way forward was through compromise with even her greatest enemies. With great distaste, but extreme practicality and believability, Mary convinced Darnley that she still loved him despite what had happened to Rizzio, and that as her husband his place was by her side. Together, they escaped the palace and went to Seton where Jean's husband and brother were waiting for her. There, Bothwell and George had raised more than 4,000 men to fight for Mary.[14] Realising the force of opposition against them, the rebels collapsed. Mary, accompanied by Bothwell, George and her other loyal lords, made a triumphant procession back into Edinburgh on horseback, where she was welcomed by a glad citizenry. Some of the conspirators escaped to England, others were punished, but Mary pursued her policy of reconciliation further, with formal forgiveness for many, and even the extension of an invitation to Moray to come back to court. Lord Ruthven fled to England, where, after writing his account of the murder, he died of his illness, exclaiming at the very end that "he saw paradise opened, and a great company of angels coming to take him". Nau, the later French secretary of Mary, Queen of Scots, added: "Others say that he died like a madman . . . It is probable that these [visions of angels] were diabolical illusions, wrought by evil spirits, who wished to delude him as he was passing away, that he might not escape them, for during his life they had possessed him with the art of magic."[15] Many of the rebels did not regret their actions in any way, but they all had their own reasons for rebelling, and Mary, Queen of Scots managed to split their ranks and divide her opposition.

It was imperative that Mary, Queen of Scots made sure that not only were those opposing her divided, but those supporting her were loyal and united. For the Gordons, Mary finally allowed the embalmed body of Jean's father to be returned home to the north of Scotland for a decent burial. Huntly was laid to rest in Elgin Cathedral in April 1566, four years after his death had precipitated the downfall of his family.[16] And, seeing the coolness between Jean and Bothwell, Mary, Queen of Scots acted decisively: she arranged a marriage for Jean's first love Alex Ogilvie. The previous marriage agreement between the Ogilvies and the Forbes had not worked out, for whatever reason, and now it was ignored, despite the fact that this meant Alex Ogilvie was sued for 'double avail' for not honouring his pre-nuptial agreements, meaning he would have to pay the Forbes family money.[17] Alex Ogilvie was instead ordered to marry one of the Four Maries, Mary Beaton, as "soon as shall be thought expedient by our Sovereign lady", that is, when Mary, Queen of Scots said so.[18] The wedding took place on 3rd May 1566, in Edinburgh. Jean's brother George was among the signatories to the wedding contract.[19]

Mary Beaton had previously been courted by the English ambassador Thomas Randolph,[20] but Randolph was well out of favour, after supporting Moray and his Protestant lords. The arranged marriage between Mary Beaton and Alex Ogilvie was an effective solution to two of Mary, Queen of Scots' problems – it removed a threat to Jean and Bothwell's marriage and it stopped Mary Beaton from becoming close to an enemy. The feelings of Alex Ogilvie and Mary Beaton, said to be "the hardiest and wisest"[21] (the bravest and most intelligent) of the Four Maries, were not taken into consideration.

Alex Ogilvie's new wife came from a family of Fife lairds and court functionaries, and her mother was one of Mary of Guise's ladies-in-waiting.[22] She was 21, two years older than Jean. A tall woman, plump and pretty with light hair and dark eyes, she was one of the most attractive, if not the most vivacious, of the Four Maries.[23] Mary Beaton was also intelligent and well-read, not only speaking fluent French after her upbringing alongside Mary, Queen of Scots in France, but also with an understanding of Italian.[24] She was said to love poetry, and wrote in looping big letters in a similar hand to the queen.[25] Besides her personal characteristics, Jean may have noted that Mary Beaton's aunt Janet had been Bothwell's mistress.

Randolph, the English ambassador, was left alone, soon to be recalled to England, and not returning to Scotland for over a decade. Mary Beaton, or 'Lady Boyne' as her new official title ran, and her new husband Alex Ogilvie remained at court so that she could continue to attend Mary, Queen of Scots. Mary Beaton was paid "100 livres tournais par an" for her job – less than the unmarried Mary Seton but still placing her among Mary, Queen of Scots' first ladies.[26]

Jean, meanwhile, went to her new home. Bothwell was in high favour at court because of his support after Rizzio's murder, and events were now relatively settled, so Jean left to manage her husband's estates while he remained in Edinburgh. Of course, after the terms of their marriage settlement, many of the lands were now Jean's own personal property. Jean had been brought up by her mother to know how to run and manage a large household and estate, and, after the years in Edinburgh, this was a return to what she knew. As Alex Ogilvie stayed at court with his new wife Mary Beaton, the change of scene and new challenges may have felt like the way forward for Jean.

Family was the most essential thing in life in the sixteenth century. Most wives would expect to move in with not only their husbands, but also their husband's family, and in particular to learn from their mother-in-law. Jean's situation, however, was slightly different. Bothwell's parents, Patrick Hepburn and Agnes Sinclair, had divorced when Bothwell was very young. Bothwell's father, a pale, tubercular man who was "fair and whitely and something hanging-shouldered", yet not unattractive for all that,[27] had laid something of a siege to Mary of Guise, believing that he had a chance of marrying the royal widow, while Agnes had retired to Morham, in East Lothian, where she lived in the tower house and was known as the Lady of Morham. Although Agnes kept in touch with her son, Bothwell had spent little time with either of his parents due to his upbringing in the north. Bothwell's sister Janet, of course, had also been married and out of the family home for many years, though she spent a lot of time at the court in Edinburgh, so could easily travel south to the Borders. What this all meant for Jean in practice was that she was coming into a bachelor household where no woman had been in charge for a while; she would be in sole control and could establish her own routines and ways of doing things. Jean brought her own servants with her and established her home at Crichton Castle south-east of Edinburgh, Bothwell's main base – and, under the very favourable terms of Jean's marriage settlement, officially now Jean's property during her lifetime. After temporarily losing her childhood home, money and status, Jean attached great importance to her ownership of property and her financial stability.

The ruins of Crichton Castle today bear the stamp of the considerable renovations carried out after Jean's time there by Bothwell's nephew, but it is possible to discern the outline of the house that Jean lived in. Like Huntly Castle, Crichton is really a collection of buildings arranged around a central square, but it is smaller, and would have been far less magnificently furnished and decorated. Placed defensively on a small rise, the original building had been built in the 1400s, but added to over time, again in a similar way to Huntly castle. Any alterations made by Bothwell or his father were relatively modest, in reflection of their generally straitened circumstances. It was also essential – perhaps even more so than at Huntly – that the castle could withstand attack, standing as it does so close to disputed Border regions, and there were man-made ditches and banks in the area round about. The most recent serious attack had been only seven years ago, when Bothwell had seized the gold sent by Elizabeth of England to the Protestant Lords of the Congregation. Crichton Castle had been besieged, captured, garrisoned and spoiled by the Protestant Lords of the Congregation's soldiers, so Jean had all sorts of work to do to make it a nobleman's home again.[28]

A small church stands very close to the castle and, as seen together on the approach up the hill to the entrance, the collection of buildings looks impressive. Inside the castle, however, some rooms were not in a good state of repair: the South wing was fit for nobility but the older parts of the building and adjoining cottages and bothies were reserved for servants. The castle had previously hosted royalty, when Mary, Queen of Scots had attended the wedding of her half-brother Lord John Stewart to Bothwell's sister Janet, though it seems that Bothwell had taken advantage of good weather to host some of these celebrations outside in the field below the castle, rather than in the Hall.[29]

Janet Hepburn's second marriage to the Master of Caithness, John the Stout, took place sometime around 1565/66, but her first son Francis Stewart was still the official heir to the Earldom of Bothwell, unless Jean and Bothwell had children. When, at other times, Bothwell and Jean were with other partners, neither of them had any trouble conceiving. Bothwell already had a young son with his mistress, Skottefruen Anna Throndsen. But there were to be no offspring from Bothwell and Jean's marriage. One reason for this is that Bothwell was simply not there: his time was taken up more and more by events at court, while Jean was left to her own devices in Crichton Castle. The other reason was the ongoing personality clash between the two.

Long after the events of 1566, when Mary, Queen of Scots' story had unfolded almost to its inevitable conclusion and she was on trial, a number of letters were produced in evidence: the 'Casket Letters'. These letters had been discovered in a silver casket in Bothwell's possession, and they were copied by Mary's enemies and used as proof that she had done all sorts of things that she should not have. The original letters were mysteriously lost and only copies and extracts were produced at the trial; only copies of these copies have survived, but, since the letters were to prove crucial evidence, they have been pored over and examined and reconstructed by many historians. Their conclusion is that this silver casket belonging to Bothwell originally contained many different items of correspondence, from several different women, and that these were forged and copied out to look like they were all from Mary, Queen of Scots. Bothwell had saved love letters from his mistress Skottefruen Anna Throndsen, letters from his wife Jean, and business letters from his Queen, and the sentiments within them all were mixed up by Mary's enemies to produce something else entirely. Historians have worked to disentangle these, with their main aim usually being to exonerate Mary, but one interpretation is that they show the story of what happened with Jean and Bothwell after their marriage.[30]

Skottefruen Anna Throndsen had returned to her native home of

Norway not long after Mary, Queen of Scots arrived in Scotland, when it had become apparent that not only was Bothwell not prepared to acknowledge her as his true wife, but that Bothwell was also out of favour at court himself. However, it seems that when she heard that Bothwell had returned to Scotland from exile, and was now in favour again, she too returned to Scotland. She may have wanted to check on their son William, who seems to have been left in Scotland, possibly in the care, or at least under the watchful eye, of Bothwell's mother Agnes Sinclair.[31] Bothwell did not want to acknowledge Anna as his former mistress, but she was the mother of his child and he was not only in some way responsible for her, but also did not want her to make a fuss, so he installed her in one of his minor houses, where he was able to visit occasionally on his way from Edinburgh to Crichton. During her lonely time waiting for her lover's infrequent visits, Anna wrote the Sonnets which were later collected in with the Casket Letters:[32] "My heart, my blood, my soul, my care," Anna pleaded to Bothwell, "you promised we should be together all night at our leisure here where I languish, my heart assailed by panic that springs from the absence of the aim of my desire. At one time fear of being forgotten grips me; at others I dread your dear heart hardened by the words of some tale-bearer; at another time I am afraid of some adventure on the road turning back my lover, some fresh troublesome mishap...."[33] Since she hadn't seen him, Anna poured her heart out on paper.

Bothwell tried to deflect attention by accusing Anna of finding solace elsewhere in between his long absences, but Anna soon knew that Bothwell was very definitely with another woman: Jean. Anna wrote more jealous outpourings, accusing Jean of only wanting Bothwell's status and money. Anna became aware of Jean's continuing attachment to Alex Ogilvie, and knew that Jean was refusing Bothwell's advances, so Anna felt she still had a chance with her former lover.

It is one thing to reject someone and quite another to be rejected. Jean had gone into her marriage clearly stating that she wanted Alex Ogilvie, not Bothwell, but that did not mean that she did not want

Bothwell to want her. Jean was horrified to hear of the existence of Anna, and of some of the details of Anna and Bothwell's long-term relationship. Anna was not just someone insignificant who had been cast away by Bothwell in the past, she was the mother of his child, still maintained in her own establishment, who had a certain amount of status in her own country, and who had believed that she and Bothwell were legally married. Anna went straight for Jean's weakness and central care, the status of her Gordon family: "Through you," Anna wrote, "and through your marriage vow / She [Jean] has restored her honour and estate. She has achieved through you a rank more great / Than any of her kin could hope to know."[34] Jean believed her family were of greater status than Bothwell, but, clearly, over the last few years at court, she had not been perceived this way by others. Jean saw her hand in marriage as a gift that could have been bestowed on a more worthy man, Alex Ogilvie. But Anna made fun of this too: "She [Jean] has had to give up nothing, save the embrace / Of a tiresome dolt she once loved dear ..." Alex Ogilvie was only a dolt, "un fâcheux",[35] an annoying person, and that was all Jean had given up. Anna, by contrast, had "gambled conscience, rank and right",[36] left her friends, family and country, and "into [Bothwell's] hands and wholly in his power [placed] my son, my honour and my all".[37] Anna talked of the sacrifices she had made, and her proven love for Bothwell. Both women, Anna and Jean, seem to have found out a lot about each other, perhaps from Bothwell himself: Bothwell was obviously talking to Anna about Jean, and even sharing intimate details of his marriage: Anna writes to Bothwell, "While you made love, she [Jean] lay with cold disdain ... / Taking no joy in your love's fervent art. / ... I saw in her none of the fear of death for you / That such a lord and husband should be due." But Jean was still Bothwell's legal wife. This sonnet of Anna's turns on Jean's change of heart. "Yet now she says she loved it best of all",[38] indicating that, however belatedly, Jean began to try to make compromises and attract Bothwell to her.

Jean thought Bothwell should be running after her trying to make her love him, not spending time with a strange foreign mistress. Jean, in her turn, now wrote to Bothwell during his absences at court. Unlike Anna, Jean, educated alongside her brothers, did not write loving, desperate poetry, but tried to appeal to him as her intellectual equal, writing what is now known as the Medea Casket Letter.[39] In this, she describes how she has seen Anna with another man. Anna, Jean says, is not worthy of Bothwell's attention. He should be spending time with his wife. "The thing I most desire and seek in the world is your good grace ... I will never despair so long as you keep your promise and tell me what is in your mind."[40] The long letter was confusing and oblique, filled with references to classical literature and situations that might reflect Jean and Bothwell's own situation.

Anna in turn heard about Jean's letter and mocked it as "writings all rouged with learning, that does not grow in her brain but is borrowed from some distinguished author".[41] The Bothwell that Anna knew did not want his women to be his intellectual equals; he wanted a lover.

Anna was right in one way: Bothwell did not want all these complications in his love life. His life in politics was complicated enough. He tried to shake things up in his married household by taking Jean to visit Haddington in May 1566: Haddington Abbey had previously been in the hands of Mary, Queen of Scots' secretary William Maitland of Lethington, but since Maitland of Lethington was in disgrace for his lack of support of Mary's marriage to Darnley and his support of Moray, control of the Abbey and its revenues had been handed over to Bothwell, and he and Jean wanted to check on this new asset.[42] Taking Jean to see more of her new financial and land assets was exactly the sort of trip to appeal to her – but it was not very romantic. As Bothwell spent more time with Jean and her household, he did not turn to Jean for companionship; instead his eye was caught by one of Jean's servants, her seamstress Bessie Crawford. Jean was cool and businesslike: by contrast, Bessie was just Bothwell's type; a dark-haired beauty willing to risk everything for love – with the added advantage that she was of low status so could not cause him too much trouble.

Bothwell does not seem to have gone to too much trouble to make sure there were no witnesses to his liaisons with Bessie, and plenty of people saw the two disappear suspiciously up into the steeple of Haddington Abbey, the couple coming back down a little later with their clothing disarranged and covered in dust. Bessie had previously been in service in Edinburgh in Lady Huntly's household, and Jean had brought her with her when she married and moved to Crichton.[43] Bessie had even helped sew Jean's wedding dress.[44] When Jean found out about this supposedly loyal Gordon servant's actions, she was furious, and Bessie was immediately dismissed. Bessie had to return home to her father, a smith named Willie Crawford, who lived in the town of Haddington. That was still very close to where Jean and Bothwell were staying, however, and Bothwell managed to make at least one more assignation with the former sewing maid. Once more, however, Jean found out, and this time Bothwell had to make amends more directly. On 11th June 1566, Bothwell drew up a deed giving to "his beloved wife (for the favour and love he bore her)" for the rest of her life the lands, castle and associated houses of Nether Hailes. Bothwell had to make practical amends for having involved two other women, Anna and Bessie, in his still-new marriage to Jean – and Bothwell had finally understood Jean's businesslike approach to marriage. She was financially in control and she would stand no nonsense from Bothwell. It might be an arranged marriage, but Jean expected Bothwell to commit to her. Bothwell and Jean finally came to some sort of understanding. Friends later testified that they "lived friendly and quietly together, like man and wife as the saying is."[45] Given the chance, they could have worked out an excellent partnership: they were both extremely intelligent, capable individuals and, once Bothwell had realised that Jean expected to be treated as an equal, they could have sparked new heights in each other. However, once again, they were overtaken by events: no one in Scotland could hope to have the time to work out how to live a settled life when they were caught up in the maelstrom of the affairs of Mary, Queen of Scots.

CHAPTER SIX

The Death of Darnley: 1566–1567

The years 1566 and 1567 were extraordinarily momentous in Scotland: so many things happened that it seems incredible that they all took place in such a short space of time. Mary, Queen of Scots was only in Scotland for about eight years, yet the events of her reign are so well known, and their consequences so far-reaching, that they take on huge significance.

Mary, Queen of Scots was working hard to establish some sort of equilibrium before her child was born. It was crucial to her that Darnley remained in favour so that there was no doubt as to the child's legitimacy, and she had to ensure that while she was in childbirth and recovery she was in a secure place and her kingdom was not open to threat. She did her best to reconcile with Moray, even encouraging both Jean's brother George and also Bothwell to make some sort of peace with him. Jean, her husband and family were now firmly in favour at court and at the centre of all these events, but once again Jean's fortunes were to go through a revolution.

William Maitland of Lethington, Mary's clever Secretary of State, also came back into favour in late 1566. He was one of the sharpest minds in Scotland, comparable to Elizabeth of England's inestimable secretary Cecil, and known as 'Michael Wily' – a pun on Machiavelli. Mary, Queen of Scots sorely needed his sound advice and firm grasp of English affairs. With his rehabilitation at court Lethington also finally got his heart's desire (despite the age gap) and married one of the Four Maries, the queen's attendant Mary Fleming. Lethington was someone Mary could go to for practical, sensible, detailed advice, but she was really relying on Bothwell and George more and more – particularly Bothwell. The Huntlys and their allies were the people she felt she could trust.[1]

Mary's son, the future James VI of Scotland and I of England, was born in June 1566, in the secure environs of Edinburgh Castle. Mary was attended during the birth by her faithful Four Maries, including Mary Beaton, now Lady Boyne, the wife of Jean's lost love Alex Ogilvie. Mary Beaton had the happy task of telling people about the successful birth.[2] The birth of a male heir to the throne, and Mary's successful recovery from childbirth, was a matter for celebration, and Mary was determined to make James' christening a major event, to show not only Scotland but the world that she was in control of her kingdom. She would include all her nobles in the ceremony to promote unity.

Handing her son over to a wet-nurse and arranging for him to be kept in a secure location with suitable carers, Mary was soon back from her brief maternity leave to make what arrangements she could to organise the baptism, and also keep her country running. It was crucial that peace and order were maintained, and her normal progress of justices went on, alongside her plans to persuade Parliament to allow her large sums of money to pay for her son's baptism. In the Borders, Bothwell was actively rounding up troublemakers to attend Mary's justice sessions when he was attacked and nearly killed by one Jock o' the Park. For Mary's main supporter to be injured in this way was a serious business, and Mary rode south to check on affairs personally. Although she was an experienced rider, it may have been too much for her after not only childbirth but also her other recent stressful experiences. After ascertaining that Bothwell had received a heavy blow to the head and face which probably left him visibly scarred but otherwise unhurt, Mary herself fell seriously ill on her way home at Jedburgh – to the point where her life was despaired of, though she too ultimately made a full recovery.

Jean is never mentioned in the retellings of this story; she would certainly not have been out with Bothwell and his men as they rounded up wild Borderers, but neither is she mentioned as taking care of her wounded husband, or as being involved in any of the care or attention given to Mary, Queen of Scots. The impression given is that Bothwell and Jean's marriage had become, although polite, very distant, and that Bothwell's relationship with his queen and service to the crown now took precedence at all times.

The baptism of the future James VI took place in December, six months after James' birth, at Stirling Castle. Plans, preparations and taxes had been set in motion as soon as James had been born.[3] In the absence of Darnley, who was sulking again, Bothwell was heavily involved in both the organisation and on the day itself, and Jean, along with many other noblemen and women and foreign ambassadors, including representatives of the monarchs of France, Savoy and England, probably travelled to Stirling for the ceremony.[4] The christening was an occasion for great pomp and ceremony; everyone dressed in their finest clothes and there was a great deal of pageantry, much of it highly symbolic, emphasising unity, peace and reconciliation, and stressing James' blessings from God and his place in the succession not only to the Scottish but also the English throne.[5] It was a triumphant Renaissance festival of the sort Mary, Queen of Scots had witnessed in France as a child – the first event of its type not just in Scotland but in Britain, and one of the major triumphs of Mary's rule in its showcasing of her strength and Scotland's importance in Europe.[6]

The proceedings were overseen by two carefully chosen masters of the household: the Earl of Argyll, a Protestant who was a particular friend of Mary, Queen of Scots and married to her half-sister Jane; and Lord Seton, a Catholic and another good friend whose house Jean and Bothwell had used for their honeymoon. In this way the two religions were brought together in their loyalty to the throne. Lord Seton wore his magnificent red household robes, a three-quarter-length, cloak-like jacket with wide sleeves, a high collar and long lapels and matching soft hat, all covered in gold embroidery. In a commemorative portrait that he sat for, Lord Seton looks undoubtedly magnificent but also surprisingly young for someone involved in such momentous events: a man of action dressed up, rather than dressed.[7] Mary also asked each of her noblemen to dress his retinue in matching colours, gifting Argyll a red suit, Moray a green lined with red and gold, and Bothwell blue (the colour of loyalty) lined with silver and white.[8]

The royal party and their guests paraded through Stirling on their way to the castle. The royal horses were draped in cloth of gold with a silver fringe. The foreign ambassadors brought their own exotic retinues and costly gifts: the English ambassador was accompanied by 80 horsemen, and Elizabeth of England, who Mary had asked to be James' godmother, had sent a massive gold font for the baptism, decorated with precious stones, weighing 28 pounds, worth £1,000 and large enough for her godson to be totally immersed in.[9] The actual christening was performed with great ceremony in a Catholic service in the chapel royal in Stirling: the French ambassador carried James from his room to the chapel, passing between two rows of lesser noblemen, all holding candles, with the important noblemen following behind him – or, at least, those who were Catholic. Bothwell, George, Moray and others all refused to attend the Catholic christening, and waited outside the door until it was over.[10] The door to the chapel was left open and the words of the ritual drifted out, but the Protestant lords would not come any closer.

At the supper afterwards, Mary's ladies, likely including Jean, were seated next to the foreign ambassadors for the meal. Moray carved the meat and George served it while Bothwell supervised the whole affair, then everyone joined in the dancing.[11] The celebrations lasted for three days, with a staged bullfight the following morning, and more feasting, music and theatre. The symbolism of the event was carefully managed. Food was served at a round table, reminiscent of King Arthur and his knights, to remind people that James had a claim to the English throne, while in the tableaux and masques Mary, Queen of Scots was compared to the goddesses Diana and Venus, bringing harmony to a world of chaos. The culmination was a mock siege of an artificial castle: the castle represented the monarchy, and combatants dressed as exotic enemies, Moors and devils – and wild Highlanders in kilts – threw themselves at the castle, only to be repelled. Mary wanted to publicly show her subjects and the foreign ambassadors that she was in control again. The whole thing ended with a fireworks display, still a novelty in Scotland.[12] Even John Knox thought it was a triumph.[13]

Darnley did not attend his son's christening. He stayed in his quarters the entire time. The Protestant lords were no longer his friends after he had betrayed them and escaped with Mary after Rizzio's murder, while Mary had not forgiven him for his part in the murder. Mary's supporters such as Bothwell didn't trust him either. Darnley had isolated himself. Mary was now focused on her son and maintaining the stability of the realm and the succession while Darnley flailed around with no clear idea of what he wanted, other than to gain more power himself. He still wanted the crown matrimonial, to be King in his own right rather than the husband of the Queen, but he could see his chances of ruling slipping away the more his son was celebrated. Darnley became involved in more and ever wilder plots, writing to Spain with ideas of re-establishing Catholicism in Scotland with himself in charge. He wrote to France, and to the Pope. He tried to arrange a ship to take him to Europe. His treasonous plotting was in direct opposition to the policy of reconciliation and balance that Mary was intent on.

Darnley was becoming a liability. It reached the point where the noblemen around Mary began to openly discuss what could be done about him. George, Bothwell, Moray and Maitland of Lethington talked to Mary directly, suggesting possible legal ways out of the situation. Divorce or annulment of the marriage were put forward as options – but Mary was a Catholic and did not want to jeopardise the legitimacy of her son and successor. There seemed to be no clear way forward. Mary appeared to be suggesting there could be a way out of this dilemma if only someone could come up with something that would just remove Darnley from the picture.

The others listened.

What truly happened to Darnley is one of the great mysteries of Scottish history. On the night of Sunday 9th into Monday 10th February 1567, Darnley was staying in Kirk o' Field house near Edinburgh, suffering from an illness which kept him weak and bed-ridden. Kirk o' Field had been suggested as a location by Bothwell and richly decorated for the arrival of the king on Mary's orders. A tub was set up so that he could take medicinal baths, and rich hangings and tapestries were arranged on the walls to keep the house cosy. The hangings were the ones that had been taken from the walls of Jean's home Huntly Castle after Corrichie. The official diagnosis of Darnley's illness was smallpox, but it was probably syphilis: one of the ironies of the whole situation was that, given just a little more time, 21-year-old Darnley may well have died of his illness.[14]

Mary visited her husband early in the evening of 9th February as she had promised to do, but then left to attend the evening celebrations of the wedding of one of her favourite servants. It was a cold evening, and there was a sprinkling of snow. At about two o'clock in the morning, Darnley's house was blown up by a huge explosion: gunpowder had been packed into the vaults or lower floors of the house and ignited. Two mutilated bodies were discovered in the wreckage; they turned out to be two of Darnley's servants. The bodies of Darnley and his valet were found a few hours after the explosion in a garden outside the town wall, about 60 to 80 paces away from the ruined house, without any marks on them. Darnley's valet wore a nightshirt and only one slipper; Darnley was naked, but his furred dressing-gown and a dagger lay on the ground near him.[15] The bodies and clothes were lying neatly on the ground, near to a chair and rope, as though they had been carefully placed there. They certainly hadn't been blown out of the building by the force of the explosion, and the presence of the chair and rope showed that they seemed to have escaped the house by being lowered out of a window before the explosion happened. They had then been surprised by persons unknown, strangled in the garden and left there. Edinburgh residents living nearby reported hearing a great deal of noise during the night, with groups of men moving around. Someone was sure they had heard Darnley's voice crying, "Pity me, kinsmen!"[16] None of the witnesses were quite interviewed properly by the authorities, and none of the statements taken seemed to match up. Rumours were circulating, and there were an awful lot of armed men suddenly patrolling the city asking questions and looking for the right answers. The people might have helped them, if only they could have been sure of the right answer and what the consequences of giving the wrong answer might be.

The murder of Darnley sent shockwaves not just across Scotland but through the whole of Europe. The era in which Jean lived is known as the early modern age: one thing that makes it 'modern' is the growing use and development of technology such as guns and gunpowder. Men no longer had to be killed face-to-face, with great physical effort. It was an extraordinary shock to the crowned heads of Europe to learn of the gunpowder explosion. It was not just that a king had been killed, but that people had tried to kill him in this new, technologically advanced way.[17] The explosion had caused a massive uproar in Edinburgh – witnesses described it as being like 20 or 30 cannon being fired all at once, or like thunder.[18] Nearby buildings shook with the force of the blast. It was like nothing the Edinburgh citizens had heard before in their lives, and when those who had been woken by the noise went out to investigate, they found the house of Kirk o' Field completely reduced to rubble. Huge stones, ten foot by four foot, had been lifted by the explosion and blown far from the house.[19] Elizabeth of England wrote to Mary metaphorically that she had heard the explosion from London: "My ears have been so deafened and my understanding so grieved and my heart so affrighted to hear the dreadful news of the abominable murder of your . . . husband and my killed cousin that I scarcely have the wits to write about it."[20]

Mary was in Holyrood Palace when the explosion happened, as were George and Bothwell. Jean, too, was there, with her husband. Bothwell later stated that he spent the night of Darnley's murder in bed with his wife.[21] During the night, however, something had roused Bothwell, and he had dressed and gone out. There had been an awareness that something was going to happen: even Mary had heard rumours that something was planned, and she had discussed this with her loyal supporters. It was not surprising that people were on high alert.

One of Jean's husband's titles was Sheriff of Edinburgh, which meant that Bothwell was officially in charge of finding out who had murdered Darnley, and who had blown up the house.[22] The trouble was, the rumours that were now flying around made Bothwell himself the chief suspect in the murder investigation. An anonymous placard was pinned to the door of Edinburgh tollbooth blaming Bothwell, his former lover Janet Beaton (who was accused of witchcraft) and several more of Bothwell's associates. A huge poster campaign followed: more anonymous placards appeared across Edinburgh on a nightly basis, accusing a variety of people from Bothwell to Rizzio's brother. Moray's name was briefly mentioned as a suspect, but Mary's bastard half-brother had conveniently left town the day before Darnley's murder, hurrying home to see his wife Agnes, who he said had had a miscarriage.[23] As with the Rizzio murder, Moray never seemed to be in town when something was happening. Moray then travelled to England – via France – leaving Agnes, miscarriage or no miscarriage, once again in charge of the Moray estates.[24] Meanwhile, the majority of the posters being put up around Edinburgh blamed Bothwell, and many contained crudely drawn pictures of Bothwell and Mary, Queen of Scots. Bothwell was a murderer, posters said, and the queen was complicit in the murder.[25]

The queen herself seemed to be in shock: she slowly ordered the court into mourning, but her health, still weakened after childbirth and her illness at Jedburgh, was giving cause for concern. Mary "has been for the most part either melancholy or sickly ever since" the murder of Darnley, it was reported to the English secretary Cecil.[26] A week after Darnley's murder Mary, Queen of Scots went to her favourite retreat of Seton to rest and recuperate. She left Bothwell and George in Edinburgh in charge of guarding Prince James, who was later removed to safety in Stirling.[27]

Bothwell had other difficulties in the background too: Jean's dowry had not been enough to clear all his financial problems and he was short of cash again, and had to sell more land – and Jean herself had fallen seriously ill.[28] She became unwell at the beginning of February, around the time that Darnley was murdered, with an illness so severe that "towards the close of the month [it] led her friends to despair of her life",[29] while Cecil in England also received word that "The Lady Bothwell is extremely sick and not likely to live."[30] It is not clear what her illness was. The rumours around Bothwell's involvement in Darnley's death, and the perceived inaction of Mary, Queen of Scots while Bothwell continued to take control of the reins of power were leading to a rising swell of opinion that Bothwell had some sort of master-plan: Bothwell, people were starting to say, had killed the king in order to control the queen and take power in Scotland. Bothwell was aiming to be King of Scots and, in order to achieve this, he would first have to get rid of his wife. Jean's illness, people whispered, might be down to poison.

Bothwell certainly did not help these rumours with his actions: he was not at his sick wife's bedside, but instead trying to cheer up Mary, Queen of Scots at Seton by having an archery match. Bothwell and Mary beat George and Lord Seton in the match, and George then paid for dinner.[31] This does seem to show a singular lack of concern for Jean not only on the part of her husband, but also from her brother George.

As Jean and her family later told the story, there was a different explanation for Jean's illness: she was worn out with the events of the last few years, and with her husband's infidelities.[32] Jean had watched her father and brother die, had been thrown out of her house, had seen her brother imprisoned, and had been forced to live with and serve the person who had brought about the downfall of her family, Mary, Queen of Scots. Then Mary had compelled her to abandon the man she loved and marry a man she disliked, while her brother had supported this decision and become one of Mary's strongest supporters. George was happy to keep Mary entertained at an archery match because he believed she was the true queen, who deserved the throne and his support. As far as George was concerned, his sister was not helping the Gordon cause by her continual complaining about her marriage. From Jean's point of view, she had been forced into the marriage, then she had discovered that her husband had not only a mistress and an illegitimate son, but he was also having an affair with her servant and still in close contact with his previous lover, Janet Beaton. Janet had specifically been mentioned on the placards after Darnley's death, and it appears that Bothwell had recently renewed his friendship with her and she was now spending time with him and offering him advice. As a mistress and a foreigner, Skottefruen Anna may not have been perceived by Jean as a real threat, but Janet was an older woman of high status through her family position as a niece of Cardinal Beaton and through her previous marriages. She was very strong-minded and had a strong personal following in the Borders; she could make Jean's new home in her adopted area very difficult. Moreover, Janet was related to Mary Beaton, who had married Alex Ogilvie, the man Jean loved. Now another member of the same family was linked with Jean's husband. It was a humiliating situation.

There are other possibilities for Jean's illness. Jean and Bothwell never had children, but they were living together as man and wife. It is possible that Jean had suffered a miscarriage. However, against this theory is the fact that, generally, a miscarriage was recognised as such – when people lived together in close proximity, as they did in Jean's times, with servants sharing their master's bedrooms at night, then it was normally known very early if a woman was pregnant or not: Mary, Queen of Scots' pregnancy with James, for example, had been rumoured early on, before she made any official announcement. Alternatively, there is some evidence that Bothwell was ill around the same time: in the later 'confession' of Bothwell's servant Paris, Paris mentions that on the night of Darnley's murder Bothwell was suffering from 'the bloody flux', which is usually understood to mean dysentery.[33] There may well have been some sort of virus going around the court, or Bothwell may have suffered from a specific long-term condition which he passed on to his wife. Jean's illness could have been any one of a number of diseases that were unknown or little-understood in the sixteenth century, exacerbated by the low mood that she was in as a result of her recent experiences. However, she finally made a slow but full recovery. By this time, her husband was on trial for Darnley's murder.

Bothwell, scarred from his recent Border fight with Jock o' the Park and now sporting a black beard,[34] cut a menacing, if dashing, figure in Edinburgh. In a short space of time he had gone from being in exile to being the main advisor of the queen with an enormous amount of influence. His rise at court, apparent enjoyment of it and ambition to rise even further was not making him new friends. To the modern reader, the story of Mary, Queen of Scots seems a tragedy because she makes so many mistakes, yet there are so many occasions when a sensible decision could have helped her cause. Although we know the outcome, we will her to do something proactive and try to see a way that she could have cut through the Gordian knot of her problems. Bothwell saw things that way too. He was both a straightforward thinker and a romantic. He saw that Mary's problems were her feckless husband and the lack of a strong king, and with characteristic bluntness he sought to chop through the entire complicated mess with a simple solution. Mary must have a new king who understood Scotland and knew what to do. Bothwell loved Scotland and was already effectively ruling things as Mary dithered and despaired over Darnley's death and what action she should take. Bothwell decided that he needed to take over. He was going to be the new King of Scots.

There has been much discussion around how Bothwell came to this conclusion, and at what point he made his choices, how much Mary was involved in the decision and how much Bothwell was involved in Darnley's death. It seems likely that Bothwell was involved in some way in Darnley's murder, but he was certainly not the only person responsible. The manner of Darnley's death – the huge amounts of gunpowder needed, and the way Darnley was eventually killed by means other than gunpowder, and by people he was heard to refer to as 'kinsmen' – shows that there must have been a large number of people involved in the Kirk o' Field murder. Several months beforehand, Bothwell, George, Moray, Maitland of Lethington and others had openly discussed at the meeting at Craigmillar just what could be done about Darnley. Mary had even been approached, though from her shocked reaction after Kirk o' Field and her belief that she too had been a target, it seems she was not privy to the details. Mary, though, had probably been guilty of deliberately keeping her head in the sand and not seeing that her repeated pleas for help with the Darnley situation would be interpreted in a violent way.

Someone had to go on trial for Darnley's murder. Elizabeth of England and Catherine de Medici of France were among the many who had written to Mary, Queen of Scots, urging decisive action: Darnley was not only an English subject but also Elizabeth's relative, and this sort of insubordination against a royal could not go unpunished. The force of public opinion after the placards was so strongly against Bothwell that he had to go on trial, but it was essentially a show trial – and it was officially brought by the private petition of the Earl of Lennox, Darnley's father, not Mary herself.[35] Some efforts were made to take witness statements, but so many people were implicated and so many were lying that there was ultimately very little real evidence to go on. Mary was not going to let her chief advisor and supporter be convicted of murdering her husband – particularly when this would implicate her – so Bothwell had to be publicly acquitted. To ensure this, Bothwell flooded the town with his supporters. Around 4,000 of Bothwell's men came to Edinburgh, armed.[36]

The trial was set for 12th April. Darnley's murder had attracted huge interest at home and abroad, and the trial likewise. From early in the morning, the streets of the city were packed with people, a lot of them imported Bothwell supporters, but also many interested onlookers. At Holyrood House, where Bothwell was staying, crowds gathered in the palace courtyard. Mary herself was seen at a window with one of her Four Maries, Mary Fleming. The queen nodded to Bothwell as he rode off to his trial. There was a "merry and lusty cheer" for Bothwell from the crowd of thousands as he left Holyrood and went up to the Tolbooth.[37] Mary saw Bothwell off, but Bothwell's wife Jean was not mentioned: she was still ill and recovering, probably at Crichton Castle south of Edinburgh.

The trial was long; the better part of the day. The only person who really wished true justice for Darnley, the only people who probably mourned him, were his parents. Darnley's mother was in England, imprisoned in the Tower of London for her part in encouraging Darnley's marriage in the first place, and when she had heard the news of his death she collapsed. Darnley's mother's grief had been so intense and worrying that Elizabeth of England had not only sent her own physician to see her, but had freed her from the Tower and sent her to be with her other son.[38] Darnley's father Lennox did not attend the trial. He had been told that he would only be allowed to bring six men with him,[39] and, as he saw Edinburgh fill up with Bothwell's Hepburn men, he felt personally threatened and outnumbered in his pursuit of truth and justice: the main aim of everyone else around him was to find the best way to move forward, whatever that might be.

The evidence was so confused and the atmosphere in town so clearly in Bothwell's favour that it was no surprise when Bothwell was completely cleared and unanimously acquitted of all the charges. The jury was not wholly rigged in Bothwell's favour, and its members included both Bothwell supporters and those who had either been previously opposed to him or who were to be opposed in the future, but there was a weighting towards Gordon-friendly members of the jury: people who, although their allegiance to Bothwell was shaky, did feel comfortable supporting Bothwell's brother-in-law and wife – members of the once all-powerful Huntly Gordons. George himself was one of the chief judges. Two of the jurors were George's brothers-in-law.[40] One member of the jury was Alex Ogilvie, Jean's former beau.[41] The foreman of the jury was the Earl of Caithness, who had been eating and drinking with Bothwell on the night of Rizzio's murder and was father-in-law to Bothwell's sister Janet. On the other hand, Caithness and Moray had strong links through their anti-Gordon feelings. Primarily, though, Caithness had his own self-interest in mind as he noted that in this new, modern Scotland it was possible for Earls to get away with the worst sort of murder – the murder of the rich and powerful – and be cleared.

Now that the trial was over, Bothwell had more placards posted, proclaiming his innocence. They did not go unchallenged, and the whispers did not stop, but Bothwell rolled onwards. Parliament met two days after the trial and Bothwell's role was prominent. After the Parliament, Mary, Queen of Scots left to rest at Seton again. She was not anxious to stay in Edinburgh, where she had seen Rizzio and Darnley die in horrible ways. Meanwhile, Bothwell marked the end of Parliament by inviting 28 notable Scotsmen to dinner at Ainslie's Tavern in the Canongate. They were served a delicious feast, and, after dinner, as they sat well-fed and cheerful with their drinks, Bothwell produced a document which, he suggested politely, he thought they might want to sign. The document stated that they, the undersigned, knew that Bothwell had been found innocent in a fair trial. It then went on to say that poor Mary, Queen of Scots was now left husbandless and without a guide. If the queen might possibly decide that the only person who could guide her, the only person who could be a good husband to her, was Bothwell, then everyone who signed this document would help promote and support that marriage. The original bond no longer exists, and there are only copies to work from: the signatories on the surviving copies do not match, so it is not clear exactly who, out of all Bothwell's invitees, agreed to sign, either on the night or afterwards. Many prominent names were attached to the document, including several senior religious figures, noblemen including George, Seton, Morton and the Earls of Sutherland and Caithness, and even Lord Ogilvie, the Gordons' old adversary. Bothwell was casting the net wide in his search for support.[42]

Bothwell had not fallen in love with Mary, Queen of Scots. She was not the dark-haired, vivacious type that caught his attraction, and, equally, he was not the tall, courtly type that she liked and she had not fallen in love with him. Perhaps the idea that he could be King of Scots had come to Bothwell while Jean had been so ill that it looked likely that he could become a widower. Ironically, perhaps Jean had shown him that a marriage could be a business contract between intellectual equals, something that brought benefits to both husband and wife that was not based on the same attraction as a love affair. Perhaps Bothwell had absorbed the idea that a Hepburn could be king from his father Patrick, the Fair Earl, after his determined pursuit of Mary of Guise.

Bothwell was also speaking a lot to two other important women in his life: his former lover Janet Beaton, and his sister Janet who was at court and also involved. The two Janets had both buried their husbands; they were tough women who got on with life and they were irritated and uncomprehending of the actions of Mary, Queen of Scots after Darnley's death. Mary was drifting, unable to take strong action. She seemed unnecessarily horrified by death. The two Janets, brought up in a tough country where men died and women remarried and fought for their own corner, could not understand Mary's cosseted upbringing. They had none of the Stewart sensitivity. They saw a woman who needed a strong man to take control, and they saw Bothwell already doing that day-to-day. Mary was almost 25 years old, the age when Scottish monarchs generally took full control and revoked any laws that had been passed in their minority, or made improvidently when they were younger.[43] Mary should have been poised to take control, but instead she was relying on others. Bothwell had been the person Mary had turned to, the one who was not only carrying the sceptre at Parliament but was also advising the Queen on what acts should be passed at that Parliament. Bothwell had more power than Darnley ever had. Why not, they thought, legitimise the arrangement? Why shouldn't a Borderer, why shouldn't Bothwell, be King of Scots? It was a clear and direct way out of chaos: that a decisive, intelligent Protestant nationalist of proven loyalty, strength and courage should lead the country.

With the tacit reliance of the queen and the written support of his peers the only thing Bothwell saw now standing in his way was his wife, Jean.

CHAPTER SEVEN

Divorce: 1567

There had been rumours that Bothwell and Jean were to divorce for some time, at least since before Jean's serious illness. It was no secret that their marriage was not a happy one, and Bothwell was so often around Mary rather than Jean that people had begun to talk. Elizabeth of England's secretary Cecil received communications from his agents in Scotland at the end of March, before Bothwell's trial had taken place, stating bluntly that: "The judgement of the people is that the Queen will marry Bothwell."[1] Bothwell's adultery with Janet Beaton was cited as being the reason that would be given for the divorce. Cecil also received copies of the wording of the placards placed around Edinburgh at the time of Darnley's murder and Bothwell's trial, including one saying that Jean and Bothwell's divorce could not be accepted, even if his adultery was proved, because Bothwell had so clearly murdered the husband of the woman he wished to marry.[2] There were all sorts of rumours flying around, and these rumours were coming from the highest places: Bothwell may have had ideas in his head and be making plans, but the other lords in Scotland were manoeuvring to see if they could take advantage of the messy situation. Cecil also received an anonymous letter which carefully informed him that: "The Earl of Bothwell's wife is going to part with her husband, and a great part of the Lords have subscribed the marriage between the Queen and him."[3] It is very hard to read the reports and know what was true, what was rumour, and what was the twisting of information to suit the informant. Cecil made a memo for himself, headed 'The matters to be considered', trying to disentangle what was important. He stated that "all means" must be used to interrupt a marriage between Mary and Bothwell.[4]

One of the few things that was clear was that Jean was totally opposed to the divorce. One of Cecil's official agents reported that Jean stated that she would "never say untruly of herself, but will die with the name of the Lady Bothwell".[5] She particularly objected to the idea that a divorce could be obtained on the grounds that her marriage had not been legal because of a prior agreement between Bothwell and Janet Beaton.

Jean had not been happy to marry Bothwell, but she had been well aware since childhood that noblewomen did not always get to choose their partners. Essentially, however, although Jean had wished to make her feelings clear at the start of their marriage, she had been prepared after that to make it work because it was the right thing for her family, and because that is what society had trained her to do. She had gained considerably from the union, having received land and income in her own name, while also seeing her family's status revived. Personally, she was now mistress of her own household, rather than the youngest daughter of a large family. The discovery of Bothwell's liaisons with Skottefruen Anna and Bessie the servant had upset the marriage, but they were women with little power, unlikely to truly derail the marriage, and Jean and Bothwell were beginning to come to a businesslike arrangement. But now Bothwell was asking Jean to say that the entire year-long marriage had been a farce, that everything she had gone through had been worthless because the entire time she had not really been married to him because of a prior arrangement with the beautiful, intelligent, powerful Janet Beaton.

Another key element was Jean's religious faith. Her conversion to Protestantism had always been half-hearted – someone, after all, had taken the trouble to get that papal dispensation before the wedding to Bothwell – and not only Jean but her entire family were slowly drifting back to the Catholic faith. A true Catholic could not be divorced.

Considerable pressure was brought on Jean to agree to a divorce from Bothwell. She had married him under pressure from her family, and now, again, it was her family that pressured her to give him up. Her brother George was by now a good personal friend of Bothwell, and in excellent standing at court thanks to this. He urged Jean to think of the bigger picture, and think of how Bothwell, together with a Catholic Mary, could rescue Scotland from the rebel Protestant Lords and the Earl of Moray. The Gordons as a whole would benefit from Jean's divorce, even if she personally lost something. Respect for the wishes of royalty and family had to come before personal choice – and hadn't Jean always said that Bothwell was not the husband for her?

Bothwell then forced events by taking the irrevocable step of abducting the queen.

While Mary had been in retreat at Seton, Bothwell had broached the subject of marriage with her, but had been rebuffed – and reminded of the reality of his wife. On 21st April 1567, Mary made what was meant to be a secret visit to Stirling Castle, with only a small entourage of trusted advisors such as George and Maitland of Lethington, and around 30 horsemen. Her son James had been established at Stirling for safekeeping. Mary spent a day there, playing with the ten-month-old. It was to be the last time Mary ever saw her son. On the way back to Edinburgh, Mary and her entourage were halted by Bothwell and around 800 of his men, all armed with swords.[6] There was some initial panic and confusion as Bothwell rode up and put his hand on the bridle of Mary's horse. Although some of Mary's party were sceptical, Bothwell easily convinced Mary that she was in grave danger and must on no account return to Edinburgh, and that the only safe thing to do was to come with him immediately to Dunbar Castle – the safe and secure royal castle where Jean's brother George had previously been held prisoner.[7]

At Dunbar, Mary was locked in and the castle surrounded by Bothwell's men, ostensibly to defend her against enemies. They were also an effective guard that could stop her should she decide she wanted to leave. Bothwell had brought to Dunbar the two Janets, his sister and Janet Beaton, to wait on the queen and provide female companionship and chaperonage, but his main aim was to get Mary on her own.[8] Once they were alone, Bothwell talked and talked to Mary: he described his life up to that point, and how he had come to his final decision that the only way forward was for himself and Mary to marry. He showed her the Ainslie Tavern bond, with the many signatures of all the important men who also agreed that Mary should marry Bothwell.[9] This was absolutely the best way, the only way, forward, he argued. He gave her no time for reflection, but continued to press her and put forward every argument. Whatever Jean felt about divorce, her husband had completely made his decision.

There is little doubt that at some point during the first couple of days and nights at Dunbar Bothwell and Mary had sex. Bothwell had to be absolutely sure that Mary would not change her mind when she left Dunbar Castle. The marriage had to be as close to a done deal as possible without actually being at the altar. Mary was coerced, either by a barrage of words, or by actual physical force. Some contemporaries state bluntly that Bothwell raped Mary.[10] Mary herself was obliged to write a version of events to various people afterwards, in order to explain to them her actions, and she said of Bothwell: "Albeit we found his doings rude, yet were his words and answers gentle."[11] Mary, by that point, had to be realistic and make the best of the situation. She had seen in Bothwell her greatest and most loyal supporter, a man she could trust. She felt she needed the support of a husband. It was clear, though, that Mary had not chosen Bothwell as her husband freely and willingly. This was not a romantic love affair.

The entourage Mary had brought with her to Dunbar were of little help and support to her. Bothwell's planned abduction had, like Darnley and Rizzio's murders, not been planned overnight: it had been discussed for some time, and several of Mary's companions, like George, were probably aware of what was going to happen – although not all of them approved. Some of them were biding their time, doubtless hoping that Bothwell would be hoist with his own petard. They also had their own confusing agendas and allegiances, and George, Bothwell and Maitland of Lethington apparently came to blows, with Mary having to intervene to stop Lethington from being hurt.[12] George had been with Mary on her journey from Stirling, and had been a supporter of Bothwell, even encouraging Jean to divorce, but he seems to have started to suffer some qualms at Bothwell's methods. It was said that Bothwell had made contact with George just before the abduction with detailed plans, but George had been appalled and had refused to take part.[13]

There was by no means a popular consensus in favour of Mary marrying Bothwell. The outside world did not take the same view as Mary was persuaded to take in Dunbar. When the citizens of Edinburgh heard that Mary had been taken to Dunbar instead of returning to the capital, the Provost tried to arrange some sort of rescue party to get her from the clutches of someone they saw as an evil abductor. The alarm bell was rung, and two guns moved out of Edinburgh Castle to a position where they could fire on Bothwell's troops as they cantered on. However, although Bothwell and the Queen's party could be seen from Edinburgh, they were well out of firing range.[14] There was little the Edinburgh citizens could actually do in practice.

Mary was brought to Dunbar at midnight on the Thursday. It seems that Bothwell at some point left Mary in Dunbar and galloped to Edinburgh to speak with Jean.[15] By that Saturday, Jean had officially started the legal proceedings to end her marriage, instructing her lawyers to sue Bothwell for divorce under the Protestant religion, on the grounds of his adultery with her sewing maid, Bessie Crawford.[16] The speed of the action suggests that Bothwell had prepared the necessary information for the courts, and Jean probably had some foreknowledge of Bothwell's plans.[17] Divorce was not overly unusual in Scotland, and women were just as likely as men to file for divorce. It was most often the wealthier section of society that went to the divorce courts, but it was not limited to the nobility, and the middle classes, such as merchants' daughters, also obtained divorces.[18]

However, Bothwell was not entirely happy with Jean's action.

It would have suited him better if she had gone with his idea that they should use his prior arrangement with Janet Beaton as the reason behind the end of the marriage. That would have meant that they could have declared their marriage null – it would have been as if it had never happened. Not only was this a tidier solution in Bothwell's eyes, but it would also have been more palatable to Mary. As a Catholic, Mary should not marry a divorced man. True, there would then have been the problem of how, if Bothwell could not have married Jean, he could marry Mary, but presumably Janet Beaton would have released Bothwell from his promise – and there would be no mention of Bothwell's unsavoury dalliance with the low-status sewing maid Bessie. There was no way, however, that Jean was going to admit that her marriage had been a farce and agree to an annulment. It would have been too much for her pride and jeopardised her ability to keep the land and money that Bothwell had made over to her. If Jean absolutely had to divorce – and now that her husband had abducted and raped the queen there seemed very little other option – she still wanted to do it on her terms, in a way that might leave her with some dignity and some assets.

Bothwell answered by raising a counter-action in the Roman Catholic Commissary Court against Jean, asking to have his marriage declared null on the grounds that he and Jean were too closely related to have ever been married.[19] This covered all his bases: he would be divorced in the eyes of the Protestant Kirk, and his marriage would be annulled in the eyes of the Catholic Church. This was a way to try to make marriage with Bothwell more palatable for Mary, and easier for her to explain to others. When she came to write to her Catholic French relatives, and to Elizabeth of England, she stated that Bothwell's previous marriage had been invalid: she was not marrying a divorced man, which would have been against her Catholic religion, and beneath the dignity of a queen. Bothwell did have the option of asking for a Catholic 'divorce', but this was really a separation: although it was possible for Catholics to legally end a marriage on the grounds of adultery, the court would only allow them to live apart – neither Bothwell nor Jean would have been allowed to marry again.[20] However, asking for the marriage to be annulled was a disingenuous move as both Bothwell and Mary, Queen of Scots were probably very aware that Jean still held the papal dispensation, applied for before their marriage, that proved that Jean was not too closely related to Bothwell.[21] The other witnesses to Bothwell and Jean's wedding may also have been aware of it. They were all manipulating the law to get the result they wanted.

Jean was granted her divorce exceptionally quickly, just over a week later, on 3rd May 1567.[22] Bothwell also obtained his declaration stating that the marriage had been null and void. Jean kept the papal dispensation she held hidden, and did not declare it to the court. However, it seems strongly likely that Bothwell, and perhaps also Mary, Queen of Scots, knew of it, and that Jean used it as leverage to get what she wanted. Jean refuted the idea that her marriage was null and void and argued that she was entitled to keep her assets from the marriage. Much to Mary's displeasure, Jean remained at Crichton Castle, the home that had been made over to her in her marriage settlement.[23] There is some evidence that Jean wrote to Bothwell several times after their divorce, probably to sort out financial matters. This particularly annoyed Mary.[24]

Bothwell kept Mary at Dunbar Castle for about a week and a half. She did not look like a prisoner: there was archery practice, they went out on horseback, and Mary spent time on her favourite hobby of embroidery. She seemed to get on with Bothwell's sister Janet, giving her clothes and taking an interest in Janet's son from her first marriage; since that marriage had been to Mary's half-brother, this child, Francis, was related to Mary. The administrative duties of the queen continued to be carried out, and Maitland of Lethington stayed with her to act as her secretary.[25] However, the situation was patently not normal. Lethington was particularly unhappy, and maintained some correspondence with the rebel lords outside of Dunbar. When Mary and Bothwell finally returned to Edinburgh, they did not make a triumphal entrance marching down the High Street to the castle, but came in by the Grassmarket. The citizens of Edinburgh, who had so recently fired on Bothwell, were uncertain whether or not Mary was a free woman, but were more reassured when she moved back to her normal residence of Holyrood. Mary made Bothwell Duke of Orkney and Lord of Shetland – raising his status high to make him a more desirable husband and king as well as restoring an ancient title of the Hepburn family – but it was also clear that Mary and Bothwell, despite their wedding plans, were not living in a romantic idyll: "There is often jars between the Queen and the Duke [Bothwell] ..." Cecil heard. Any mention of Jean was a particular trigger for arguments between the two.[26]

At ten o' clock in the morning on 15th May, Bothwell and Mary were officially married.[27] It was a completely different wedding to Mary's first two: nothing like the choreographed display of splendour of her first marriage to Francis, and with none of the passion of her union with Darnley. Bothwell had had some difficulties in finding both a minister and a venue when the independent Protestant preachers of Edinburgh had demanded personal assurances from the queen that she was not a prisoner. Mary had to officially announce that, although she had initially been angry at Bothwell's removing her to Dunbar, she had now decided that, because of "his good behaving to her" and his record of loyal service she completely forgave him. In contemporary Scots law, rape was less of a crime if the woman afterwards acquiesced, particularly if she was happy to marry her rapist.[28] If Mary now wished to proceed with the wedding, and there was nothing anyone could do. The marriage contract between Mary and Bothwell was signed by George, and a selection of both Bothwell's friends and enemies among the nobility. The wedding was a Protestant ceremony, held in Holyrood, and, as a widow, Mary wore black mourning clothes. Attendees included George and the Earl of Sutherland, but by no means only the friends of Bothwell – it was a small ceremony, but there were public and ceremonial aspects to it. The public were allowed in to observe the wedding feast, but this meal was held in solemn silence.[29] There was 'neither pleasure nor pastimes' as were wont to be held 'when princes were married'.[30] Meanwhile, Jean's brother George was rewarded with the final official reversal of all forfeiture of Gordon lands – resetting Gordon possessions to essentially the way they had been before Corrichie.[31] Even the feud with the Ogilvies had been sorted out, with a compromise that gave George and Jean's brother Adam the lands and castle of Auchindoun and Keithmore.[32]

Bothwell and Mary had uninterrupted rule for only around five weeks after their marriage. Bothwell started immediately to take control in a practical way, which certainly contrasted with Darnley's approach. Recently rediscovered documents at the Museum of Edinburgh show Bothwell in action as king: he signed a paper granting ground at Newhaven to London merchants, one of a number of practical documents relating to tradesmen found by the museum.[33] As well as dealing with day-to-day concerns of traders and townspeople, Bothwell also re-enacted the declarations about religion which Mary had made when she first entered Scotland, which reconfirmed the country as Protestant while still allowing Mary herself to practise her Catholicism. He began work to reform the Privy Council to enforce more regular attendance, and wrote tactfully to Mary's allies, such as Elizabeth, maintaining with Mary a public front of amiability and co-operation.[34] But when even loyal and trusted followers like Maitland of Lethington quarrelled with Bothwell and left the court – then wrote their own versions of events to Elizabeth – there was little chance of Mary receiving any support from either the majority of her lords, the majority of Scots, or her nearest neighbouring queen. Jean's brother George was one of the few noblemen left at court and even he apparently asked Mary for permission to leave, uneasy at Bothwell's arrogance, Mary's obvious unhappiness and the situation developing around him. Mary refused him permission and angrily said that George wished to do the same as his father had done – i.e. rebel against her as Huntly had done at Corrichie.[35] Given what George's family, and he personally, had gone through after Corrichie, and their subsequent forgiveness and support of Mary, this was a shocking statement from the queen. Mary, Queen of Scots was not acting with the care and diplomacy needed to build up her shaky support.

Meanwhile, the other lords went into outright rebellion and

battle against the royal couple, publicly declaring that Bothwell had murdered Darnley and ravished the queen, and that the outcome of Bothwell's earlier trial for regicide was false.[36] Mary, finally roused out of her lethargic state by necessity, joined in the military preparations as she had during the Chaseabout Raid with Darnley. She and Bothwell hastily raised as many fighters and what finance they could: the solid gold font which Elizabeth of England had given as a christening gift to the Prince James, and which Elizabeth had said should be kept to baptise Mary's subsequent children, was partially melted down and converted into coins to pay their soldiers. However, it was so big and heavy it was not possible to melt it completely.[37]

The captain at Edinburgh Castle, who had been given his post by Bothwell, now decided to switch sides and support the rebel lords. Whoever held the castle had a good chance of holding the city, and the rebels now easily took Edinburgh, forcing Mary and Bothwell to make the first of their retreats, back to the security of Dunbar. They counted on Jean's brother George to go for reinforcements, but George ended up in Edinburgh Castle with his in-laws, the Hamilton family. It is not totally clear whether George remained there by choice or by force. What is clear is that George was swithering: he no longer felt he could support Bothwell wholeheartedly, either because of Bothwell's own actions, Mary's perceived lack of support for the Huntlys – or because Jean had started to talk to her brother about her feelings towards her ex-husband. George's inaction was a key turning point.[38]

Meanwhile, the rebel lords took control of the young Prince James and called the citizens to arms. Mary's army and that of the rebel lords finally met at Carberry Hill, near to Edinburgh, on 15th June. Mary still had a loyal personal following among some Scots, particularly among Catholics, but her marriage to Bothwell, the man seen as Darnley's murderer, had alienated many. The rebel lords took full advantage of this, and carried a flag showing an image of Darnley's naked corpse next to a picture of Prince James crying out, "Judge and revenge my cause o lord".[39] Mary and Bothwell were tired after days on the march, and Mary had been forced to borrow clothes after making an escape dressed as a man: when she rode the length of her own army, many of the men could not believe that this was the queen they wanted to win. In an era when many people never saw their sovereign, and when clothes were a massive signifier of status, bound around by legal rules that allowed only the rich to wear decorative fabrics, Mary's soldiers saw, instead of a regal woman in the best finery, a ragged, pale, tall redhead, in a borrowed rough skirt of the type that ordinary women in Edinburgh wore. Mary, always an excellent horsewoman who sometimes even followed her mother-in-law Catherine de Medici's eccentric example of riding astride, normally needed an extra-long riding habit to cover her long legs – but as she rode past her army at Carberry Hill, the men were able to catch a glimpse of her short skirt and red petticoat, which only came down to her knees.[40] Some commentators both at this point, and immediately after Carberry, drew attention to Mary's rounded stomach. She was in fact in the very early stages of pregnancy, carrying Bothwell's twins.[41] Even in the first month, a second pregnancy could have already been visible, particularly as it followed soon after her first child, and as she was carrying two children. In an ill-fitting, borrowed dress, Mary may well have looked visibly pregnant, but her detractors also wished to spread rumours and focus people's minds on the idea that her relationship with Bothwell was of long standing – pre-dating Darnley's murder, and consummated before their official marriage. There were murmurings and restlessness from the queen's side as the two armies faced each other in a stand-off. The queen's army were at the top of the hill, looking down on the lords.[42]

Bothwell, seeing himself as king of Scots, the chivalrous protector of the queen's honour, felt that the best way forward was to challenge the rebel army to send their best champion over to face him in single combat. He and his opponent would fence in front of the two armies and God would decide the winner. Bothwell was a man out of time, promoting a medieval idea of warfare wedded to an ancient code of honour in a time of gunpowder. After some discussion, the rebel army suggested that William Kirkcaldy of Grange could fight Bothwell.[43] Bothwell began to put on his armour, but Mary forbade him to meet a traitor and a man of lower status than himself. Only the Earl of Morton would do as an opponent, Mary decided. The rebel army conferred again, and Morton accepted the challenge, but (perhaps thinking that he was 15 years older than Bothwell) he nominated Lord Lindsay as his proxy. Lindsay began to put on his heavy armour, then took it off again as Bothwell and Mary discussed whether or not he really was a suitable opponent. Both armies wanted to delay. The rebel army was carefully watching the queen's forces, who were beginning to drift away. It was a hot day, and there was not enough for Mary and Bothwell's army to drink – while the rebel army, at the bottom of the hill, were camped near a stream. The French ambassador, who had spent the past few weeks trying to stop civil war in Scotland, urged the two sides not to fight, until the impossibility of his task grew obvious and he rode off to Edinburgh in disgust.[44] And Mary had a personal desire not to see her husband go into battle. Despite all this, Bothwell finally got into his armour and went to the appointed place to meet his opponent. There, he waited. And waited.[45]

The rebel lords watched more of Mary's army slip away. Mary and Bothwell waited anxiously for George to appear with reinforcements, but he never came. Then the lords began to advance – not only Bothwell's agreed-upon opponent, but the whole army. The main body of men came slowly towards Mary, while Kirkcaldy of Grange started to lead a flanking movement of around 200 horsemen. Bothwell saw that if battle was joined it was going to mean a massacre. He had to change tactic, and he walked back to Mary and urged her to parley. Mary, exhausted, knew that it was finally over, and sent messengers to ask about terms for surrender. Seeing Bothwell, standing ready in his armour to fight for her as a champion, a man out of time, wedded to the romantic idea of chivalry and facing the entire implacable Protestant army of the rebel lords, Mary finally turned to her husband and embraced him, as both armies watched. They kissed, and Mary told him he was forgiven, and that she would always be his loyal wife. Their hands clasped one last time, then Bothwell went to his horse and jumped up into his saddle and, with only a dozen of his loyal friends, rode away as the sun went down. Mary offered herself up as a prisoner. The rebel army put her on horseback and led her into Edinburgh, where it was clear to her that not only had she lost her army and her husband, she had also lost the support of the ordinary people.[46] Riding next to the banner showing the corpse of Darnley, Mary heard and saw through her tears the crowd of citizens rushing around her, shouting out, "Burn the whore!"[47] Bothwell's project, Mary's rule, the revival of the fortunes of the Huntly family – everything was at an end.

Jean had thought that she could hold on to Crichton Castle and her Border lands, but the rebel lords made no distinction between Bothwell and his ex-wife: they rode to Crichton and, although Jean tried to hold the castle, it soon fell and all of the assets that were considered to be Bothwell's – even those that Jean argued were really hers – were seized. Jean had to act quickly, and sensibly in order to stay safe. In August 1567, she travelled to the safest place that she knew: to see her cousin, Agnes Keith, the wife of the Earl of Moray.

Jean had always been close to her mother and her mother's side of the family, and despite Agnes' loving marriage to the head of the Protestant, anti-Marian faction in Scotland, Jean had maintained links with her cousin. The two women wrote to each other, and Jean knew that Agnes would not turn her away. Whenever Moray left the country, as he often prudently chose to do in uncertain times,[48] he left Agnes in charge of his affairs: like Jean and Jean's mother, Agnes was one of the extraordinarily capable, managing Keith women, more than able to look after the Moray estates. She generally lived in the south of Scotland, and kept an eye on the northern estates from afar, while making sure that she was up to date with events at court. Most recently, she had spent time with the captured Mary, Queen of Scots in her prison at Lochleven.[49] Moray had returned to Scotland, and his wife, by 11th August, and, as his rapturous welcome by the citizens of Edinburgh showed,[50] it was clear that he was now going to be in charge. What Jean wanted to do was to publicly disassociate herself from Bothwell, whose status in Scotland was diminishing even more rapidly than it had risen, and she wanted to align herself with the new powers in Scotland, so she went straight to her cousin Agnes, who she knew would take her in, and who she realised would soon be the wife of the Regent and therefore one of the most powerful women in the country. Jean told Agnes in conversation that she would "never live with the Earl of Bothwell, nor take him for her husband",[51] safe in the knowledge that Agnes would pass the information on. It also reinforced the action that Jean had taken when she had hidden the dispensation for their marriage: Jean knew that if that was ever discovered the annulment, if not the divorce, could be brought into question. The annulment was the aspect that Mary herself had chosen to stress, and Jean knew that the rebel lords would be keen to somehow get Bothwell away from the queen and undermine his marriage with Mary. Jean had to be aware that she could have been remarried to Bothwell. In fact, the lords had already approached Mary with the idea of either divorcing Bothwell or annulling her marriage to him, and Mary had refused to consider this because she knew that she was pregnant.

With her position made as clear as possible, Jean made her way back north. After a couple of days in Edinburgh, Jean had passed on to "northern parts" by 22nd August,[52] the day of Moray's official investiture as Regent.[53] There was no question that Moray would be foremost among the Scots lords, and he was pleased to take up the position he had always thought was his by right: this son of James V was going to take the throne of Scotland, nominally as Regent for Prince James, but in actuality the sole leader of a Protestant country with Agnes at his side.

The whole Gordon family, enemies of Moray, were retrenching and returning to their power base: after some attempts to negotiate with the rebel lords, Jean's brother George went back north as well. The entire family were returning to Huntly Castle. Jean's interlude in the south of Scotland was over, her time as Bothwell's wife was over, and from now on her story was once again the Gordon story.

CHAPTER EIGHT

North: 1567–1572

As Jean had made her way northwards, Bothwell had already travelled the same route. He had ridden from the battlefield of Carberry
Hill to Dunbar, but then, when he heard that Mary had been imprisoned at Lochleven, he took a boat north and then west, trying to
rally his supporters like the Hamiltons. However, when several of
his supporters and co-accused were captured to stand trial for the
Darnley murder, Bothwell chose to sail north again, to the person
he had considered his greatest ally in Scotland: his ex-wife's brother,
George, Earl of Huntly. He was, however, to be disappointed.

When Jean returned to her family, she had no compunction about
telling them exactly what she thought of Bothwell. A later Catholic
narrative, written long after the events described, and after Jean's
reconversion to the old religion had been consolidated, gave this
version of Jean's separation from Bothwell: it stated that Bothwell
"first endeavoured to prevail on her [Jean] by flattery and entreaty to
consent to a separation or divorce. He found, however, his prayers
and persuasions of no effect, for his wife absolutely refused to take
part in so iniquitous a proceeding, and he therefore determined to
remove this weight from his neck by an act of violence. He carried
Lady Bothwell to Crichton Castle, and when alone with her in her
chamber presented to her a cup of poisoned wine, requiring that she
should either drink it or sign her name to the paper approving the
divorce. She agreed to have the notaries summoned, as a means of

escaping the immediate danger to her life, but she would not sign until she had declared in their presence that she did this unwillingly and simply under compulsion".[1] Another version describes Jean as being "heartily disgusted with his [Bothwell's] vagaries, and desirous of being rid of as 'naughty a man a liveth, and much given to the most destestable vices'", adding that she suppressed the papal dispensation that had allowed them, as two Catholics distantly related to each other, to be married "because its production would have bound her to him [Bothwell] for life".[2] Jean's brother George might have chosen to be Bothwell's friend for a while, but family always came before friends – especially when those friends were of a different religion. With Moray as a firmly Protestant Regent, Scotland was Protestant. Once Jean was back with her family, and as they embraced their Catholicism more strongly again, George's loyalty to Bothwell wavered, particularly as the situation looked more and more bleak for the pro-Bothwell party in Scotland. The English ambassador reported that Bothwell had asked George for help, but George "will not adventure much for him".[3] George was now ready to support his sister Jean over his friend – though his allegiance to his queen remained strong. The Gordons were to become the leaders of the Marian, pro-Mary, Queen of Scots, party in Scotland, and increasingly the visible champions of the Catholic faith.

Mary had been sent to Lochleven, the castle in the middle of the loch, where she was closely guarded and essentially powerless as those around her decided what to do. The lords who had delayed and delayed at Carberry Hill wished to get rid of Mary in a way that was somehow both permanent but also preferably non-violent. They could not put on trial nor kill an anointed queen. Maitland of Lethington suggested to the new English ambassador Throckmorton that Mary could be sent to an abbey in France, or to her grandmother the old Duchess of Guise, to live out her life in exile, perhaps even with her child James, while a council of noblemen ruled Scotland.[4] The idea had some aspects to recommend it, but it was imperative that the lords of the small country of Scotland did not do anything that France or England might consider as an insult, or anything that would lead either of these countries to intervene. Elizabeth was not keen on the idea of lords taking over from royalty, while Catholic France did not like the idea of Protestant lords in charge. The lords' stated main aim at this time was still to get rid of Bothwell, and another suggestion was that Mary divorced Bothwell and promised to rule under the guidance of her lords – but Mary herself refused this, as she knew that she was pregnant and would not risk her baby being declared illegitimate.[5] Throckmorton wrote to Cecil that he: "Never saw greater confusion amongst men, for they change their opinions very often",[6] and contributed to the ferment by passing on the idea that the baby Prince James could be sent to his godmother Elizabeth of England for safekeeping.[7] Elizabeth and Throckmorton were also becoming increasingly concerned that law and order in Scotland, particularly in the Borders, was breaking down as the lords and the queen focused on their personal struggles. A considerable number of the letters flying up and down to England were not about the queen, but about wider problems of instability as the country lurched through the crisis and people took advantage of the lack of central control.[8] The Borders were of concern to Elizabeth of England, but it was the same in the north and north-east where Jean was now. Meanwhile, the lords leaned towards the idea that James should be crowned as King, with Regents to guide him until he came of age. Mary herself, as she got more rest, did not despair: she knew that Bothwell was still at liberty and felt secure in the knowledge that she was queen and there were limits to what the lords would do: "though her body be restrained, yet her heart is not dismayed".[9]

After Jean's family had refused to help him, Bothwell and the dozen or so men who stayed with him had remained in the north-east of Scotland, going to Bothwell's former home of the enormous palace of Spynie, near Elgin, where he had spent some of his childhood with his great-uncle, Patrick Hepburn the Bishop of Moray.[10] The Bishop of Moray lived a dissolute life, being one of those Catholic clergymen whose way of life could be said to have contributed to the pressure for the Reformation: he had numerous illegitimate children and lived in luxury in the grand palace buildings, funding his various mistresses through the rents he controlled. He was also a savvy political operator, who had used his relative isolation in the north to avoid the excesses of the Reformation and keep his position unchallenged. His sheltering of his great-nephew Bothwell, however, led to Moray's government trying to intervene to stop his rent collections and, although the Bishop was welcoming, some of the Bishop's children tried to betray Bothwell, most likely for money or personal gain, though perhaps even motivated by loyalty to the Regent. An English spy, Christopher Rokesby, was being held prisoner in Spynie, and three of the Bishop's illegitimate sons offered him his liberty if he would either capture or kill Bothwell. They desired Rokesby to ask the English ambassador Throckmorton which course of action Elizabeth of England would prefer. At the same time, they planned to murder the Bishop himself. Throckmorton found the convoluted plot "very cruel and abominable", and passed the problem on to the Scottish Secretary of State, Lethington.[11]

Bothwell and the dozen or so men who accompanied him were ready for the Bishop's sons though, and when they tried to put their murderous plan into action, Bothwell killed one of them, then had the rest and all their servants thrown out of Spynie.[12] Jean's brother George seems to have had some foreknowledge of the plot, particularly since his other sister Margaret was now apparently having an affair with one of the Bishop's illegitimate sons, Patrick of Kinnoir. It is unclear whether or not this particular son was involved in the Rokesby plot, but George did not intervene on either side, and Bothwell saw that he would receive no more help by staying in Moray.

Bothwell was the hereditary Admiral of Scotland and, putting this together with his newly acquired title of Duke of Orkney and Shetland, Jean's ex-husband decided that his way forward was to go yet further north in Scotland – this time by boat. He got together five boats, manned by 300 men, and fully equipped them for a voyage.[13] Roads in the north of Scotland were poor, and going by sea was a logical choice, shortening the length of journeys considerably, as well as giving the element of surprise: boats could sail up without warning, whereas a party of horsemen traversing the north would have attracted attention. Sailing across to the Cromarty Firth, where Cromarty was the main port, Bothwell then added to his small fleet by capturing a boat that was carrying food for the Earl of Moray, but had stopped to shelter from bad weather.[14]

In Lochleven, Mary, Queen of Scots miscarried Bothwell's children: twin girls. Weakened from her experiences, Mary had little choice as she was forced to abdicate in favour of her son. Meanwhile, Bothwell sailed up the coast, making for Orkney. On the way he passed by Caithness, where his sister Janet and his brother-in-law were based, but his connections there were of little use: much like in the Borders, people in the north of Scotland were taking advantage of the chaos at court to settle old feuds, and Caithness, Sutherland and the Mackay clan were becoming embroiled in a tangled series of events; events that George and Jean were to become involved in and which were to shape the rest of Jean's life.[15] For the moment it meant that Janet Hepburn could not help her brother Bothwell. Bothwell had more family connections in Orkney though, through his Sinclair mother, and he was hopeful of a warm reception in the northern isles.

Bothwell did not receive the welcome he had hoped for in Orkney, however, and he stayed only two days before sailing on to Shetland. Here, he was more fortunate. He added to his fleet by chartering two ships for two months, including a large double-masted boat called the *Pelican*, which was normally used to import flax, hemp, iron or tar from the Continent to Scotland, and which was well-equipped with guns to defend itself against pirates. The *Pelican* was loading a cargo of fish at Sumburgh Head at the southern tip of the Shetland mainland for its return journey when, as its owner Bremen merchant Gerdt Hemelingk later explained, "a Scottish Lord with some hundred men . . . seized my ship, cast fish and other wares on shore to my appreciable and irretrievable loss and forced me to agree to sell the ship belonging to me and my associates or to charter it for two months". Bothwell drew up a contract, and said that he would pay 50 crowns a month for the boat, and 1600 crowns if the *Pelican* was not returned.[16]

However, the Regent Moray was now taking control, and he sent four large ships, the *Primrose*, the *James*, the *Robert* and the flagship the *Unicorn*, fully equipped with guns, 400 men and accompanied by several smaller vessels, all racing after Bothwell. One of the main men in charge of this expedition was Kirkcaldy of Grange, who Bothwell had refused to fight in single combat at Carberry Hill because he was too low in status. Kirkcaldy of Grange had no reason to like Bothwell. "Albeit I be no good seaman," he said, "I promise ... if I may once encounter him [Bothwell] either by land or sea, he shall either carry me with him or else I shall bring him dead or quick to Edinburgh."[17] Kirkcaldy of Grange and his four ships sailed quickly to Shetland where they surprised Bothwell, who was onshore eating his lunch with some of his men while his boats were lying at anchor in Bressay Sound. Sighting their pursuers and their superior numbers in the distance, Bothwell's men hurriedly set sail. In the confusion, one of Bothwell's ships sailed dangerously close to a reef. It just managed to scrape over, but the pursuing ship, the *Unicorn*, captained by Kirkcaldy of Grange was less lucky: it struck hard and sank. Kirkcaldy of Grange, that poor sailor, nearly drowned. The Regent's pursuit was temporarily called off. The treacherous rock is still called Unicorn Rock to this day, after the ship. Meanwhile, Bothwell gathered what men he could and escaped overland, catching a small local boat to Yell, and rejoining his own ships near the very northern tip of the Shetland Isles, at Unst. He sent one of his ships, the one least able to defend itself as it mainly contained his personal effects such as fine clothes and jewellery, back down to the southern part of Shetland, to Scalloway, to collect the men he had been forced to leave behind in his mad overland dash.[18]

It was not to be expected that Kirkcaldy of Grange would give up, and the Regent Moray's force soon located Bothwell's position. A sea battle took place, lasting for three hours, and the Regent's men captured one of Bothwell's ships, and shot away the main mast of the *Pelican*. Fortunately for Bothwell, the weather and the expert seamanship of his crew were on his side: a south-westerly gale sprang up and his small, battered fleet ran before the wind across the North Sea to Norway, where they made landfall at Karmøy Island.[19]

Bothwell and his men were in rags, dirty and battered by the storm. They had been on the run for about two months, riding and sailing around Scotland in stealth and secrecy; they had just fought a three-hour sea battle, followed by a hair-raising voyage in bad weather across a wild North Sea in a boat which had one mast shot away. They had no provisions and only a hazy idea of where they were. They staggered into safe harbour, guided to safety by a friendly Hanseatic merchant ship, and put down their anchors ready to head ashore. Immediately they were challenged by a Danish warship, which was patrolling the waters for pirates. The captain[20] demanded to see their papers. All of Bothwell's papers and riches were on the ship that was lost to them, left behind in Shetland, but Bothwell was not fazed. He drew himself up to his full height and announced that he was the King of Scots. He did not need any papers, as he was in supreme command of his country. He was the man who issued papers to others.[21] He was the husband of Mary, Queen of Scots, and he was here to offer his services to the King of Denmark, the supreme leader in charge of Scandinavian waters.[22] Jean's ex-husband was not short of courage.

The Danish warship captain could not believe his ears. This ruffian, surrounded by about 150 desperate-looking sailors, was claiming to be a king. It was true that the Danes did need manpower, in their ongoing seven-year war with Sweden, but the whole story seemed so unlikely. However, the Danes were outnumbered, so their captain proceeded cautiously. As Bothwell explained that events in Scotland had necessitated a precipitous departure, the Danish captain cleverly divided up Bothwell's men, inviting some, including Bothwell himself, on board his own ship for food, while letting others go ashore, where they were met by an unhappy peasantry who were well-primed to look out for pirates.[23] Once on board the Danish boat, Bothwell was informed that he must accompany the captain to Bergen to sort this out. Bothwell had little choice but to agree.

Once in Bergen, Bothwell had the most extraordinary bad luck:

a karmic revenge for youthful broken promises that led to consequences and punishment far greater than the crimes he had committed. First, he was entangled in legal querying over his ownership
of the two vessels he was commanding: not only did he not have
the documents for his purchase of the *Pelican*, whose owner started
legal proceedings for compensation, but the owner of the other
Hanseatic merchant ship he had acquired in the Shetlands turned out
to be accused of piracy, and Bothwell became mixed up in his legal
proceedings. Secondly, Skottefruen Anna was in Bergen. She may
have only just returned from Scotland herself, having finally given
up on her relationship with Bothwell after his marriages to Jean and
to Mary.[24] Anna, the daughter of a Danish admiral, had status in
Bergen, and she had Bothwell summoned before the Court, where
documents that she claimed proved their marriage were read out.[25]
Bothwell had always maintained that theirs was a handfasting, not a
legal marriage, but in Scandinavia a handfasting was seen as binding:
"Mrs. Anne, the daughter of Admiral Christopher Throndsson
charged the Earl of Bothwell that he had taken her from her native
land and her father's home and led her into a foreign country away
from her parents and would not hold her as his lawful wife which
he with hand and mouth and writings had promised them and her to
do."[26] Bothwell had to agree to pay Anna an annuity – and to hand
over one of his ships to her.

After this trial was over, Bothwell was sent to Copenhagen for
the Danish government to decide his fate. However much he continued to insist that he was King of Scots, to the Danish he was a man
mixed up in piracy, who had stolen the ships of honest merchants,
a multiple adulterer who had tricked and abandoned an important
Scandinavian woman in the worst way. His insistence on his status
was a curiosity: he might be a useful and important prisoner or
bargaining tool, but he was clearly a man with a chequered past
and many enemies. Like Mary, Queen of Scots, Bothwell was now
imprisoned, with no idea when he would again be free.

Back in Scotland, Moray declared peace in Scotland on 15th
September 1567.[27] By December he was holding his first Parliament,

which all the nobility attended, even former opponents of Moray, like Jean's brother George. George had not attended the coronation of the young James VI after Mary's forced abdication. He had been discharged of the Lieutenancy of the North[28] and he had not been involved in any of the discussions over the regency, but Moray's overwhelming support among the other nobility left George with few options other than to try to reconcile himself with the new Regent.[29] In return for George's allegiance, Moray reconfirmed Mary's restoration of George's title and lands – on the condition that George gave up all claims over the Moray lands. Moray also suggested a marriage alliance between his daughter (aged two) and George's son (aged five).[30] Moray was working hard to provide the stability that Scotland needed – and to increase his own power. He was now king in all but name, as he had always wanted to be. In many ways, he would have been an ideal leader, but the dubious legality of his claim to power combined with his personal ambition and character meant he was not universally liked. Meanwhile, the religious differences that underpinned many of the conflicts of Mary's time in Scotland were to remain of paramount importance for the next one hundred years, if not longer. One Regent was not going to be able to instantly solve all of Scotland's problems.

In spring of the following year, Mary, recovered and restored to some of her former vitality, escaped from the island prison of Lochleven Castle in the most romantic and daring way possible, charming one of her young male captors into rowing her ashore while she was in disguise as a servant girl, under cover of the chaos of May Day festivities. The dramatic escape was the catalyst for her supporters, like George, to reform and reassert their opposition to Moray. It was one thing for George and his family to oppose Bothwell as king, but another to support Moray as king in all but name.

Mary, Queen of Scots went to Hamilton family territory, and publicly revoked her abdication. The Hamiltons were the traditional Regents for the Scottish throne, next in line for the succession after the Stewarts, and they saw Regent Moray as usurping their rightful place. They were also George's in-laws, and George hastened to gather together a force of men and make ready to head down to help the Queen of Scots. Many of the Catholic nobility came out in support of Mary, but several Protestant nobles did too, including the powerful Earl of Argyll and several others.[31]

The Regent's position was by no means assured, and Mary had a genuine possibility of returning to her throne, but Moray had a steely determination to hold onto power and a belief that God was on his side: he was not going to back down now. He knew that his main chance was to attack Mary before George and his supporters had time to get down from the north. Moray had two excellent and loyal commanders in the Earl of Morton and Kirkcaldy of Grange, and seasoned, hardened troops. Moray and his force attacked his half-sister at Langside less than a fortnight after her escape from Lochleven and won a decisive victory.[32] Among the captured at Langside was Jean's former beau, Alex Ogilvie, still fighting for Mary, Queen of Scots alongside the family of his wife, Mary Beaton.[33] Alex Ogilvie and many others were sent to Edinburgh Castle. There, several of the prominent names were convicted of treason and sentenced to be executed – but the next day, apparently at the behest of John Knox, the Regent Moray pardoned them all. Everyone who paid a fine received remission for their crimes.[34] Alex Ogilvie, and others, were free to return home.[35] Moray needed people who were grateful to him.

Mary had to escape again. Given the choice of where to go, she did not go deeper into her own country, up to the north of Scotland where her major supporters were, where she would have had to negotiate with George and work with him instead of talking about Corrichie and loyalty as she had done in the final days of Bothwell's administration. Mary instead decided to gamble on going to England, and Elizabeth. She forgot everything she had learnt about Scotland in the brief period between Rizzio's death and Carberry Hill, everything she had learnt about the different parts of the country and the balancing act between the Borders, the Highlands and the Lowlands, everything she had learnt about the need for reconciliation and subtle manipulation of the different factions among the lords. She was once again seeing only the bigger picture: Catholic vs Protestant; the position of France and England. She had always focused on her right to succession to the English throne, and she had always seen Scotland as a pawn in the larger European game, encouraged by her upbringing which was firmly positioned in France. Now, she saw herself increasingly as a Catholic monarch, answerable to the Pope, part of a wider continental picture. Her brief moment of understanding, epitomised in Jean and Bothwell's marriage, that she was actually in control of a small country that was yet deeply complex within itself, not just within the context of its surrounding nations, was gone. She was not interested in the skirmishes that were happening in the Borders since her capture after Carberry Hill, not focused on the truly shocking events that were taking place in Caithness and Sutherland. Instead, Mary looked only to a big picture constructed by an upbringing that had assumed she would be not Queen of Scots but queen of France and England. Mary escaped south where she was not welcomed by Elizabeth but instead placed into an indefinite holding limbo; a gilded captivity.

George and his men did not make it to the south of Scotland. There was not a lot of time for him to get there, and Moray did his best to guard the routes south: some sources say that the Forbes helped to block the Gordons' route. Others say that George, Jean, their siblings and followers were distracted at the crucial moment by the death of Jean's mother, old Lady Huntly.[36] In the complex web of loyalties and allegiances of Scottish life, there was also the possibility that Mary's treatment of George just before Carberry – her goading about Corrichie and the dissolution of his sister Jean's marriage – had not encouraged him to rush to her rescue. Mary was still the woman who had ordered the killing of his father and brother and, although George was to become the most fervent supporter of the Marian cause in principle, he was not too fond of Mary herself.[37] Jean had after all just spent time with her cousin Agnes Keith, who was now the wife of the Regent, and Agnes "bitterly reproached" George for taking Mary's side.[38] Regardless, the Marian party, once galvanised, did not give up. For about the next five years Scotland was on the verge of civil war, as the queen's party attempted to set up an alternative government and Parliament. The Marian party had strong support and covered a wide area in Scotland: the Hamilton family, whose head was George's father-in-law the Duke of Chatelherault, controlled a good part of south central Scotland and the Earl of Argyll and his supporters were in the west. George was their acknowledged leader, controlling a vast territory in the north of Scotland where he "virtually established a provisional Marian administration".[39] In this, George was supported by other Gordons, and by the Grants, Forbes, Ogilvies and also clansmen like Mackay and the Mackintosh chief of Clan Chattan – not all of whom were Catholic, but all of whom wished to serve their true queen.[40]

Jean was based at Huntly Castle, where the mood was very much one of support for Mary, Queen of Scots – or, perhaps more aptly, of lack of support for the Regent Moray. Mary, Queen of Scots was able from her prison in England to get some news of how matters stood in Scotland, and she communicated with George directly, sending a letter to him suggesting French aid might be available. George wrote back with details of how matters stood, and assuring her of support in the north, but his communication was intercepted.[41] The distance between George in the north and Mary in England was a great hindrance to the Marian cause, as lines of communication were virtually impossible to keep open, with several letters intercepted so plans unable to be made.[42]

In the autumn of 1568, George, supported by his younger brother Adam, was focusing on gaining the support of the city and Provost of Aberdeen, primarily through force. They attacked the Provost's house with around 1500 men, and Adam took over control of Aberdeen.[43] Meanwhile, Moray was working hard to get back control, and took advantage of any weakness on the Marian side. In the south of Scotland, he managed to overpower the opposition, while his legitimacy as Regent was bolstered by support – both verbal and financial – from Elizabeth of England.[44] Elizabeth's support of Moray was encouraged by her realisation that a Catholic Mary, Queen of Scots, in England, even in prison, was a catalyst for rebellion: the north of England, where Mary was currently being held in genteel captivity, had a high proportion of Catholic nobility, who tried to organise at this time. Mary was not just writing to George and Bothwell,[45] but also to the northern English lords, who wished to depose Elizabeth of England and put Mary on the throne in her place. It became imperative that Elizabeth support Moray's regime and reduce Mary's power even further.

The Earl of Argyll in the west then capitulated to Moray, and, as encouragement to others to do the same, was totally forgiven. George still controlled most of the north, but he was too isolated to continue and had to acknowledge Moray's authority in May 1569. George's influence in Aberdeen had always been weaker than in the countryside, and Moray immediately came north with his men and established them in the town: he forgave the people of Aberdeen and their Provost on the grounds that they had been coerced, but levied massive fines on people from other parts of the north such as George himself, and others from Elgin and Inverness.[46] Moray also purged Kings College in Aberdeen of its remaining Catholic staff, and encouraged the development of a reformed, Protestant university.[47]

With a few notable exceptions, Moray was gradually gaining total control over and allegiance from the nobility and people of Scotland. Had he been given time, history may well have viewed Moray in a very different light: his personal failings, dubious legal claim to the throne and over-deference to England could have been overlooked if he had given Scotland years of peace and good management. However, after less than two years as Regent, Moray was shockingly assassinated.[48]

Moray was progressing through Linlithgow as he travelled from Stirling to Edinburgh. A crowd had come out to watch the Regent and his retainers, and the crush of people meant that Moray and his followers could only travel very slowly down the High Street. Sitting high on his horse, Moray was an easy target for the assassin crouching, hidden, at an upstairs window overlooking the street. The assassin was well-prepared and had only to wait until the Regent was in his sights. Taking aim, the gunshot rang out and Moray was hit in the pelvis. The crude weapon sent the bullet tearing through Moray's stomach before hitting a horse.[49] The gunman made his escape unhindered as Moray fell. Bleeding heavily from the messy wound, Moray managed to make it into Linlithgow Palace, but he died from the injury just before midnight. It was the first-ever recorded assassination by a firearm, and both the murder itself and the method attracted huge amounts of attention. As with the attempted murder of Darnley by gunpowder, it had never really occurred to the crowned heads of Europe before that the improving technology of guns meant that a quite ordinary person could shoot and kill a king from a distance. In England, Elizabeth increased her personal security dramatically.

The assassin in this case was a Hamilton. The Hamiltons, George's in-laws and stalwarts of the Marian party, had hoped that once Moray was dead people would flock to their side and spark another uprising, but the horrific manner of the shooting, and Moray's dignity in death, had the opposite effect. The people of Scotland were tired of instability, and Moray's death, and particularly the shocking method of his death, united people in grief: 'The death of my lord regent wes the caus of great dolour to all them of Christ's religion, and the caus of raising of great tumult and uproar in this realme amang the nobilitie thereof, for he was the defender of the widow and the fatherless . . .'[50] The primary emotion was horror at Moray's passing, and John Knox in Edinburgh preached a sermon at Moray's funeral that brought the congregation of around three thousand mourners to tears, telling them of the stability and leadership they had lost from the 'Good Regent', a man almost a Protestant saint. The line "judge and avenge my cause" from Psalm 43, the 'blood-feud psalm', was invoked in Moray's memory – and with it the memory of the same line being used after Darnley's death, on the banners showing the infant James VI. The villain was still Mary, Queen of Scots and her supporters – and the assassination of Moray left a dangerous power vacuum in Scotland.[51]

In the north of Scotland, at Huntly Castle, it was not to be expected that Moray would be much mourned, other than perhaps a passing sympathy for Jean's cousin Agnes, now their near neighbour in charge of the Moray estates, who was pregnant with her late husband's last child.[52] Jean had returned to her family, and was now living again with George and her other siblings. Her sister Margaret's marriage to the Master of Forbes had irrevocably broken down, so she too may have returned to George's house. The rest of Jean's family were all in Huntly Castle as well. The Gordon siblings were a tight-knit and increasingly formidable grouping. George was particularly supported in his efforts to maintain power by his brother Adam, or Edom, the brother who had been pardoned after Corrichie because of his youth. Adam was Jean's closest brother in age. Known locally by the name Edom o' Gordon, Adam's earlier pardon at Corrichie had not made him into any sort of pacifist. George and Adam were backed up by the youngest brothers Patrick, Robert and Thomas. Middle brothers James and William had both gone into the church, but they too were not shy of speaking up for their beliefs, embracing ever more strongly their Catholic faith. For the boys, this meant a violent path for the time being. For Jean, the reaffirmation of her Catholic faith meant that she was in the uncomfortable position of having to consider herself, despite the Protestant divorce, still linked in some way with Bothwell, the husband of the queen the Gordons were trying to reinstate. Indeed, for some years Mary, Queen of Scots in England pursued various routes to try and annul her marriage to Bothwell, including arguing to the Pope that Jean and Bothwell were still married. This came to nothing, but Jean, part of the leading family in the Marian cause, must have been aware that it was a possibility.[53] Practically, however, the recognition of Jean's marriage to Bothwell brought some benefits: as George struggled financially to pay the huge fines that Moray had imposed and to continue to raise money to fight for Mary, Jean was able to keep the lands in the Borders that she had gained through her marriage with Bothwell, and to draw revenue from them. She did this for the rest of her life,[54] and Jean's descendants in the Gordon family continue to hold lands in the Border to this day. Supporting Mary, Queen of Scots, and the true Catholic Church was a strange mixture of idealism and pragmatism for the Gordons. The true allegiance, however, for the close-knit siblings, was to family. Gordon interest came above everything.

Moray's replacement as Regent was the Earl of Lennox, grand-father of King James VI and father of Darnley. This was as unac-ceptable to Mary's supporters as the choice of Moray had been. George derisorily described him as "an alien, a lackey of England, a traitor bought by English gold".[55] George had a point. The choice of Lennox was almost universally unpopular; he had lived a lot of his life in England, his lust for power and promotion of the crown matrimonial for his son Darnley had caused many of the problems of Mary's reign, and he was fully supported by Elizabeth of England. It was not difficult for the Marian supporters to begin to gather again, and Huntly began to march a large body of men south, while Argyll and Chatelherault gathered their forces. They had ambitious plans to call a Marian Parliament; an alternative government to Lennox's Regency.[56] Lennox's own attempt to assemble his government ended in shambles: in Edinburgh, William Kirkcaldy of Grange, the man who had lined up against Mary at Carberry Hill, written on numerous occasions to the English, who had chased Bothwell to the Shetland Isles, and who had ridden at the front of Moray's funeral procession, had stunningly changed sides to support Mary, Queen of Scots. He could support Moray, but not Lennox. Kirkcaldy of Grange was now holding Edinburgh Castle for the Marian cause. As Lennox tried to hold his Parliament in the capital, Kirkcaldy of Grange shot cannon fire at them, causing Lennox's men to repeatedly fall to their knees and crawl around in an attempt to hide from cannon shot and falling masonry: it became known as the 'creeping parliament'. Kirkcaldy of Grange and George, now allied in the same cause, even discussed holding their Marian Parliament in Edinburgh itself, as Lennox with-drew to the safety of Stirling Castle.[57]

George and Kirkcaldy of Grange arranged an attack on Stirling, and, in the skirmish, Lennox was killed, shot in the back.[58] He was the second Scottish Regent to be assassinated in less than two years. The confusion continued as a replacement was quickly sought.

George's wider activities in the interest of Scotland and his actions in the south were backed up by his family in the north. The Gordons were fighting for the Queen's party and for the wider cause of Catholicism, but there were also northern quarrels being settled. The Earl of Mar was made Regent, and as he tried to deal with the ongoing problems with Edinburgh Castle, in the north an old feud between the Gordons and the Forbes broke out again. The Forbes' and Gordons' long-standing enmity had been partially healed when Jean's sister Margaret was married to John, Master of Forbes. However, not only had the marriage broken down, but Baron Forbes (the leader of the clan) had been named by the King's party as lieutenant in the north – the same position that the Queen's party had given to George. With George in Edinburgh, it was up to Jean's next oldest brother, Adam, to take the lead.

At the beginning of October, Adam heard that the Forbes were assembling at Tulliangus, and made his way there. Adam split his force into two, giving one-half to his younger brother Robert to command, and attacked the Forbes on two fronts, beginning a "cruel skirmish".[59] Adam, Robert and their men comprehensively defeated the Forbes, killing 120. The Master of Forbes, Adam's brother-in-law, fled the battlefield and made his way to Edinburgh, where he passed on the news of Adam's victory to the Regent Mar, who sent him north again with 800 men.[60] Meanwhile, George sent 40 soldiers up from Edinburgh by sea to assist Adam, and to warn him of Forbes' arrival. Adam laid waste to the northern countryside to make sure that Forbes and his approaching army would not be able to find food or shelter. The two sides, Gordon and Forbes, fought again at Crabstane and once again Adam, well-prepared by his brother's warning, was victorious. Three hundred Forbes men were killed and 200, including Adam's brother-in-law, the Master of Forbes, were taken prisoner.[61] The Master of Forbes was conveyed to Spynie Palace – Bothwell's childhood home and recent residence – where he was held in the genteel captivity reserved for men of high birth. Bishop Patrick Hepburn was supporting the Gordons, but also working in his own interest and building up his rent money again by renting George lands at Spynie. Forbes was also forced to pay all expenses accrued during his captivity.[62] Jean's sister Margaret visited Forbes in prison and showed her disdain for her husband by flaunting her new relationship with one of the Bishop of Moray's illegitimate sons.[63] Margaret and Forbes were subsequently to officially divorce.[64]

Meanwhile, Jean's brother Adam commanded a (Catholic) service of thanksgiving to be held in Aberdeen, while sending his soldiers to occupy and retain the houses of the defeated Forbes.[65] He wanted to be as sure as possible that there would be no further uprisings from the Forbes, and that Gordon word was law in the north. His soldiers were commanded to use considerable force, but this was taken to extremes: at one of the Forbes residences, the recently built Castle of Corgarff, the lady of the house refused entry to Adam's soldiers, and fired on them from the roof. Adam's soldiers eventually set the house on fire, and the lady and 27 others, including women and children, were burnt to death.[66] This effectively ended any Forbes opposition to the Gordons in the north, but it irrevocably blackened Adam's reputation. A popular ballad, "Edom o' Gordon" commemorated the event, describing the brave lady of Corgarff shooting from the rooftop, her children pleading with her to open the castle door as the fire takes hold, and finally one child thrown from the window wrapped in sheets in a desperate attempt to save her from the flames – but 'on the point o' Gordon's sword she got a deadly fall'. Jean's brother was given the sobriquet 'the Herod of the North', and became in the popular imagination of the north-east a child-murderer and bogeyman for generations to come.[67]

Adam veered between brutal violence and extreme religious display to justify that violence, still acting as his brother's trusted agent in the north. Even as he became the target of vitriolic popular song, Catholic commentators praised his ferocity in defence of the true faith, describing him as "the illustrious Adam Gordon".[68] As George pursued his enemies in the south, Adam pounced on any of them that attempted to assemble in the north. At Brechin very early in the morning of 5th July 1572, Adam surprised a group of nobles collecting their forces, bursting in on them at 1am with "the ferocity of a Highland chief".[69] He took all the ringleaders and 200 of their men prisoner. They were kept waiting while Adam went to the Kirk of Brechin, where he spent an hour thanking God for his victory. The prisoners were then called to stand before him. Adam stood at the front of the assembled group, and berated them at length, expounding on all the wrongs that had been suffered by the Gordon family; the death of his father, the beheading of his dashing brother John after Corrichie and the slaughter of those loyal to Queen Mary and Catholicism by the Regent's party. The terrified prisoners had no idea where this diatribe by the Herod of the North was leading when Adam suddenly paused: 'My good brethren and countrymen,' he said, 'be not afraid; fear nothing, for you shall be treated as brethren, and I shall do to you after the commandment of God in doing good for evil, forgetting the cruelty done to the Queen and her faithful subjects, and receiving you as her faithful subjects in time coming.'[70] Adam then gave the prisoners the option of being freed, if they could provide security for their loyalty (i.e. if they gave him money or provisions). The Regent called on the freed men to ride with him against Adam, but they refused, on account of the mercy Adam had shown them, the promises he had secured from them, and their fear of the unpredictable Adam himself.[71]

The Gordon siblings seemed to be almost out of control, both defending the strict rule of Catholicism yet flaunting the law as it suited their needs, with Margaret ready to divorce the Master of Forbes, Jean's own complicated position with regards divorce, George's taking up of arms for his queen, and Adam becoming increasingly violent and unstable. In this, they were reflecting the mood of the entire country. The lack of clear leadership in Scotland was exacerbating every division, whether it was a religious difference or a long-standing feud – and bad weather and the constant demand for men to leave their land and farms to fight was causing famine.[72] Each individual choice assumed massive significance as, with no person in overall charge, small actions were magnified in importance and consequences were unpredictable. In Edinburgh as well as the north, the king and queen's parties committed ever worse atrocities, unforgiveable acts that seemed to drive them further and further from any hope of reconciliation. In the north, where Jean was, the regular systems of law and order, the justice ayres that Mary, Queen of Scots had always been so careful to resume no matter what else was going on, had virtually broken down. Major landowners like George were distracted by the fighting further south. The clans realigned themselves with whichever noble seemed most powerful at that moment, to try to advance their own local causes. Crimes were not reported and criminals not brought to court.

To understand the next part of Jean's story we have to go back in time again, to the momentous year of 1567, when Jean divorced Bothwell and Mary, Queen of Scots was first deposed, and look in more detail at what was happening in the Far North of Scotland at that time and after, and how Jean and the Gordons became entangled in an extraordinary poison plot.

CHAPTER NINE

Further North and Further Back: 1567–1573

Unlike Mary, Queen of Scots, Jean and the Gordon family never lost touch with what was happening in the north of Scotland. After Huntly had been defeated at Corrichie, the Gordons had lost a significant amount of power in the north and north-east, and other families had been trying to consolidate their positions. This included not only the Earls, such as Moray and Caithness, but also the clans. One of Jean's brother George's most pressing issues was to try to deal with the Earl of Caithness. The feuds between Caithness, Sutherland and Huntly, with the constant interventions of clans like Mackay, were to lead to Jean's second marriage, to another Earl.

The Earl of Caithness was George Sinclair. Along with the Earl of Sutherland, Bothwell and George, Caithness had come into favour at court not long after the murder of Rizzio.[1] He had been dining with Bothwell on the night of Rizzio's murder, and celebrating the marriage of his son and heir John the Stout, the Master of Caithness, with Bothwell's sister Janet. In this way, Caithness was part of the new Highland-Border alliance that Mary, Queen of Scots had hoped would be a counterbalance to the power of Moray and his associates. The problem was that Caithness did not always get on with his close neighbours in the north, particularly the Earl of Sutherland, as they battled for power and resources in an area that was also strongly contested by the clans.

The Earl of Sutherland's territory was next to Caithness' land.

Sutherland had traditionally been a strong ally of the Huntly Gordons, since a marriage between their families in the early sixteenth century, when the daughter of the Earl of Sutherland had married a son of the Earl of Huntly. This couple had then taken over the Sutherland succession, bringing several Gordon retainers from Moray to Sutherland with them when they moved into the Sutherland seat of Dunrobin Castle.[2] The grandson of this Sutherland-Huntly marriage, John Gordon, was now the 11th Earl of Sutherland. He was sometimes known as 'Good Earl John'.[3] After the battle of Corrichie, Good Earl John had been exiled into France because of his support of Jean's father. Caithness had not been exiled, and had used the time while both the Earl of Sutherland and the Huntly Gordons were significantly out of favour to try and boost his power in the north. However, as a Catholic, and as a relatively minor lord with a reputation for violence including an outstanding murder charge for killing a servant, Caithness had not been able to gain much standing at Mary's court in her early days in Scotland.[4]

Good Earl John had only just returned to Scotland, via a brief period of captivity in England, when the Rizzio murder happened – as Bothwell and George were escaping Edinburgh Castle to plan for Mary's rescue, Good Earl John's main concern had been to get back home to the north. However, he, like the Earl of Caithness, had played his part in the subsequent events of Mary's reign: Caithness had been on the jury at Bothwell's trial; Caithness and Good Earl John had both signed the Ainslie Tavern bond promoting Bothwell's marriage with Mary, Queen of Scots; Good Earl John had been a witness at Bothwell and Mary's marriage. The animosity of close neighbours who jostled for territory in the north had been put aside in the larger concerns of the nation. So, when Good Earl John, his wife and son were invited to dinner by a relative of the Earl of Caithness in summer 1567, they had no reason to think it was anything other than a meal shared with friends.

It was the summer of Carberry Hill; the lull after Mary, Queen of Scots had just been defeated, when she was imprisoned in Lochleven. Attention was focused on the south of Scotland. No one knew yet just how events were going to pan out. The Earl of Caithness had been made hereditary justiciar in Caithness earlier that year, and he had hoped that this position would help him consolidate his power in the Far North: it meant that he was in charge of justice, with power to banish and kill criminals as he thought fit, or pardon any crime (except treason).[5] Caithness had continued to support Bothwell throughout his trial for Darnley's murder, where he was foreman of the jury, but after Bothwell's abduction of Mary, Caithness had gone a different way from his neighbour the Earl of Sutherland and from George, and had stood with the rebel lords. Caithness' support of Moray was half-hearted, however, and his main interest remained his own position in the north.[6] However, Caithness had found himself in the uncomfortable position of having backed the winning side (Moray), but now being ignored by that side, and totally cut off from them: whatever power Moray and his supporters had in the south of Scotland, in the north the Sutherlands and George in the north-east were still firmly on the side of Mary. Caithness was surrounded by his former friends and allies, who he had let down at the crucial moment by switching sides, while his new allies were no longer interested in him. This put him in a vulnerable position, and he seems to have tried to think of a creative way out; a way to make sure that he was not overwhelmed by the combined forces of his former allies the Earl of Sutherland and George.

Our understanding of events at this time in the north is heavily weighted towards Gordon interests, as the main written sources were composed some time after events by Gordons, but the story of the Helmsdale poisoning, even when told by those supporting Caithness, is shocking.

Good Earl John of Sutherland and his wife, Marion Seton, were staying at a hunting lodge near the River Helmsdale, accompanied by Sutherland's son and heir, Alexander. Marion was Sutherland's third wife, after he had been made a widower twice before, and she was pregnant with their child. That day, the Sutherlands' supper was to be organised for them by Isobel Sinclair, the Earl's aunt, a high-ranking member of the Sinclair-Caithness family who had married into the Sutherland Gordon family.[7] Good Earl John's son Alexander was late home, as he was still out hunting, but Sutherland and his wife sat down to start their meal without him. As soon as they started to eat and drink, they both immediately started to feel violently ill with stomach pains. Alexander walked in, but his father managed to drag himself to his feet and overturned the table, pulling off the tablecloth, smashing all the dishes and scattering the food and drink on the floor; crying out that he had been poisoned and that Alexander should flee for his life back home to Dunrobin. Isobel Sinclair had hoped to poison all three of them, which would have made her own son next in line to the Earldom of Sutherland.[8]

Meanwhile, in the kitchen of the hunting lodge, Isobel Sinclair's own son[9] had unexpectedly arrived. He knew nothing about his mother's plot on his behalf. Thirsty, he called to the servants to bring him a drink. The servants, too, knew nothing of the poisoning plot or the drama unfolding at the dinner table elsewhere in the lodge, and Isobel's son was given a drink – but it too was full of poison.[10]

As Caithness was in charge of dispensing justice in the region, he was soon involved. Good Earl John and his pregnant wife managed to follow their son back to Dunrobin Castle, where they died in agony about a week later. Isobel Sinclair's own son had taken so much of the poison that he had only lasted two days. The nature of their deaths and the appearance of the corpses made it clear to onlookers that poison had been involved and that these deaths had been deliberately planned.[11] Caithness acted swiftly and arrested and executed the Earl of Sutherland's servants from his hunting lodge, blaming them for the poisoning, but Good Earl John's followers were not convinced. There was no motive for the servants to have carried out such a wholesale action. Instead, they alleged that Isobel Sinclair was the poisoner and that her motive had been to stop the Earl of Sutherland from coming back into his full powers in the north, and that she had wanted place her own son in his place – and, furthermore, that Isobel had been encouraged in this by her Sinclair relatives, in particular the Earl of Caithness, but also William Sinclair of Dunbeath, who was worried that the Earl of Sutherland would find out about some land deals he had transacted in Sutherland's absence.[12] Isobel was apprehended and sent to Edinburgh, where she was tried and found guilty. She died the night before her execution was to take place, and it was popularly believed that she committed suicide, distraught at the failure of her plan and in particular the death of her son.[13]

The Earl of Sutherland's friends were able to bring Isobel Sinclair to trial, but with Alexander, the Earl's son, still underage at only 15 years old, the Earldom was not strong, and Caithness was able to take advantage of this.[14] Alexander was officially in the charge of his elder sister, Margaret, who at the time of the poisoning was with Mary, Queen of Scots.[15] Unable to leave the queen as she was at Lochleven, Margaret chose a suitable man to take over the official duties of her brother's 'warding': the Earl of Atholl, who was related to the House of Sutherland.[16] Holding someone in ward meant essentially controlling their title for them, taking over things like decisions over land, collecting of rents etc. – it was a position of responsibility, and one which could mean financial gains for the person holding the wardship, but also a great deal of time and effort for them. Unfortunately for Alexander, however, Caithness persuaded Atholl to sell him Alexander's wardship.[17] The Earl of Caithness was now in official control of the Earldom of Sutherland – and now that he had control on paper, he wanted to make sure that he had control in reality.

Since the poisoning, Alexander had been living at the castle of Skibo, in the nominal care of the castle's heritable constable John Gray, and the Bishop of Caithness. Like most children of his status and time, he had not been brought up by his parents, but had been fostered out nearby from a young age.[18] He was the son of the Earl John of Sutherland and his second wife, Lady Helenor Stewart, and had one brother, who had died in infancy, and three sisters: Margaret, who was older than him, and two younger sisters Janet and Elinor. For much of Alexander and his siblings' childhood their father had been in exile (after Corrichie). Their mother had died during this period of exile, and it was their stepmother, Marion Seton, who had been poisoned alongside his father at Helmsdale. Unlike Jean, whose childhood was relatively stable and secure, with her mother and siblings nearby – even when her father was in exile – Alexander was used to living with many different adults.

After the Gordon-biased account of the poisoning, there are now a variety of different interpretations of the subsequent events. From Jean's point of view, the Earl of Caithness was now firmly in opposition to both Sutherland and her own branch of the Gordon family, he was a murderer who would stop at nothing and whose every action was now open to negative interpretation. Others did not necessarily see it that way. It was not only the lords who were involved in events in the summer of 1567. Caithness first secured the help of the Bishop of Caithness, who agreed that the Earl should have control of Alexander, and persuaded the captain of Skibo Castle to agree to this.[19] However, the clans were trying to take advantage of events as well.

From the clans' point of view, all the Earls were pretty much equally bad: the Corrichie defeat and the squabbles between Caithness and Sutherland had all meant encroachments on clan lands, and the clans were prepared to ally with whoever seemed most helpful to them at the time, with little regard to the royal situation. The processes of law which the Earls set great store by, the positions of wardship and land deals, were all biased against the clans. There was little hope that the clansmen could get what they wanted by going to the courts, as the courts generally treated them as second-class citizens whose rights over the land were not recognised, subservient to the Earls in every way. Consequently, the clansmen tended to look to the power of the sword as the only power they would trust. The Mackay clan had lost power in the north when Caithness, Sutherland and George had all worked together – now that there was dissension among the Earls, the Clan Chiefs wanted to exploit it. Alexander was in Skibo Castle, which was in Murray territory. The Murrays did not want Caithness to have any sort of hold in their lands, so were opposed to Caithness taking over Alexander's wardship. Meanwhile, the powerful Mackay clan were unhappy with the Murrays. Despite the fact that the Mackays had previously pledged allegiance to Jean's brother George, Caithness and chief Aodh Mackay now formed an alliance. Aodh Mackay led his men to Skibo, where he laid waste to the castle and surrounding lands, and burnt the nearby town of Dornoch. Many Murrays were killed, and Caithness took Alexander away with him to his own home.[20]

Caithness' main seat was Girnigoe Castle, almost at the very tip of the north of Scotland. It was as far away from the Gordon territory of Sutherland and Huntly as Caithness could go. After years of local fighting and minority successions, most of the castles in the Far North were far less luxurious than Jean's home of Huntly Castle, and Girnigoe was a defensive set of buildings in a dramatic location, perched at the top of cliffs on a small piece of land which jutted off the coast. A natural inlet was extended into a moat so that Girnigoe was virtually surrounded by sea, meaning access over the causeway to the main gate could be strictly controlled.[21] Caithness' family grouping was more disparate and less united than Jean's family as well: his wife was Elizabeth Graham, daughter of the Earl of Montrose. Elizabeth seems to have been ruled by her violent husband: there is a record of her renouncing a contract she had agreed to on the grounds that she had only agreed to what her husband said 'through fear' – but she seems to have found solace in the church and was a pious Catholic.[22] The couple had four sons and five daughters.[23] Caithness' sons seem to have taken after their violent father. John the Stout, the heir and Master of Caithness, was used to accompanying his father to court in Edinburgh: Jean knew him as he was married to Janet Hepburn, Bothwell's sister. Janet Hepburn and John the Stout had five children, and their eldest son and heir was called George. Janet's son from her first marriage, Francis, may also have spent at least some of his childhood in the north of Scotland among the extended Caithness family.[24] Both Francis and George, though still young, were to grow up into formidable men, like their Caithness forbears. Fortunately Alexander, used to fitting in with different adults in his various foster homes, had a pleasant and undemanding character which generally made him popular.[25] As Earl of Sutherland, Alexander was also a valuable person of status, so his time with Caithness, despite the intimidating people around him, was not an uncomfortable confinement in a prison – but Alexander was constantly watched by Caithness' men, his movements curtailed and his place in the household minor.[26] Caithness was very definitely in command, ruling over his dysfunctional brood.

Next, the Earl of Caithness informed Alexander that he was going to be married: to Caithness' daughter Barbara. Barbara was 32, while Alexander was 15.[27] They first went through a handfasting ceremony, where the couple held hands and promised to marry – a legally binding agreement, which supposedly went ahead with both their consent. Since the Earl of Caithness was officially in charge of Alexander's wardship, that made it legal for him to choose Alexander's bride – and since the rest of Scotland was concerned with Mary being deposed, there were few people ready to take issue with events in the Far North. Alexander and Barbara were married in Girnigoe Castle by the Catholic priest from Wick in the morning of Saturday 9th August 1567, in front of a number of witnesses.[28] Caithness reaffirmed his Catholic religion – and had also resumed his support of the Queen's party, though, characteristically, mainly in name only, as he preferred to focus on his own problems. At the same time, Caithness also arranged marriages for his other two daughters, 'by which means the Earle of Caithness made himself strong and potent in friendship and alliance within this diocese'.[29] Having now bolstered his position, Caithness took his daughter and his new son-in-law, and the rest of his brood, including his ally Aodh, the Chief of Mackay, and installed them all in Dunrobin Castle, the home of the Earls of Sutherland, a much more well-appointed castle than his own. Caithness continued to exercise his powers as justiciary across the whole of Caithness and Sutherland, but his sweeping actions were not well received, and even his supporters acknowledge that he exercised his power "in a very oppressive and tyrannical manner. He was cordially detested by the inhabitants and by some of the principal families..."[30] Some of the Gordon families in the area left when Caithness came to Dunrobin, and moved over to Aberdeenshire and the safe haven of Jean's family territories.[31]

Jean and her family viewed this situation as an abduction and forced marriage, and an invasion of Gordon territory; a Gordon heir stolen away by enemies in league with the treacherous clansman Aodh Mackay, who had forgotten his allegiance to George.[32] However, alternative viewpoints are given by others: one wonderful (pro-clan) description of the situation was that it was "a common outcome of such a situation among the Anglo-Norman barons, whose traditional practices had outlived the Middle Ages in this corner of Europe" – a harsh assessment of the Earls, but one which undoubtedly contains a grain of truth: the veneer of civilisation and recourse to the law rather than the sword that early modern times were bringing to Scotland had fairly comprehensively broken down in the north at this time.[33] Meanwhile, a history of the Clan Mackay says that Caithness treated Alexander "with great kindness, as one of his own children".[34] Subsequent events show that being treated as one of Caithness' children was not necessarily a good thing.

Not all the Gordons had left Sutherland after Good Earl John's poisoning and Caithness' takeover. Golspitour was an important Gordon holding, a substantial dwelling-house on a hill, near Dunrobin and with a good view of that castle, owned by a branch of the Gordon family descended from John Gordon of Drummoy, who was linked by blood and marriage to the Earls of Huntly, and who had moved to Sutherland many years before when the Gordons of Huntly first married into the Sutherland Earldom.[35] These Gordons were in communication with Jean and her family, and reached out as well to the Murrays, who were Mackay's enemies. Their chance to act came in 1569. Caithness left his extended family at Dunrobin while he went down to Edinburgh. Moray was the Regent and Caithness was currently supporting him, while the Gordons, promoting Mary's cause, remained in the north. The Gordons believed that Caithness, seeing that neither Barbara nor Alexander were happy in their forced marriage, was also using his trip to Edinburgh to further a plot to enforce the marriage of Alexander's older sister Margaret (still based in Edinburgh) to his second son William, then Caithness would kill Alexander, thereby gaining control over Sutherland.[36] The family of John Gordon of Drummoy had to act fast, taking advantage of Caithness' temporary absence from Dunrobin, and stopping matters developing further away from Gordon interests. They "came quietlie, vnder silence of the night" to the burn of Golspie, not far from Dunrobin Castle, "and ther they lay in ambush".[37] Then the second son of the family, Sidderay,[38] dressed himself as a pedlar, and went into the castle, where he was able to communicate the rescue plan to Alexander. Alexander was constantly surrounded by Caithness' servants, but he convinced them that he needed to go out to 'take the air' that morning before breakfast – and walked straight to the Gordons, hiding nearby.[39] Alexander's Gordon allies rushed him down through Sutherland, hotly pursued by Caithness' men. As the two companies ran further south, a great storm blew up: Alexander and his companions had reached the Dornoch firth and, as they crossed on the ferry they were nearly drowned. Despite the "great tempest" Caithness' men made it over on the ferry as well, but only just. Battered by the weather, they gave up the chase at Portnaculter, the peninsula that formed the ferry's landing point just across the firth (close to the start of the Dornoch bridge today).[40]

As the only scapegoats left in the Far North, the Murrays came in for the brunt of Caithness' displeasure. John Murray was a principal agent in Alexander's escape, and he was imprisoned in Skibo, while a number of other Murrays were also taken prisoner.[41] Aodh, Chief of Mackay, and John the Stout, Master of Caithness, marched together with their men to the town of Dornoch, where the remainder of the Murray clan were making their last stand. " …in the night season",[42] Mackay and John the Stout burnt the church and town.[43] The Murrays were reduced to hiding in the church steeple, the only unburnt and defendable part of that structure left, and in the castle. They had little hope of holding out against the combined Caithness and Mackay force, however, and after about a week of sustained assaults the Murrays negotiated conditions for surrender. Three sons from the principal Murray families were handed over to the Caithness/Mackay force as 'pledges' – security to show that the Murrays meant what they said and would stick by their promises and do as they agreed, submitting to Caithness and Mackay's superior force and rule in the north. However, the Earl of Caithness himself, returning from Edinburgh to find his ward Alexander safe in the hands of Jean's family, refused to ratify the agreement. Going against what his son John the Stout and Mackay had agreed, Caithness acted unilaterally, executing the three Murray hostages by beheading.[44] John the Stout, Master of Caithness, and Aodh Mackay were horrified. They had negotiated a suitable agreement with the Murrays and the three hostages had been handed over in good faith: the executions went against all the moral codes of the clans and the legal codes of the earls. Caithness' high-handed management of the situation in the north had gone to extremes, and it caused a bitter break between him and his ally Aodh Mackay – and an irreparable break with his own son and heir, John the Stout. John the Stout, Master and heir of Caithness, moved out of Dunrobin and went to live with Aodh Mackay in the Mackay clan lands of Strathnaver.[45]

In Huntly Castle, Jean and her family were jubilant, and Alexander was welcomed with open arms. Used to being moved around from house to house, his opinions unconsulted as the adults around him planned his marriage and life, Alexander now found himself with the large family of loyal Gordon siblings, much closer to him in age than Caithness or his wife Barbara, who respected him and welcomed him as a distant cousin and promised to restore him to power as an Earl. They even searched out his younger sisters Janet and Elinor to bring them into the family as well. After a childhood where his father had been exiled, his mother had died, then his returning father and stepmother were brutally poisoned by his aunt to die in agony in front of him, the close-knit family of Gordon siblings was a revelation to Alexander. His recent experiences hiding in the ruinous castle of Skibo then being captured by Caithness were now just a memory – and a memory he could be revenged upon.

The Gordon men who had helped Alexander escape from Dunrobin stayed with him as his entourage. Huntly Castle, despite the items looted by Mary, Queen of Scots, after Corrichie, was still a more luxurious home than Alexander had ever known, while the people around him were his father's relations, who talked about his lost parents with affection. This group of handsome young people were all of the same Catholic religion, dedicated to the cause of the beautiful and wronged Queen Mary, and they invited Alexander in. Alexander threw his lot in with Jean's family completely, and his loyalty to them never wavered from this moment.

Back in Caithness and Sutherland, Mackay and John the Stout had to decide what to do next. Mackay was in law the vassal of the Earl of Sutherland. If Alexander was now free, and supported by the powerful Gordons, and wanted to take revenge on his captors, Mackay was in a very tricky position. Fortunately for him, Jean's brother George was struggling to legally get control of Alexander's wardship back from the Earl of Caithness, and George came to the conclusion that the only way for Alexander to regain power in Sutherland was to ally with the Mackays.[46] George sent one of the Murrays who had escaped with Alexander back to Sutherland, to talk to Aodh Mackay.

Affairs in the north of Scotland had been settled by Caithness over the last few years by the power of the sword, but all parties concerned knew that there was a legal code in Scotland, and were keen to twist it to their advantage. While Mary, Queen of Scots, was in Lochleven and the Regency unsettled, the law had been slipping, but once Moray was Regent Scotland looked like it might be in for a period of more settled calm, when there would be a reckoning and people brought to justice. Aodh Mackay, like everyone involved, walked this fine line between the law and the sword, and it now suited him to switch sides and support George and the Gordons again. Legally, in return for some money and a pledge of allegiance, George returned to Aodh Mackay official power over the Mackay Strathnaver lands. And, by pledging allegiance to George, rather than Alexander (who was still underage) Aodh Mackay effectively stopped Alexander from taking any future revenge against him.[47]

Caithness was not happy when he heard that Aodh Mackay had pledged loyalty to George. He believed that Aodh and his own son John the Stout were now plotting against him. Caithness sent several messages to Aodh and John, claiming that he wished to make up their quarrel, and, eventually, John consented to visit his father at Girnigoe Castle. Aodh did not trust Caithness, but John persuaded him to come along as well. The two men rode to Girnigoe, where they were welcomed by Caithness himself, who saluted them as they rode over the drawbridge.[48] Mackay, still suspicious, was unconvinced by this affable greeting, and slowed down to look around. He saw an unusual number of armed men lounging around the castle walls, and, making a split-second decision, turned and rode back along the drawbridge as fast as he could, leaving John behind him to face his father alone.[49] As John came into the main hall, he was seized by the group of armed men. John was a large man, and there was a severe struggle, but eventually Caithness saw his son put into fetters and thrown in chains into the dark dungeon of the castle, watched over by three jailors.[50]

As the Regent Moray was assassinated and replaced with Lennox in the south of Scotland, in the north George and Jean's family continued to grow in power. Alexander remained with them, supporting George in 1570 when he tried to call a Marian Parliament, the name of the Earl of Sutherland adding extra legitimacy to George's roll call of supportive noblemen, particularly as Alexander, through his mother, was related to Darnley's Lennox Stewart family. After the Regent Lennox was stabbed in the back, Alexander and his Sutherland men helped Adam Gordon fight against the Forbes at Crabstane, the victory whose aftermath gave Adam or 'Edom o'Gordon' his vicious reputation. Alexander's men were notable bowmen and archers, and they 'set upon the back and flanks of the Forbes footmen' while Adam and his brother Robert took the Gordon musketeers to ambush and kill the Forbes at Crabstane itself.[51] After several of the Forbes men were imprisoned, Adam gave many of their houses and possessions to Alexander's Sutherland men.[52]

The Regent Mar had taken over after Lennox's assassination, but his reign too lasted only a short time: he died suddenly in October 1572, not long after the battle of Crabstane. It was said that he died of a broken heart, unable to resolve Scotland's problems.[53] Scotland had now gone through three Regents in less than five years. Mar was succeeded by the Regent Morton, a ruthless operator who barely had a heart to break. John Knox, on his deathbed in 1572, just before Morton was elected Regent, had asked Morton if he had killed Darnley. Morton said no, but he might have been being economical with the truth.[54] Douglas man Morton, with his shock of ginger hair and squint, was for several years to provide stability for Scotland – though a stability borne out of violence.

The Regent Morton inherited a Scotland that was moving into a new phase of its religious war, caught in the current of wider European events. In the early days of Mary, Queen of Scots' rule, it had seemed possible to have Protestants and Catholics living together in some sort of harmonious compromise. Now, each sides' opinions had hardened. John Knox, the guiding light of the reformed Scottish church, died, an old man, as Morton assumed the title of Regent. Meanwhile, public opinion against Scotland's Catholic former queen was influenced by events in France: in what became known as the St Bartholomew's Eve Massacre, mob violence against Protestants was triggered by Mary's former mother-in-law Catherine de Medici when she ordered targeted assassinations of prominent Protestants.

As Jean's family had held out for Mary, Queen of Scots in the north of Scotland, in the south one of the focal points for Marian resistance was Edinburgh Castle. After Regent Moray's death, Kirkcaldy of Grange had been unable to bring himself to support Darnley's father Lennox as succeeding Regent and had taken possession of the castle. Whoever held the castle held Edinburgh. William Kirkcaldy of Grange, never previously a strong supporter of Mary, prominent in the fight against Bothwell and admired by John Knox, was an unlikely champion of the queen's cause. William Kirkcaldy of Grange had been joined by another equally unlikely person: William Maitland of Lethington. Lethington, Mary's 'Michael Wily' Machiavellian secretary, had felt unable to support his queen in her marriage to Bothwell but, like Kirkcaldy of Grange, felt that disposing of Bothwell was one thing while forcing the queen to abdicate was another. Lethington, Scotland's Cecil, was an extremely able administrator but more than a dry man of papers – his pursuit of and marriage to the much younger Mary Fleming showed his streak of Scottish passion. As Knox lay on his deathbed, he had said special prayers for Kirkcaldy of Grange, and sent a messenger to deliver notice of these prayers up to Edinburgh Castle. Kirkcaldy of Grange, who used to attend Knox's sermons with his friend Agnes Keith, Jean's cousin and wife of Regent Moray, had wavered – but the rational Lethington, the one man in Reformation Scotland who attracted the insult 'atheist', persuaded Kirkcaldy of Grange to stand firm, and even sent Knox a jokey reply.[55] Now the two Williams, Lethington and Kirkcaldy, joined forces in a supremely Scottish last stand of high principle; a doomed and heroic fight for the romantic lost cause of Mary, Queen of Scots, a cause that neither of them had wholly believed in before, but which they felt they now had to stand up for because it was the only, right, moral thing to do. Kirkcaldy of Grange and Maitland of Lethington, a soldier and an administrator, with their ragged band of followers, held Edinburgh Castle against the Regent's forces for over two years. It became known as the war between Edinburgh and Leith, as all the queen's forces stayed in the city, while the Regent's men had to move out of firing range down to the port of Leith.

The war between Edinburgh Castle and the Regent in Leith had grown increasingly bitter over the two years. In the castle, Maitland of Lethington had suffered some sort of stroke, and was now unable to move: reduced to his most brilliant and distinguishing feature, his mind, he lay flat on his back, directing events from his bed. His influence was so great that no one questioned him despite his infirmities. It was by no means just hardened soldiers who were holding out, and women, children and servants were still able to enter and leave the fortification: Lethington's wife, the young Mary Fleming, stayed loyal to the end, and Mary, Queen of Scots' half-sister Jane, Countess of Argyll, who had saved Holyrood from the flames by catching up the overturned candles on the night of the Rizzio murder, also remained, even though her husband, outside the castle, switched sides.[56] Kirkcaldy's wife was also in the castle, supervising the rationing as the Regent attempted to starve them out but this did not go well, partly because Kirkcaldy of Grange was carrying on an affair with her maid, and partly because she was seen to be too strict with the rations.[57]

The people of Edinburgh had suffered greatly, as shots had rained down on them from both sides, and great damage had been caused to buildings and several people killed. The defenders in the castle had by far the superior weaponry, but the help they longed for from Mary, from Jean's family in the north, or from France, was not forthcoming. The previous Regents had not been able to muster the forces to make a concerted attack. Morton, however, managed to secure the backing of Elizabeth of England and bring English troops north. Now the castle could be bombarded continually: the noise started to drive Lethington mad with shellshock. The two sides had become so bitter that unforgiveable atrocities were committed, and a peaceful resolution seemed impossible. Some Edinburgh citizens were hanged for helping Kirkcaldy and Lethington, including a pregnant woman who gave birth as she died on the scaffold.[58] Atrocities were committed on both sides, and it has been argued, convincingly, that Lethington's and Kirkcaldy's legacies and reputations are irreparably damaged by the suffering they caused the Edinburgh citizenry to endure.[59]

Finally, the water supply to the castle was poisoned in an attempt to force the dwindling defenders outside. Eventually it was all too much: Kirkcaldy of Grange appeared on the castle walls waving a white rod one early evening in late May 1573 – they would agree to parley. There were 164 men, 34 women and ten boys left inside the castle. They surrendered to the English troops – not to Regent Morton – and marched out of the castle, wearing armour, and surrounded by guards. The guards were for their own safety, as the people of Edinburgh, weary of the continual bombardment, the deadly fires and sniper shot, jeered and threw stones at the castle defenders as they were walked down the High Street.

Kirkcaldy of Grange and Maitland of Lethington were at first lodged with the English, but Elizabeth of England had gained little from the ending of the siege: it had cost her a good deal of money (she had been so worried about cutting costs that she had sent her soldiers out to crawl round the foot of the castle rock during the bombardment to pick up cannonballs to reuse[60]), and Lethington had made sure that any important papers within the castle had been destroyed. The castle defenders had none of the foreign, Catholic money that people had expected to find – they truly had been holding out on their own. Elizabeth ordered her men to return home and give up their prisoners to the Scots. Once Morton had hold of Lethington and Kirkcaldy, they could expect no mercy.[61] Lethington died in Leith Tolbooth the night before he was to be hanged – some said by his own hand. His loyal wife Mary Fleming, mother of his two children, petitioned effectively for his body to be released to her and not 'dishonoured by mal-treatment' – that is, not put on trial as Jean's father's corpse had been.[62] Kirkcaldy of Grange was put on trial and sentenced to death. He was hanged in front of a huge crowd of onlookers, protesting his loyalty to God and his queen to the last. His body was quartered and beheaded, and his head stuck on the castle walls, a gruesomely visible sign of the end of the hopes of Mary, Queen of Scots to ever return to the Scottish throne. The Marian cause was effectively dead.

When it had become obvious that Mary's cause was lost, George became pragmatic. Better to try to negotiate with the Regent Morton and salvage what he could for the House of Huntly than to die like Kirkcaldy of Grange and Maitland of Lethington. He had already seen what had happened after Corrichie; the brutal death of his brother and the indignities suffered by his father's corpse – not to mention his own long imprisonment. George was threatened again with the loss of his lands and title. His personal dislike of Bothwell and disapproval of Mary's choices meant that his commitment to the queen had never been total, and since his retrenchment in the north, his interest often seemed more focused on his home rather than national affairs. The great chief of the Mackay clan, Aodh Mackay, died in 1572; the Earl of Sutherland was living at Huntly Castle; the Earl of Caithness had imprisoned his son and heir – what would that all mean for the north of Scotland? These were becoming the more pressing issues. The endless civil war for a queen who seemed ever more distant in imprisonment in England was wearing Scotland down. There were problems with crops and famine.[63] A period of stability seemed more appealing.

Once Elizabeth of England had chosen to intervene on behalf of Morton, the Regent's position had become more tenable. George met with the Regent Morton and they came to an agreement: George would be forgiven for everything he had done, his land and titles would be secure, and in return George would stand down his army and free his prisoners.[64] He signed the Pacification of Perth in 1573, recognising the authority of the Regent and King James VI.

George abandoned Mary's cause and let down the defenders of Edinburgh Castle for what he believed was the greater good of his family – but, for once, the Gordon family was divided, as not all of his siblings agreed with him.

CHAPTER TEN

The House of Gordon: 1573–1575

For the first time since Jean had returned home to the north-east of Scotland, the unity of the Gordon siblings wavered. George and Adam, the two senior and most powerful figures in the House of Huntly, disagreed with each other. Jean was used to her siblings working together: William and James were in France, but still pursuing the Catholic Huntly cause; Margaret too had re-embraced her Catholic faith and returned to her Gordon family as she divorced the Master of Forbes; and younger brothers Patrick and Thomas normally supported George. Robert, Jean's remaining younger brother, had fought alongside Adam against the Forbes – but on 25th April 1572 Adam's supporter Robert was "killed accidentally".[1]

Robert was 'slain by a man of his own, recklessly, as he was cleaning his gun'.[2] Enemies of the House of Huntly observed piously that: 'So can the Lord, when he pleases, cause the wicked each one to destroy the other, so that this may be a beginning of their further destruction!'.[3] Robert's death, just before the disagreement between Adam and George, shook the family. George became committed to peace and the end to civil war in Scotland, while Adam wanted to carry on the fight for the Catholic Marian cause. One of the conditions George agreed to when he signed the Pacification of Perth was that he would release prisoners – including the Forbes. Adam was horrified by this. His crusade against the Forbes had been long and violent and earned him his nickname 'the Herod of the North';

Adam saw it as not only a religious struggle for his queen, but also a personal struggle for the honour of his sister Margaret. Margaret's divorce took a long time to finalise, and although originally her supposed adultery with one of the Bishop of Moray's sons was cited, in the end the divorce from Forbes was partly granted because of 'differences in religion'.[4] Feelings on the Forbes side ran no less high. Adam knew his life would be in danger if George released the Forbes prisoners.

Sure enough, the very first thing the Master of Forbes did when he was released from Spynie Palace was to gather together his supporters and march out, searching for Adam.[5] Adam reacted just as quickly, and took his men on a march through the night to meet his enemy and, before they were aware of his presence, "rushed in like a mountain torrent, carrying everything before him." Forbes and his allies fled, and there was 'great slaughter of both sides'.[6] George hurried north from Edinburgh to remonstrate with Adam, and Adam, disgusted with his brother's new pacifism, retired to France with half a dozen of his main supporters.[7] Before he left, Adam also sold his lands of Auchindoun to his and Jean's younger brother Patrick.[8] Auchindoun had originally been Ogilvie land, which Adam had managed to hold onto after the resolution of the feud between his family and James Ogilvie – it was land that was important to the Gordons.[9] Adam was the closest brother in age to Jean, and his departure was a big change for the Huntly household. From France, Adam, and also his brother James, continued to work for Mary and for Catholicism, and Adam was 'very kindly and honourably entertained at Paris by King Charles IX of France'.[10]

George, Jean and the other Gordon siblings, meanwhile, increasingly focused on the north and how things would be arranged there. Rumours were beginning to circulate that Bothwell had died in prison in Denmark. Although untrue, Jean's belief that Bothwell died in 1573 was enough to release her from even the strictest Catholic definition of marriage. She was now a free woman, able to marry again.

Who, though, could she marry? The man she had been in love with, Alex Ogilvie, was settled with someone else. His marriage had prospered, as Mary Beaton delivered him three sons and heirs. After Mary, Queen of Scots' court had broken up in Edinburgh, the queen's supporters had necessarily moved away, though Mary, Queen of Scots still paid Mary Beaton in her absence. According to her accounts for 1573, when Mary, Queen of Scots was in captivity, Lady Boyne was still on the payroll for 100 livres a year, the same amount she received while at court in Edinburgh.[11] Alex Ogilvie was not only seemingly happily married to Mary Beaton, the father of a growing family, but they had also both come to Jean's country in the north of Scotland. Mary Beaton and Alex Ogilvie were Marian and Gordon-supporting and were involved for many years in the affairs of Mary, Queen of Scots, taking up arms for Mary at Jean's brother's request, so Jean would have seen and heard from them regularly.[12] Moreover, Alex Ogilvie had embarked on an ambitious building project, moving his main seat from the Craig o' Boyne on the coast, and building Mary Beaton the huge Boyne Castle slightly further inland. Alex Ogilvie had the confidence in his finances and his family to build a large new home in a time of political uncertainty.

Today Boyne Castle is a particularly impressive ruin, but the outlines of a grand house, three stories high, can still be seen. In a naturally defensive position high above a river, it was not only a castle that could withstand attack, but obviously also a show-stopper of a residence, designed to impress. Boyne Castle is one of the most evocative sites associated with Jean Gordon: the castle is fully overgrown now, unmanaged by any tourism operator, hidden at the end of a short tramp through fields and forest. The massive structure is slowly being taken over by nature, but the intrepid explorer can still find the entranceway, which was over a raised and walled causeway. The castle is perched high above the burn of Boyne, famous for its trout fishing.[13] Entering by what would have been the grand front door, where a drawbridge could once have been pulled up, you come into the enclosed courtyard that Jean would have known. Architectural experts point out that the castle seems to differ in plan from all other castles of the period in the north of Scotland, with multiple towers, still visible today, and clever use of the surrounding river and gorge to add to the castle's defences.[14] The walls, up to five feet thick in places, now protect nettles and thistles growing to head-height, and their ruinous state mean any decorative features that Jean would have known are long gone, the plaster and paintings that once decorated the inside only a memory:[15] the only preservation work that has been done to the castle is some shoring up of the walls to stop dangerous collapse. After walking through the ruined courtyard and peering out through the narrow windows, it becomes clear that this was the middle floor of the castle, where the hall and a withdrawing room would have been. Alex Ogilvie's private apartments would have been over the top of the hall, but the staircases in the towers have long since crumbled away. Underneath in the basement, the vaulted cellars can still be seen, with the remains of a huge range or fireplace, and oven. People have obviously lit their own fires in the ruins, and the scratched initials of later lovers are all over the stonework, but the sheer weight of the stone and the unsupported and unmanaged condition of the castle prevents too much further exploration. There were once gardens and an orchard outside, but these too are long gone.[16] One of the outside towers has a full-grown tree right through the middle of it. It is a romantic ruin in every sense of the phrase – but it was Alex Ogilvie and Mary Beaton's romance: Jean did not live here.[17]

However, although Jean may personally have wished that Mary Beaton had not married Alex Ogilvie, even without her the Ogilvies would still not have been considered by the Gordons to be ideal marriage material. The fallout from the Ogilvie saga that had kickstarted the Corrichie defeat continued to drag on: Jean's brother Adam had laid claim to some of the Ogilvie lands after dashing John had been executed by Mary, Queen of Scots, and Alex Ogilvie was ranged with the wider Ogilvie family network in rebutting the Gordon claim.[18] Jean had to look elsewhere for a husband.

In the same year that Jean believed her ex-husband Bothwell had died, the Huntly's ward Alexander, Earl of Sutherland came of age. Jean was a few years older than Alexander,[19] but they had been thrown together at Huntly Castle, and in some ways had a lot in common: both of them had been forced by their family circumstances into marriages that weren't of their choosing, and both of them had been swept along by forces and personalities that were stronger than themselves. Now, they were both dedicated to the Gordon family, the place they had both found comfort and sanctuary. It was decided that Jean should marry Alexander Gordon, Earl of Sutherland.

For Jean, marriage meant taking agency and control of her life again. Women's place was with their family; their parents, siblings or children. As the sister of the Earl of Huntly, Jean had lower status at Huntly Castle than she had had as Countess of Bothwell, second to both her sister-in-law and (formerly) her mother, as well as her brothers. This does not mean her contribution was not valued, but she had little scope for developing her own ideas or managing the estates – her role was solely to support her brother George, something that she had been happy to do, but which was far removed from her time in control of property in the Borders. Now, with marriage to Alexander, she could step out of her brother's shadow while remaining within the wider Gordon family. The marriage would join the Huntly Gordons and the Sutherland Gordons. It was the perfect situation for Jean.

Women generally did remarry, and the family trees of the time are peculiarly complicated as their remarriages are often within the family group, and within the limited pool of others of their own status. For example, Jean's cousin Agnes Keith, widow of the Regent Moray, had remarried the year before, to the heir to the Earldom of Argyll.[20] Marriages for a widow were very much a matter of free choice for the woman: there was not always a need for a noblewoman to remarry as, like Jean or Agnes, they could be left financially secure from their first marriage, and were no longer wholly answerable to their fathers or brothers when making their choice of husband. Second marriages for noblewomen were rarely a matter of necessity: Jean was making her own choice.

Alexander himself would be a very different sort of husband from Bothwell, although, as an Earl, he was of similar status to Jean's first husband – certainly higher status than Alex Ogilvie. Jean, as the daughter of an Earl, was Alexander's equal. Like Jean, Alexander was linked by blood to the royal family, since his mother had been a Stewart (and Darnley's aunt). Alexander was described later by his son as a man of clemency, 'very liberal', who was always ready to talk to his enemies and work for appeasement, a man of his word who was 'very upright in all his actions, unfit for these our days, wherein integrity lies speechless and upright dealing ready to give up the ghost'.[21] Alexander was a gentler man who had no desire to involve himself more than necessary in the Scottish affairs, and had none of Bothwell's ambition. With a husband like Alexander, Jean could take agency again, after her life had been dominated by strong characters like Bothwell, Mary, Queen of Scots, or her mother, father and brothers. Jean's own strong personality was finally to be given scope, and this, and the couple's mutual devotion to the wider Gordon family cause, were to be the foundation of the marriage.

For Alexander, coming of age and choosing his own wife meant that he could go back to Sutherland and, with his new brother-in-law's support, take back his home of Dunrobin Castle. He would no longer be living in a place that did not belong to him, and he would be able to take charge of his own affairs. George's pardoning of the Forbes had impacted Alexander and his supporters, because Alexander's men had been quartered in homes that had been taken as spoil from the Forbes men – after the Forbes men had been released, Alexander's men needed new homes. Alexander could now take his Sutherland men back home, and count on the strong and lasting support of the Gordon family he had come to feel part of. He had a sense of belonging, both to the land, and to a strong family network.

First, Alexander had to divorce Barbara, the daughter of the Earl of Caithness – but this did not prove to be too difficult. The circumstances of Alexander's stay with Caithness, and his subsequent escape, made it easy to show that this marriage was coerced. There had been no children from the match. Barbara had never been happy in the union either, and, at some point either during their stay in Dunrobin Castle or before, she had become the mistress of Aodh, Chief of Mackay. Since Alexander had left Sutherland, Barbara and

Aodh had had a daughter.[22] The divorce was granted. Poor Barbara died either shortly after or during the process of divorce.[23]

Not all commentators have viewed the marriage of Jean and Alexander as a happy one, pointing out their age difference and seeing it as another "bizarre" forced marriage for Alexander.[24] However, the main description of Jean and Alexander's time together comes later from their son, who testifies that they were a particularly happy and contented couple. Jean and Alexander's child saw marriage as an institution where there should be real affection between husband and wife; marriage could be "the greatest cursse or blisse that can happin yow in this world" and so should not be rushed into, but carefully considered, making sure that the couple were well-matched socially, coming from a similar area, preferably of the same religion, and both healthy. Once a couple were married they should be faithful to each other.[25] Jean and Alexander's years together include no mention of any strife, and they had a long family. It might not be the love story, heady and romantic, that Jean had hoped for with Alex Ogilvie, but Jean and Alexander's marriage benefitted them both: as a couple, they worked well together.

Jean and Alexander were married quietly at Huntly Castle on 13th December 1573. There were no great public festivities as there had been during Jean's marriage to Bothwell, and the wedding was celebrated mainly within the family. There were no wedding portraits commissioned this time, but a later picture of Alexander shows a careful man with light brown hair and a neat goatee and moustache. His expression is nothing like the lively, watchful look of Bothwell, but instead shows a man in repose, with thoughtful, almost sad eyes. Jean and Alexander were shortly to set out for their rightful home of Dunrobin Castle in Sutherland – but they knew that they would have years of fights ahead of them. The Earl of Caithness had to be kept away from Dunrobin and prevented from making his home there again, while the Clan Mackay, now nominally on the Gordon side, would still have to be watched carefully. Jean was marrying a rich man, but one who would have to be prepared to fight for his inheritance. On his own, young Alexander was hardly capable of it, but with the backing of the Gordon family it should be possible. It was very much a marriage where both parties were bringing something to the union; the sort of union that Jean had eventually hoped to make with Bothwell when they had worked out a compromise. This time, however, Jean was in her late twenties and already knew what she wanted.

The legal steps necessary to get Alexander's estate back were not wholly straightforward. It did not happen automatically as soon as he turned 21. Alexander had to fight Caithness through the courts. The case should have been brought in Inverness, but Inverness, said the Gordons, was "in such a condition of feud" that was not possible. Instead, George helped Alexander to bring the case to court in Aberdeen – where George was sheriff principal and Alexander could select the jury. Unsurprisingly, Alexander won, and was now in legal possession of his castle. Alexander immediately sent a messenger to Caithness to tell him to leave Dunrobin: Caithness had the messenger killed, but he knew Alexander was following with Gordon support. Alexander was coming home and Caithness had to clear out.[26] It was clear to Caithness that the House of Huntly was going to give the House of Sutherland their full support, as a joint House of Gordon. Indeed the link between the two families was strengthened again soon after when Alexander's younger sister Janet was married to Jean's younger brother Thomas.[27]

The journey to Dunrobin was in sharp contrast to Alexander's flight from that castle four years earlier. Now that Alexander was of age, and allied with the powerful Huntly Gordons, Caithness did not fight his return, but removed himself from Dunrobin Castle. Not only the Earl of Caithness but also all his followers left Dunrobin, the nearby town of Dornoch and all the surrounding areas, retreating north to their own lands. Alexander's followers and all families loyal to him were to re-establish themselves 'peaceably' in Sutherland.[28] The newlyweds and their entourage would have travelled by horseback to the coast and then by boat up and across to Sutherland, avoiding the land journey through the sometimes hostile territory of Moray. Agnes Keith was still in charge of her late husband's Earldom, but was in the middle of a dispute about her lands, which both the new Regent Morton and Mary, Queen of Scots (arguing from captivity in England) thought should revert back to being crown land.[29] Morton and Mary, Queen of Scots were not only exercised about the Moray lands, but also wanted to know what had happened to some of Scotland's crown jewels, which had slipped into Agnes' possession when she was wife of the Regent. Agnes said she would only give the jewels back if the crown paid the debts it owed her and her late husband, and hung onto them.[30] Agnes, as strong-willed and determined as ever, held on to her children's inheritance, and the Moray lands remain in the hands of her descendants even today. The Regent Morton remained interested and active in the north of the country, however, taking a large body of men with him to tour the north-east in 1574. George's wariness of the new situation in Scotland was proved correct when Morton put George in prison for the duration of this north-east tour. Morton argued that George was aiding his brother Adam in France to plot treason against the crown. Huge fines were imposed on Catholic and Marian supporters in the north-east, including George. However, once Morton returned south to Edinburgh George was let out of prison, and most of the fines went unpaid – after the battles of the Marian civil war years, George and his neighbours and allies simply did not have any cash left. Scotland as a whole was in an impoverished position.[31]

Some descriptions of Scotland at this time focus on this poor state of the country, arguing that the landscape had changed little since medieval times in the rural areas, with small clusters of settlements confined to the coast, or isolated in larger glens.[32] Certainly Jean's new home in Sutherland could be bleak. But on the long, clear night of a northern winter, Dunrobin lay under a blanket of stars, the land sloping gently down from the castle to the sea. Jean and her family came to see it as a beautiful place. Dunrobin was of course much smaller in the mid-1500s than the Versailles-inspired white turreted castle on the site today, but it was still surrounded by gardens and orchards. They were planted with "all kynds of fruits, herbs and flowers", including good pears and cherries. Sutherland was windswept, but, with careful management, it was possible to grow many things. A deep well in the centre of Dunrobin Castle court-yard gave up cool, sweet water. The surrounding land, dotted with lochans, still with remnants of great forest, was full of an abundance of wild game – deer and rabbits, salmon and trout – and Jean's family were enthusiastic hunters, not just for food but for sport. There were still wolves roaming the north of Scotland, foxes and badgers, wild-cats, and so many different types of birdlife.[33] It was mountainous, though not as much so as the Western Highlands or the Cairngorms further south – the flat peatlands are far more striking to the visitor. Nowadays, the Far North has a small population, but the Gordons knew a pre-Clearance area which, although it obviously had fewer people than Scotland's major towns, was still an area where Jean's children could describe hunts and occasions where six or seven hundred "of the common sort of the inhabitants" assembled.[34] The land also gave up pearls and silver, and was rumoured to have gold.[35] The towns and churches were perhaps not so dramatic as the land-scape, but they boasted some good buildings. It was the landscape and light that people remembered though: in the summer, the hours of darkness are very short, with endless Scottish summer twilight pausing only briefly in night before the sun begins to rise again.

Jean's thoughts, however, were elsewhere: she was now expecting her first child. A first pregnancy is a momentous event in any woman's life, and, for Jean, it had come a little later than she might have expected. Most noblewomen would expect to be married around 19 – the age Jean was at her first wedding – and to have their first child shortly after. Jean was 29, older than the average woman of her status when having her first baby. She was not too much older than the average first-time mother, however, as poorer women tended to have their first babies a little later than their richer sisters, waiting until they and their husbands had established themselves financially and generally giving birth in their early- to mid-twenties.[36] Jean's age would not have caused undue concern, but the birth of an heir to the Earldom of Sutherland was a great event, and she was surrounded by the best attention possible.

Childbirth was surrounded by ritual. The labour suite was generally a woman's space that men were not admitted to, but one of the unintended consequences of the Reformation in England and Scotland was that the way that women gave birth altered forever.[37] During labour, midwives often relied on repeated phrases and talismans to calm the woman down, just as today labouring women are taught to count or to control their breathing. In the sixteenth century the natural touchstone was religion: women repeated prayers or held holy relics, often passed down through the generations. When the Catholic Church and its attendant rituals were swept away, midwives faced a dilemma: what should these traditional prayers be replaced with? Every time a woman died in childbirth after abandoning traditional religious practices, a midwife could experience a moment of doubt: having abandoned the traditional Catholic religious practices in a woman's hour of need, had God abandoned them? Religion had been an emotional support to women, not only in labour but also afterwards, as ceremonies such as 'churching' (where the woman went to church one month after the birth to be purified and welcomed back into their role in society) and baptism had regulated their lives after childbirth: now the role of the church must be completely changed. In England, during Henry VIII's desperate quest for a male heir, he had let male doctors into the birthing room for the first time: he found the result effective, as Jane Seymour gave birth to Prince Edward.[38] Meanwhile, the spread of literacy and printing encouraged medical textbooks to be printed talking about childbirth, allowing the knowledge of the birthing room to be taught to male students. For the first time, female midwives' superiority was challenged. Midwives later became prime suspects in the witch craze: their rituals were attributed to Satanic influence.[39] Women's traditional support networks and systems were challenged directly by the new church and by male doctors. The role of women within the Protestant Church was both subtly and brutally different from the Catholic Church; the Reformation was in many ways an ongoing battle, and childbirth and the labour suite were one of the fields in which it was fought. Jean, no less than her brothers on the battlefield, made a stand for Catholicism in the way she chose to live her life, give birth and bring up her children.

Jean had flirted with the new reformed religion while married to Bothwell, but from the moment of her return north she had returned decisively to Catholicism. She and her new husband Alexander openly supported the Catholic Church and were to bring up their children as Catholics. Jean would have followed traditional practices in childbirth, praying for a safe delivery. In the absence of a structured medical system, women relied mainly on their families, alongside trusted midwives. Alexander's mother had died many years ago, and his stepmother had been poisoned when Dunrobin Castle had been occupied by the enemy Earl of Caithness and the Gordon support network in the area disrupted: there were few trusted older women in Sutherland to guide or support Jean through her pregnancy. Alexander's power base and safe haven was still very weighted towards Jean's family lands in Aberdeenshire, and consequently Jean probably journeyed back to Huntly Castle to have her first child. Although Jean's mother was dead,[40] Jean could rely on her sister, sister-in-law and other trusted Gordon women at Huntly Castle. Noblewomen would expect to reduce activity before the birth and go into confinement a little before the expected due date, so Jean would have travelled from Dunrobin some time before the baby arrived. The journey between Aberdeenshire and Sutherland was one that she and Alexander made regularly for many years: Jean lived in a world where the main method of transport was not roads and the land, but often boats and the sea. The linking of the opposite coasts of the Moray Firth is a crucial way into understanding Jean's worldview. Boats could pull up in what was essentially Dunrobin Castle's garden. Even using an overland route, the journey from Sutherland to Moray involved only four short regular ferry crossings, and engagement between the two areas was high because of the ease of travel across these regularly used routes.[41] Through Jean's marriage, the Gordon family were cementing and strengthening the links between the north and north-east coastlines.[42]

On 1st November 1574 Jean gave birth to her first child, a healthy daughter. She was named Jane, after her mother. In Scotland inheritance of titles could pass through the female as well as the male line, unlike in England, and a daughter was no less valued than a son. Jean and Alexander were first-time parents delighted with their growing family.[43]

After Jane's birth, Jean and Alexander returned to Dunrobin. It was usual for noblewomen to find a wet-nurse for their children – rich women did not normally breastfeed. Breastfeeding on demand, with the necessity for the woman to remain close to the child and, generally, the home at all times in order to feed, rest and eat when it suits the baby, was incompatible with the life of a noblewoman. Noblewomen were expected to act as hostesses in their houses, entertaining people, visiting tenants, working as a team with their husbands as they managed their lands. They attended social events and visited the court in Edinburgh; they did not sit at home and breastfeed. Stopping breastfeeding also increased fertility, not only because feeding has a contraceptive effect but also because there were taboos against having sex while nursing. A successful countess gave her earl many children.[44] For all that modern women are sometimes given the impression that breastfeeding is a natural process only recently abandoned in the modern world, as far back as Jean's time in the sixteenth century it was already surrounded by social conventions. The difference was that instead of formula milk being available, there was an industry of women working as wet-nurses. Breastfeeding could be difficult, unpleasant and painful, even as it is now: women, especially noblewomen, could opt out of doing it. There are vivid descriptions of the English envoy waiting to see Mary, Queen of Scots, after the birth of James VI: Mary sent word that she would see him as soon as the pain in her breasts had subsided. Although her milk had come in, the young Prince had been immediately handed over to a high-ranking noblewoman for nursing. Mary was described as being as well as could be expected for a woman in her condition.[45] Mary chose one of her attendants as the wet-nurse; for the Gordon family there were retainers and distant kinsfolk who they usually went to. The Gordons from the family best known as of Embo, based at Golspitour, the family who had helped Alexander escape from the Earl of Caithness, were the family that the Earls of Sutherland chose as their nurses.[46] Children were brought up, as Jean herself had been, within a large family grouping of the wider Gordon family, a system that encouraged awareness of and loyalty to the entity of the House of Gordon.

Now Alexander had come of age, the crown supported him and he was regaining control of the lands that had been ruled for him in his minority by others. His supporters, including branches of the Gordon, Murray and Gunn families, who had been forced out of Sutherland by the Earl of Caithness, had all returned.[47] According to the Gordon chronicler, Alexander had 'pacified the country of Sutherland, and the clans thereof, with such admirable and happy dexterity, that there was not one drop of blood shed . . . he procured the love of all his country-men, even of such as had been formerly most eager against him'.[48] As surviving receipts from the estate show, Jean was involved in managing the household in various ways, including receiving and authorising payments from tenants and to merchants, purchasing items including oxen, and travelling around the estate.[49] Alexander and Jean seem to have managed their return to Dunrobin particularly adeptly. Jean was healthy, her new daughter Jane was healthy, and they looked forward to a future where they could continue to develop their power in the north, push for more recognition at court and hopefully grow their family. There was "a comparative degree of quietness in the north" compared to the years that had just passed.[50]

Jean had security in this new marriage, in comparison to her early days with Bothwell. She also maintained her interest in the Crichton Border lands that she had received from that first marriage, and now jointly administered them with Alexander, gaining an income from this to add to their income at Dunrobin.[51] Jean and Alexander received rent in both money and in kind: the money income amounted to £1,702 os 4d – but almost half of this came from Jean's properties which she had kept from her marriage to Bothwell. Expenditure could be high, including servicing historic debts stemming from the previous years' instabilities, but rent in kind made up a large part of Jean and Alexander's income, the equivalent of £2,588 os 4d, providing them with the items they needed, such as foodstuffs.[52]

Jean's relative financial security contrasted with what she might have experienced had she married Alex Ogilvie: in 1575 Alex Ogilvie and Mary Beaton developed financial difficulties. Mary Beaton was still supposed to be the attendant of Mary, Queen of Scots, but the queen's captivity in England continued. Their position as Catholic, Marian supporters was less tenable in a Scotland ruled by Protestant Regents. Mary Beaton had to turn to her old friend the former English ambassador Randolph to intercede for her with the Regent Morton. Randolph asked, "that the lady of Boyne" – Mary and Alex Ogilvie had now been married nine years – "may ever remain in . . . good grace and favour under [the Regent's] defence against her adversaries, and be holpen in these suits she has".[53] The ambitious building project at Boyne Castle had stretched them too far, and Alex Ogilvie was in considerable financial difficulties. He had to borrow large sums of money from a relative, Sir George Ogilvie of Dunlugas. By November 1575 Alex Ogilvie was supposed to pay his relative almost £18,000: when he was unable to raise this huge sum, his lands were apprised – valued for the purpose of paying his debt. Ultimately, perhaps with the help of the Regent, Alex Ogilvie and Mary Beaton managed to reach an agreement with Sir George Ogilvie and did not lose their lands of Boyne, though Sir George "seems to have exercised considerable control over the estate with very extensive powers".[54]

Meanwhile, for Jean and Alexander the only blot on the horizon was their neighbours. The great chieftain Aodh Mackay had died the year before Jean and Alexander's marriage, some said tortured to the end by grief over the fate of his former friend and ally John the Stout, who was still imprisoned by his father.[55] The Earl of Caithness – thwarted in his desire to take over the Earldom of Sutherland – was now manoeuvring to establish control over the Mackays instead. Just as Caithness had captured the young Alexander after the deaths of the Earl and Countess of Sutherland, he now abducted Mackay's son Uisdean.[56] Uisdean was only 11 years old, younger than Alexander had been, and he did not have the advantage of powerful Gordon relatives. In fact, in contrast to the unity of the Gordons, the Mackays were beset by in-fighting. Aodh had been married twice – in addition to his liaison with Alexander's ex-wife Barbara – and Uisdean had two half-brothers with competing claims to the title of Chief of Mackay. Uisdean was the son of Aodh's second wife, a Sinclair of Caithness, and the Earl of Caithness naturally supported this branch of the family which was linked to his own. Uisdean's older half-brothers were the children of Aodh and Helen Macleod of Assynt – but Helen had been Aodh's cousin, and now the Earl of Caithness argued that this close relationship had invalidated Aodh's first marriage. Uisdean's older half-brothers were illegitimate, the Earl of Caithness argued. Uisdean was the true heir to the title of Chief of Mackay, and, while he was underage, Uisdean would be guided in all things by his loving relative the Earl of Caithness.[57]

Uisdean Mackay was installed in Castle Girnigoe with the motley collection of relatives ruled over by the Earl of Caithness. It was an extraordinary household living in an extraordinary castle, built into the sea stacks on the very edge of the northern coast, constantly battered by the sea and scoured by the wind. Caithness' eldest son, John the Stout, was still imprisoned in the dungeon underground, permanently estranged from his father, but John's wife Janet Hepburn seems to have hung on in the north for as long as she could. As Bothwell's sister, she had few options – she was hardly going to be immediately welcomed at court, her father was dead, and her mother seems to have also died around this time. Both Bothwell's lands and the lands belonging to Janet and Bothwell's mother had all reverted to the crown because of Bothwell's actions. Janet was effectively stuck living with a father-in-law who had imprisoned his own son, her husband. The atmosphere in Girnigoe can only be imagined – or perhaps deduced from the personalities of those who grew up there: Janet's son from her first marriage was Francis, known in later life as The Mad Earl or the Wizard Earl. Janet's eldest son from her second marriage to John the Stout was George, in later life known as The Wicked Earl. Uisdean, meanwhile, was to grow up and acquire the nickname 'Dark Uisdean of the Battleaxe'. The Mad Wizard Earl, the Wicked Earl and Dark Uisdean of the Battleaxe grew up together in Castle Girnigoe and all three of them, particularly Francis and George, became known as fierce opponents. Francis, George and Uisdean, along with George's two younger siblings James and John, formed a band of young boys growing up in an exceptionally dys-functional household in a lawless land where the example set for them by their protector, the anti-Gordon Earl of Caithness, was of extreme violence. These were Jean's closest neighbours of her own rank, neighbouring Earls who could have been her allies, but were something else instead.

Jean's former sister-in-law Janet Hepburn pleaded her case as best as she could, and by 1575 she convinced the crown to give her the lands of Morham, which had belonged to her mother. She divorced John the Stout (still imprisoned at this time) and left the Highlands to take up residence there, south of Edinburgh.[58] Her son George, as the heir to the Earldom of Caithness, seems to have been left behind, and George's younger brothers James and John also later inherited land in the north so Janet probably also had to leave these children with the Sinclairs.[59] Janet's elder son Francis from her first marriage may have gone south with her, but the familiarity he showed with the north of Scotland in later life demonstrates his continued affinity with Caithness. Uisdean, of course, had to stay with the Earl of Caithness, so he was there to see the final denouement of the Earl of Caithness' quarrel with his son and heir John the Stout.

John the Stout had been in prison for around six years.[60] He had had one chance of escape, when he had almost persuaded one of his jailors to help him, but the plot had been discovered and stopped in advance by John's own brother, William. The unfortunate sympa-thetic jailor was hanged. John the Stout's brother William Sinclair of Mey was the second son of the Earl of Caithness, and he had benefit-ted greatly by the imprisonment of his elder brother: William had been given all of John the Stout's former privileges, lands and castles, and enjoyed the favour of their father the Earl. John, a massive hulk of a man, was enraged by the death of the unfortunate jailor and by William's taunting afterwards. Although John was chained up, when William next visited the prison John managed to catch hold of his brother. John strangled William with the chains he was bound in. The Earl of Caithness was distraught at the death of his favourite son and commanded that all food and water should be withheld from John for five days. Then, John was sent a plate of salt beef. John ate greedily, but when he called for water to go with his food, he was refused. John died "of a raging thirst"[61] on 15th March 1576, and was buried in Wick. John the Stout's gravestone called him a "noble and worthie man".[62]

Meanwhile, the Earl of Caithness and Uisdean's claim to the chieftainship of Mackay was not unchallenged: in Uisdean's minority, the leadership of the clan was first assumed by a senior member of Aodh's family, John Mor Mackay (Big John). Big John was inclined to support Alexander and Jean, which did not go down well with Caithness.[63] Caithness worked with some of Big John's clan enemies, the Macleods of Durness and Edderachillis, to lure Big John to Castle Girnigoe, where he was imprisoned. Big John died soon after – exactly how is not recorded.[64] Uisdean's half-brother John Beg Mackay (Little John) then took over the leadership of the clan. Little John was "a prudent man ... and peaceably inclined",[65] and he came to an arrangement with the Earl of Caithness, where Caithness (by now characteristically) brought Little John's two younger brothers to Girnigoe to bring them up under his watchful eye. Little John managed to hold onto power for seven years, but even his peaceable nature and willingness to let Caithness control his young relatives was not enough to save him, as Little John too was later murdered in conflict with another branch of the Mackay clan at Durness in 1579.[66] The Earl of Caithness' involvement in this murder was murky, but Uisdean, brought into Girnigoe at a young, impressionable age, remained, for the time being, loyal to the Earl of Caithness.[67] He had very little other choice.

Janet Hepburn was no less martial than the men in her life,

and within three years of her divorce from John the Stout and her departure from the north and the Girnigoe house of horrors she had remarried to Archibald, a Douglas who had been present and stood trial for his part at Kirk o' Field. The murder of Darnley may be one of the great mysteries of Scottish history, but both Jean and her former sister-in-law Janet were two of the people who could probably have told the whole story of that night, of who killed the king of Scots, and whether Bothwell and Mary were truly guilty. But times in Scotland were moving on. Jean's time in Edinburgh and with Bothwell was fading into her past as she now came into her full powers as Countess of Sutherland.

The Living Tomb, Mummification and Transcendental Peace

Times in Scotland may have been moving on but one man remained literally trapped in the past. Jean's ex-husband Bothwell actually did not die, as Jean believed, in the early 1570s: he was still in prison in Scandinavia.

The Scottish Parliament asked for Bothwell to be sent back to Scotland in 1570 but when he was not, he was gradually forgotten.[1] Jean was not the only person who believed he was dead; his wife Mary, Queen of Scots, who had written to him at the beginning, believed he was gone and was ready to consider remarriage with an English Catholic nobleman – anything to end her own prolonged captivity. Unlike Mary, though, who was still living in relative comfort, Bothwell was moved to increasingly meaner prisons as his relevancy to Scottish and European current affairs diminished. By the summer of 1573, the year that Jean married Alexander, Bothwell ended up in Denmark's state prison at Dragsholm.[2] He may as well have been in a living tomb: Bothwell reportedly ended his days in a sunken room, chained to a pillar half his height, unable to stand upright. Food was thrown down to him at regular intervals, but the active Scotsman was treated worse than an animal. He went entirely mad, yet probably lived another five years in the worst conditions, not dying until 1578.[3] Whatever Bothwell had done in life, he did not deserve this fate, or this death.

Bothwell's corpse, mummified by the sea air and with its reddish-brown hair still visible, was then left on public display until the 1930s. Bothwell's partisan biographer Robert Gore-Brown describes visiting Dragsholm and viewing the body in 1935: "Dried and shrunken flesh covers head and chest. The long, folded arms are now but bone. The stamp of personality and individuality persists in this three hundred and fifty year old corpse ... Matter seems to fade away, while a crisp, sharp personality has been preserved in decay, moulded out of dust."[4] The head was separated from the body, and there were stories that children had at one point used his head as a football. In the 1970s an American called Fred Bothwell became interested in his namesake's story, and, along with his brother, lawyer Anthony Bothwell, they tried to raise awareness of Bothwell's fate, primarily through an article in the international *Mensa Research Journal* and the setting up of a group, the International Friends of Bothwell.[5] Fred Bothwell received letters from people all around the world[6] – "most notable among them", said Fred in an email to me several years later, "was one typed on Buckingham palace stationery and signed by an equerry. It said that a member of the household expressed interest in the cause". Fred Bothwell believed that a personal intervention from the Danish queen (who is related to the British royal family) resulted in the removal of Bothwell's body from public display and the sealing of Bothwell's coffin.

Interest in Bothwell again revived in the late 1990s/early 2000s, when a movement, spearheaded by one of Bothwell's distant descendants Sir Alistair Buchan-Hepburn, by the Americans Fred and Anthony Bothwell, and supported by well-known French novelist Catherine Hermary-Vielle, as well as a collection of history enthusiasts, tried to have Bothwell's body repatriated and his reputation restored. Ultimately, it came to nothing. However, Sir Alastair Buchan-Hepburn wrote to me some years later, after another visit to Bothwell's grave: "I went to Denmark and visited the Crypt where Bothwell lies in a fine large sealed wooden coffin provided by the Queen of Denmark. I felt an almost transcendental experience when there – Within me there was a contentment and that Bothwell was at peace where he lay."

PART TWO

The Gordon Years

CHAPTER ELEVEN

Death and Land: 1576–1581

The year 1576 was an important one for Jean. She was focused on her new life as Countess of Sutherland, wife and mother – though this too would not be without its dark moments and death.

Jean's brother Adam was one of the last prominent supporters of Mary, Queen of Scots, though he was still in France until the summer of that year. Adam's support for Mary from afar was well known, but George had always pleaded for him, even going as far as writing to Elizabeth of England to protest Adam's innocence on any charge of treason.[1] George wrote the letter to try and put himself in a better position: the Marian party in Scotland had dwindled, the Forbes were pushing against him, and Regent Morton had grown in power – George was trying to prove that he was not a major threat. He had managed to balance his desire to hold onto power in the north of Scotland with his loyalty to his family, and was rewarded by being made Sheriff of Aberdeen and Inverness again, with the power to collect taxes. Despite continuing in his personal Catholic beliefs, George did recognise and fulfil obligations to the Protestant Kirk, for example presenting ministers to benefices in his patronage.[2]

Adam, meanwhile, had his own troubles, as the Forbes had followed him to France. In a vivid illustration of how Jean's sister Margaret's marriage had irrevocably broken down and created a vicious feud, Margaret's former brother-in-law Arthur went to France to hunt down Adam. The son of Lord Forbes and nephew of a man that Adam had killed at Tilliangus,[3] Arthur Forbes travelled to Paris, where he 'aquainted himself with some desperate swaggerers and nightwalkers ... called Enfans de la Mat, men ready to enterprise any kind of desperate mischief'.[4] Arthur Forbes persuaded this band of ruffians for hire to murder Adam Gordon one night, promising them that as a reward they should have the heavy chains of gold which Adam and Adam's followers ostentatiously wore round their necks.[5] Adam had used his family connections to make friends in France, and was visiting the lodging of the Archbishop of Glasgow, the Scottish ambassador in the country. Arthur Forbes and his hired assassins lay in wait outside the lodging at the University of Paris, not far from the Port of St Jacques "under silence of the night", until Adam and his men left on foot to return home. As Adam walked past their hiding place, Forbes and his men fired their pistols. Adam was hit in the thigh and fell to the ground. Believing that he was dead, Forbes fled, hotly pursued by Adam's friends. As they ran through the twisting streets of Paris, Forbes managed to escape, but he dropped his hat behind him in the rush to leave: tucked inside the hat was a piece of paper noting the rendezvous point for Forbes and his men. As Adam – badly hurt but not killed – was helped to a place of safety, a messenger was sent to King Charles of France, who authorised Adam's servants and a number of armed men to go to the rendezvous point and apprehend Forbes and his accomplices. Adam's friends rushed to the Forbes house where, 'being impatient of delay', they entered 'with hasty violence' and killed Arthur Forbes. All of Forbes' men were captured, and they in turn were executed. Treated as highway robbers, they were subject to the barbarous and ignominious punishment of being broken on the wheel. Meanwhile, Adam made a full recovery and decided to return to Scotland.[6]

Adam was immediately put in prison on his return, and kept there for several months but George stood surety for him, promising that he would look out for his brother, returning him to jail if need be, but in the meantime keeping him at Huntly Castle. When they next visited Huntly, Jean and her husband Alexander, were able to meet not only with George, but also with Adam, and their youngest brothers Thomas and Patrick. Jean was pregnant for the second time, and it seems that she once again travelled east to her old family home not long before the birth. At this crucial point in her life, when Jean was embracing her role as Countess of Sutherland, we get a new and invaluable source of information about her life: her own letters.

There are a handful of letters, written by Jean herself, preserved in the Sutherland archives.[7] Nothing compares to being able to read Jean's own thoughts, in her own handwriting; to being able to pick up the piece of paper that she herself handled, unfold a letter that she herself closed and sealed. The immediacy of her family concerns and the sheer modernity of many of her sentiments is striking, and it brings the history alive in a new way. This was a woman who knew legendary Scottish historical figures like Mary, Queen of Scots and was married to Lord Bothwell – yet we can read of her own day-to-day concerns and family life.

Some of Jean's letters are more personal than others, especially later ones written to her sons, but writing was still an unfamiliar activity in her time and letter delivery erratic, so pen was most often put to paper for important matters. The first preserved letter we have from her, like other subsequent ones, is partly a business letter. Jean was writing from the cathedral town of Elgin, near to her former home at Huntly Castle, on 5th May 1576. She was about six or seven months pregnant at the time. The letter is to Agnes Keith, Jean's cousin, formerly Countess of Moray and now Countess of Argyll. Agnes and Jean had kept in touch, and Agnes had helped Jean in the break-up of her marriage to Bothwell, but there was a tension between the two women because of their identification with the different sides in the Reformation and the Marian Civil War: Jean was very definitely a Catholic, while Agnes was of course a Protestant. The letter walks that balance between the family connection and friendship, and a more formal relationship. Agnes' tensions with the new Regent Morton, however, who wanted her to give up the lands of Moray, may have made her more ready to listen to Jean, as a Gordon who had no real reason to love Morton. Jean's reason for writing to Agnes, though, was also about the touchy subject of land ownership.

Jean wanted to re-establish her husband Alexander's claim over the lands of Kintessack. This piece of land near Forres had belonged to Alexander's uncle, and Alexander should have inherited it after his uncle's death. Alexander was named after this uncle (his father's brother) who had died falling from his horse just before Alexander was born, so the Kintessack lands had some family sentimentality attached for Alexander.[8] Jean needed Agnes and her second husband the Earl of Argyll, as major landowners, to sign a legal document called a 'Clare Constat' agreeing that the land belonged to Alexander, as his uncle's heir. Alexander and Jean were pursuing a number of similar transactions at this time, trying to sort out the tangle that had been made of Alexander's legal affairs while he was in his minority.[9]

The interesting thing about the letter is that it is Jean and Agnes who are in control of the estates and legal documents, active in the management of land, and politics.[10] The written legal status of women appears to show them as subservient – for example, they could not be called as witnesses to court – but the reality for noblewomen was different: Jean and Agnes were actively involved in the practical legal details of running the lands that their families owned. 'I don't doubt that your ladyship will seal and subscribe the said precept of Clare Constat with pleasure and good will', Jean wrote, 'and . . . will cause my lord, your husband, to do the same'.[11] Jean finished the letter by reminding Agnes of their family connection: 'I have ever found your ladyship's good favour in all my turns' and adding the hope that Agnes would continue to treat Jean and her husband in the same way, signing off 'your ladyship's cousin . . . Jeane Sutherland'.[12] Agnes and her husband were happy to sign off the document, and Alexander took possession of the Kintessack lands. Agnes may have been less happy with what Alexander did next though, as he decided to gift the lands to her adversary, the Regent Morton, in exchange for help against the Earl of Caithness and in the hope that Morton would reduce the Earl of Caithness' powers of justiciary over the north of Scotland. It was not a good deal for Alexander, and strengthened the Sutherlands' dislike of Morton, as Morton took the land, but apparently did not help much.[13] The dispute over who had power of justiciary in the north was one that would rumble on, through the courts, for many years.

In the midst of these legal manoeuvrings, Jean gave birth for the second time. The baby was a healthy boy, who was named John after Alexander's father, the Earl who had been poisoned. Baby John would in turn grow up to be Earl of Sutherland himself. There was a joyful family reunion that autumn at Huntly Castle, as Jean celebrated the birth of her new son with her wider family. Alexander and Adam, who had fought the Forbes together, met again, and Jean and Alexander heard the story of Adam's near miss in France. Alexander saw his sister and her husband, Jean's brother Thomas. Head of the family George was in "high spirits"[14] by the end of the visit, when Jean and Alexander left to return home early in the morning of Saturday 20th October 1576. After Jean left, George went to nearby Winton's wood, to hunt, and killed three hares and a fox. He returned to dine at midday, making plans for a game of football after lunch. He was most put out when no one could find a ball, and jokingly took his purse out and threw a coin over to a retainer with orders to go and procure one. Over lunch and for a short while afterwards George argued in an exasperated but friendly way with a man called Murray, who had some sort of quarrel with his mother which George wanted to help resolve. The Laird of Grant and Adam then came to chat, and George called for a late lunch to be prepared for them, but the planned football match finally got underway between 3 and 4pm. George had only kicked the ball twice when he suddenly fell upon his face. He managed to rise and stagger over to sit and rest his back against a peat-stack at the side of the pitch, but George felt strangely faint. "I believe I shall not play more at this time", he said, as his younger brother Patrick rushed to his side. "I am something sick – bring me my cloak." Patrick did so, and, wrapping it around him, helped George to his feet. George could barely stand, and Patrick and the other Gordon men who were playing football had to take a grip of his arms to lead him up to his room. 'I will be well enough soon, believe me,' said George as they led him on, but as soon as they released their grip he staggered and fell again. Once he was finally laid down on his bed, he began to foam at the mouth and nose. He tried to speak, but could only say, "Look! Look! Look!", before he started to vomit black blood. Three hours later he was dead.[15]

George was declared by those around him to have never been in better health or spirits than he had been that morning when he said goodbye to his sister Jean, and his sudden and unexpected death afflicted his household with a sort of hysteria. Adam, as the next eldest Gordon brother, immediately took command, and, as his brother's body lay in the room known as the Leather Chamber (because of its decoration), Adam called for the family strongboxes and keys. He quickly made an inventory of the money and important papers George had stored in there, before re-locking the boxes safely and then locking the boxes into the room where George lay, and giving the keys to George's most trusted man to guard. With candles lit, Adam then took first watch over the dead, standing guard outside the Leather Chamber. Securing the chest, and especially important charters and papers, was very important. Many blood feuds were the result of debate over land ownership – Alexander's claim to the Earldom of Sutherland, for example, would have been much more difficult to fight for if his father hadn't providentially stored his charter chest with a relative, where it was out of reach of Caithness.[16]

Early the following day, which was the Sunday morning around 7am, 14 or 15 men stood together in the chamber adjacent to the one in which George's body lay, lamenting the death and questioning what was to happen next. One man, standing with his back to the fire, was loud in discussing what the effects might be for him personally – when all of a sudden he fell forward onto his face, just as George had done the day before. The men around him pulled him upright and threw open the doors and windows to give him air, but he was unresponsive and burning hot to touch. They carried him to a bed and laid him down, and after half an hour he suddenly roused up sobbing and crying, 'Cold! Cold!' and agitatedly rubbing his hands and feet to try and warm them. He suffered like this for 24 hours more before he recovered.[17]

After this odd occurrence the Gordon household was more on edge than ever, and the following day, the second after the earl's death, another man was struck down: in the middle of gathering spices to prepare a meal he suddenly cried out, 'I am very sick!' and fell, once again in the same manner as George had and with the same deathly pallor, then he repeated, as the other man had, 'Cold! Cold!' While they were busy tending to him, a third man fell down with the same ailment.[18]

George's body was prepared for burial, and his body taken to the chapel until the funeral. But the mysterious happenings had not stopped: George's brother Patrick, along with 14 or 15 other men, heard a great noise coming from the Leather Chamber where George's body had been lying. Thinking that someone had been locked in by mistake, they called for the key to be brought to them to open the door. There was nobody in there, protested George's steward, but he unlocked the door anyway. In the dim early evening light they could see nothing inside, and were greatly afraid. Patrick went to the great hall to call for assistance and candles, and when they came back upstairs the noise was as great as before – but they could still see nothing inside the room. 'The story would go through the country that the Earl of Huntly were risen again!', cried one man, and Patrick, afraid of starting rumours, made everyone around him come near and promise not to repeat what had happened.[19]

The story made its way out despite this, and much of the afore-mentioned embellished description comes from a near contemporary account, from someone who was 'credibly informed by a gentlewoman who heard it from a gentleman who was present at the death...'[20] Jean, too, would have heard the shocking story of her brother's death after her return to Dunrobin. People made their own take on the story, with those opposed to George considering it a divine punishment. Considering the similar manner of George's father's death it seems likely that they died of similar causes – a hereditary heart condition or stroke for example. George's retainers had been affected only with hysteria, and recovered. George was buried in Elgin, and much mourned by Jean and the rest of his family, who accounted him a 'valiant, liberal and constant man'.[21]

Adam, now the oldest male in the Gordon family, took control. Although legally other people were involved in the management of the Gordon lands, Adam o' Gordon was the real power at Huntly Castle.[22] George's heir was 14 years old, and currently at court, where he was being brought up as a companion of James VI. James VI was said to admire and look up to him. However, at court the Regent Morton was in charge and he was not popular with the Gordons, since he had not helped Jean and Alexander and had so recently put Adam in prison. Adam and the Gordons decided to remove George's son from court and send him to the continent – despite James VI being left in tears at his departure. Adam sent his nephew, who was still in his early teens, abroad to France, where he would be welcomed both by his other uncle James, the Jesuit, and by Adam and James' influential friends. George's son Lord Huntly, the 6th Earl of Huntly and later also to be the 1st Marquis of Huntly,[23] was to be given a Catholic and cosmopolitan education on the continent, at the University of Paris and at the court of Henri III.[24]

Adam ruled the Gordon lands with "daring and masterful policy", but it was not to be expected that the Forbes would take his promotion lightly, and the Forbes-Gordon feud was renewed in 1579. The trigger was a quarrel among some cadet branches of the family, which most unfortunately took place in front of King James VI, but there were also disputes over land grants to the Gordons behind the resurgence in animosity. There were "forays, dire bloodshed and tumult" across the north-east.[25]

There was a streak of ruthlessness in Adam that meant his unwelcome nickname 'the Herod of the North' continued to be applied to him, even if the events that led to the nickname were more rumour than hard fact. This ruthlessness was a family trait which Jean, the closest Gordon sibling in age to Adam, sometimes shared. Adam and Jean were entirely devoted to the Gordon family, and their desire to advance the family in the way they thought was best balanced on a fine line between a familial devotion that was praiseworthy and a selfish ignoring of anyone else's claims. They used whatever means they thought necessary to protect and future-proof their family's claim to power.

After Jean had given birth to her healthy son John, Alexander was convinced to put in place some legal trickery that put his lands and title in the hands of his one-year-old heir.[26] This in some ways was a fairly common safety device that was meant to make it certain that property and titles were handed down from father to son,[27] and the official record of the Sutherland family argues that Alexander did this "having learned by his own experience the evils of ward-ship during the minority of an heir"[28] but to put a one-year-old in possession of the fee of his entire Earldom, while retaining only the liferent for himself, was a drastic action. The Sutherland book judges it "prudent", and wholly justified by subsequent events, but what Alexander was doing was putting a huge amount of power into the hands of his wife's family. A later Gordon chronicler stated that Alexander also made an entail specifying that if his son did not inherit, the Earldom of Sutherland should go to the House of Huntly.[29] Alexander, according to this later interpretation of events, even specifically wrote out his daughter from the succession, saying that should she marry, she would lose the surname of Gordon, and he did not want the Earldom of Sutherland to go to any but a Gordon.[30]

Alexander is sometimes described as weak in some way, suffering health problems, though this is not wholly consistent with his actions on the battlefield. He may have suffered from the effects of his kidnapping by the Earl of Caithness, or have had some underlying health condition, but the mental effect of his time under Caithness' control was probably equally important to his decision: he was still experiencing some problems in taking back full control of the Earldom of Sutherland and all the rights that his father had exercised before he was poisoned. He was only able to continue working for this with the help of the powerful Gordons, and was willing to acquiesce with all Gordon suggestions. He saw his wife Jean and the other Gordons as his only friends and was willing to throw his lot in with them entirely. He did not see the Earldom of Sutherland as a separate entity, he saw it as part of the wider Gordon family, stretching from

Aberdeenshire to the opposite coast in Sutherland. Later generations did not see it quite the same way, and reinterpreted their history to fit their present reality,[31] but the reality for Alexander was that his wife Jean was an extremely important, if not the senior, partner in their marriage, and Jean's brothers were their most important allies and friends. Jean's brother Adam now had control of the Huntly lands in Aberdeenshire while his nephew was growing up in France and, through Jean, the Gordons also had a measure of control over Sutherland lands. By making over titles to Jean's son, Sutherland was becoming more of a Gordon territory. Siblings Jean and Adam were working together to raise the Gordon interests.

In the Far North, Jean and her husband Alexander were also watching events within the Mackay clan. Before George's son, Jean's nephew, had gone to France, he had signed over the ward of Strathnaver, the Mackay lands, to Alexander.[32] At the time when John the Stout had been imprisoned by his father Caithness, the great chieftain Aodh Mackay had offered his allegiance to George, partly to stop being obliged to either Caithness or the Earl of Sutherland. Now, Alexander had legally taken back the control the Earldom of Sutherland wanted over the Mackays. But again there was a mismatch between the legal and actual positions: Alexander might have a piece of paper that said he was the person that the Mackays should be loyal to, but Uisdean Mackay was still living with and under the control of the Earl of Caithness. Caithness took care to oversee the marriage of his daughter[33] to Uisdean in 1578 just before Uisdean came of age in 1579. Uisdean was essentially led by Caithness, and Caithness urged Uisdean to lead Mackay men into battle against the Clan Gunn: the chieftain of the Clan Gunn at this time[34] had 'begun to depend' on Alexander, and paid rent from Clan Gunn lands direct to Alexander and Jean. The problem was that the boundary between what was Clan Gunn land and what was Caithness land was a little hazy, and Caithness believed that rent money should be coming to him. Accordingly, Caithness used Uisdean and the Mackays to try to reinforce his claims over Clan Gunn. Uisdean's half-brother Little John Mackay, who was still officially Chief of Mackay at this time, was not informed in advance of what Uisdean was going to do, and when Little John found out he was 'much offended': Clan Gunn and the Mackays had been friends, and Uisdean had ridden right through that carefully nurtured alliance with violence. Uisdean's first foray against the Gunns was not a success, particularly as it brought reprisals against the Mackays from the Earl of Sutherland: Alexander invaded the Mackay lands of Strathnaver and killed many of Uisdean's followers and made off with 'a great prey of goods', taking the booty to be dispersed among the Clan Gunn.[35] This conflict was called Creagh-drumi-doun.[36] Tensions between the clans and earls continued to run high. The Mackays were to find that their relationship with both Caithness and Sutherland was to continue to be of the first importance, while the Gunns, always a clan who were slightly different and problematic compared to those around them, did not fare any better, even if they were temporarily in favour. For Uisdean it was a steep learning curve, but after the death of Chieftain Little John Mackay – which, most conveniently, happened the same year that Uisdean reached his majority – it was not too difficult for Uisdean, supported by Caithness, to take up his full role and title as Chief of Mackay.[37]

Uisdean was not the only young man feeling his way to power in 1579: James VI, at 13 years old, was beginning to make his presence felt. Ever since Mary, Queen of Scots had left her infant son and been trapped in captivity in England, James had been brought up carefully and strictly, in the full knowledge that he was to one day be not only King of a Protestant Scotland but also, as Elizabeth of England continued to refuse marriage offers, perhaps King of England as well. The effect of James' harsh upbringing was to teach him to move with secrecy and patience when negotiating his way around the multiple allegiances of the Scottish court. His utilitarian upbringing did not, however, include much kindness, and it did not breed in him any strong love of Scotland or of the harsh Scottish men who had brought him up. When James was first offered attention, love and respect, he reacted violently and passionately: in September 1579 his glamorous French cousin Esmé Stuart, Sieur d'Aubigny came to Scotland and became the first of James' many male favourites at court. Esmé was a connection of the Guise: Mary, Queen of Scots had not been able to bring up her son or even establish any meaningful communication with him, but of course neither she nor her French relatives had forgotten him. However, Esmé swiftly realised that the most profitable allegiance for him was going to be with James VI: converting to Protestantism, Esmé declared himself the King's man, and focused on promoting his own cause, rather than anyone else's.

James was fascinated with his tall, well-dressed cousin, and loved the fact that Esmé listened to him, rather than telling him what to do, as everyone else around him did.[38] Esmé was promoted first to the title of Earl of Lennox, then Duke of Lennox, then high chamberlain of Scotland, and showered with gifts. Jean's husband Alexander, hearing of Esmé's arrival, presently went to meet him, reminding Esmé that he was related to the Gordons[39] 'and remained with him for the most part of the time, until he returned into France'. In return, Esmé 'dealt earnestly with the king for his majesty's favour to the Gordons'. The Gordons status at court rose because of their friendship and connection with the new arrival.[40] Jean and her siblings may have prioritised northern relations for a while, but they were still playing national politics – as soon as there was an opening they were back at court. They still believed they should be one of the foremost families in the country.

Of course, Esmé's promotion did not endear him to all the Scottish noblemen at court, and, together with the new friends he had made, Esmé encouraged James VI to exert his authority and punish those unsympathetic lords. James was not unwilling to take revenge on the men who had brought him up so strictly. The first casualty was to be the ex-Regent Morton, which suited the Huntly and Sutherland Gordons just fine.

Despite the deal with the lands of Kintessack, Alexander had not bought the assistance of the Earl of Morton in his disputes with Caithness. In 1578 Alexander was still trying to sort out the position of justiciary within Sutherland: as matters stood, Caithness had the commission of justiciary, which meant that legally he could hold everyone in the north to account – including Alexander, Earl of Sutherland.[41] Morton tried to stop Alexander from changing this, but was eventually overruled. Only eight days after this legal verdict was delivered, however, Morton was forced to resign his position as Regent. James VI was now supposedly in full control – with a lot of help from the Earls of Atholl and Argyll, who had taken possession of both the king himself and Stirling Castle.

Jean and Alexander's interest in dealings in the south of Scotland was distracted, however, by family tragedy closer to home. Alexander had three sisters: the oldest, Margaret, he had little contact with since she had started the train of events that meant the Earl of Caithness had been able to buy the rights to the Earldom of Sutherland while Alexander was underage; Janet was married to Jean's brother Thomas; and the youngest was Elinor. Elinor was living in Sutherland, and a good marriage was arranged for her with the Laird of Fowlis. Preparations got underway to celebrate a joyful wedding, and Elinor spent the night before the wedding in Dornoch. However, she suddenly died during the night, 'and that day, which was thought to have been the day of marriage and of mirth, fell forth to be a day of mourning and of sorrow'.[42] No explanation is given for how Elinor died.

Perhaps there was a sickness around, because it was a time of death: during the four-year period between the birth of her son John, in 1576, and 1580, Jean had two more sons, Alexander, named after her husband, and Adam, named after her brother. Both died in infancy, and nothing more is known of them than their names and the fact of their brief existence.[43] Infant mortality was much higher in the sixteenth century, and it was not uncommon for children to die young – it was one reason why noblewomen were encouraged to have such long families, after all. That did not make the deaths any easier to bear.[44]

Meanwhile, as Jean's brother Adam and the Forbes continued to try and settle their feud through the courts, Adam too was finally struck down. Adam had gone to Edinburgh in 1580, accompanied by Jean's husband Alexander and 39 other supporters, ready to stand in front of James VI to hear the judgement on his feud with the Forbes. But, only three days before Adam was supposed to hear the verdict, the 35-year-old died. It was no fight or foe that finally took out the 'Herod of the North' but 'ane bledin', a mysterious illness.[45] According to the Gordon family chronicler, he was 'much regretted and lamented by his friends', as being a 'very resolute and active gentleman, a good soldier, and a wise and fortunate captain'.[46] Jean's brother Adam's allegiances were always to the Gordon family and the Catholic cause. Adam's memory in the popular imagination of the north-east veers between his family and the Catholic Church's loving assessment, and the damning and sticking description of him as 'Herod of the North'. For Jean, the loss of her closest brother in age was undoubtedly a wrench. Of the close-knit band of 12 original Gordon siblings, at least six had now died. Jean's older brother James was an active and prominent Jesuit in Europe, while her other older brother William lived a quieter existence in France, also based with a religious order.

In Scotland, Margaret's divorce from the Master of Forbes had been finalised in 1574, but for the time being she remained in the north-east, close to her children but now returning to her Gordon family and the Catholic religion. It is possible that Jean may also have welcomed Margaret to Sutherland.[47] Jean's younger brothers Patrick and Thomas were also in the north-east. Patrick, as the next in age to Adam, and still residing at Huntly Castle, took over both the running of the Gordon Aberdeenshire estates, and the title of Laird of Auchindoun, which had belonged to Adam. Jean's nephew, the heir to the Huntly title, was still in France, but began to put in place plans to return home to his Earldom. He made it back to Scotland in either late 1580 or early 1581.

While Alexander was negotiating with Esmé and working at court to restore the Gordon reputation, Jean was noted as controlling the Sutherland estates in his absence. Jean was a more than able administrator, and, as a Gordon, she was extending the power of the House of Huntly over Sutherland. Surviving accounts for 1580 and for 1583–85 show Jean involved in managing day-to-day affairs: feu duties were paid directly to her, she authorised payment to creditors, and she was in charge of spending money too, signing off on purchases of oxen and on merchants' bills.[48] She travelled from Dunrobin to other properties on the Sutherland estates, staying in different areas to oversee what was happening in different places.[49] All this she did while pregnant again, with her fifth pregnancy. Jean's fourth, and second surviving, son was born when Jean was 35 years old, on 14th May 1580. He was named Robert, after Jean's brother who had died in the gun accident eight years earlier. Since it was this son Robert who grew up to be the family chronicler, we know several details about his upbringing, which he wrote about as an adult.

Robert, like his brothers and sister, was fostered out from an early age. His foster-mother was Margaret Mackreth, the wife of John Gordon of Drummoy, a man from a cadet branch of the Huntly Gordon family who had settled in Sutherland in the time of Alexander's father.[50] These Gordons were linked to Jean by blood through descent from younger sons of the Huntly Gordon earls, and marriage.[51] Jean's husband Alexander trusted them completely as John Gordon's second son (Sidderay)[52] was the person who had helped plan Alexander's own escape from old Caithness – their property at Golspitour was where the escape was planned and was probably one place where Jean's children grew up. Robert's foster-mother Margaret Mackreth had also previously been in service with the Countess of Sutherland (either Alexander's mother or his step-mother), and her and her family's services to the Sutherland family were not forgotten. Widowed with seven children, Margaret had had to find ways to support herself, and in her middle age and later years she was pleased to foster Jean and Alexander's children. Robert described his contented upbringing in a busy family household with many visitors, describing Margaret as a 'very virtuous gentlewoman, much given to hospitality, both towards rich and poor'.[53] Robert had a lifelong friendship with this family, especially the Sidderay branch.

In Edinburgh, the year after Robert was born, Esmé's influence reached an apogee as the former Regent Morton was arrested – and charged with the historical crime of the death of James VI's father: the murder of Darnley. Catholics and supporters of Mary, Queen of Scots, such as Alexander and the Huntly Gordons, felt this was a sign that James VI was going to return things to the way they were before. James VI might even intervene on behalf of his mother and remove her from captivity in England, remove the friends of Morton and the extreme Protestants from government – there was even talk of Catholic priests being able to return to Scotland. "Our chief hope is in Scotland", a letter to the General of the Society of Jesus (Jesuits) ran, "on which depends the conversion not of England only, but of all the north of Europe; for the right of succession to the English crown, on the death of the present occupant [Elizabeth], passes to the Queen of Scotland and her son. Of this son some hopes have begun to be formed, especially since the execution of the Earl of Morton..."[54] Morton was beheaded with a forerunner of the guillotine, called the Maiden, at the beginning of June 1581. James VI had been particularly displeased that, even after Morton had resigned the Regency, the English had continued to deal with him rather than coming to young James directly.[55] James had never known Morton very well – Regents were debarred from looking after the monarch, a system which allowed for some separation which could theoretically make things fairer, and which also freed the Regent to carry out their duties of travelling throughout the country to keep order – but James' distance from Morton also made it easier for him to see the Regent as someone who wanted to steal his place. James had been worked on by those around him – not just Esmé but also others who had no reason to like Morton such as Alexander, and Agnes Keith's husband the Earl of Argyll, who had a long-standing disagreement with Morton on behalf of his wife over the jewels and land which the Regent claimed belonged to the crown and which Agnes wanted to keep.[56] James wanted to exercise his power, he wanted to be king and show that if he disliked someone he was able to do something about it. Meanwhile, Alexander and the Gordons rejoiced that their enemy Morton was dead: he had 'been privy to the murder of Henry Stuart, King of Scotland,' the Gordon chronicler stated later – one of the few times that Darnley was ever given his official title. 'This Earl of Morton was a man full of partiality in the administration of justice, greedy, and much given to the pleasures of the flesh; all which he confessed, with great remorse, at his death.' The chronicler then goes on to find quotes from other people who also found Morton greedy and unfair, damning him completely.[57] Morton was undoubtedly not a man whose kindness was his overriding feature, but he had ended up in an impossible position. To be near the Scottish throne was still to court danger.

James VI was still a very young man, however, and it was not to be expected that he would have his own way from this moment on. The noblemen who opposed his actions were still a very strong party, and, in the Ruthven Raid of 22nd August 1582, a group of them took control of the king himself, kidnapping James and taking over the reins of power once more. James VI, tearful and powerless, remained under their rule for about a year. Esmé left the country, 'not being able to abide the contentious factions which were then in Scotland', and died young in Paris, in 1583, leaving his title of Duke of Lennox to his son Ludovick.[58]

This was not the endgame, however: Jean and her family were no longer lurching from success to disaster as it had seemed in Jean's youth and early adulthood. It was not the bouleversant early days of the Reformation any more, where someone as powerful as Jean's father could be brought down unexpectedly: the Scots nobles had lived through that time and had become cannier about holding onto power. The uncertainty of Mary, Queen of Scots' time was not totally gone, but James VI was a young, healthy male heir to the throne who had been trained to rule: there were to be ups and downs for him, and for his subjects like Jean, but this was now the daily struggle of life. Jean and Alexander were working through setbacks with the strength of a united family behind them.

CHAPTER TWELVE

Neighbours: Two Companies of Pretty Men: 1582–1585

As James VI was taken prisoner in the Ruthven Raid on 22nd August 1582, the nobles of Scotland gathered in Scotland's capital to assess the situation. Alexander and Jean's neighbour and adversary the Earl of Caithness was in Edinburgh at the beginning of September when he died, aged about 55.[1] Caithness was buried at Roslin, where his Sinclair family had ancient roots, but before burial his heart was taken from his body and encased in a lead casket, which was returned to the Highlands and placed in the Sinclair aisle in the church in Wick.[2] Even if his heart was in the Highlands, Caithness was not much mourned in the north: for his neighbours, he 'had lived too long'.[3] However, not long after old Caithness' grandson succeeded to the title of Earl of Caithness, the people of the north were soon wishing for the good old days: Caithness' grandson and heir "inherited much of the talents of his grandfather, with, if possible, greater cruelty of disposition".[4] The grandson and heir was the son of John the Stout and Bothwell's sister Janet Hepburn, and soon gained the nickname of Wicked Earl George.

Jean and Alexander had gained an extraordinary new neighbour. The relationship between Jean and Alexander's Sutherland family and their near neighbours, both earl and clans, was to be the theme for the next few years.

Wicked Earl George was 16 years old when his grandfather died, and his accession to his title was not wholly straightforward. Caithness, at the time of his death, was still unhappy at his son, Wicked Earl George's father John the Stout. There was nothing Caithness could do about who inherited the title of Earl, but he could make things difficult for John the Stout's son in one way: Caithness left all his money – and it was supposed to be a considerable amount – to his third son, Wicked Earl George's uncle. So George inherited the title to an Earldom – but without the money to run that Earldom.⁵ Accordingly, Wicked Earl George started his career with little love for his grandfather, and by trying, as James VI had been attempting to do, to avenge the wrongs done to his father. John the Stout's jailors, David and Ingram Sinclair, were well known and still at large, having been rewarded by old Caithness for their part in John the Stout's downfall. At the time when Wicked Earl George took over the Earldom, David and Ingram Sinclair were arranging Ingram's daughter's wedding. The Wicked Earl George received an invitation and rode down from Girnigoe Castle to celebrate the bridal-feast. After dinner, a football match was arranged. Once George was certain that the Sinclairs were wholly absorbed in watching the football, and that any defences they had were down, he, "without any other preamble", walked up to Ingram and, drawing a pistol, shot him in the head.⁶ As the horrified wedding guests looked on, George then drew his sword, turned to David Sinclair and simply "ran him through". Wicked Earl George then went coolly to his horse, "turned his horse's head towards Girnigoe, and rode off with as little concern as if he had merely killed a brace of moor-fowl".⁷ Since George was in charge of dispensing justice in the county, and had now comprehensively terrified everyone into being unwilling to cross him, there were no reprisals for him at all.⁸

Wicked Earl George continued to live at Girnigoe, surrounded by much the same motley household as his grandfather. His mother, Janet Hepburn, Bothwell's sister, seems to have been a frequent visitor, as she ultimately ended her days there. Although Janet had got her mother's lands in Morham and had remarried to Archibald Douglas, Janet was feeling wary at the new rule of James VI, particularly after the execution of the Earl of Morton. Her new husband Archibald Douglas was as heavily implicated in the murder of Darnley as Morton had been, and if James VI was going to start punishing people for Darnley's death, Janet and her new husband were not in a great position. Archibald Douglas was indeed put on trial, though he was eventually acquitted.

Jean cannot have been thrilled to hear that her former sister-in-law was back in Caithness – however established Jean was now as Countess of Sutherland, her previous life as Countess of Bothwell still haunted her. Janet Hepburn would continue to visit her son Wicked Earl George in the north of Scotland for about another decade. We have no pictures of Wicked Earl George: what did Jean see when she looked at him? He was a powerful man. Was he imposing in stature like his father John the Stout? Or did he look like his mother's family – could Jean see a resemblance to his uncle, her ex-husband Bothwell? The Wicked Earl George was still a young man though, and Jean and Alexander were becoming very experienced. The new Earl soon realised that Sutherland was slowly getting power back from Caithness. Wicked Earl George had been brought up in a household where might was the decider in all fights: quarrels were settled with physical violence. Caithness was closer to the clans' way of thinking than the earls'. Jean and Alexander, spending more time at court, had realised that the way forward was not only through the sword, but also through the power of the law. A key moment in the process of Sutherland establishing itself as free from Caithness' power was the conclusion of the long-drawn-out legal process Alexander had put in place to try and free himself from Caithness' powers of justiciary: the old Earl Caithness had had the power to bring anyone in the north of Scotland to justice, and Alexander had challenged this in the courts by an action before the lords of session. This "tedious process" finally came to an end a few months after Wicked Earl George succeeded to the Earldom of Caithness, when the case was found in favour of Alexander.[9] Wicked Earl George put in a protest, but Alexander replied with a counter protest, and, by 1584, Alexander had won again – decisively this time.[10]

Meanwhile, Jean was pregnant again and, just as Wicked Earl

George was taking over the Earldom of Caithness, Jean gave birth to her second daughter who she named Mary. She and Alexander now had a family of four surviving children: Jane, the eldest, was about eight years old; John was six; there was a small gap because of the two boys who had died young; Robert was two, and now, born on 14th August 1582, there was Mary. Sons were important as heirs to property, but daughters were no less valuable to the maintenance of Sutherland power, as they could be used as marriageable assets. When Mary was about a year old, Jean and Alexander had an extended visit from Laird George Ross of Balnagowan, who was entertained at Dunrobin for several months. Ross of Balnagowan was a landowner in Ross-shire; his status was not as high as that of an earl, but the land he owned was between the Sutherland lands and the Huntly Gordon lands, so was potentially very useful to Alexander and Jean to help establish connections between the two Gordon heartlands, in addition to Ross-shire being good, arable farming land. George Ross had a young family as well, and it was agreed that George Ross' eldest son and heir David would marry Mary.[11]

The proposed marriage alliance was designed to bring the Rosses and the Sutherlands closer together, and the arrangements made were very comprehensive. If Ross of Balnagowan's son David died, then his next eldest son was to marry Mary. If Mary died, then David was to marry any other of Jean and Alexander's daughters who were still living. If all of George Ross' sons died, then his eldest daughter Jean Ross was to marry Jean and Alexander's son John. And, further, George Ross, the Laird of Balnagowan, was not to marry off any of his daughters without first consulting and getting the consent of the Earl of Sutherland. The Laird of Balnagowan was to give a bond of manrent to the earl, promising to do as the Earl wanted and to serve him, and promising that all his relatives were to do the same, in exchange for Alexander's protection. Manrent was a pledge from a weaker man or clan making them a vassal to a superior. If the contracts for marriage or manrent were broken, then there was a scale of monetary fines agreed, depending on the severity of the broken promise, from 10,000 merks up to £20,000 Scots.[12]

It was clearly a contract in which Alexander and Jean, as Earl and Countess of Sutherland, were the senior partners. They were arranging for Ross of Balnagowan to be married to their second-eldest daughter – perhaps because Mary and David were closer in age, but perhaps also because their eldest daughter Jane would have been more of a prize. The Earldom of Sutherland would gain most of the land, and they would get the large financial compensation if the agreement fell through. So, what was in it for Ross of Balnagowan? For a start, the marriage took Ross up a level on the social scale. Secondly, Alexander and Jean promised to give their daughter a handsome dowry. And finally, the Sutherlands promised to support Ross of Balnagowan against all potential enemies (with the careful exception of the Earl of Huntly: if Huntly ever took up arms against Ross of Balnagowan, the Sutherlands would of course never go against the other Gordons). To be allied with the Earl of Sutherland gave Ross of Balnagowan a powerful friend, which, as the north was full of warring clans and, as Wicked Earl George's actions showed, still teetering on the brink of lawlessness and constant violence, was an extremely important incentive.

The money that Jean and Alexander offered seemed to be one of the most important incentives. The marriage contract was treated as being as binding as a marriage itself, and Mary was invested with the lands of Ross of Balnagowan almost immediately, while a history of Sutherland notes that Ross of Balnagowan went even further than he had agreed in his land deals: "the laird of Balnagowan, for no apparent adequate reason, granted a charter selling to the Earl of Sutherland evidently his whole estate", a long list of lands including those with fishing rights, rich forests and land where profitable mills were based.[13] Ross of Balnagowan may have thought that he was getting a good deal, but Jean and Alexander seem to have comprehensively outmanoeuvred him, as he would later realise.

Faced with the violence of their neighbours, the clans and Wicked Earl George, Jean and Alexander were choosing to fight back, not only on the battlefield, but also in the lawcourts. While the teenaged Wicked Earl George was terrorising the countryside with random acts of violence, Jean, now in her late thirties, was using the excellent education she had been given as a child at Huntly Castle, the same training in writing and logic that had enabled her brother James to become a well-known Jesuit, or her brother George to maintain and re-establish his powerbase. Jean and Alexander understood, from their time at court, that the world was changing. Wicked Earl George, the lairds and the clans were still living in an almost medieval manner at times whereas Jean and Alexander were fully embracing the modern. They knew that agreements on paper could outfence the sword.

Jean and Alexander were happy to arrange marriages for their daughters, even though Jean had been very unhappy in her arranged marriage to Bothwell and Alexander had annulled his arranged marriage to the daughter of old Caithness. Perhaps the happy union of Jean and Alexander's own marriage had convinced them both that arranged matches were the best way forward – so long as they were arranged by a loving family and within the best family interests. Judging by later events, Jean had not forgotten her lost love Alex Ogilvie, but, at this point in time, Jean definitely had total commitment to her husband the Earl of Sutherland, and to the wider Gordon family, and that was her main concern when thinking of her daughters' marriages. Perhaps Jean thought that by arranging matches for her children so very young, she could avoid for them the unhappy situation she herself had been in, developing feelings for someone her family did not approve of. She may also have been influenced by the uncertain times she had lived in, and have believed that securing Gordon power was the only way for her children to avoid the situations she had found herself in: her father and brother killed, her family dispossessed, her husband involved in regicide. Jean's daughter Mary would grow up knowing exactly what was in store for her, in an environment that was as secure as Alexander, Jean and the Gordons could make it.

Once James VI escaped from the conspirators of the Ruthven Raid in mid-1583, the Gordon family seemed to get another boost. As he established his personal rule, stepping out from the influence of others, James VI did not forget Lord Huntly and his Gordon relatives. Alexander was appointed royal lieutenant and justice-depute within the bounds of Sutherland and Strathnaver.[14] Strathnaver was the traditional home of the Mackay clan. After old Caithness' death, the young chief Uisdean Mackay had continued to support the Earldom of Caithness: Uisdean had, after all, partly grown up with the new Earl of Caithness, Wicked Earl George, and they were personally friendly. However, the legal situation, these bits of paper that Jean and Alexander were collecting, was that Strathnaver and the Mackay clan owed allegiance still to Lord Huntly (George's son and Jean's nephew). Alexander was one of Lord Huntly's curators, advising him on how to run his estates, and in 1583, Jean's nephew transferred the superiority of some of Mackay's lands to Alexander. Alexander now had superiority over the lands and barony of Farr, and also the sheriffship of Sutherland. The sheriff was the permanent representative of central government, who could act as judge, who collected and handed out government money, and who was in charge of the local militia.[15] In return, Alexander gave Lord Huntly lands in Aboyne.[16] Alexander was now officially Uisdean Mackay's superior. Neither Uisdean nor Wicked Earl George were happy about this, and they did their best to change the situation. Alexander, however, ignored them and proceeded to engage in more legal trickery, and use his new crown connections, by giving the lands up to James VI, who then re-granted them to Alexander and Jean's eldest son John.[17] Taken along with the Balnagowan land deal/marriage settlement, Alexander and Jean had now extended their influence both north and south.

Meanwhile, Jean's nephew Lord Huntly was slowly stepping out of the shadow of his powerful Gordon uncles. He was unwaveringly loyal to his childhood companion James VI during the Ruthven Raid and after, and from this loyalty a strong personal relationship developed.[18] The two men were close in age, but Lord Huntly was just that little bit older, and his time on the continent had given him a polish that perhaps reminded James VI of his former favourite Esmé: Lord Huntly was exactly the sort of man that James VI liked to look up to. Jean's nephew stood on excellent, easy terms with the king he called 'his cousin',[19] and their growing alliance was to be of considerable importance to the Gordon family fortunes. There were still a few years to go, however, before Jean's nephew could be anything other than his family's protégé, and in 1584 Jean's brother James, the Jesuit, made a dramatic return to Scotland.

Two of Jean's older brothers were in holy orders. William lived more quietly in France, but James was a prominent figure. He had a strong influence on Jean's nephew and the rest of the Gordon family; they were all proud of his commitment and service to the Catholic faith. Jean's nephew had lived in France and seen him there, while Jean's sister Margaret had returned to Catholicism, and Margaret's two sons, disgusted with their father's treatment of their mother, were also leaning towards Catholicism.

Jean was delighted to see James return. James had entered into the Society of Jesus (Jesuits) in Cologne in 1563 and had studied theology in Rome. He had then been sent to Vienna in 1571, and had started to teach, becoming professor of controversial theology, and writing and publishing his ideas.[20] James was well-travelled, cultured, and used to debate, a "quiet and dispassionate person", "virtuous and prudent ... held in great estimatation", having given up his position in a first family of Scotland for his religious faith.[21] With James VI of Scotland now in charge again, the Jesuits sensed an opportunity, and sent Father James Gordon and another Jesuit, William Crichton – known for his contrasting "vehement temperament"[22] – home to their native Scotland to try to promote the Catholic faith. Over the next few years Jean's brother James made several trips to Scotland: his movements are sometimes hard to follow as he was supposed to move secretly and he sometimes worked under an assumed name,[23] but Father James always traded on his high rank, assuming, correctly, that people would rarely challenge the son, brother and uncle of an earl.

Father James Gordon and William Crichton made their first journey by boat from the Continent to Scotland, hiding their identities as Jesuits. By bad luck, the vessel they were travelling on was seized on the high seas by Dutchmen. The Protestant Dutch were engaged in revolt against their hereditary Catholic ruler, the king of Spain. When the Dutch discovered the boat was en route for Protestant Scotland, they set it free again, but the merchant who had chartered the vessel had realised that Father James and William Crichton were Catholic, and left them behind to the mercies of the Dutchmen. Father James and William were taken to the coastal city of Ostend (which was then under Protestant Dutch control). When Father James' full identity as a Gordon was discovered, the Dutch became uneasy: the Huntly name was well known, particularly the power and status of Lord Huntly and his friendship with the Scots king. There was a story that once, returning to see James VI after time spent at Huntly Castle, Lord Huntly forgot to bow in greeting before his king. Realising his mistake, he excused himself by saying he had just come from a place where everyone bowed to him. James VI just laughed.[24] This close relationship between Lord Huntly and James VI was well known, and the Dutch worried that there would be reprisals if anything happened to Father James Gordon – so Father James was allowed to continue on to Scotland. His companion William Crichton only escaped a certain death after the timely conclusion of a treaty between the Protestant Dutch and Elizabeth of England, when Elizabeth personally requested that he be sent to England for her government to deal with.[25]

Even though Father James made it to Scotland, his cover had been blown, and he was not able to meet with any Scottish priests. His presence in Scotland was known and tolerated by King James VI, but any open Catholic activity would have been enough to have him, at best, instantly expelled from the country. At worst it could put his life in immediate danger.[26] However, Father James Gordon was free to take stock of the situation in Scotland, and sent word to his superiors that he thought it was worthwhile sending more priests over, if it could be arranged for them to land at Aberdeen, as they might receive a better reception in the north, where Lord Huntly and his Catholic family had more power. Father James himself decided to make his way north to his family at Huntly Castle. He was greeted in the north with open arms. His nephew Lord Huntly had gathered around him at Huntly Castle some family members who Father James had not seen for many years. With George and Adam gone, and his nephew and younger brothers grown up, Father James would have found things greatly changed, but the youngest Gordon brothers Patrick and Thomas were still there – though Thomas was now a widower, as his wife Janet (Alexander's sister) had recently died.[27] Father James was pleased, too, that his nephew adhered to the Catholic faith, that his sister Margaret encouraged her sons to follow in his own footsteps and take up orders, and that Jean and Alexander were still strong Catholics and providing the Gordons with a serious powerbase in the far north of Scotland as well as the north-east. Father James and Jean grew closer, and it seems very likely that she made one of her regular trips to Huntly Castle to meet him during his visit, as from this point on Father James regarded his sister Jean as an important Scottish contact.

Father James held out hope that his own considerable powers of oratory and persuasion could have a big impact in Scotland, but realistically the Protestant defeat of Catholicism was firmly entrenched by this time. However highly he was rated, by himself and his loving Gordon family, others found Father James to be optimistic to the point of stupidity.[28]

King James VI, however, seemed likely to at least try to continue the policy of tolerance that his mother had initially hoped to pursue, and the Catholic Lord Huntly continued to be an important person at court. James VI needed Lord Huntly as well, in order to try and maintain order in the north of Scotland. Lord Huntly began to be the official peacemaker between Caithness and Sutherland, intervening between Jean and Alexander, and Wicked Earl George. The nephew, all grown up, was now telling his aunt and uncle what to do. Jean and Alexander had been clashing with Caithness over some complicated disputes involving, once again, the Mackay clan.

There were several branches of the Mackay clan, and Uisdean Mackay had not automatically gained support from all of them. One branch became embroiled in a dispute over ownership of land in Assynt, and started to call on their allies. One by one, many of the families in the north were drawn into the clan debate, starting with the Laird of Fowlis, soon involving Macleods and Gunns, and working up to the Earls of both Caithness and Sutherland.[29] Strong family ties and complicated allegiances meant clan squabbles had a habit of escalating in this way.

James VI did not want this sort of situation to keep happening, and he hoped that by encouraging Lord Huntly to intervene, he could promote stronger allegiances that would prevent fights breaking out. The Earls wanted to establish final superiority over the clans, while James VI wanted to tie the Earls' allegiances firmly to the crown. James VI saw Lord Huntly as the way in.

Using neutral intermediaries, Lord Huntly managed to convince Wicked Earl George and Alexander that they should meet in Elgin. Here, Lord Huntly proposed the idea of marriage between his own sister and Wicked Earl George. This would hopefully have the effect of bringing Caithness indirectly under James VI's influence, while also placing a Gordon in the Caithness camp and so bringing those two families closer together. Maybe marriage would even sober the young and Wicked Earl George. The unfortunate woman on whose shoulders this allegiance rested was a namesake of Jean's: her niece, eldest daughter of Jean's brother George. She was shortly married to Wicked Earl George and they went on to have four children together, but she herself did not leave much trace so perhaps did not have the strong personality and longevity of her aunt Jean.

However clever Lord Huntly thought he was being, both he and Wicked Earl George were young men compared to Jean and Alexander. The average age of the nobility in the 1580s was around 27.[30] Alexander was in his early thirties, and guided by Jean, who was 40 in 1585. They had been working together now for over a decade, and Alexander's upbringing and Jean's time at Mary, Queen of Scots' court had exposed them to all sorts of conspiracies: they were experienced operators who had learnt from the best, and learnt from the mistakes of those around them. Alexander had always supported Jean as she put Gordon interests first, and that was still their joint aim: except now they focused more and more on the interests of the Gordon Sutherlands, not the Huntly Gordons – that is, they focused on their own interests and those of their children. The Gordons saw not only Caithness as a threat to their power, but also saw that the clan system, with these escalating feuds, could destabilise the north of Scotland and threaten their legacy. The clans were a system that was in opposition to the legal government, an unwelcome problem in a modern Scotland. The nobility had already taken much of the power from the church when lands were divided up in the Reformation; now, in this battle of the alternative three estates of nobility, church and clan, the nobility were looking to the clans. Of course, the clans and the nobles were not completely separate – they were united, notably, in the person of the Earl of Argyll, who was also head of the Clan Campbell – but one of the stories of Jean's life was the widening gap between the two groups. It was to be a long and bitter battle that raged for many years. Jean and Alexander were only one part of it, but their family and the attitudes they set, and the way these trickled down the generations, were to be an emotive and important part. Jean, as a woman, was not involved in fighting on the battlefield, and did not always take part in official meetings, but she knew what Wicked Earl George did not: that violence was only one way get what she wanted – the law courts were another way.

Jean and Alexander were used to using the legal courts now to get what they wanted, and they understood the importance of using words to win people over to their side. At the meeting in Elgin, Alexander acquiesced with Lord Huntly's proposal that Caithness and Sutherland should be officially reconciled and Wicked Earl George married to a Gordon. Wicked Earl George was flattered to be taken into the established order of Earls – accepted by the powerful Lord Huntly, talked to by people like Alexander who were close to the King. However, Alexander then persuaded Wicked Earl George that actually they had a common enemy: the clans, and specifically the unfortunate Clan Gunn. During the dispute among the Mackays, the Clan Gunn had switched their allegiance: so recently tied to Alexander and Sutherland, they had decided instead to support Caithness.[31] The Clan Gunn were effectively trapped between the two Earldoms, and their method of dealing with this had been to continually switch sides to whoever seemed most like they were winning – this had worked for a while, but eventually had the end result that neither Caithness nor Sutherland fully trusted them. Their last switch to Caithness and Wicked Earl George seems to have been the final straw for Jean and Alexander and the Sutherlands. All their recent troubles, Alexander gently suggested to Wicked Earl George, were actually the fault of the Clan Gunn. If only they got rid of them, then everything would be fine. In the earliest example of the Sutherland family wanting to totally get rid of clansmen from their lands, one historian argues that Jean and Alexander's policy was to "liquidate" Clan Gunn.[32]

The Clan Gunn, says Jean and Alexander's son Robert in his later history of the time, 'were judged to be the principal authors of these troubles and commotions which were likely to ensue in that area'.[33] He then went on to describe the Clan Gunn in what come across as rather racist terms: they are very definitely positioned as the Other, not only unlike the Earls, but not even like the other clans. Earlier in his chronology, Robert had explained that there was a story that the Gunns were descended from Danish royalty, who had moved to Scotland.[34] The Gunns are described as a 'tribe', 'a race of people dwelling within the diocese of Caithness, [who] are divided among the three countries of Sutherland, Caithness and Strathnaver [Mackay country]. They are very courageous, rather desperate than valiant. They have such intelligence and correspondence among themselves, that they run all one course when any of them is pursued in either of these countries. In time of war they have always served the Earl of Sutherland and Mackay; in time of peace they have still made their gain and profit of the Earl of Caithness and his country: but he [Caithness] can hardly trust them with any service, chiefly against the Earl of Sutherland and Mackay; neither do they repose any great confidence in time'.[35] A smaller clan than some, the Gunns did not fit in, nor had they made the strong ally system that the Mackays, for example, could sometimes benefit from. Jean and Alexander hoped that with the help of Wicked Earl George they could be less one clan problem.

However, when Wicked Earl George got back to Caithness, with his new Gordon bride, he had second thoughts about Clan Gunn. They had so recently been his allies, whereas the Sutherlands were his traditional enemies. The clans were not alien to him – he had been brought up alongside Uisdean Mackay, after all. Wicked Earl George warned the Gunns what had been said. Lord Huntly then travelled to Jean's home of Dunrobin, and ordered Wicked Earl George and, for good measure, Uisdean Mackay, to come and meet with him. Wicked Earl George made the visit, but there was no way Uisdean was going to risk it.[36] In retaliation, Alexander, using his newly ratified powers of justiciary, declared clansman Uisdean Mackay officially a rebel. Wicked Earl George was persuaded once again to go against Clan Gunn – but once again quietly informed them when a join Sutherland-Caithness attack was planned. By this point Clan Gunn had no idea who to trust.

Alexander gathered together a host of Sutherland men to attack Clan Gunn and headed north. However, on the way the Sutherland men came, by chance, upon a group of Mackays. The unfortunate Mackays had been in the middle of a cattle raid: they had just successfully taken away the cattle of a Sutherland man. Alexander immediately changed his plans and engaged the Mackays in battle. Alexander rescued the cattle from the Mackays and sent them back to their owner, and then continued for the rest of the day to chase the Mackays back towards Strathnaver – on the way managing, after all, to pick off some of Clan Gunn. The skirmish became known as Claw-tom-Richi, or the day of the heather bush, as the companies of Sutherland, Mackay and Gunn men scrambled around the hills and heather of the Far North all day.

As Alexander chased the Mackay men right up to Caithness, the Gunns, alarmed by the reports they were hearing, had started to assemble. As evening was falling, and the Sutherland host had made it almost as far as Caithness, the Mackays and Gunns met by chance in the hills. Quickly, the Mackays and Gunns decided to join forces.

As they were swearing loyalty to each other, they suddenly saw Wicked Earl George bearing down on them with a host of Caithness men. They had no idea which side Caithness was currently on. The Gunns' position was now literally one of being trapped between a Caithness force and a Sutherland force, those "two companies of pretty men".[37] The Mackays wanted to fight Alexander's men, arguing that not only were they definitely the enemy, but also that they would be tired after fighting and travelling all day – but the Gunns instead chose to risk their luck and fight Caithness. There were far fewer Gunns than there were Caithness men, but even the Sutherland Gordons became grudgingly impressed by the bravery of the stricken Gunns: 'they had in mind, that nothing was before them but enemies, the deep and bottomless ocean behind them, no place of retreat, no surety but in valour and victory: so, having the advantage of the hill, they set upon the enemy with a resolute courage. The Caithness men came short with their first flight of arrows; [but] the Clan Gunn spared their shot until they came hard to the enemy...' – they then let lose their arrows to great damage. The Clan Gunn defeated Caithness, killing seven score (140) men, including the captain, who was Wicked Earl George's own cousin. The only reason any of Caithness' men escaped was that darkness fell and so they could run away.[38]

For the Mackays, it was a sore victory; the dead captain was not only cousin to Wicked Earl George – but also the uncle of Uisdean Mackay. The Mackay forces took out their confusion and fury by pursuing the fleeing Caithness men with no mercy. Meanwhile, Alexander, unaware, because of the slowly falling darkness, of Clan Gunn's desperate last stand in the hills, had returned home. From the Sutherland point of view, though, things had turned out surprisingly well. They might not be rid of Clan Gunn as planned, but what had happened was perhaps even better: Caithness and Mackay were a lot weaker. That chance meeting between the Mackay cohort and the Gunns in the hills had far-reaching consequences. Wicked Earl George protested to everyone who would listen that he had not wanted to go against Clan Gunn in the first place, but now that they had killed some of his allies, the Mackays, he pursued the Gunns with ferocity. Uisdean Mackay was caught in the middle. Since some of the Mackays had allied with the Gunns, Uisdean was urged by some of his kinsmen to kill Wicked Earl George in retaliation. Uisdean's hold over the entire Mackay clan was still slightly shaky because of his background being brought up by Caithness. It was an untenable situation for Uisdean: he was linked to Wicked Earl George by marriage and upbringing, so could not bring himself to kill him, but neither did he want to antagonise his clansmen. Uisdean ended up leaving Caithness entirely, and retiring to the Mackay lands of Strathnaver. The Caithness-Mackay links were weakening.[39]

Lord Huntly tried desperately to keep control of the north. Anxious not to have the Caithness-Sutherland alliance break down, though perhaps not fully understanding the clan situation, he sent Jean's brother Patrick to promote a friendly meeting between Alexander and Wicked Earl George. Once again Wicked Earl George was persuaded to go with the Sutherlands against the Clan Gunn. The Clan Gunn appealed to Uisdean Mackay for help, but Uisdean saw that the Earls' combined forces were too much for him. Uisdean 'discharged [Clan Gunn] from his country'.[40] The broken Clan Gunn were forced to retreat entirely, leaving their home in the north and heading en masse towards the Western Isles. As they travelled west, the Caithness and Sutherland host, which included Jean's brother Patrick, caught up with them at a place called Leckmelme. Caithness and Sutherland had, according to another historian, a "determinate resolution to exterminate them".[41] There was a "sharp skirmish" and most of the Clan Gunn were killed. Alexander's company took one symbolic prisoner, returned home, and sent that prisoner to Wicked Earl George. George received the prisoner with an outward show of cheerfulness, but inwardly it was thought that he was not only jealous of Alexander's military success, but also horrified by the consequences of all of this. It was dawning on the Wicked Earl George that, not only was he now estranged from Uisdean Mackay, but that Alexander had legal superiority over the Mackay lands of Strathnaver.[42] The Gunn prisoner rubbed salt in the wound by telling Wicked Earl George to his face that it was 'a sorry victory ... dear bought, without gain or credit in the attempt; two Earls to join against a poor handful and a [small] family sheltered under their patronage'.[43] The Gunn prisoner was later quietly released, but the damage to Caithness was done.[44] Jean and Alexander had not only got rid of some of their clan enemies but they had also comprehensively outmanoeuvred and weakened Wicked Earl George.

While the clan troubles absorbed Wicked Earl George and much of the north, Jean and Alexander took care to keep an eye on the wider picture within Scotland. This was one of the advantages they had over Caithness: they were involved in several games at once, and never lost sight of either the complicated smaller clan scene, or the bigger picture. Jean and Alexander's goals were always the preservation of the Gordon family, but they saw the Gordon family not only in the context of the north of Scotland, but also across the north-east, down to the capital in Edinburgh, and across to the continent – and still strongly linked with the cause of Catholicism. King James VI continued to not only offer friendship to the Catholic Lord Huntly but also to turn a blind eye to Father James Gordon's preachings. Encouraged, a few other Catholic priests managed to land in Scotland to continue Father James' work.[45]

Elizabeth of England was not pleased and wrote to James VI, strongly urging him to take action. Elizabeth was worried by what seemed like a revival of Catholicism in Scotland, James VI's friendship with Catholic favourites like Jean's nephew Lord Huntly and the continued plotting of James VI's captive mother Mary, Queen of Scots with Catholic noblemen in England. Elizabeth felt that for the security of her kingdom she could not let the situation continue, and in November 1585 there was an English-backed coup in Scotland. James VI was once more taken under the control of ultra-Protestant lords and as a consequence Father James Gordon had to leave Scotland early in 1586.[46]

CHAPTER THIRTEEN

Creachlarn: The Great Spoil and the Three Weddings: 1585–1590

Early in 1585, on 5th March, Jean gave birth to her final child. She was 40 years old and had been married for the last 12 years: for most of her marriage she had either been pregnant or recovering from childbirth. She named her last son Alexander, her husband's name. Most noblewomen spent their married lives in this cycle of constant pregnancy, but Jean had also remained active in many other ways, constantly working on maintaining and running the Sutherland estates, as well as her own lands in Crichton,[1] especially when her husband was away at court, and keeping up her links with her family and promoting Gordon interests in addition. She and Alexander had comprehensively retaken Sutherland as their own, and built up Dunrobin Castle to "the werie heart and center of [their] countrey, and the most pleasant habitation", with its brew-house and little tower.[2] Conflicts with the clans and with Caithness loomed large over the next few years, but Jean did not forget her brother James the Jesuit or her commitment to the Catholic faith. Wider events happening in Scotland and Europe, including the Spanish Armada, had a big impact on the north of Scotland. It was certainly not time for this energetic woman to rest: Scotland was about to enter a time of challenges, not only on the world stage, but also at the practical local level as the beginning of a period of high inflation and a succession of poor harvests.[3] It was imperative that someone, as Jean had already been doing, kept an eye on estate expenditure if Earls were not to get into horrendous debt. Jean's aim was to continue to work for herself and her husband, but now that her nephew had taken over in Huntly Castle, her focus gradually became less about the wider Gordon family and more about her own children and the Sutherland lands they were to inherit – particularly as her nephew Lord Huntly became embroiled in his own damaging blood feud against the Morays. The House of the Sutherland and the House of Huntly still worked together as the joint House of Gordon, but to a lesser degree than before.

Jean's cousin, Agnes Keith, had been holding the lands of Moray for her young daughters. In 1580 Elizabeth, the eldest child of Agnes and the late Regent Moray, was married, aged only 15, to a tall and very handsome 13-year-old boy called James Stewart. This James Stewart, so good-looking that he became known by the sobriquet of 'Bonnie', was not a particularly high-ranking nobleman[4] but he was very well-connected, and King James VI was in favour of the match. Agnes Keith and her second husband the Earl of Argyll continued to guide the new bonnie young 2nd Earl of Moray and his youthful bride. Then in 1584, while on a visit to the Moray castle of Darnaway, Agnes' second husband died. Agnes was now in charge of the Argyll estates – but with no experienced older man in charge, not only the Earldom of Argyll, but also the Earldom of Moray, was weakened. There was room in the north for someone new to step in and take up the reins of power. The Gordons, in the shape of Jean's nephew Lord Huntly, were obvious contenders. Rashly, the Bonnie Earl of Moray thought he could stand against them – but, however highly he thought of himself, the Bonnie Earl was "an immature novice" when ranked against Lord Huntly. Lord Huntly was already not disposed to look kindly on the Bonnie Earl because Agnes Keith's daughter had been suggested as a bride for him when he was a child, something that would have brought him all the Moray lands. The Gordons had not forgotten their interest in the Moray lands, or their hatred of the Regent Moray for his actions so long ago at Corrichie against Jean's father and brothers. The long-standing Gordon-Moray enmity was to develop into one of the most publicised and notorious blood feuds in Scotland.[5]

From about 1584, while Lord Huntly was patronisingly telling his aunt Jean and her husband to simmer down their quarrels with Wicked Earl George, he was involved in an exceptionally violent blood feud himself. Supporters of Lord Huntly and the Bonnie Earl of Moray did charming things to each other, like the time that a Grant (a Moray supporter) was bound hand and foot by some Gordons, hung up and suspended by his testicles before being beaten to death.[6] Lord Huntly was not personally involved in these incidents, but the fact that he allowed kinsmen to carry out acts like this unpunished, demonstrates the violence that simmered underneath his veneer of cosmopolitan European culture.

When I argue that Jean was in control of the Sutherland estates, it should not be forgotten that she was a woman in a man's world: she may have been a power behind the throne, but she was in no way stepping into a man's role. Financial management and discussion of tactics was perfectly acceptable women's work, but she was living in a world where the most powerful Earls in the land were violent adolescent boys who were dealing with the confusing aftermath of a brutal reversal of every religious belief their ancestors had held dear while succeeding to their titles at a young age – often with no guidance, as their elders had died young as a result of conflict. Their king, James VI, was himself barely an adult, surrounded by people he did not always trust and buffeted by the reaction from events on the continent – but he was becoming remarkably adept at maintaining both his power and Scotland's image as a cultured kingdom. Even though Lord Huntly was a favourite, James VI put a lot of time and energy into trying to show Lord Huntly the error of his ways and reconcile him with Moray. In Edinburgh in 1586, James VI made Lord Huntly and the Bonnie Earl of Moray come to Holyrood, where, in front of everyone, they had to shake hands and drink to each other's health. Then the king made them walk hand in hand up the High Street to the Mercat Cross, where a great banquet was held.[7]

James VI finally reached his majority – 21 years old – in 1587. It was a momentous time. James VI's mother, Mary, Queen of Scots, had been held in captivity now for almost 20 years, since she had fled to England in the confusing aftermath of her and Bothwell's surrender at Carberry Hill. Elizabeth of England had procrastinated superbly: she kept her royal cousin in cosseted confinement in a series of castles, and the two women and rivals never, ever met. At last, with James VI's majority looming, and with a constant fear of Catholic revival exacerbated by events like Jean's brother James the Jesuit's trip to Scotland, Elizabeth was finally persuaded by her clever secretary Cecil that Mary, Queen of Scots was a problem that had to be dealt with, rather than ignored indefinitely. After producing evidence of Mary's continued plotting with English Catholics – much of that evidence being gathered after Cecil had placed double agents – Elizabeth of England was convinced that Mary had to be put on formal trial, and, when that trial was concluded against Mary, that she had to sign a death warrant for the Scots queen. Elizabeth was enormously reluctant to authorise the execution of another royal queen, as she never wanted to do anything that might jeopardise the power of royal women, and even the final signature was something Cecil had to pretend to get by stealth: Elizabeth knew exactly what she was signing but she wanted to go through the form of having someone else she could blame if necessary, and Cecil was obliged to hide the death warrant in among a sheaf of other papers awaiting signature. Elizabeth signed them all.

Elizabeth of England tried to control the final execution as much as possible, holding it in private, and with as little opportunity as possible for Mary to make a final statement. It was not possible of course, and every detail of the manner of Mary's death was recorded, as she deliberately went with the dignity of Catholic martyr to the execution block. The key, however, was how James VI would react. James VI had never known his mother personally, and his whole life he had been taught that she was evil. He made some attempts to alter the way she was remembered, and it was not advisable to speak badly of her in front of him, but there was no real familial connection. She was, in fact, another barrier to him assuming full power in Scotland: if she was released from prison, then she could claim the throne instead of him. In addition, James VI was always very focused on his potential succession to the English throne. It was ultimately more important to maintain a good relationship with Elizabeth of England than it was to lead some sort of pointless raid to avenge the death of a woman he did not know and did not approve of. After Mary, Queen of Scots was beheaded, James VI ordered his court into mourning, but that was the extent of his actions. He was not without his critics – Francis, Bothwell's nephew, for example, motivated by family feeling, chivalry and nationalism, wanted to be revenged on England and forcefully advocated for military action on the border – but James VI held firm.[8]

For Jean, when Mary, Queen of Scots died, she was witnessing several deaths: the death of the true Catholic monarch, whose restoration her brothers George and Adam had fought for, yes, but also the death of a tiresome, impulsive woman who had destroyed the most powerful defender of the Catholic faith in Scotland: Jean's father the Earl of Huntly. Jean was hearing of the execution of the woman who had caused her father and beloved dashing elder brother John to die and the woman who had imprisoned her brother George. She was hearing of the death of a cousin whose capricious temperament she had got to know well as she had lived with her and seen her daily at court, whose charm she personally had never fallen for, but a woman who Jean's own mother had been happy to serve and to take risks for. She was hearing of the death of the woman who had taken her ex-husband and forced her into a scandalous and possibly illegal divorce which went against all her religious beliefs. But, perhaps most of all, Jean was hearing of the death of a woman from the past: a woman who had not been directly involved in her life for many years, an old, ill woman with grey hair. Jean could still picture red-headed Mary, slim and beautiful like her mother, as she sat in her finery. It was like a picture from another world: now, the court was ruled by a young man; violent boys who had not even been born when Jean was first married were in charge of the countryside. Jean was never a woman who looked backwards. She was always focused on the present and the challenges of the day she was living in. She did not forget what had happened, and she did not necessarily forgive, but nor did she wallow in the past. Mary, Queen of Scots was dead: what would happen next?

In Jean's Far North of Scotland, what happened next was continued disturbances between Caithness and Sutherland. Wicked Earl George was desperately trying to gain back some control, particularly over the Mackays. He appealed directly to Lord Huntly, asking for the superiority of Strathnaver to be returned to him instead of Alexander. Lord Huntly wavered, but, when Alexander heard of this, he made it clear that there was no way he was giving up any power over Strathnaver and the Mackay lands.[9] It was a brief moment of discord between Lord Huntly and Alexander, but Jean's brother Patrick intervened and smoothed down the situation. Patrick could do little to soothe the Wicked Earl George though, and, in 1587, 'flames of dissension and discord did burst forth between the Earls of Sutherland and Caithness'.[10] The catalyst was a silly dispute over horses' tails.

Directly on the border of Caithness' land lived a man called George Gordon of Marle.[11] Marle was not only well aware of the history of the Sutherland-Caithness tensions, but linked to it: there were no bystanders in the north, with the complicated family relationships of blood and name. Everyone was involved somehow in what was going on, and many took great pleasure in playing their own small parts. Marle, a man described as "a daring, insolent libertine"[12] took great exception to Caithness' actions, and intercepted some of Wicked Earl George's servants as they led the Earl's horses past Helmsdale river, travelling on their way to Edinburgh. Marle cut the horses' tails off and jeered at the servants. Wicked Earl George was mightily offended when he saw his ragged-looking horses, who did not at all present the sort of sleek look he wanted to project in Edinburgh when he brought his retinue in front of the young king.[13] George resolved to have revenge on the man who had made him look so stupid. Lord Huntly advised Wicked Earl George to pass the problem on to Alexander, since Alexander should deal with Gordon men in Sutherland, but George did not want to go to Alexander with the problem: he thought that he would seem ridiculous if he complained that one of Alexander's tenants had cut off his horses' tails. Actually, Alexander might have supported him in this instance, as he was already displeased with Marle, having learnt that the man 'did entertain his own wife's sister as concubine'.[14] Marle, realising that he had now invoked the displeasure of both the Earl of Caithness and the Earl of Sutherland, hastily tried to make amends with at least one of them. Judging that the crime the Wicked Earl George was angry about was the least serious, Marle sent his brother direct to Wicked Earl George to plead for forgiveness for cutting off the horses' tails. Hearing that Alexander was angry with Marle, Wicked Earl George pretended that his enemy's enemy was his friend and said to the brother that Marle had nothing to fear from him any more. What Wicked Earl George really thought was that Alexander probably would not mind him taking revenge on someone who was so out of favour with Sutherland already. In the silence of a dark and cold February night, Wicked Earl George brought an entire army down from Caithness to Marle's house. Marle barricaded himself in and resisted furiously, managing to kill some of Wicked Earl George's men. Eventually though, Marle decided his best chance was to make a break for it: he ran out of his house and somehow made it through the thick press of his enemies, before jumping into the icy River Helmsdale. Here, though, his luck run out, and the unfortunate Marle was shot and slain with arrows as he tried to swim away.

This ridiculous fight over horses' tails was the trigger for renewed hostilities between Wicked Earl George and Alexander. Even though Alexander was certainly not a fan of the revolting Marle, Wicked Earl George could not be allowed to get away with riding into Sutherland country and killing Gordons. By March, Alexander and Wicked Earl George were facing off at the heads of two massive armies. Wicked Earl George called on all his allies: Uisdean Mackay and the Mackays who were still loyal to him were persuaded into the fight, and joined by Orcadians, and other friends, while ranged against Wicked Earl George was Alexander and his Sutherland men, bolstered by Mackintosh, Mackenzie, Munro, Hutchinson and some of the Mackays. The two armies met at the River Helmsdale in March 1587. Guns and arrows were shot across the water, with the Sutherland archers proving particularly deadly.[15] With neither side able to cross the icy swollen river, Alexander sent a Mackintosh clansman over to speak to Mackay, Gael to Gael. The Mackintosh tried to persuade Uisdean Mackay to come to Alexander's side, and submit to him as the legal superior of Strathnaver and the Mackays. The Mackays refused.

While this Gael talk was going on, other mediations were happening between the Earls, with more success. A truce between Wicked Earl George and Alexander was agreed – but then Alexander made his condition: Mackay, he said, was the vassal of Sutherland, and must submit to him. Mackay still refused – but Wicked Earl George would not support him. The Earls were reconciled, the armies were dissolved and Mackay was left as the sole rebel. Alexander appointed a meeting with Wicked Earl George in Edinburgh in 1588, and persuaded him that Uisdean Mackay must be their mutual enemy.[16] It was a union of Earls versus Gaels; a repeat of the successful tactics Alexander and Jean had operated against the Clan Gunn.

Uisdean Mackay felt he had little option. He was not supported by all his own clan and he had lost the protection of Caithness. He agreed to meet Alexander on neutral ground, in Inverness. They discussed the situation, and appointed a second meeting, this one to be held in Elgin in November 1588. At the second meeting, Uisdean Mackay finally capitulated: he acknowledged Alexander as his superior, becoming the first Mackay chief to ever submit to an Earl of Sutherland and, moreover, switching up the allegiances again: Uisdean agreed to work with Alexander against Wicked Earl George.

Alexander, having subdued the clans to his satisfaction, now went all out for Wicked Earl George. While in Edinburgh, Alexander had persuaded James VI to give him a letter of special protection for himself and Jean: in the letter, which was clearly directed against Wicked Earl George, James VI stated that the kirklands of Caithness were now annexed to the crown, and all feu duties from them were now payable to James VI. If Wicked Earl George did not give up this money, Alexander was allowed to go against Wicked Earl George, and, furthermore, Alexander must have the support of Lord Huntly, of Jean's brother Patrick, of Ross of Balnagowan, Lord Lovat, the Mackintoshes, the Munros of Foulis, and a list of other notable northern men.[17] Alexander also sought an additional commission to go against Wicked Earl George for the murder of Marle.[18] They were paper documents that were not wholly matched in practice, especially the list of men who were supposed to aid Alexander, but what Alexander was doing was making sure that he had the whole force of the law behind him before he embarked on a violent raid of his neighbour's territory.

Using the horses' tails incident once again as the catalyst, Alexander demanded that Wicked Earl George send to him the men that had killed Marle. Wicked Earl George refused, so Alexander sent a trusted Gordon of Golspitour, that family who lived so close to Dunrobin and had done so much for Sutherland, to go into Caithness at the head of a host of 200 men. The force returned with a number of cattle. Alexander then took another force, this time co-led by his new ally Uisdean Mackay, and bolstered by a few vengeful Gunns, and this one made it all the way up to Wicked Earl George's main stronghold at Girnigoe Castle, where they camped for 12 days.[19] While some of the force were encamped, others laid waste to the countryside. They advanced on the town of Wick, and set it alight. The church was one of the few buildings spared, but the Sutherland men entered even there, looking for things they could take. Inside the church, they came across a curious lead box: opening it, they discovered that it contained the ashes of the heart of the old Earl of Caithness. The ashes of the heart were scattered into the wind.[20] The frightened inhabitants of Wick and wider Caithness fled, as more cattle and goods were taken. Seeing that Wicked Earl George was unable to protect them, people in Caithness began to make their own deals with the Sutherland men, promising allegiance to Alexander in exchange for being left alone. Wicked Earl George, safe in Girnigoe Castle, could have withstood the siege for longer, but reports were filtering through to him of what was happening outside. A mediation group was hastily organised, and representatives of Caithness and Sutherland met halfway between Girnigoe and Wick. Alexander promised to stop his men from causing any more damage, and both sides agreed to further negotiations. Lord Huntly was once again appointed to be the man in charge of future peace talks.[21]

The Gordon chronicler claims that only one Sutherland man was lost in the whole campaign, a straggler who drowned, but the more balanced reports, and the magnitude of the operation, suggest the number of dead were in the hundreds.[22] The series of events became known as 'Creach Iarn' and 'La na creachmore', passing into folk memory as 'the great spoil'.[23] Either way, it was definitely a victory for Alexander, Jean and the Earldom of Sutherland. It was not the last time Alexander sent a force into Caithness, and nor was it the last time Wicked Earl George tried to assert his authority – while the 'common' people in Sutherland and Caithness, who had, of course, suffered the most, took several opportunities to try and revenge themselves on their neighbours independently of their Earls[24] – but there had been a massive shift the moment that Uisdean Mackay had changed sides. Uisdean began to spend more time at Dunrobin, as Alexander's guest, and acted for the Sutherlands in other military engagements.[25]

As Jean's husband went between these military engagements in the Far North, his entertaining of Mackay at Dunrobin and his trips to the capital to check in on the young King James VI and keep up his legal proceedings, Jean also heard from her brother, James, the Jesuit. Although James VI had not taken any direct steps to avenge the death of Mary, Queen of Scots, it was felt that the execution of the Scots queen, now seen as a martyr, could lead to an opening for the revival of the Catholic faith. James VI, now officially of age, was seen as being sympathetic to Catholics: if a priest could get to talk to him at this moment, and speak to him of his mother, it was felt that there might be a way to get through to him. Father James Gordon thought he was the man for the job, and returned to Scotland.

Jean's nephew, Lord Huntly, was still openly Catholic. King James VI remonstrated with his friend for not embracing the Protestant faith, and Lord Huntly took the chance to reply that "there was an uncle of his own in Scotland, to whom he would much more willingly entrust the salvation of his soul than to any of that heretical ministry". Lord Huntly suggested that Father James Gordon be brought to meet with King James VI. "Let him come," said the King, "we are not afraid of him."[26] Father James Gordon dressed carefully in his official robes, and appeared before the king and eight of the king's trusted ministers. As King James VI watched carefully, the ministers opened debate with Father James. They questioned him closely on the intricacies of his beliefs, asking him to defend the Mass. Father James put all his training to good use, and argued clearly and logically, overruling the Protestant ministers and steadfastly holding his ground. King James VI, seeing his ministers descending into confusion, entered the debate himself, arguing with all the tools his strict education had given him. The debate descended into "noisy clamours and strong language".[27] Jean's brother Father James was an extraordinary public speaker, charismatic and incredibly persuasive, and demonstrably able to defeat and throw into confusion even the best minds in Protestant Scotland. Some called him "the most learned papist in Europe".[28] Father James would have been a worthy and effective opponent to the charismatic John Knox – but he was at least 20 years too late. Afraid of what might be sparked, King James VI prohibited Father James from discussing religion anywhere save in the king's own presence. Father James remained at court for two months, pushing for further debate with the Protestant ministers, certain that he could in this way influence the king and perhaps the religion of the whole country. But every time he saw the ministers assembling for debate, James VI went out hunting. Father Gordon even followed James VI to the chase, hunting alongside him and making every effort at conversation, but with no success. There was growing disquiet over his presence at court, so Father James decided to head north, to his family in Aberdeenshire.

Now that he was out of reach of the king, Father James decided to accede to the request of several noblemen in the north and hold a public debate and discussion on religion. A Mr George Hay "the most learned of ministers, a man of good birth, fairly versed in Greek and Latin literature, and occupying the first place among [Protestant] preachers" was selected as Father James' opponent.[29] A great number of noblemen and women came to watch the two men debate. George Hay might have been the best preacher in the north, but at the public debate Father James wiped the floor with him. Hay tried to defend himself with biblical quotations that proved his views, but Father James outquoted him. Hay sent to his house for a "whole horseload" of books, and picked out passages that supported his arguments. But the well-read Father James capped each short quotation that Hay could produce with an explanation of the context of that quotation, each time showing to the satisfaction of the audience that Hay was mistaken. "This occurrence made a great noise," exulted Father James' Catholic supporters, and a number of nobles in the north did return to the Catholic faith as a result of the spirited debate. James Gordon personally "not only touched the hearts of many persons by the holiness of his life", said one of his fellow Jesuits, "but, further, being a man of great learning, he openly defeated the ministers of the heretics".[30]

Two more of Jean's nephews were affected by Father James: Margaret's sons. Angry at their father's treatment of their mother after the divorce, eldest son William had left home to fight in wars on the continent. Eventually he decided to embrace religious life, entering a monastery as a Capuchin Friar in Ghent, Belgium. He became known as 'Brother Archangelus' and devoted his life from then on to working with the poor. William had kept in touch with his younger brother John and when a dynastic marriage was planned for John Forbes, John chose to leave his Forbes family, disguised as a shepherd, to follow his brother to Belgium. William encouraged John to ask their uncle James the Jesuit for advice. William and John's father the Master of Forbes was horrified: he had remarried and had children with his new wife, and now tried to cut his sons with Margaret out of their inheritance and stop them from receiving his title.[31]

Catholicism was not really increasing in popularity, however. James VI may not have felt that his mother's execution required a military response, but on the continent Mary, Queen of Scots had not been forgotten. She was always a monarch of European, not just Scottish significance. King Philip II of Spain, the greatest Catholic monarch, whose mighty Empire extended across western Europe and over to the New World, was personally angered at the death of his relative, adding it to his list of reasons to dislike Elizabeth of England. The Spanish Armada, 130 ships stuffed full of troops, was prepared to invade England. They started to assemble in spring 1588, and were sighted in the English Channel by July. However, as the Spanish fleet anchored at Calais, the English, under the command of Sir Francis Drake, loaded up old boats with flammable material, and sent these fireships to cause chaos and scatter the Spaniards. The English then followed up with a fierce attack from their fast fleet – but what really finished off the Armada was the weather: storms, the 'Protestant Wind', drove the fleet off course, and many of the ships, trying to sail home round the north of Scotland, were shipwrecked. To Jean at Dunrobin Castle, perched on the coast, the Spanish Armada was a real and present event, not something that happened in far-off Europe. Throughout the summer months of July and August, Scotland "was in a state of keenest anxiety".[32] Beacon signals were arranged along the coast and, as Spanish ships continued to be sighted all around the north, the General Assembly of the Kirk spent their time "in prayers, sighs and sobbing", and directing much of their anxiety over invasion towards any Scottish Catholics, such as Lord Huntly or Jean and her husband.[33] For years afterwards there were semi-apocryphal stories of Spaniards washed up on the beaches of the north of Scotland and in the western and northern isles, and reports of subsequent generations of Highlanders with dark, curly hair and swarthy European skin. Some Spaniards did indeed land in Scottish territory,[34] and by the end of 1588 there were reports of around 660 Spaniards in Scotland. Catholics in Scotland, such as Huntly, were thought to want to help them, and certainly seem to have been willing to do so, but James VI had to be careful to be seen by Elizabeth of England to do what she thought was right. Some Spaniards were sent away from Scotland by boat with safe-conduct passes, but these passes meant little once they were out at sea, and English ships could attack them.[35] With Catholics from an attacking force actually landing in Scotland, the mood was very jumpy. As Lord Huntly was seen as the most senior Catholic in Scotland, and someone who clearly had the confidence of King James VI, Jean's nephew had to submit to constant harassment by various church ministers. When Lord Huntly protested to the king, James VI said that Lord Huntly must sit and listen to these ministers and, afterwards, Jean's nephew had to publicly swear his allegiance to the Protestant Kirk.[36] James VI had no intention of losing his friend, but being openly Catholic in Scotland at the time of the Spanish Armada was not going to work. Lord Huntly's public 'conversion' and open avowal of Protestant values "gave the greatest satisfaction" to the Kirk – though there were still those who were suspicious that he remained secretly committed to Catholicism.[37] Lord Huntly was still in high favour with King James VI, whatever the Kirk thought of him.

Three weddings affected Jean in the years 1588–89, and the first was that of her nephew Lord Huntly. James VI had spent some time arranging a suitable marriage for his favourite, and in July 1588, as the Spanish Armada approached, the wedding had finally taken place. As a young man, Lord Huntly had fallen in love with what seemed like a suitable young lady, but she had not been good enough for James VI, and the king had made Lord Huntly stay with him until his passion wore off – even though Lord Huntly had made himself ill through being miserable.[38] James VI's relationship with Lord Huntly sometimes overstepped friendship between two men and moved into something else: the power balance was always that of a king's relationship with a subject, but modern commentators sometimes draw other conclusions.[39] Any understanding of James VI's relationships with his favourites has to be seen in the historical context, however, and, in the sixteenth century, noblemen looked for wives. The only woman that James VI agreed would be good enough for Lord Huntly was the eldest daughter of his very first favourite Esmé: Henrietta. Fortunately, although there was a delay of two years between arranging the union and the actual wedding, once Lord Huntly finally met Henrietta she turned out to be an excellent choice and their marriage worked extremely well.

James VI took a strong interest in the marriage of Lord Huntly. If his friend and favourite had to marry, James VI wanted nothing but the best for him. Henrietta was his close blood relative, and James VI referred to her as "his doughter, and beloved of his blud", going so far as to provide her dowry and pay for her travel to Scotland from her home in France.[40] Even in a time of scarcity in Scotland, James VI made sure to arrange for venison and wild fowl to be served at the wedding breakfast, and even started to write a masque to be performed after the wedding ceremony, which he himself would have played a part in – though this touching idea to celebrate his friend's wedding was never quite finished. James did play his part in the ceremony though, as he gave Henrietta away.[41] Henrietta was judged by her new relatives to be 'a virtuous wife, and prudent lady; who providently governed her husband's affairs'.[42] She was very much in the mould of the strong Huntly Gordon women, an astute political operator who not only provided Lord Huntly with a long and healthy family but knew how to manage both her own family connections and the Gordon ones, working together with her husband over the years to promote their interests and remain on excellent terms with the Scottish crown.[43] By marrying Henrietta, Lord Huntly gained a helpmeet and strengthened his connections to James VI: not only was he married to the daughter of James VI's beloved Esmé, but, through Henrietta and her family the Lennox Stewarts, Lord Huntly's children were directly related to James. Lord Huntly's existing bloodlinks to the Scottish crown, although meaningful to Jean and the other Gordons, were historical, and receding into the past: this marriage brought the Gordon link to the throne and the relevance of the Huntly Gordons to Scottish politics bang up to date. The only thing that still hindered the Huntlys' rise to prominence was that Lord Huntly's religious convictions outweighed his desire for power: despite being married according to Protestant rites, he could not genuinely give up his Catholic faith. For the Gordons, Jean, her nephew and the wider family, Catholicism had become a central part of their identity.

During the winter of 1588–89, after his wedding to Henrietta, Jean's nephew Lord Huntly pretty much lived with James VI at Holyrood, spending all his time with the king.[44] At the beginning of the following year, however, Elizabeth of England wrote to James VI accusing Lord Huntly of "a vile conspiracy".[45] Her spy network had intercepted coded letters from Lord Huntly to the king of Spain, in which Lord Huntly promised his allegiance to Catholicism, and expressed his sadness at the fact that the Armada had not been able to land safely in the north of Scotland, where they would have been welcomed. Lord Huntly protested that the letters were forged, and James VI refused to read them, but Elizabeth of England produced more proof and would not be ignored. Anxious not to go against Elizabeth, and aware that Lord Huntly was not universally trusted and popular, James VI had no option but to endorse Lord Huntly's imprisonment in Edinburgh Castle. Jean's nephew was in comfortable confinement, and soon welcomed the king for a cosy dinner, where James VI "kissed him often, protesting that he knew he was innocent".[46] James VI's position on the throne was ultimately more important to him than his favourite, however, and although Lord Huntly was soon released, he had to retreat north, where he remained.

Huntly, along with other sympathetic lords, made an abortive attempt to rebel against James VI, and the king made his first trip north to Huntly's territory – in pursuit of his friend, as Huntly's foe. The rebellion was soon put down. James VI then went on to Inverness and Cromarty, seeing them for the first time.[47] Like his mother Mary, Queen of Scots, James VI saw this trip north as an enjoyable holiday: there was no sense that it was in any way strange for it to have taken so long for James VI to view this part of his kingdom, or that it was necessary to see the land that he ruled further north, where Jean lived in Sutherland. One of the reasons the clan system was still so strong in the Far North was that it was so far removed from the seat of power in Scotland: it would have been possible for several generations of ordinary people in the Mackay clan to go without ever seeing their monarch. Like her son, Mary, Queen of Scots had not made it much further north than the Black Isle. Further back, James V and IV had likewise not travelled further north, and what they did for the Highlands was often done through negotiation with chiefs, or through the crown's representatives the Earls, rather than by the King visiting and doing work on the ground.[48] Jean and her husband, as Countess and Earl of Sutherland and the crown's representatives, were literally as close to royalty as many people in the north ever saw. When class and the feudal system were rigid and people had little social mobility, this mattered: Jean and her husband sometimes saw the clans as being something 'Other' than themselves – and, likewise, ordinary people could see royalty and the nobles as entirely separate from themselves. Protestantism's challenge to this was still radical. James VI returned to run his increasingly centralised kingdom from Edinburgh. Meanwhile, Jean's nephew was busy maintaining his estate in Aberdeenshire, embarking on an ambitious programme of renovations to his castles, including Huntly Castle itself. Lord Huntly focused on his northern concerns, not forgetting his feud with the Bonnie Earl of Moray who had lately returned from France and now had even fewer elders to guide him, as Agnes Keith had recently died. Meanwhile, James VI tried to forget the absence of his best friend.

The King had plenty to distract him, as in the summer of 1589 he celebrated his own marriage – by proxy, as his bride, Anne of Denmark, had not been able to travel to Scotland. The religious and political situation on the European continent was one that James VI kept a close eye on: the actions of powerful Catholic Spain of course; while in France, King Henri III, the brother-in-law of Mary, Queen of Scots, was suddenly and brutally assassinated. Protestant Denmark, meanwhile, was entering a period of relative stability after the succession of Christian IV. James VI, looking for a high-born Protestant wife, was betrothed to Christian's sister, the 14-year-old Anne.

Meanwhile, in the north of Scotland, the third marriage that affected Jean took place in late 1589. After his marriage and before his denouncement by Elizabeth of England, Lord Huntly had found time to send Jean's brother Patrick to intervene in the feud between Caithness and Sutherland. Patrick had actually arrived just as Alexander was setting out at the head of an army, but managed to talk his brother-in-law into arranging another meeting with Wicked Earl George instead.[49] Jean's family was enjoying the peace that had followed that meeting, but it was clearly a shaky peace that would not last, and the House of Sutherland was not resting in the promotion of their interests. Uisdean Mackay was still supporting Alexander and staying at Dunrobin Castle, and was being encouraged to cut even more of his ties to Caithness. Uisdean had been married to Elizabeth Sinclair, the aunt of Wicked Earl George, since he was a young man. The marriage had been arranged by old Caithness in much the same way that Alexander had once been betrothed to Elizabeth's sister Barbara, and now Alexander encouraged his new ally to make a break with his wife. Conveniently, Uisdean's wife Elizabeth was found to have been committing adultery with a man named as Neill-Mack-ean-Mack-William, a relative of Uisdean's, and Uisdean used this as his reason to 'put away and repudiate his wife'.[50] Now, Alexander and Jean wanted to help Uisdean to contract a new marriage, one that would tie the Mackays to the Sutherlands. Startlingly, Uisdean was engaged to be married to Jean's eldest daughter, Jane.

Jane was 15 years old, while Uisdean was 28.[51] For Uisdean, the benefits were clear: Alexander agreed to ratify various legal titles to guarantee Uisdean the Mackay lands,[52] he was uniting with the House of Sutherland and, as his new son-in-law, he would gain Alexander's almost guaranteed protection. The Mackay clan history says that Uisdean found the proposal "fascinating, and even irresistible".[53] Uisdean was also gaining financially: when he had made feudal submission to Alexander as his superior at the end of the previous year and come over to the Gordon Sutherland side, Uisdean had acknowledged that he owed Alexander money from things like rent in Strathnaver: back payments were calculated at around £50,000

Scots.[54] Alexander agreed to write this off if the marriage went ahead, and Jane, as was customary, would also bring a dowry to her marriage. For Jean and Alexander, the benefits must also have seemed considerable: the House of Sutherland could not defeat Caithness when Caithness was allied with Mackay, and would even struggle to defeat the strong Mackay clan if they chose to stand alone or unite with other Gaels. They might be in the ascendant over Wicked Earl George right now, but as Jean's nephew's situation showed, Gordon power was not unassailable. By formally uniting the House of Sutherland and the Mackays through marriage, particularly when Uisdean (despite his age) had acknowledged that he was the junior partner in the marriage because he was marrying his superior's daughter, Jean and Alexander were aiming for control over the north of Scotland. Personally, Jean was not sending her daughter away to the north on her own: Uisdean, brought up in Castle Girnigoe, had no established Mackay stronghold of his own,[55] and he and Jane would be making their home at Dunrobin, where Jean and Alexander could keep an eye on things. Castle life meant that men and women lived fairly separately, so Jean would keep her daughter safe with her. Even for Jane, there were visible benefits: she would not inherit the Earldom of Sutherland as that would pass to her younger brother John, but with this marriage she would have high status as the wife of the Chief of Mackay, a major landowner with numbers of families loyal to them. Her daily status at Dunrobin would instantly have changed, as people had to treat her with more respect because of this. Just as Jean had gained land, property and independence as Countess of Bothwell – despite the obvious drawbacks of actually being married to Bothwell – so Jean could encourage her daughter to look on the positive side. Uisdean was apparently also an attractive man: strong and dark and powerful. However, surely Jean must have felt at least some small qualm at marrying off her eldest daughter to a man known as 'Dark Uisdean of the Battleaxe', a man whose formative years had been spent under the guidance of old Caithness as the friend and childhood companion of 'Wicked Earl George' and 'mad Wizard Earl Francis'. Uisdean was a man who Jane's father

---

and uncles had spent several years fighting on the battlefield, who was just divorced, who was a different religion – since the Mackay clan was nominally Protestant – and who, importantly, was a Gael and a clansman: someone who the Earls saw as being very different to themselves, lower in social status, almost a race apart.[56]

Jean's son said the best way to bring up children was "in obedience, yet without too much austeritie" – a comment on Jean's approach? He argued that daughters should have their marriages organised or they will marry themselves and organise it their way, and added that they should be married to "men of lower degree than [their parents] so that they and their issue will follow you and your house" – the practice Jean seemed to be following.[57] Jean's early romance with Alex Ogilvie had not brought her happiness but instead years of pain, and the notoriety of her unhappy marriage to Bothwell, experiences that years of contented marriage to Alexander did not wipe out. When Jean organised her daughters' marriages she was not thinking of making them love-matches as she had missed out on hers, but instead of what she thought would be best for them and their family, drawing on her own experiences.

There do not seem to have ever been any other marriages proposed for Jane – there were no childhood betrothals or promises as there had been for her younger sister Mary. Jean and Alexander would have always wanted their daughter to marry well, by marrying someone who would be useful to the family and able to keep her in the style to which she was accustomed. Given Uisdean's very recent change of sides, and previous marriage, his arrival as a potential suitor seems to have been a quick decision. Who else could have been considered as a potential match for Jane? One of her Gordon cousins from Aberdeenshire would probably have been thought too close a relationship, while other cadet Gordon families were not high enough status to marry an earl's daughter. Status would also have been a problem for the eligibility of other local landowners in the north of Scotland. Loyalty to the Sutherland Gordons was also an issue. Not just the clans but also some local lairds still saw the Sutherlands as Gordon Aberdeenshire incomers: Alexander and

Jean may also have taken fright as their younger daughter Mary's planned marriage seemed to be faltering. The father of her promised match, Ross of Balnagowan, unhappy at the power Alexander had gained over him, had been supporting Wicked Earl George, and Balnagowan and Alexander were currently going through the courts to resolve this.[58] Later Gordon sources do their best to show Jean and Alexander's superiority over Caithness as an inevitable victory, but the reality is that the tensions and battles would not have lasted so long if both sides had not been fairly evenly matched. Jean and Alexander could not know what the outcome would be. Since there were no other contenders likely for Jane's hand, as allegiances still shifted around in James VI's court as it continued to adjust to the king's newfound and growing hold on power, Alexander and Jean may have decided that the Mackay marriage was one that had the advantage of being able to be settled immediately, without the problems of a long engagement. Since Jane had probably not had any serious contenders in mind – unlike when Jean was a girl and had met Alex Ogilvie – that made adjusting to the marriage to Uisdean easier to transition into. Jean's eldest daughter Jane, 'a lady of excellent beauty and comeliness, witty . . . with sundry good qualities both of mind and body'[59] was married to Uisdean Mackay in December 1589.

There was one final reason why Jean encouraged her daughter's wedding to Uisdean, the virile Chief of Mackay, and encouraged the couple to make their home at Dunrobin Castle. In a time and place where a strong male head of household was essential for security, Jean's husband Alexander was getting sick.

CHAPTER FOURTEEN

Jean's Two Nephews: 1589/90–1594

PART I: A GRANDSON AND A NEPHEW

Jean's husband Alexander is sometimes described as being a physically weak man.[1] His actions in the battlefield against Wicked Earl George belie this, but from about 1589 his health does seem to have deteriorated and become a cause for concern. An undated portrait of Alexander shows a man in around his thirties, richly dressed, a nobleman with a carefully tended goatee, a long falling ruff trimmed with detailed lace covering his neck and shoulders, white lace at his sleeves and a ring in his ear – but also wearing armour: what looks like a shiny metal breastplate and coverings for his shoulders and arms.[2] The mix between courtly fashion and armour shows how Alexander lived his life – and by presenting it in his portrait, how he wished to be remembered.

Jean was looking after her husband as his health deteriorated, and also helping her daughter Jane through the early years of her marriage – always with an eye to the Gordon future. Family concerns were national concerns: two of Jean's nephews, her brother's son Lord Huntly and her ex-husband's nephew Francis, the Mad Wizard Earl of Bothwell, battled for the attention of James VI and the growth of their own personal power. These battles affected Jean directly – both through the Mad Wizard Earl Francis' continuing links with his half-brother the Wicked Earl George in Caithness, and on the battlefield at Glenlivet. Jean and her family were intimately involved in the blood feud between the Gordons and the Bonnie Earl of Moray which widened out into a much larger conflict, and in the continuing struggle between Catholic and Protestant.

Although there was officially a truce between the noble houses of Caithness and Sutherland, the people of those two areas, as the story of the horses' tails shows, were all invested in the quarrel between their two Earls, and violence and reprisals could not be so easily stopped now that they had started. The people in both counties had suffered heavily as Alexander and Wicked Earl George had run their raiding parties over their land, and 'there remained still in the hearts of the inhabitants of these parts and countries, some hidden sparks of rancour, which did again burst out into a flame'.[3] Horses and cattle were stolen and taken away from both sides, while individuals took out their frustrations on people they had been taught to see as their enemies. Wicked Earl George and Alexander wrote to each other, sending overtly friendly, complimentary messages to try to keep the peace and figure out a way to work together and stop their followers from killing each other. However, when he did not receive the response he hoped for, Wicked Earl George once again assembled a force to enter Sutherland, in October 1590.[4] There was a problem for the Sutherland troops: Alexander was sick, and so they had no head to guide them, 'which made them fall at variance'.[5] Alexander's army was made up of different families, including Gordons and Murrays. Even though the Gordons certainly did not consider themselves a clan in the way that the Mackays did, they still operated in much the same way, with a strong sense of family feeling and pride. The different families fought alongside each other, but as distinct units, and without Alexander to lead them they descended into arguments about who should take precedence. 'A multitude of commanders and commandments is a plague to all good order, and specially to military discipline, which consisteth only in authority and order,' said the Gordon chronicler, with the benefit of hindsight.[6] The Murrays wanted to be at the front, arguing that was their traditional spot, given to them because of their good service to the House of Sutherland, while the Gordons disagreed. Taking the huff, the Murrays removed themselves completely from the fray, and watched proceedings from a standpoint on a nearby hill. The Gordons, led by the Gordons of Golspitour, saw the Caithness men driving a huge herd of cattle before them as they made their way northwards, decided, 'more rashly than wisely', to fight on.[7] They were at Clyne, a bad place for a battle, with the sun and wind against them, and outnumbered 12 to one, but they engaged the Caithness men 'with much courage and variety of fortune', fighting until nightfall. The Sutherland men chased Wicked Earl George's archers – which they counted at around 1500 men – back three times but the archers' commander rallied them and arrows, and some gunshot, fell like hail all around. There was almost equal slaughter on both sides, but at nightfall the Caithness men made the decision to withdraw, leaving behind the cattle.[8] Wicked Earl George went back to Caithness, but when he got home he found that Uisdean's Mackay troops had taken advantage of his absence to 'ravage' the area – taking much booty.[9] Uisdean, used to command, did not need to wait for Alexander to tell him what to do. The new alliance between Uisdean Mackay and Alexander of Sutherland, cemented by Uisdean's marriage to Jean's daughter Jane, meant that Wicked Earl George was in the uncomfortable position of having enemies on two borders of his land: if he went one way to attack one of his enemies, the other could take advantage to come in from the opposite direction. Wicked Earl George had not only lost the cattle he had tried to drive home from Sutherland, but also much of the goods he had thought would be safe at home. At a time of scarcity, these losses were important.

At Dunrobin, Jean's daughter Jane had become pregnant soon after her marriage. Jean's eldest son John was still only in his mid-teens, and with Alexander sick and unable to protect them, it was important that Jean continued to maintain good relations with her son-in-law Uisdean Mackay. There were many reasons for Jean to ensure that Uisdean's wife, her daughter, had the best care as Jane gave birth to the baby who they hoped would become Uisdean's heir.

Jane, aged 17, gave birth to her first child in February 1591. It was a healthy boy, strong and dark like his father, and he was named Donald. Jean was a grandmother for the first time. Jane recovered at Dunrobin with her mother, and Donald was soon sent to be fostered with the loyal Gordons of Golspitour, part of the same family that had fostered Jean's own sons. Like her mother, there was little question of Jane breastfeeding: the situation among high-ranking clanswomen was not significantly different to that of noblewomen, in that they were used to seeing their children fed by wet-nurses and raised by extended family. There was considerable overlap in how the clans and nobles behaved, especially in their loyalty to family, though the cultural and, particularly, legal differences were becoming more pronounced. Uisdean Mackay had already been so well integrated with the noble families of the north that his lifestyle, while still retaining distinctive cultural clan attributes such as his love of bagpipe music, was not noticeably different from that of the Earls of Caithness and Sutherland. Women in early modern Scotland retained their surnames so Jane was still completely a Gordon, and Uisdean made no attempt to have his son fostered with a Mackay family, so Donald was clearly to be brought up among Gordons. The fostering system was an important way of promoting friendship in the Highlands, and it was acknowledged that bonds between children and foster-parents could be very strong, overriding blood ties: "[fostering] is accompted the strictest poynt of amitie and freindship among all the Hielanders of the kingdome of Scotland, [children] preferring oftentymes their fosters and foster-brethren vnto their parents and neirest kindred; they will follow and depend vpon them, before their naturall lords and masters".[10] Despite Alexander's illness, the Gordons were still the Mackays' legal superiors and Uisdean still a junior partner. Jean and Alexander were still very much in control.

The family that Jean's grandson baby Donald was placed with were the Gordons of Golspitour. Part of the extended family of John Gordon of Drummoy, they were the trusted retainers of the Sutherland Earls, the same family who had fostered Jean and Alexander's own children, and who had helped Alexander numerous times, including his escape from the old Earl of Caithness. Baby

Donald was being placed with a family that was rooted in Gordon tradition – rather than a family that would have emphasised his Mackay heritage.

In addition to their house at Golspitour near Dunrobin Castle, one child of the Gordons of Drummoy had also bought more property in Embo in the late 1580s, and his family were now often known as the Gordons of Embo. Each of the children of John of Drummoy, in fact, had ended up owning parcels of land. The Gordon chronicler said that although they had been born to 'small means', 'yet have they so faithfully and truly behaved themselves in serving their masters, the Earls of Sutherland, that by their liberality, connivance, and suffrance of their masters, together with their own industry, they have purchased to themselves reasonable means'.[11] Donald was to grow up alongside Young Golspitour (otherwise known as John Gordon of Embo the younger), who became not only his ally and foster-brother but his best friend.[12]

Wicked Earl George had argued desperately that Uisdean's first marriage was still valid, but the birth of Donald effectively closed that argument. Uisdean's first wife Elizabeth Sinclair, Wicked Earl George's aunt, was discarded, along with her children. The Sinclairs no longer had any claim over any of the Clan Mackay titles or property; Jean's new grandson Donald would get it all. Alexander and Jean told Wicked Earl George that any complaint on behalf of his aunt would have to go through the courts and legal proceedings.[13] Wicked Earl George knew how experienced the Sutherlands had become at pursuing legal rights through the courts – and how they continued to pursue claims against Ross of Balnagowan and broker deals that benefitted their supporters such as the Gordons of Golspitour.[14] Faced as well with constant attacks from Uisdean, Wicked Earl George capitulated and tried, once again, to broker a new peace between Caithness and Sutherland.

Deals between Caithness and Sutherland were, as was now usual, overseen by Jean's brother Patrick, and her nephew Lord Huntly – but Lord Huntly was less interested in the Sutherland Gordon affairs as his time was taken up more and more by his own intrigues. Lord

Huntly Castle, Aberdeenshire. Jean's childhood home was
substantially remodelled in her lifetime by her nephew.
Photo by Jennifer Morag Henderson

Findlater castle, near Portsoy, Banff. The former Ogilvie stronghold was held by Jean's brother against Mary, Queen of Scots.
Photo by Jennifer Morag Henderson.

The marriage miniatures of Lady Jean Gordon, Countess of Bothwell
and James Hepburn, 4th Earl of Bothwell.
Scottish National Portrait Gallery.

The ORKNEY Portrait
of
MARY QUEEN of SCOTS

Portrait of Mary, Queen of Scots, from Dunrobin Castle.
This painting is known as the 'Orkney portrait': several versions of this
image exist, which appear to be based on an earlier miniature.
Sutherland Dunrobin Castle Trust.

Stained glass window showing preacher John Knox.
From the John Knox House in Edinburgh.

Alexander Gordon, 12th Earl of Sutherland: Jean's second husband.
Sutherland Dunrobin Castle Trust.

Spynie Palace, near Elgin. Bothwell's childhood home, to which he later
fled after his defeat at Carberry. Also the site of imprisonment for Jean's
brother-in-law the Master of Forbes, and the English spy Rokesby.
Photo by Jennifer Morag Henderson.

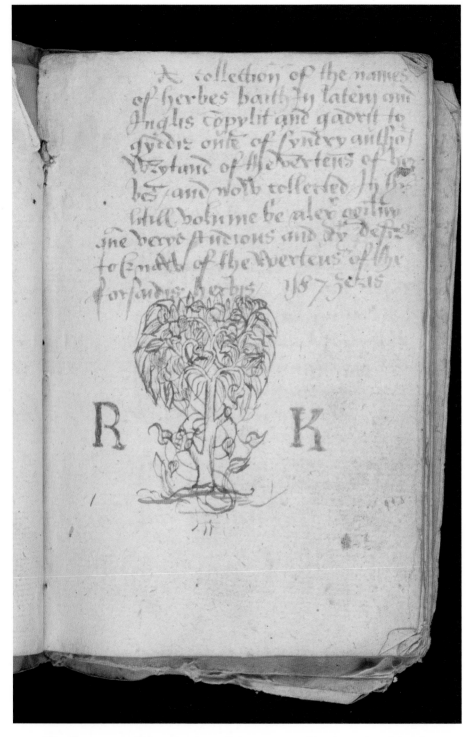

The first page of 'A collection of the names of herbes…' written by Alex Ogilvie, dated 1587. The initials 'R' and 'K' have been added in different ink. National Library of Scotland / Altyre Estates.

Sinclair-Girnigoe Castle, the home of the Earls of Caithness. The impressive ruin shows the remains of the new castle remodelled by Wicked Earl George. Photo by Jennifer Morag Henderson.

Sir Alexander Gordon, Knight of Navidale. Jean's youngest son. Painting attributed to Adam de Colone, 1631. Sutherland Dunrobin Castle Trust.

Sir Robert Gordon, the Tutor of Sutherland, c1621. Jean's middle son, the family historian. Sutherland Dunrobin Castle Trust.

Letter from Jean Gordon to her son Robert, discussing servants, Caithness and estate business. 'Loving son, I have written these few lines…' Showing her handwriting and spelling in the old Scots style. National Library of Scotland / Altyre Estates.

Lady Jean Gordon, Countess of Sutherland. Attributed to George Jameson,
c1620. Sutherland Dunrobin Castle Trust.

Mackay's regiment, landing on the continent, 1630. The regiment of Jean's grandson, Donald Mackay, shown wearing their distinctive plaids. Image based on an old German print.

The author at the romantic ruin of Alex Ogilvie's Boyne Castle. Photo by Andrew Thomson.

Huntly had been in high favour with King James VI just before Jane's marriage to Uisdean, but the discovery of his Catholic-supporting letters to Spain had sent him away from the court and back to the north-east. Here, Lord Huntly and his hard-working wife Henrietta were doing their best to consolidate their power, particularly against the Bonnie Earl of Moray. The feud between Lord Huntly and the Bonnie Earl intensified when James VI unexpectedly left Scotland.

After James VI's bride, Anne of Denmark, had her journey to Scotland interrupted by bad weather, the couple had been married by proxy. Anne was storm-bound in Norway. In late 1589, James VI decided to embark on a rash and uncharacteristically romantic journey out of his kingdom to collect his bride, sailing from Leith with 300 men. It was difficult for a king to leave his country, but although James VI was only supposed to be away for 20 days, he actually journeyed back to Anne's native Denmark after their wedding ceremony and only finally returned to Scotland in May 1590. It speaks volumes for James VI's burgeoning authority – and the importance of securing the succession – that he felt confident enough to go away. In the meantime, James VI left a council of Regency in charge of Scotland.[15] Notable among the lords of this Regency were two rather unlikely suspects: Ludovick Stewart, the son of James VI's favourite Esmé and inheritor of the title of 2nd Duke of Lennox, was left as official governor of the kingdom despite being only 15 years old; while Francis Stewart, the Mad Earl of Bothwell, was Ludovick's vice-president.[16]

Francis Stewart was the son of Janet Hepburn (Bothwell's sister) and Lord John (half-brother of Mary, Queen of Scots). Jean would have known Francis first when he was a baby, when she was married to Bothwell and he was her nephew; and then again as a young man, when he lived with his mother Janet and Janet's second husband John the Stout in Caithness. Sometimes, people who like to believe that Mary, Queen of Scots and Bothwell were truly in love try to imagine what would have happened if that couple had managed to hold onto power in Scotland, and if Mary, Queen of Scots had not miscarried Bothwell's children. Francis, the offspring of a Hepburn and a royal Stewart, might be a cautionary tale for these romantics.

His time in the Far North in the dysfunctional household of Old Caithness, with his stepfather John the Stout imprisoned in the basement and the company of the young Wicked Earl George and Dark Uisdean of the Battleaxe, had set him up nicely for a latter career where Francis himself was known as both 'the Mad Earl' and 'the Wizard Earl'. By the 1590s, this intelligent but wayward young man had long ago left his mother's house, graduated from St Andrews University and inherited the Earldom of Bothwell, though not without some manoeuvring because of his uncle's reputation. He was married, though one week after his marriage he had been forbidden to go within 20 miles of his new wife, 'by reason of his youngness.'[17] Leaving his wife behind, Francis travelled through England, where his lows and highs included being arrested, and spending time at the court of Elizabeth of England. Elizabeth thought Francis might have potential. Francis then continued his lifelong love of learning by going to the continent and matriculating at Angers University in France. He became fluent in several languages,[18] and during his time abroad also explored his religious beliefs, though he remained a Protestant. After returning to Scotland, he was trusted by James VI, but tried to play the other side as well, telling everyone what they wanted to hear.

In a time when violence was more common than now, Francis Stewart, Earl of Bothwell still managed to gain a reputation for inconsistent wildness, and his response to most things was to use a peculiarly smart and directed nasty violence. He was not a thug but an intelligent man, with something of the direct, yet romantic attitude of his uncle, added to the romantic and intelligent Stewart heritage, and mixed with his own peculiar streak of difference. He was certainly as much of a loose cannon as his uncle had been, taking his own erratic route at an angle through the following years. He has been described as being worth three of any other Scottish noblemen of the time – for both wickedness and valour.[19] He remodelled Jean's old home of Crichton Castle, and his schizophrenic personality still comes through vividly in the ruins of that castle today, almost obliterating the older memories of Jean and his uncle's time there. He chose to remodel the building after some of the effects that he had seen on the continent, and oversaw the creation of a castle where, on the outside, "menacing, wide-mouthed gunholes appear alongside handsome corbelled bartizans".[20] The castle was rebuilt with defence in mind, but inside elaborate ornamentation took over, and the most striking feature is the façade of the courtyard, a huge wall covered in diamond-faceted detail that looms over you as you stand in the centre of the ruin; the vivid imprint of disturbing personality.

Francis created his own group of friends, alongside his colourfully named half-brother Hercules Stewart,[21] and had a growing, though inconstant, friendship with Jean's nephew, Lord Huntly. Lord Huntly had a huge following in the north of Scotland, and Francis, despite his errant personality, commanded a similarly large base of support in the Borders, making their friendship an echo of the Highland-Border alliance once promoted by Jean and Bothwell's marriage. Setting the poacher as gamekeeper and leaving Francis as one of the people in charge of Scotland when James VI went to collect Anne of Denmark was surprisingly successful, and James VI was able to come back and show his new bride a kingdom no more unsettled than when he left, where the English even remarked that the Border was more peaceful than it had been for years.[22] Elizabeth of England was so pleased that she not only forgave Francis for what she had previously seen as his part in a Catholic Spanish plot that threatened her, but even agreed to be godmother to his daughter.[23] This shows, however, that his position in charge of Scotland had certainly not mellowed Francis' ambition. During his time in charge of Scotland, Francis' meddling had begun to open up new sources of future problems, not just around what James VI saw as the threatening developing friendship between Francis and Esmé's son Ludovick – two Stewarts of royal blood with strong claims to the throne – but also, pertinently for Jean in the north, in his involvement in the worsening feud between Lord Huntly and the Bonnie Earl of Moray (another Stewart) – and around James VI's growing fascination with witchcraft.[24]

During his time in Denmark, James VI developed a growing interest in witchcraft and demonology.[25] Surrounded by noblemen with shifting allegiances, and fearful for his own personal safety, James VI's obsession with unseen forces is understandable. Living in a changing religious situation where the relationship of God and the Devil to man was constantly questioned, James VI was not the only one to have an interest in magic, and Francis Stewart chose to explore what benefits sorcery might be able to bring him, earning his other nickname of 'the Wizard Earl'. A kingdom without a king was a vulnerable place, and while James VI was in Denmark, it seems that some witches tried to take advantage of the situation: at North Berwick, a cat, baptised in the name of Satan, was cast into the sea with the aim of raising storms which would smash into splinters the ship King James VI and his new bride were travelling home on. Along with the reluctant cat, which tried to swim ashore, the witches also threw into the water dead body parts. Other rituals followed, involving roasted toad, and wax images which were to be dropped in fire, accompanied by dancing a reel in a churchyard in the dead of night.[26]

The women who carried out this plot were captured and later put on trial. In speaking to one of them, James VI believed that she was able to tell him private things that he had said to his new bride Anne of Denmark on their wedding night, things that no one else should have been able to discover.[27] James VI's belief in the power of witchcraft was confirmed, and he saw the women on trial as being genuine threats to his life. The witches then went on to say that the instigator behind their attempt to endanger the king's life, the prime motivator behind their Satanic conspiracy, was Francis, Earl of Bothwell.

For Francis and his peers, for people like Jean and her family, the Reformation meant a lot of different things: a change in religious worship and belief, but also the opening up of land ownership as areas were transferred from the church's control, the transfer of riches, and possibilities for advancement – and even a fundamental questioning of things previously known and believed: if God was not the way the Church had told them, what was the Devil? If God was walking among them, if their relationship to God was the personal, direct relationship of private Protestant prayer in their own language, rather than through the intermediary of a priest and the Latin language, then their relationship to the Devil also changed: the Devil too could speak and be spoken to directly. Belief in God meant a corresponding strong belief in the Devil and his works. The accusations against Francis were taken very seriously by James VI, and, despite denying everything, Francis was imprisoned in Edinburgh Castle.

Francis' time in jail did not last long, however, as he persuaded the night-watchman to help him escape two months later. He had too many supporters for James VI to be able to pursue him successfully, but not enough support to cause too much trouble.[28] James VI ordered Francis to be captured, but Francis rode around Edinburgh quite openly and nothing was done. No one had enough power to take control, and the whole situation seemed to be finely balanced yet unable to move in any direction. After a while, Francis went to the Borders – James VI tried to find him there, but Francis kept on the move. His wife was warded in Aberdeen, and Francis too headed north – not to his wife, though, but to a further-away and much safer sanctuary: he went to the Far North, where the Rosses of Balnagowan (the family Jean and Alexander had tried to secure a marriage alliance for their youngest daughter Mary with) once again ferried him over Inverness, Cromarty and Dornoch firths to the home of his half-brother, Wicked Earl George in Caithness, where he lay low for a while.[29] Wicked Earl George remained close to Francis, naming one of his sons after him.[30]

Francis had decided that the Protestant side of the debate in Scotland was the one most likely to win, and had allied himself with that, and with Protestant England – but not so long ago he had been friends with Jean's nephew Lord Huntly and involved in writing to the Spanish. Francis still got letters from Spain, but he now showed them to James VI, saying that he was really a double agent, who could bring in useful Spanish information while, of course, remaining on the Protestant side.[31] Lord Huntly, whose Catholicism was committed, had an uneasy relationship with Francis, and James VI now started to use these two nephews of Jean to balance each other.

At least a balanced situation, even if it was a stalemate, was a peaceful situation. But Francis' response was to increase his alliance with Ludovick, Duke of Lennox and with the Bonnie Earl of Moray, two men who were Stewarts by birth, and so his distant relations. The Bonnie Earl of Moray was still the implacable enemy of Lord Huntly, and, despite the efforts Francis had made to bring the two men together when James VI was away, the Huntly-Moray blood feud was getting worse.

PART 2: ANOTHER NEPHEW AND GLENLIVET

Since Lord Huntly had been banished to the north, he had been building castles and trying to consolidate his powerbase, splitting clan alliances and weakening the power of others, all with the ultimate goal of getting rid of the Bonnie Earl of Moray. The Bonnie Earl was not doing well, with the death of his father robbing him of his best advisor, and the death of his wife in childbirth taking from him the legitimation of much of his power and wealth. The Bonnie Earl decided to throw in his lot completely with Francis. Still trying to maintain that delicate balance of the scales of power in Scotland, James VI decided to rehabilitate his old friend Lord Huntly, and ask him to find and apprehend the other two men. Lord Huntly interpreted this as carte blanche to do whatever was needed to get rid of the Bonnie Earl of Moray.

Francis and Lord Huntly were very different men, but they both became gripped by obsession: they both came from families which were of the first importance, yet not quite as important as they had once been; and they were both powerful, but not quite as powerful as they wanted to be. Lord Huntly had an equally high opinion of himself and his noble background, and as vivid a memory as Francis of what his family had once been capable of, but, like Francis, he could not quite get the power he wanted, and Lord Huntly's hatred coalesced around the Bonnie Earl of Moray. Both men were continuing the power battles of their elders; Francis was the product of his upbringing, the result of his mother Janet's stories about his father, his uncle, and his godmother Mary, Queen of Scots; Lord Huntly was the product of the Gordon siblings: his father George and his aunt Jean, and his other Gordon uncles and their stories of Gordon power. The battles that Jean was fighting; her marriage to Bothwell; the downfall of Mary, Queen of Scots; the arguments over religion that her generation started, were still being played out through both her nephews, Lord Huntly and Francis.

In 1592 the Huntly-Moray feud came to an apogee. An earlier incident in 1591 at the Bonnie Earl's stronghold of Darnaway Castle in Moray had seen Lord Huntly ride up with a group of armed men and surround the building. Darnaway was an impregnable stronghold, so the Bonnie Earl sat tight until Lord Huntly had to give up and leave, but lives were lost and tensions were high. Learning that the Bonnie Earl would be staying at his mother's house of Donnibristle in Dalgety Bay in Fife, Lord Huntly decided to finish what he had started. Taking with him around 60–80 men, Lord Huntly rode to Donnibristle in the fast-fading February light. His men fanned out, surrounding the building, and shouted for the Bonnie Earl to come out. As shots were fired – both from inside and outside the building – Lord Huntly's men started to gather together the brushwood that had been stacked for winter fuel, and lay the flammable material around the house. This time they were outside a large country house, rather than a well-built castle, and it was soon alight. Inside, the Bonnie Earl oversaw the evacuation of his family and servants, but would not give himself up: it was clear from the responses outside that there would be no mercy for him if he did so. He waited until the increasing darkness of evening gave him at least a chance of escape, but as he made his way out he was so badly burnt that he could no longer hold a weapon to defend himself. He managed to escape the building, but a ribbon on his steel helmet was set alight as he ran, and acted as a beacon, alerting Lord Huntly and his followers to his position. The Bonnie Earl was shot at, and bullets hit his body. He was chased and caught, then the Gordon men hamstrung him, cutting the Bonnie Earl's legs so he couldn't run. Lord Huntly stood to the side, having given the order to kill, but Huntly's men, unhappy to be implicated alone in the killing, made Lord Huntly step forward – and deliberately slash the Bonnie Earl's face twice across. A stab wound to the heart was the final deathblow. The Bonnie Earl's final words were supposedly addressed to Lord Huntly: 'You have ruined a better face than your own.'[32]

The Earl of Moray was only 24 years old, still that Bonnie Young Man, and his death became notorious. His family, particularly his redoubtable mother,[33] determined that they would seek justice, and that the extent of his injuries would be made abundantly clear to as many people in Scotland as possible. In life, the Bonnie Earl had been little more than a silly and good-looking young man. In death, he became many other things: he was a Protestant martyr killed by the Catholic Lord Huntly; he was the successor to the beloved Regent Moray, and parallels were drawn between the assassination of the two Earls of Moray. The feud between the House of Moray and the House of Huntly was extrapolated backwards in time, and people talked of Jean's brother's attitude, of Jean's father's attitude, of Corrichie... The whole of Edinburgh, the whole of Scotland, was talking about the murder of the Bonnie Earl of Moray. Moray's mother took his body to Edinburgh with the intention of parading it through the street: if someone was murdered there was a belief that their wounds would bleed when the corpse was in front of the murderer, and the Bonnie Earl's mother wanted to challenge the people she saw as responsible. Stopped from showing the body publicly, the Bonnie Earl's family and friends still managed to tell as many people as possible as lurid tales as they could of the Donnibristle night. The Bonnie Earl's mother had her son's body embalmed and laid on display in Leith. She then took the bloody shirt her son had been wearing and fashioned it into a banner, and walked down Edinburgh High Street carrying it. Ultra-Protestants took advantage of the situation to push for the Catholic Lord Huntly to be punished. Meanwhile, the Bonnie Earl's mother commissioned a macabre death portrait, in life-size. The massive picture shows the pale dead body of the Bonnie Earl, with bullet wounds and knife wounds, starkly painted in still-bleeding red. As her son's body was still refused entry to Edinburgh, the Bonnie Earl's mother wrapped the painting in cloth and took it to James VI to demand justice. James VI refused to look at it. Lord Huntly was to be brought to trial in March, and James hoped for a speedy resolution, but it was not to be. Jean's nephew was allowed to go north again, but the Bonnie Earl's supporters refused to let his embalmed body be buried until justice was served. It was to lie unburied for several years more. The Bonnie Earl's mother died before her son was buried, as a result, her supporters said, from the smoke inhalation she had suffered as Donnibristle House had burnt.[34]

Rumours and counter-rumours were flying around Edinburgh, as the citizens tried to work out which side was which. Lord Huntly and the Bonnie Earl were enemies. James VI still officially supported Lord Huntly, but the Bonnie Earl was on the side of Francis, whose star was rising at court. However, the slur of witchcraft would not leave Francis, and he started to cause more trouble for James VI again. As usual, other families were drawn into the argument: Francis' Bordermen were as loyal and factious as the clans in the north; the Forbes enjoyed their traditional enmity with Lord Huntly by taking the banner fashioned out of the Bonnie Earl's bloody shirt into battle; and the coincidentally timed death of Moray supporter the Thane of Cawdor continues to be discussed as something of a mystery even today.[35] The soon-to-be well-known Scottish folk song, the "Ballad of the Bonny Earl of Moray" presents the conflict in black and white, showing Lord Huntly as having directly disobeyed the King's order and killing the Bonnie Earl – "Ye Highlands and ye Lowlands / O whare hae ye been? / They hae slain the Earl o' Moray / And hae lain him on the green / Now woe be to thee Huntly! / And wherefore did ye sae? / I bade ye bring him wi' you / And forbade you him to slay . . ."[36] – but the reality was more complicated. James VI could not publicly support Lord Huntly's actions, but he was still his friend. In fact, they wrote to each daily throughout the summer of 1592, and on into 1593.[37] Jean's nephew was once again banished to the north – but his wife Henrietta remained at court, becoming a confidant of Queen Anne. Francis, after some scuffling of a more or less serious nature, was no more popular – and now facing renewed accusations of involvement in witchcraft.

There were an enormous amount of things going on at the one time, and the different 'sides' were not really united. James VI's great strength was in learning how to balance everything so that his kingdom always stayed mostly stable. Threats came in, however, not just from within the Scottish nobility and their ongoing feuds, but also from outwith the kingdom. As Francis' offer to be a double agent shows, Spain was still very interested in the situation in Scotland, and Spanish agents and the Jesuits, including Jean's brother James, continued to see Lord Huntly as a possible way in to Scottish politics. Elizabeth of England intercepted several letters which were destined for the king of Spain. Among them were eight clean and blank sheets of paper, with nothing on them but the signatures of Lord Huntly, of Jean's brother Patrick, and other, Catholic-supporting noblemen.[38] Seals were enclosed with the signed pieces of paper, ready to be appended once something was written. It was not clear who the letters were for, but they appeared destined for someone of high rank. The messenger carrying the letters at first insisted they were to be used as letters of credit on the continent, but soon the information was extracted that it was all part of a plot to enable Spanish troops to land in Scotland and turn Britain Catholic again.[39] Jean's Jesuit brother Father James Gordon was named as one of the principal movers in the plot. Lord Huntly was soon telling James VI that Father James the Jesuit had told him the letters were to forward to his superiors if he was expelled from Scotland – or perhaps something to do with paying off Jesuit debts.[40] Father James had left Scotland in 1589, feeling the atmosphere was too anti-Catholic, but had returned again by 1592.[41] James VI had applied his principle of constant negotiation when faced with Father James before, and had continued to use the Catholic party to balance out the views of the stricter Protestants around him, but by the end of 1593 it was clear that stronger measures would have to be taken, and, in the fallout from the Spanish Blanks affair, and under pressure from England, a decree was issued in November 1593 saying that James VI was happy to pardon everyone involved in the Spanish Blanks affair, if they would renounce their faith and show their loyalty. If they would not, they should leave Scotland.[42]

Jean's nephew Lord Huntly, Jean's brother and Lord Huntly's advisor Patrick, and Jean and her family themselves were all Catholics. This decree directly affected Jean: it was interpreted as all Catholics being told to give up their religion or leave the country. However, from where Jean was sitting, it certainly didn't look like James VI had the power to enforce this. She and her husband Alexander had the Far North under control, and her nephew Lord Huntly had Aberdeenshire – and Moray – pretty much under control as well. Instead of doing as they were told, Jean and the Gordons settled in for a fight. Jean's brother James the Jesuit was briefly heard of in Rome, but back in Scotland once more by summer 1594.[43]

1594 was a crucial year for one other reason: at the start of the year, James VI and Anne of Denmark had a son, Henry Frederick, an heir for the Scottish throne. A healthy male heir, a healthy king and queen, the possibility of more children in the future, a stable country – these were all the things the Stewart kings and Scotland had wanted for so long.

Francis was one of the noblemen who tried to work out what the new heir would mean and turn the situation to his advantage. He had been publicly tried in a show trial which he had helped to engineer, to be found officially not guilty of witchcraft, but his personal relations with James VI had continued to sour, especially after he attempted, once again, the tactic of kidnapping the king. With some support from Elizabeth of England, who now saw Francis as an important Protestant counterweight to the Catholic Lord Huntly, and who continued to hector James VI by letter to rule Scotland the way she wanted it to be ruled, Francis tried to use force to get back his power – but James VI had reached the end of the line, and wanted to be rid of the Wizard Earl. James VI sent a band of men to capture and subdue Francis, and, although Francis and his supporters were able to fight them off in this raid of Leith, Francis was unable to follow up his victory, and ended up fleeing south to the Borders and on to England. Here, Francis was approached by an unlikely friend. Even though Francis had openly supported Protestantism for some time now, Lord Huntly and his allies made an appeal to him: would Francis consider, for 25,000 crowns, switching sides and supporting the northern Catholic earls in their fight against James VI?[44] Francis, feeling desperate, accepted Lord Huntly's offer.

Even though he was in exile again, Francis could still command a huge following: he had left after victory in battle after all, it was only his inability to follow up military success that had stopped him, so Lord Huntly's motivation in asking him to join them may have been to increase his numbers. Lord Huntly knew he was going in to a fight where he was outnumbered. Francis had been friends with Lord Huntly before, and they were related by blood. However, it seems highly unlikely that Lord Huntly would have truly welcomed Francis, a man who had been his enemy, who had sided with the ultra-Protestants and who had been a supporter of the Bonnie Earl of Moray. In addition, Lord Huntly was still advised by Jean's brother Patrick, and by Jean and Alexander themselves: only very recently Francis had been in Caithness with the Gordon family enemy Wicked Earl George, and Jean personally had little reason to like her ex-husband's nephew. Was Lord Huntly playing a clever game? Lord Huntly, Jean and Patrick, after all, had so recently and cleverly used a combination of negotiation, legal steps and force to wipe out Clan Gunn and subdue both the Earl of Caithness and the Chief of Mackay. Francis was known to switch sides when it suited him, but perhaps Lord Huntly realised that James VI had been playing a balancing game and wanted to tip the scales once and for all: to find out what would happen if Francis was not constantly raised up as Lord Huntly was cast down. In the event, Francis' desperate acceptance of Lord Huntly's offer was the beginning of the end for him: his change of sides and renunciation of his religion for money was seen as unforgivably mercenary, and he was deserted by the kirk and by Elizabeth of England. Nor did he actually help Lord Huntly on the battlefield.[45]

The battlefield was where Lord Huntly was now heading. He and his family and supporters had ignored James VI's call for them to renounce their faith, and they were now declared traitors, whose estates were forfeit. James VI gave a commission to the Earl of Argyll to bring these rebels to heel. Even Henrietta, Lord Huntly's wife and the daughter of James VI's favourite Esmé, was finally dismissed from court.

Lord Huntly did do what he could to avoid a fight: he had been James VI's close friend, they had embraced and made up many times in the past. Adding credence to the idea that his approach to Francis was a ruse, Lord Huntly now explained to James VI that actually he had met with Francis in order to reconcile their differences over the death of the Bonnie Earl of Moray – and offering to hand over Francis to James VI so James could deal with him as he saw fit. The king answered sorrowfully that alliance with Francis was the one thing that he could not forgive Lord Huntly for – and added that Francis had already been in touch with a similar offer to hand over Lord Huntly.[46]

Where Lord Huntly did win against Francis was that his devotion to the Catholic faith was sincere. Father James had arrived in Scotland in July. He had considered landing at Jean's home of Dunrobin, but eventually made landfall at Aberdeen.[47] Once again, he was recognised as a Jesuit – this time by "a local invalid taking a constitutional" who saw him disembarking[48] – and Father James and his travelling companion were arrested, but the authorities in the north-east were too afraid of going against Lord Huntly to take further action, particularly when Lord Huntly showed up to meet his uncle with a train of 700 horsemen who menaced the town of Aberdeen with the threat of fire.[49] Father James and his companion were allowed to go free, and their possessions, including a large sum of money (10,000 gold crowns), were returned to them.[50] Lord Huntly welcomed his uncle (and his money) gladly.

The money that Father James brought with him was used to finance the resistance that Lord Huntly was building. Archibald Campbell, the 7th Earl of Argyll, now that he had his commission from James VI to go against the Catholics in the north, was gathering men together.

By October 1594, Argyll was on the march at the head of a force of six or seven thousand, made up of his own large and powerful clan house, Protestants and men who disliked the Gordons, and including the Campbell, Forbes, Stewart, Murray and Grant families, supplemented by the Clan Chattan confederation (which included Mackintosh and Macneils among others). As usual in Scotland, allegiances and motivations were mixed and changeable – 19-year-old Argyll was, if you remember, the son of Jean's cousin Agnes Keith and her second husband,[51] and, like his followers, Argyll would have known his intended foes personally. Battle was a more normal part of life than now, but never prepared for lightly: men knew what it was, though they sometimes looked to the positive side. Argyll's followers were 'a rabble of rascals', some of whom brought with them sacks for the booty they anticipated their victory would bring them.[52] Argyll also had a small number of Irish mercenaries. Jean's nephew Lord Huntly had spent the last few months trying to negotiate with his former friend James VI, trying to think of a way to avert open war – but now, he decided that "it would be more for [his] honour, in so just a cause, to die sword in hand, than to be murdered in their own houses".[53] Lord Huntly and his allies gathered together what men they could, but could only muster around about two thousand people, or between one-quarter and one-third of the king's forces ranged against him. The two armies met at Balrinnes in Glenlivet.

Lord Huntly sat on his horse, alongside his uncles, Jean's brothers Patrick and James. He asked Father James to bless the army before they went into battle. Father James, along with two or three religious companions, ostentatiously heard the confessions of the entire army, and gave them communion. They sprinkled their weapons with holy water, and marked white crosses on their arms and coats "to let the enemy see that they were fighting in defence of the cross of Christ".[54] Jean's brother Patrick was the sole exception: when he was asked to put a cross on his armour, he answered that he did not have time, as he rode up and down the front line, arranging his troops. Father James and his companions then fell to their knees and prayed loudly as, around 11 o'clock in the morning, battle was commenced. They kept up their loud prayers as the engagement continued into the afternoon.[55]

Argyll's troops also prayed, under the guidance of a Protestant bishop. But Lord Huntly gave the order to fire: Lord Huntly was the proud owner of half a dozen artillery pieces, technology that was rarely used this far north, and the effect of the shots on Argyll's praying troops was immediate: although they did not cause huge loss of life, the shots came, as far as Argyll's men were concerned, unexpectedly and from out of nowhere, blowing the head off a noted Hebridean warrior among their ranks.[56] The combined efforts of Patrick, Father James and the artillery led to a feeling of euphoria and invincibility among the Gordon troops, outnumbered as they were, and as they approached Argyll's men they attacked fiercely, one section wheeling around to come in from the rear, while the cavalry charged up the side of a steep hill to the ridge where Argyll had taken up position. The name 'Glenlivet' means 'a deep narrow mountain valley of the slippery smooth place', and it was difficult terrain to ride up.[57] Argyll caused arrows and bullets to be fired towards Patrick as he led his horsemen forward, but the Gordon men had two advantages over their foes: they might be inferior in number, but not only did they have superior weaponry, but they also had more horses. The Gordons were always noted for their horsemanship, and knew that horses were well-suited to the terrain. Lord Huntly had used Father James' money wisely, offering a generous pay of up to £40 Scots a month to well-equipped horsemen willing to join him, tempting in not only Highlanders but also sure-footed Borderers and even some of the king's own men.[58] Argyll's foot soldiers broke before the lances carried by the mail-clad cavalry. The cannonballs delivered into the midst of Argyll's army caused extra panic – many of them were raw recruits, and they were facing an army that might have been smaller, but which was more experienced and far-better equipped. As 2,000 of King James VI's men fled immediately, it was said that they cast their heavy weapons into a nearby small lochan so that they could run faster: it became known as the Loch of the Swords.

Argyll's remaining men fought back, firing bullets and arrows onto the horsemen and horses – around 150 horses were killed, and several prominent Gordon men fatally wounded, one of them hit by three bullets which 'carved his armour into him',[59] but men on foot could not stand against cavalry for long. Even the elements favoured the Gordons, as the sun, which had been shining into the eyes of Lord Huntly's army, went behind a cloud, while the wind changed and blew the smoke from the artillery into the eyes of Argyll's men.[60]

It was a stunning victory for Jean's family, who lost only about 70 men to around 400 dead on Argyll's side. Many legends grew up around the Battle of Glenlivet, often emphasising the religious aspect of the conflict, but also including the traditional folk song "The Ballad of Balrinnes", which emphasised the victory of the small army over the larger – some reports put Lord Huntly's losses as low as 12 men: 'Huntly...'s men / Could scarce be thirteen hundred called / The truth if ye would ken. / And yet Argyle his thousands ten / Were they that took the race / And tho that they were nine to ane / They caused them take the chase'.[61]

With clansmen on both sides, Glenlivet has entered mythical clan history as well as the more political history of Scotland, and a vivid illustration of that is shown in the restoration of a sword used in the battle. The Clan Cameron fought on the side of Lord Huntly and the Gordons, and were led into battle by Allan Cameron of Locheil, the 16th Chief of Clan Cameron. In 2016, Paul Macdonald of Macdonald Armouries in Edinburgh carried out restoration work on Lochiel's clam-shell two-hander sword. The sword was originally crafted in 1588, and, despite its size, weighs only 3¾ lbs. The Highlanders that Jean's nephew and brother commanded were wielding light, fast weapons. It was an exceptionally well-made sword too, unlike the more makeshift weapons of Argyll's men: Lochiel's sword is one of the earliest attributed to legendary Scottish-Spanish swordmaker Andrea Ferrara. The blade is carved with Ferrara's name, and a running wolf mark, and the Latin motto: "*Spero dum spiro*" (while I breathe, I hope). The hilt is marked with the name of an Aberdeen craft guild. Restoration work on the sword revealed what appeared to be battle damage and subsequent repair, with the guard having been cut through and then fixed. Lochiel survived the Battle of Glenlivet and his sword was handed down in an unbroken line through the generations. It hangs in the Clan Cameron family home today.[62]

The defeated Argyll was said to have left the field weeping bitterly as Lord Huntly's army sang a traditional hymn of joy and thanksgiving over the battlefield. It was said that no man with a cross on his armour died during the Battle of Glenlivet – but, although the numbers of dead on the Gordon side were smaller, it was senior members of their family that had been lost, among them Jean's brother Patrick, who had not had time to affix the cross to his armour. Struggling to control a horse maddened by the sights and sounds of battle, Patrick led the charge of the cavalry in an almost suicidal fashion, and was unhorsed by a shot. He was then dirked and beheaded by Argyll's men, who waved his severed head around as a trophy.[63]

James VI was said to be torn by the result of the fight: on the one hand furious at his loss, but on the other still glad his friend Lord Huntly was unharmed. There was no way James VI could let his army's defeat go unavenged, however, and the interception of a letter in which Lord Huntly described the king's campaign as a 'gowk's storm' angered him even more.[64] Lord Huntly, unsettled and unadvised after the loss of his uncle Patrick, did not follow up his victory: he could not bring himself to attack his king. James VI and his men advanced into the north, fining and punishing those who had supported Lord Huntly, until they came to Huntly Castle itself. The beautiful building, Jean's childhood home, was pulled down.[65]

James VI did not stay long in the north though – he lacked enough money to pay his troops to stay with him indefinitely, and they were running out of food. Glenlivet was a strange victory: all of Lord Huntly's enemies were gone – Moray was dead, Argyll was humiliated, there were few families who could challenge Gordon supremacy in the north-east – but Lord Huntly could not stay and exercise his power. Father James preached one last Mass in Elgin Cathedral, and pleaded with his nephew to stay, but Lord Huntly made for the safety of Sutherland, and his aunt Jean's house, before moving further north to his sister (married to Wicked Earl George) in Caithness.[66] Jean's nephew Lord Huntly decided to go into exile in Europe, and her brother Father James felt he was left with no choice but to return to the continent as well. They were gone by mid-March 1595. One of Father James' Jesuit colleagues stayed for a short while longer though, entrusted with taking important papers out of Huntly Castle and delivering them to Jean for safe keeping, travelling by sea from Huntly Castle via Caithness. He then lived in comparative safety at Jean's home, Dunrobin Castle, where he used the time to tutor Jean's children.[67] Meanwhile, Lord Huntly's wife Henrietta was allowed to stay at court, and the person that James VI put in charge of the Gordon estates while he was gone was the trusted Ludovick, 2nd Duke of Lennox – who was of course Henrietta's brother.

Francis, too, was in the north, but he was in a far worse state: he had not helped Lord Huntly at Glenlivet, but he was fatally and irrevocably out of favour with James VI. This once-exuberant man drifted like a shadow on the fringes of events, excommunicated by the Edinburgh presbytery, his property seized, and betrayed by his former friends. Elizabeth of England was preoccupied now with events in Ireland, so Francis could no longer count on his English supporters, while his Scottish supporters were too disgusted with Francis' conversion to Catholicism. Francis was left with almost nowhere to go, and he too ended up getting help from his half-brother Wicked Earl George, who had so recently also sheltered Lord Huntly. When Francis heard the news that his most trusted adviser[68] had betrayed his half-brother Hercules Stewart to King James VI it was the final straw.[69] It was said that Hercules was "not a wicked man, nor an enterpriser, but a simple follower of his brother".[70] Despite this, and their blood relationship, James VI showed no mercy and Hercules was hanged at the Mercat Cross in Edinburgh.[71] Francis collapsed, unable to help himself. His other half-brother Wicked Earl George procured for him, by piracy, two ships, and Francis left, as his uncle had done so many years before, for Orkney.[72] From Orkney, Francis sailed to France, and so started many years of sad exile. Francis was gone by the end of March 1595, only weeks after Jean's other nephew Lord Huntly had left, but Jean's two nephews' futures were very different. Francis had to leave France after he broke the law by duelling, and went on to Spain, where he consolidated his conversion to Catholicism, and became a soldier of fortune.[73] His health broke down and his fortunes dwindled until he was living in true poverty. Francis eventually died 17 years later, in 1612 in Naples, under suspicion of necromancy. His son did not regain his Earldom, and the sad story of the Earls of Bothwell was at an end.[74]

Jean saw the end of both Francis' story, and the temporary resolution of her other nephew Lord Huntly's story as he went abroad – but she was preoccupied throughout with caring for her husband Alexander. Alexander had never recovered his strength after his illness, and was not able to fight with the other Gordons at Glenlivet. Jean's second husband died at Dunrobin Castle on 6th December 1594, and was buried in Dornoch Cathedral.[75] He was in his very early forties, and Jean was 49.[76] It was a 'doleful' time for Jean, coming so soon after her brother Patrick's gruesome death in battle.[77] Alexander, the family said, was 'an honourable and high-minded man', one who was respected by his peers and his retainers. Alexander's life was defined and set by the poisoning of his parents. The Huntly Gordons rescued him and took him in, and his loyalty to them afterwards never wavered, as he tried to build up the power of the Sutherland Gordons. Honourable and loyal to those who helped him he may have been, but, as his family admitted, Alexander was 'one that loved much to be well followed'.[78] As he aimed to regain his position as Earl of Sutherland and master of Dunrobin Castle, and build up the power of the Gordons, Alexander had not let opponents like the Clan Gunn stand in his way.

Alexander had not been Jean's first choice of husband, but they forged a good relationship together and she never let him down. She brought him not only the protection of her family but also her not-inconsiderable intelligence and gifts of estate management. Jean and Alexander created a comfortable home together, united in their belief of the superiority of the Gordons. They shared qualities of loyalty and steadfastness, and had a quiet partnership which emphasised negotiation over violent feeling – though their commitment to legal rather than violent solutions to problems could be no less ruthless. "Constant and resolute"[79], Alexander was genuinely mourned by his wife Jean, their children and the wider community in Sutherland.

CHAPTER FIFTEEN

Salt: 1595–1598

After the death of her husband Alexander, Jean went to Edinburgh where she established herself in lodgings in the Canongate, the part of the Royal Mile closest to Holyrood Palace. Under Scots law, widows received one-third of their husband's goods after debts were paid,[1] and either terce (the liferent of a third of their husband's heritable estate as it stood at the time of their marriage) or a fee in place of this. This was not land that a widow could sell, but it could give her a source of food or income, and somewhere to live. Marriage contracts, particularly among the nobility, could alter some of this, but a Scottish widow was generally in a good position – certainly better than her counterpart in England, where husbands could leave wills that left nothing to their wife and children. The written law did not always correspond to what happened in reality – as we will see later with Jean's daughter-in-law's terce portion – but widows were often financially independent and able to continue life without dramatic disruption. For example, sometimes they would take on their husband's business.[2] Jean and Alexander's eldest son John, aged 18, had inherited the title and lands of the Earldom of Sutherland. Jean, used to managing her husband's estates for many years now, continued to be responsible for a large part of Sutherland, working alongside her still-youthful son. However, since Alexander's death had come at a time when their family were in open rebellion on the battlefield against the king, Jean had to make certain of her position – and

James VI ordered that she should come to Edinburgh and remain there until he had decided what was to be done.[3]

James VI was generally sympathetic to petitioners, in line with his policy of constant conciliation and balance among the nobility, and he was particularly sympathetic to the wives of errant subjects.[4] Jean was soon successful in regaining the king's favour. A 'remission' was granted to "Dame Jehane Gordoun, Countesse of Sutherland". It was dated only with the year, 1594, but no month or day – but it must have followed quickly on the events of Glenlivet, which had taken place in autumn 1594.[5] It was a comprehensive document. Jean was forgiven for 'her treasonable receipt and intercommuning' with Lord Huntly her nephew, and with 'others his Majesty declared traitors, Jesuits, excommunicated persons, and other rebellious and unnatural subjects, at diverse times, against sundry [of] his Highness' acts, laws and proclamations made to the contrary; and for all action and crime that may follow thereupon, or be imputed to the said Dame Jean therewith; and that precept be directly followed hereupon, with extension of all causes necessary'.[6] Jean had been forgiven for sheltering her nephew and her brother the Jesuit. This letter from James VI was followed by another, giving Jean official permission to leave the capital and return home. Again, the day and month have been obscured – torn off – but the letter is dated 1595, so Jean's stay in Edinburgh was probably a few months long. 'We,' said the letter from James VI, 'give and grant our licence to Dame Jeane Gordoun, Countesse of Suthirland, to depart and pass furth of our burgh of Edinburgh and the Cannogait to whichever parts she please without any pain, crime, skaith[7] or danger to be incurred by her as she goes either in her person or goods.'[8] Jean was now free to go home.

Back in Sutherland, Jean's immediate concern was to decide what her children should do. Her eldest son, John, was now the 13th Earl of Sutherland.[9] He was 18 years old and, because of the legal safeguards that Alexander and Jean had already put in place, was already nominally in charge of much of the Sutherland estate.[10] Earl John had been sent to school locally in Dornoch and had been well-trained by his parents, who had always focused on the maintenance and hoped-for longevity of Gordon succession to the Earldom of Sutherland – but 18 was still officially underage. Jean took on 'the managing of all the affairs of [the] house [of Sutherland] a good while'.[11] She had already been running the estate during Alexander's lifetime, and she continued, too, to manage and collect a not-inconsiderable amount of money from the land she had obtained in the Borders after her first marriage to Bothwell.[12] Jean was extremely competent, and 'always managed her affairs with so great prudence and foresight that the enemies of her family could never prevail against her, nor move these that were the chief rulers of the state for the time to do anything to her prejudice'.[13] A woman who could so speedily receive such a comprehensive pardon from the king for having been involved in an uprising while part of a banned religious group was a formidable asset to the House of Sutherland. Jean performed her duties 'with great care, to her own credit, and the benefit of that family [the Gordons]; all being committed to her charge by reasons of the singular affection which she did carry to the preservation of that house, as likewise for her dexterity in managing of business'.[14] Her son John had a lot to live up to.

After Jean returned from Edinburgh, her son Earl John was sent on two diplomatic visits to demonstrate to his neighbours that the House of Sutherland was in control. Jean controlled decisions behind the scenes, but the male Earl of Sutherland would always be the face of power, the leader of the House in the field, and ultimately take over all duties from his mother. Earl John's first important action was to go to Aberdeen and pay court to the current lieutenant of the north, Ludovick, Duke of Lennox. Ludovick had been appointed lieutenant in the north after Jean's nephew Lord Huntly had been forced into exile.[15] Ludovick was, of course, related to Earl John through both blood and marriage,[16] and he was in high favour with James VI. Earl John stayed with him in Aberdeen until Ludovick departed, and Ludovick 'entertained him kindly and lovingly, as his near cousin'.[17] That visit was a success. Then, Earl John paid a visit to the other person in the north that it was important he was on good terms with: Wicked Earl George.[18] Although Earl John thought that he left Girnigoe Castle "great friends" with Wicked Earl George, raids from Caithness into Sutherland continued. Earl John 'being young, and not able to endure such dealing' wanted to immediately revenge himself on Caithness by leading a raiding party, but Jean and the other adults around him prevailed on him to remain calm.[19]

Earl John was still young, and his fiery reaction to what he saw as Wicked Earl George's treachery and false friendship showed that he was still learning – but there were plenty of adults around to guide him into what they thought was the wisest course. People reacted differently to age than they do now: there was, of course, a natural tendency to stick with contemporaries, such as Jean's grandson Donald Mackay was to do in his strong friendship with his foster-brother, but when an Earl could succeed to his title at 16 or 18 and immediately lead an army into battle, or when a girl of 15 could marry and have children, then pulling rank by virtue of age could be unwise. Men and women of all ages worked together. The Gordons were a close family, and there was certainly no doubting the loyalty of the Gordons to their House, but this did not mean they were close in quite the way that a modern family would be: the fostering system, where Jean's children were placed with cadet families, necessarily changed her attitude to them. Jean seems to have always expected her children to treat her with respect, but equally she expected them to behave as adults: ready to take her advice, particularly on subjects she knew a lot about, but also ready to take action when necessary. She wanted a network around her like that of her siblings when she was younger: strong men like her late brother Adam who were constantly loyal to her but very independent. Jean was a leading part of the House of Sutherland Gordons, backed up by her nephew Lord Huntly, and by the wider Gordon family, including the cadet families like those at Golspitour, and not forgetting her son-in-law Uisdean Mackay. She drew on this supportive family network as she guided her children into adulthood.

Jean was carefully supervising the education of her other two sons, Robert and Alexander, aged 15 and ten respectively, who were still studying and boarding in Dornoch with the same schoolmaster,

Mr William Pape, who had taught their elder brother the Earl John – though Robert was to leave the following year, 1596, when he was 16. The Papes were a respectable family, who seem to have become linked to the loyal Gordons of Golspitour through marriage. Gordon loyalty was always the most important lesson to learn.[20] Jean's daughter Mary was 13, but unlike her brothers is not mentioned as attending school outwith the home. Like Jean, Mary was probably taught at home, perhaps by Jean herself. Jean's education seems to have been superior to that of her daughters, though mainly we suffer from simply not having enough information about Jane and Mary to know how educated they were: unlike Jean, they did not spend their twenties unmarried, so their time was quickly taken up with family. Eldest daughter Jane, still only in her early twenties, was already on her way to becoming a mother of four, two boys and two girls.

Jean's nephew, Lord Huntly, did not remain in exile long: Jean's pardon from James VI was only one step towards the rehabilitation of the Gordons, and at court Henrietta continued to work diligently to promote their interests. Henrietta 'carefullie solicited [Lord Huntly's] business at home during his banishment from Scotland' from March 1595 until June 1596.[21] She became particularly close to Anne of Denmark and people said that she was responsible for Anne's growing interest in Catholicism.[22] Lord Huntly, secure in his place as a former favourite of James VI and husband of Esmé's daughter, had never taken his exile too seriously: immediately after Glenlivet, Ludovick the Duke of Lennox had been sent to take over Huntly Castle and its lands – but, since Ludovick was Lord Huntly's brother-in-law, Lord Huntly could be certain that his affairs would be in safe hands while he was out of Scotland. In truth, Lord Huntly's wife Henrietta, like Jean in Sutherland, continued to be essentially in charge of the family estates. In the nights before Lord Huntly left for exile, he had actually stayed with his brother-in-law Ludovick and "was found dancing with two gentlewomen until midnight".[23] This had caused uproar and James VI knew that even if his friend was allowed to return to Scotland, Lord Huntly had to be seen to be chastised, and complying with his king.

Lord Huntly was told that if he wished to remain in Scotland, he had to publicly subscribe to the Protestant faith. Lord Huntly replied that was not a problem. The Kirk in Aberdeen was outraged once more: this was not a true conversion, they said, it was clear favouritism on the part of James VI. The king was no more willing to accept challenges to his authority from the kirk than he was from his Earls: eventually Lord Huntly,[24] in front of an audience of noblemen and gentlemen in Aberdeen, "made open confession of [his] apostacy, renounced papistry and swore never to decline again, but to defend the religion presently confessed".[25] Then everyone celebrated by drinking copious amounts of wine, smashing their glasses and spilling excess drink on the ground. They did exactly the same thing in Edinburgh a couple of months later, in August 1597, when they were officially declared, to accompaniment of the blast of a trumpet, to be no longer rebels. The Gordons had their Aberdeenshire lands back.

Things were not the same as they had been, however. Lord Huntly had to send his eldest son to be educated at a place of James VI's choosing – which would mean, of course, in the Protestant faith.[26] James VI essentially believed that Catholics were immature and simply needed education in order to progress to Protestantism.[27] For a family like the Gordons, who relied on absolute loyalty to their House, and who were used to sending their children to loyal cadet families, this would turn out to be a crucial break. Lord Huntly's hold on the north had been considerably weakened, and clans like the Grants and Mackintoshes who had fought on the opposite side at Glenlivet, no longer offered their allegiance. Clan and factional violence "reached almost epidemic proportions", while other noble families, like the Keiths, took advantage to increase their influence.[28] And, although his personal friendship with James VI was renewed, Lord Huntly's influence at court never wholly returned: he never held public office after his return from exile, and stayed focused on the north, especially the rebuilding of Huntly Castle. His earlier renovations had been partially destroyed after Glenlivet, but Lord Huntly thought about what he had seen in exile, and started again in even more ambitious style: the results of his renovation, especially the oriel windows looking out onto the garden with a massive inscription of his name and Henrietta's name carved right along the top of them, are still visible today. The carved fireplaces and grand doorway emphasise heraldic and symbolic imagery designed to show the importance of the House of Huntly and their loyalty to the crown: there are coats of arms of Huntly, and of Henrietta's family of Lennox, placed beneath an exceptionally fine and detailed carving of the royal arms of James VI and his Queen Anne. The huge carved frontispiece above the doorway shows the same two coats of arms – with the eye then led upwards to the only thing more important than the Huntlys and the king of Scots: religious carvings showing Jesus Christ and finally topped with a depiction of the day of the Last Judgement, with Good triumphing over Evil.[29]

Lord Huntly's true conversion to Protestantism was as suspect as the Kirk in Aberdeen believed but, for now, he had to conform. As Lord Huntly resettled in Scotland, another member of Jean's family also made a return: Father James the Jesuit. After Glenlivet, Father James had believed that, although he was leaving the country, he was quitting "with the full prestige of victory".[30] Now, only a short while later, even his nephew had publicly converted to the Protestant faith. Conditions for Catholics in Scotland were not good. A contemporary letter from around the time of Glenlivet described how the Jesuits working to spread the Word in Scotland had to move in a clandestine fashion: "We live in caves, in secret and unfrequented places, perpetually moving from place to place, like the gipsies, and we never lodge two nights in the same locality, for fear of falling into the hands of the enemy. Spies and officers are posted at all the inns, and in every parish, to discover our whereabouts, and give us up to the authorities. On my first arrival I was taken prisoner, together with my companions ... After being robbed of all I possessed, I was committed to a guard of soldiers, whom I had to keep at my own expense, and who were charged to hold me in safe custody ..."[31] Now, matters "grew worse" – to give someone the name of Catholic was "odious and abominable... It is worse than calling a man a heathen, or a member of the vilest sect on earth ..."

Father James had not received a letter posted from his nephew asking him not to return to Scotland, and, still believing that his nephew's sentiments had remained unchanged and that the name of the Gordon Huntlys would protect him and undaunted by any other reports he had received, Father James set sail from Calais on 4th June 1597. He made landfall in the north of Scotland a week later, arriving in between his nephew's public conversion to Protestantism in Aberdeen, and his later, equally public recanting of his faith in Edinburgh. It was the worst time for Lord Huntly to be seen receiving his uncle.

Father James confidently sent a messenger to Lord Huntly to alert him of his arrival, but did at least take the precaution of landing secretly. He soon learnt that a "great change had taken place".[32] There were only three Jesuit fathers left in Scotland, not counting Father James himself, and up until now they had all been able to live under the protection of Lord Huntly – but now they had been obliged to go elsewhere, keeping themselves concealed, and under constant threat of death. When Lord Huntly received Father James' messenger his "confusion was very great".[33] He sent a reply to his uncle, saying that he could not possibly receive him, and that he would have to write to James VI, to let the king know of Father James' arrival, then wait until the king told him what to do: "He was resolved to follow the royal commands whatever they might be, for fear of the loss of his property and position," stated Father James.[34] Father James did not bother to wait and find out what the king of Scots wanted done with him and the other Jesuits, instead sailing to a port he thought would be safer: Cromarty.

Cromarty was a safe port in more ways than one: first of all, it was a calm harbour to anchor in, and second, Father James knew that by landing there, towards the north of Scotland, he was more likely to find Catholic supporters. Cromarty was en route to his sister Jean's territory and Jean welcomed Father James, giving hospitality to him and his companions.[35] "We had no want of friends," Father James reported gladly to his superiors, "who abundantly supplied our wants, in spite of the threatening orders issued by the government against me."[36] This was not Father James' true homeland, however: he was used to the north-east and Aberdeenshire, and he shared some of Jean's prejudices against the Highland clans. Jean and Alexander had spent time making alliances with Clan Mackay, but they had never remained in any doubt that the nobles of Scottish were far superior to the Highland clans, and Father James thought so too: the clans might be Catholics, but he described the people he was staying with as "the Highland tribes of Scotland". Father James was very clear to his superiors that here in the north he was on the periphery: these were good simple Catholics, but not the people with the true power in Scotland. Another Jesuit priest of the time, Father James' friend William Crichton, "linked the men under the Earl of Sutherland with those under the Hebridean chiefs as, together, 'barbarorum et semiinermium' (savage and semi-clad)".[37] The best he would allow any of the people in the Far North to be was 'semibarbarorum' – semi-savage. 'Barbarorum' could have been a shorthand for Gaelic, or non-English, speaking, but by linking it to the adjective 'semi-clad' the Jesuits were certainly making a value judgement. The north and north-east of Scotland were seen as far more remote than they had been in the time of Father James' father – there was no way that Aodh Mackay would have ever been dismissed in the way that Uisdean Mackay was.[38] Power in Scotland was centralising at the court in Edinburgh. Jean may have fought hard for her family to be recognised, and would continue to do so, but she and the other Gordons were guilty of seeing themselves as lone civilising influences. The diminishment of the north of Scotland was well underway, and the reduced power of Lord Huntly was only adding to this.

Lord Huntly eventually heard back from James VI, who allowed him to help his uncle on one condition: Father James must leave Scotland soon. Father James took full advantage of the time left to him – just over a month – reasoning that it allowed him to move around freely and unmolested. He left his place of hiding and boldly made contact with the other Jesuits in Scotland, spoke with loyal Catholics, then issued a public challenge to all the Protestant ministers of Scotland to debate with him in front of the king. He wrote out his challenge and made sure it was widely disseminated across Scotland, as well as sending a copy to James VI himself. Father James Gordon was nothing if not confident.

The kirk replied that they would have to wait for the meeting of the General Assembly to decide what to do. Father James was happy with this, and said piously and martially that his "armour is spiritual, not carnal, and our sword is the word of God, by means of which Christ our Lord is accustomed to rout and overthrow the armies of Satan".[39] He made his way to Aberdeen, ready to sail for Edinburgh to see the king. While in Aberdeen, he took the opportunity for a practice run, making a very public appearance in front of an audience to propound his views. Then he left Scotland, fairly punctually by the deadline James VI had set him, but went only to Norway, where he waited confidently for his invitation back to Scotland to debate in front of the king, using the time to write a detailed letter explaining his activities to his superiors.[40]

Father James waited in vain for his invitation back, and by winter, despite the bad weather, he decided to return anyway. He had a small window of time before the sea in the harbour froze over and his boat would be unable to leave, but managed to charter a vessel and catch a last period of calm weather for an easy sail to Scotland. Father James decided that this time he would not go to his family, but would head straight for King James VI – he was concerned about exposing his family to danger for sheltering him, and he wanted to go direct to the top. He landed at Leith on St Andrew's Day, the feast day of the patron saint of Scotland, and disembarked at nightfall – late afternoon in November – and went straight to Holyrood Palace. By 7pm Father James had talked his way into Holyrood Palace and made it as far as the door of the king's chamber without anyone knowing who he really was. The doorkeeper told Father James that the king was having a meeting with his Privy Council. Father James knew one of the councillors, a Gordon supporter, and he requested the doorkeeper to ask him to step outside. It had been so long since Father James had been in the capital that his friend did not at first recognise him, but eventually Father James persuaded him to ask the king if he would grant him an audience. "James [VI] himself and all present were surprised",[41] unsurprisingly, to receive the message that a notorious Jesuit was waiting outside, and eventually it was decided to convey Father James to a secure location in Edinburgh Castle – not quite a prison, but a comfortable holding-place.

Father James traded heavily on his family name and connections, and described meeting with old friends and kindness wherever he went. Unluckily, though, some Englishmen arrived at the same time as he did, and when they were discovered the public feeling was that Father James was the advance guard of a Catholic conspiracy or invasion. The unfortunate Englishmen were actually neither Catholic nor Jesuit, but soldiers looking for a night out, who "had come to Edinburgh for no other purpose than to drink wine with their boon companions, which they had so often done before, that they were well known to nearly every one in the town".[42]

The feeling against Catholics ran high, and James VI was disinclined to give Father James the platform for public debate he so desired. Instead, Father James was given some Protestant texts by an eminent Scottish minister. These did not convince him, so Father James now made the Scottish minister his pen-pal, writing responses to his texts with the hope that the king would also read what he had written. Unfortunately for Father James, his new minister pen-pal died suddenly and unexpectedly, which was held to be a very bad omen, and Father James' malign influence was blamed for, in some way, causing the death.

It had now been 20 days since Father James arrived in Scotland. Lord Huntly arrived in the capital and took responsibility for his uncle, paying off all the debts he had incurred, getting him released from the castle and setting him up in a house in town. Father James blithely continued to instruct everyone he met in the ways of the true religion but soon realised that none of the ministers would enter into debate with him. He then went to the house of the friendly Seton family, just outside Edinburgh, where he lived in luxury. This situation could plainly not continue if James VI did not want to be accused of favouring Catholics: the people of Edinburgh were hearing weekly sermons about Jean's brother's actions and whereabouts, and the ministers were constantly clashing with the king over what should be done. The Privy Council eventually passed an act of 'perpetual banishment' on Father James. Father James was ordered to Leith, where he was told he would be put on the next available ship out of Scotland – but bad weather meant he was delayed and his visit extended even more. It was not until May, five months after his arrival, that Father James finally set sail for Denmark, his ship's expenses paid for by his nephew, Lord Huntly. He was armed with documents promising safe conduct, and Queen Anne, who may have secretly sought Father James' advice on converting to Catholicism, even entrusted him with letters to her brother, the King of Denmark.[43] Father James used his noble connections to the House of Huntly to obtain remarkable treatment for a Catholic Jesuit, and his own confidence, intelligence and undoubted public speaking skills took him even further, but his mission was never likely to succeed. Jean never saw her brother again: his age, and the unchanging hostility to Catholics in Protestant Scotland meant that after this, Father James did not make any further journeys home. He remained in France, teaching philosophy, scripture and Hebrew at what became the Scots college, and focusing too on his own religious writings.[44]

Lord Huntly, no matter how much he would help his uncle the Jesuit personally, continued his official acceptance of the Protestant faith. James VI knew that he had to have the outward acceptance of his friend to the Protestant religion, and he did not forget the rest of Lord Huntly's family. Jean, along with the Countess of Huntly Henrietta, and Lord Huntly's sister the Countess of Caithness, were ordered to subscribe to the Confession of faith under pain of excommunication. That sentence, though, was never carried out, even though Jean seems to have made no effort to subscribe.[45]

While Father James had been in Edinburgh, Jean's son Earl John had also decided to make his way to court, and he "took up his residence in Edinburgh for a considerable time".[46] He turned 21, the age of majority, not long after arriving in the south of Scotland, officially placing him in control of all of his estates and money. In practice, however, Jean continued to administer everything in Sutherland. Jean was a very strong personality; she had been used to running things for her late husband, and she enjoyed being in charge. It would be difficult for her son to take over all at once. Either Earl John himself, or Earl John advised by those around him, seems to have decided that the best course for him was to strike out on his own. It was not unusual for young noblemen to spend several years at court and on the continent, and this is what Earl John set out to do. Seen as an alternative to university, the forerunner to the Grand Tour was a way for young noblemen to obtain the relevant 'polish'. It meant John could break free of his mother and become his own person while, from Jean's point of view, it meant that she could carry on with her work in the north uninterrupted.

Spending time at court also reminded James VI of just who the new Earl of Sutherland was: Earl John spent quite a lot of time jockeying for position, and ensuring that he and his allies did well. He was present at the Parliament where his cousin, Lord Huntly was finally restored, and claimed at this Parliament his hereditary right of bearing the sword of state before the king.[47] Wicked Earl George was also at the Parliament, and was outraged at the fact that Earl John was being given precedence: Wicked Earl George wanted the titles of Earl of Caithness and Sutherland to be on equal footing. Earl John took up the fight with relish, and, already ill-disposed to Wicked Earl George, maintained a simmering feud with him for the rest of their lives. It often played out in the law courts, rather than on the battlefield as it had with Earl John's father. Earl John had learnt well from his mother.

Earl John knew that he could safely leave Sutherland under his mother's control. Jean did not have it all easy, as renewed clan fighting flared up, but 'diligent and earnest mediation' prevailed to keep the peace.[48] After spending a year or so in Edinburgh, Earl John applied to James VI for permission to go abroad "to France, Flanders, and any other places beyond sea". His stated reason was that it was 'not only for his recreation, but likewise thereby to enable himself for the service of his prince and country'.[49] A visit to France was still practically obligatory for Scottish noblemen, who strongly believed in the cultural ties between the two countries even if their official religions now differed – and for a Catholic like Earl John there was added incentive, including the probability of seeing his uncle James the Jesuit, who had so recently left Edinburgh. Earl John, and the good friends he travelled with, stayed abroad and enjoyed their 'recreation' for just over two years; hopefully they also enabled themselves for service of their king.

In Sutherland, Jean's other sons, Robert and Alexander, had by now both left school. Robert had just as strong a personality as his mother, and was very intelligent. 'Wearying of that idle life which he then led in his brother [John]'s absence, and considering the loss of his time (which was irrecoverable)', Robert 'dealt so with his mother, the countess, that she yielded to send him and his younger brother ... to the university of St Andrews, to be instructed in learning and virtue'.[50] Robert was not going to stay at home stuck in the north of Scotland while his elder brother had all the adventures – he was leaving too, whether Jean liked it or not. After six months in St Andrews, Robert and Alexander then transferred to the University of Edinburgh, settling in the capital, where they expected Earl John to return soon. Robert, never backward in singing his own praises, said that 'he behaved himself in such sort, that he was beloved by the principal [of the University of Edinburgh] and regents there'.[51] He certainly made the most of his time, not only studying at the university, but also taking extra private lessons from tutors at the college. Robert, a worthy successor to his uncle the Jesuit Father James in application and confidence, was determined to do his best, and stayed in Edinburgh for three years, 'employing that time seriously in philosophy, and other studies, to his own contentment and profit'.[52]

Back in Sutherland, Jean oversaw the wedding of her youngest daughter Mary. Mary had been betrothed to the heir of Ross of Balnagowan since she was a baby, but it had not been a smooth engagement: Ross of Balnagowan had become unhappy with the arrangements that had been made with the Sutherlands at the time of the agreement to marry, particularly the Sutherland appropriation of his land rights. Ross had then sided with Wicked Earl George in the struggles between Caithness and Sutherland, and had last been heard of helping Francis north to Caithness. However, before leaving for the continent, Earl John had met with George Ross of Balnagowan, and had agreed to resign the rights that Alexander had gained over his land. The two men had worked out a new succession to the land rights – if Ross' heir, David Ross of Balnagowan, and Mary had no children, then other Rosses would take over the succession. If there were no Rosses left though, then the land reverted to a list of Mackays (Earl John's sister and brother-in-law's family) or Gordons (the Gordons of Golspitour) or other Gordon-approved families. Mary was to take a good dowry to her marriage, and a further marriage was arranged between the family of Ross and the Gordons of Golspitour, that loyal family linked to the Earls of Sutherland through blood and fosterage.[53] Earl John had thus sorted out the problem of his sister's marriage, with some loss of land but no loss of face, and worked to resolve a hostility that had been ongoing between his family and the Rosses for some years. Mary was 15, the same age that her older sister Jane had been when she married Uisdean Mackay, but Mary's marriage never seemed to work so well as Jane's: it produced no children.

As well as overseeing her children, Jean had other major projects to work on. Her aim was to increase productivity on the Sutherland estates. She oversaw the drainage of land by diverting water from a loch and burn, creating good new farm land,[54] and in 1598, she oversaw the establishment of the first salt pans at Brora, just a few miles north of her home at Dunrobin.[55] With two sons at university and a third son abroad, Jean needed to find a source of money: the system of paying rent in kind was not going to fund her sons' desire to go to the cities and participate in court life. Even a second son, Robert, was not content with life on the Sutherland estate. He expected education and opportunity, and Jean wanted to give him that. In order to do this she had to find a way to move the House of Sutherland into the future. There were salt-making centres elsewhere in Scotland and Jean could have seen salt from the Firth of Forth on sale in Edinburgh, while the salt industry had been burgeoning since the time of Mary, Queen of Scots. Mary, Queen of Scots had introduced a salt tax as the industry grew, but higher taxes on salt in England over the years meant it was worthwhile for Scottish producers to consider exporting salt there.[56] Salt pans were a way to extract the salt from sea water: the water was put into large iron pans, then heated underneath by coal fires. A natural coagulant was added to draw out the impurities, such as pieces of shell, sand or seaweed, from the water – egg white was one option, but ox blood was another. The salters constantly monitored the temperature, continuously skimming off the coagulant and impurities as the water boiled, so that no trace or taste would be left on the salt. As the water evaporated, more sea water was gradually added then boiled away, until a large quantity of salt crystals were visible along the bottom of the pan, ready to be raked out. Large amounts of coal were needed, but Jean knew that her late husband's father had found a seam of coal at Brora and had planned to work it before his untimely death, and she went back to this site. The coal, extracted from surface pits, was conveniently located near to the sea which provided the constant supply of salt water needed – water was collected in 'bucket pots' (large man-made hollows in the rock) along the shoreline. The salt obtained was used locally and elsewhere, with records showing that it was shipped as far away as London. Secondary products, such as cured fish, were valuable commodities as well: salmon fished from nearby lochs and rivers were regularly sold to people from Inverness, Elgin and Aberdeen, and the salt curing process meant fish was able to be transported longer distances than fresh fish, including as far as France, where it could be sold.

Recent archaeological excavations on the beach at Brora have uncovered the evidence of large-scale and sophisticated construction work, showing the scale of Jean's project, which ran for many years.[57] Remains of a long building, probably a store, can still be seen, including remnants of work done by specialised craftsmen such as smiths, working on iron fixtures, and masons, who carved the doorways and left their official signature, or mason's mark, on the stonework. This was a major building project, financed by the Sutherland estates. While financial records for the earliest period are scarce, later records show that the equipment and setting up of the salt pans was costly, but that this was money well invested as they generated income running into several hundred pounds.[58] Other archaeological evidence, of broken pottery and animal bones showing signs of butcher's marks, show that many people were working and eating regularly at the site, though there are no records of who the workers were. Did Jean recruit local workers, or did they come in from further afield, such as men brought in from Gordon territories in Huntly or Aberdeenshire? Likewise, there is no record of what their work was like: modern workers in salt pans – which still exist, running on similar methods, in poorer countries – talk about health problems associated with working with salt, such as over-absorption of salt into bare hands and feet which can cause skin problems, though the main focus of their complaints is usually around poor wages.[59]

The archaeological work at the site is ongoing, and there are potentially more discoveries to be made and understood. Brora was the most northerly coal mine in the UK, though the coal was not of the best quality: it was very sulphurous and even susceptible to spontaneous combustion, partly because it came from a coal field that was relatively 'young', geographically speaking (160 million years old as opposed to 310 million years old). The fires in the salt pans would have burnt slowly with this coal, and made a lot of smoke. It would have been a hot, unpleasant place to work for long periods, especially for men more used to fishing and farming outside, though they would have been used to the smoky atmosphere around peat-burning fires in the smaller blackhouse residences. The coal in Brora continued to be mined until the 1970s.[60]

The whole site was one of the first major industrial developments in the Highlands, an area which at the time was being noted for its wildness rather than innovation in industry. The Highlands, and specifically clan lands, were being positioned as barbarous and savage areas that needed to be controlled: James VI famously wrote in his "Basilikon Doron", or book of advice to his son and heir, that the Highlands and Hebrides were full of savages.[61] The most he would allow was that the northern part of his kingdom was slightly better than the west; they were "barbarous for the most part and yet mixed with some show of civility".[62] James VI's main aim was always the consolidation and expansion of his power, and he did not want challenges to it from the alternative system of clanship and clan loyalty. Everyone in Scotland should be loyal to the king – to be otherwise was to be a savage in an uncivilised region. The distance of the Highlands and the Far North from Edinburgh, and the defeat at Glenlivet of Lord Huntly, meant James VI could step up his rhetoric, laying the foundation for ideas that persist today. However, the north of Scotland was not as isolated as it at first seemed: the reality was that there were established trading routes from the Highlands to Scandinavia and elsewhere,[63] and there are numerous examples of people from the north of Scotland travelling in Europe in various different contexts, from commercial to military.[64] The north Highlands was an established stopping point for trade routes – not a major port, but of some importance. Jean, the daughter of the Cock o' the North, certainly never saw her home territory as anything other than of equal importance to any other part of Scotland. She looked for opportunities as a businesswoman would anywhere.

Jean's establishment of the salt pans at Brora is of major significance and can be interpreted in many different ways. It is a tangible reminder that women were prime movers in estate management, and illustrates how much control and influence Jean had. More settled times meant more development was possible, and this is early evidence of the House of Sutherland seeing the land as something that could be developed and industrialised. The salt pans are also early evidence of the House of Sutherland needing to operate within a cash economy: in an area where many rents were paid in kind, the salt and the produce cured with salt could be sold for ready money. Jean was the first from the House of Sutherland to grapple fully with this problem of how to make the land around her pay. She wanted it to produce cash that would benefit her family. The primary goal was not to improve the life of tenants or the wider Gordon network of cadet families; it was to produce a commodity for export to bring in money in order to benefit Jean's most immediate family. In lieu of records of what life was like for the people working at the salt pans, our primary account comes from Jean's son Robert, who saw them in terms of what they brought to the Sutherland estate, not what they brought to the people of Sutherland. It was an attitude on the part of the House of Sutherland that could be seen to develop over the years to come.

In some ways, the salt pans were a huge achievement that prove that the Highlands were not backward, and that women had agency. They also indicate the growth of a cash economy, and the nobility wanting to control the land in new ways in exchange for the cash that would enable them to participate fully in that new economy and advance personally in the south.

CHAPTER SIXTEEN

Alex Ogilvie: Family and Clan: 1599–1603

The situation in Sutherland remained calm enough for Jean's son Earl John to stay abroad, leaving estate management to his mother and others. Wicked Earl George tested the boundaries of what was possible by asking to hunt on Sutherland and Mackay land, but not only was Jean an able administrator and manager, but she could also rely on the military force of her son-in-law Uisdean, who remained loyal to the Sutherlands. Uisdean was well able to negotiate and delay with Wicked Earl George, even when George sent messages to him through various other Mackays, and threatened to bring a suspiciously large party of armed men to the hunting.[1]

Seeing the power of Sutherland over Caithness, and watching her nephew in Aberdeenshire, Jean could see that, despite the vicissitudes of Scottish history and her nephew's recent troubles, the Gordons were still "one of the foremost dynasties in Scotland", and the "Sutherland earldom certainly remained a jewel in the Gordon crown" at the turn of the sixteenth century.[2] In some ways, the younger generation seemed to be successfully taking over. Jean's contemporaries, who had been of such importance only a few years before, were gradually fading from the scene – for example, Janet Hepburn, the sister of Bothwell and mother of Wicked Earl George and the Mad Wizard Earl Francis, died in 1599.[3]

Jean's son Robert wrote in his chronicle of the family history that Jean's next decision was made 'for the utilitie and profite of her children'.⁴ Although Jean may have spun it that way – a chance for her to take a step back and let Earl John and his brothers find their own path – it actually looks a lot like Jean finally got to do something for herself rather than her family: she married her childhood sweetheart, Alex Ogilvie, Laird of Boyne.

Alex Ogilvie's wife, Mary Beaton, had died two years before, in 1597.⁵ Now that both Jean and Alex Ogilvie were widowed, they saw their chance and seized it. Despite her two arranged marriages, Jean's notion of romantic love would not have been so very different from our own: Shakespeare's *Romeo and Juliet*, for example, with its lovers thwarted by their family circumstances, had received its first performance only around five years beforehand. Jean loved in much the same way that we do. She and Alex Ogilvie had been in love when Jean was a teenager, but had been separated. Jean, a pragmatic Juliet, had done what her family had needed her to do; she had not been unhappy. Alex Ogilvie, married to Mary Beaton, had three sons (James, Andrew and Robert), and was owner and manager of a substantial amount of property: he had not spent his years without Jean pining either.⁶ However, by outliving many of their contemporaries they gained extra time for themselves. Average life expectancy at the time was only about 35, though this did not mean a young population as figures were influenced by war, violence, high rates of death in infancy, and disease – but it did mean that Jean and Alex Ogilvie had significantly beaten the odds to live to healthy old age.⁷ Mary, Queen of Scots' tragic fate had enmeshed itself in the lives of her contemporaries and claimed Jean's first husband Bothwell, Darnley, and many others involved in the Marian intrigues and civil wars that followed. It is sometimes said that no one associated with Mary could escape her bad luck. It was extraordinary that Jean and Alex Ogilvie should finally find love together; a remarkable happy ending for two people from the unhappy court of Mary, Queen of Scots.

Jean and Alex Ogilvie's wedding contract was drawn up in Elgin on 10th December 1599.⁸ The contract follows the regular pattern for such documents, but it reveals that there was a great disparity in Jean's and Alex Ogilvie's income. Alex Ogilvie's support for Mary, Queen of Scots had not come without a cost, and he had run into considerable debt. The ambitious building project of the new Boyne Castle had been too much, and the castle and his estate had passed into the hands of another branch of the Ogilvie family, to Sir George Ogilvie of Dunlugas. Since 1575, Alex Ogilvie had fallen in and out of debt, struggling to pay off Sir George, borrowing and owing money to Lord Forbes, and entering what sound like shady business deals buying Norwegian ships with Sir George Ogilvie and others.[9] Marriage contracts usually made sure that the bride would be provided for, and there is some complicated legal manoeuvring in this contract to enable Alex Ogilvie to support his new wife financially, even though he is in debt.[10] The contract also made sure that Jean would keep her financial affairs in some way separate. She still retained control over the income she gained from the lands that Bothwell had given her, and the income she was entitled to from the Sutherland estates, including keeping control over all the profits from her particular projects, the salt pans and coal heuchs. And careful provision was made to ensure that neither Alex Ogilvie nor his sons would have any claim over the Sutherland land.[11] Jean was once more an extremely practical Juliet, making sure that she would lose nothing, not even her title of Countess,[12] but the absence of financial gain for either Jean or Alex Ogilvie points again to this being a love match. There was no need for either of them to marry; it was something they chose to do.[13] Neither was it really 'for their children', as Robert had said, as neither Alex Ogilvie nor Jean seem to have involved themselves as stepparents. It certainly would have been strange for Alex Ogilvie, a minor nobleman, to advise Jean's eldest son, an Earl who was over 21.

So who was the man Jean had married? Since Alex Ogilvie was not as wealthy as the Earls of Sutherland, nor as notorious as the Earl of Bothwell, there are no fine portraits of him or descriptions of his personality. His name is recorded as being on the Marian side, but beyond that there is little more. However, some documents I found tucked away in the Gordon archives shed some more light on his character. Here, stored among miscellaneous papers belonging to Jean's son Robert, there is small and unusual booklet. Folded and bound together by an amateur hand, a collection of beautifully written notes has been given a cover made from some scrap paper from earlier centuries. On it, the contents of the booklet are described:

'A collection of the names
of herbs both in latin and
English copied and gathered together out of sundry authors
writing of the virtues of herbs / and now collected in this
little volume by Alex Ogilvie:
one who is very studious and aye desiring [always wanting]
to know of the virtues of the
foresaid herbs'.[14]

It is dated 1587. Obviously a work that has been put together with great care, it gathers together and lists alphabetically a huge amount of information about the kinds of plants and herbs that could be grown in the north-east of Scotland, including their Latin and English names and their uses.[15] Herbs were used for both food and medicine. The impression is of a landowner who is interested in what he can grow and what it can be used for, a gardener connected to the land and keen to learn more from whatever sources he can read. As a 'gentleman gardener', Alex Ogilvie was following the fashions of the time. Alex Ogilvie and his first wife Mary Beaton had wanted to build up a library,[16] and in a time when books were scarce, information like this, which could be of great use to landowners, had to be painstakingly gathered together. In the marriage contract between Jean and Alex Ogilvie, specific mention is made of the orchards and lands of Boyne. The atmospheric ruins of the castle today, with trees now growing up through the towers, show that it would have then been surrounded with its own garden growing herbs and plants for food and medicine. At Jean's home of Dunrobin Castle too, Alex Ogilvie could have felt at home in the extensive gardens, where, over time, exotic items such as "an abundance of good saphron, tobacco, and rosemarie" were grown.[17]

Each entry in the herbal is carefully copied, with heading and description in slightly different script, with neater, bigger letters for the headings. In order to keep the main booklet looking good, Alex Ogilvie used the front cover as a scrap page, testing his pen here, writing a few words there. Best of all, there is a little drawing of a kindly older man with long hair and a long beard, shady sunhat in one hand, a stick in the other hand, and wearing what look like gardening clothes. Could this be the only surviving sketch of what Jean's Alex looked like? – the studious gentleman gardener who always wanted to learn more.

Marriage to Alex Ogilvie probably meant that Jean, now Lady Boyne, spent more of her time back in the north-east – though she certainly retained her interest in the Sutherland estates, where she was always sure of a home next to her children.[18] Jean had spent most of her married life flitting between Sutherland and her Gordon family at Huntly Castle, and she continued to divide her time between the north-east and the far north, travelling between the two on horseback and across the firth by boat.

Jean's marriage to Alex Ogilvie was happy, and, like many happy couples, they fade out of history – it is the dramatic failures of a Mary, Queen of Scots or a Bothwell who blaze across our memories, while the steady warmth of a contented couple is part of the background. After waiting for each other for 35 years, Jean and Alex Ogilvie deserved their private time together. However, her third marriage was by no means the end of Jean's story.

When Jean's son Earl John finally came home from France to Scotland for good, he knew his Earldom was in a good state, so did not hurry back to Dunrobin. Earl John's younger siblings Robert and Alexander were in Edinburgh, so Jean and her daughter Jane and son-in-law Uisdean were still involved with managing the Sutherland estates in their absence. Earl John remained in the south of Scotland, spending time in the capital with his brothers and putting forward the Sutherland cause at the court of James VI.

James VI and his Queen Anne were by then in a strong position, as they welcomed another son, Charles, in 1600 – the future King Charles I, though as his golden older brother Henry was still alive no one knew this yet. Earl John aimed to show James VI the importance of the Gordons and the Sutherlands, making sure at all times that he was given precedence over Wicked Earl George, the Earl of Caithness.[19] Earl John's cousin Lord Huntly had already moved another step forward in his rehabilitation when he had been created the Marquis of Huntly just before Earl John had returned to Scotland.[20] Jean's nephew still spent more time in the north than at court, and was still under suspicion for his lightly held Protestant conversion, but the Gordons were certainly not being forgotten by James VI. Meanwhile, Jean's efforts in promoting the salt pans and coal industries at Brora were recognised not long after Earl John's return when Brora was erected into a "free burgh of barony and regality" in 1601. This confirmed the prominence of the town of Brora in the area, and gave the town and the people who lived there certain privileges, including the right to hold four fairs annually which would then bring even more money and people into the area, and which in turn helped with Earl John's plans to expand the export of coal and salt out of the local harbour.[21]

Meanwhile, the troublesome relationship with Wicked Earl George in Caithness was mitigated somewhat – not because George stopped trying to prove the worth of Caithness, but because in order to do so George decided to focus his energy on a major rebuilding project at his home of Girnigoe, renaming it Castle Sinclair, after his family name.[22] Rather than the old defensive Girnigoe, with its miserable dungeon where George's father John the Stout had been put to death, now in a relatively more peaceful time Wicked Earl George wanted to create a more modern, comfortable dwelling – with grandeur in mind. His wife, Jean's niece,[23] saw the improvements her brother Lord Huntly was making to Huntly Castle, and she and Wicked Earl George have been described as "amateur architects".[24]

They had the western gatehouse, the first thing the traveller saw as they entered, enlarged and embellished and, further into the castle complex, put up a new central tower house. Local material, such as Caithness stone and slate, was used, while other things they wanted were traded in: timber from Ross, for example, as well as crafts-men.[25] The castle now comprised several buildings, all perched just off the Caithness coast. Wicked Earl George retained apartments on the upper floors, with a commanding view.[26] George's wife's involvement was very much in keeping with the involvement of all the women in her family in running their lands: it "further signalled the participation of women in the management of the estates and buildings as elsewhere in Scotland".[27]

Earl John's other action on returning to Scotland was to choose a suitable wife: Jean soon gained a new daughter-in-law as her son married Annas Elphinstone,[28] the eldest daughter of the fourth Lord Elphinstone. Lord Elphinstone was Lord High Treasurer of Scotland, and the marriage of his daughters was a major event: at the same time Annas married Earl John, her younger sister married the 9th Lord Forbes.[29] A joint wedding was held in Edinburgh, attended by King James VI, Queen Anne and most of the nobil-ity – probably including Jean as proud mother of the groom. The weddings were considered to be such an important occasion that the official start of Lent was delayed in order for the bridal feasts to take place.[30] Earl John was doing well in advancing the Sutherland cause, while the linked wedding of a Forbes – traditional enemy of the Gordons – showed once again how James VI liked to see the relationships between his noblemen negotiated, forcing them always to compromise and work together. Jean's new daughter-in-law, Annas Elphinstone, was "a lady of good inclination, of a meek disposition, and very provident" – though her 'meekness' did not stop her clashing a little with her new mother-in-law.[31]

Jean's son Earl John also got on well with the Mackays. However, cordial relations did not mean that Earl John saw his brother-in-law Uisdean Mackay or his ten-year-old nephew Donald as being his equals in rank. As Earl John pushed for greater recognition for the Earls of Sutherland from James VI, he made sure to emphasise to the king that the northern Earls were not the same as Highlanders or clansmen, who James VI saw as threats to his authority. John, fresh from the continent, emphasised the idea that the Earls were northern, but not Highland. The Sutherland Earls were loyal subjects of the throne, and James VI had no need to be wary of them. However, since Earl John's elder sister Jane was married to the Chief of Mackay, this situation had to be clarified: at the moment, Jane had a son and heir, Donald. Earl John had, as yet, no children – and he and his new wife had the worst beginning to their attempts to start a family, as their first-born children died in infancy.[32] Neither of Earl John's younger brothers, Robert or Alexander, were married yet or looked to be married soon, and his other sister Mary, Jean's youngest daughter who had been married to Ross of Balnagowan, also had no children. Earl John took after his father Alexander, and was not always in the best of health. The possibility existed that the Earldom of Sutherland could be inherited by Donald Mackay, rendering a Highland clan chieftain one of the most important Earls in Scotland.

This was not what Jean and Alexander had intended when they had arranged their daughter's marriage to Uisdean: Jean had always worked for the promotion of Gordon interests. When Jean's husband Alexander had been ill, then when Earl John was young, the best thing to do had been to rely on Jean, Jane and Jane's strong husband Uisdean, but perhaps when Earl John returned from the continent to take up full duties he felt that his brother-in-law was encroaching on his territory. Earl John did not want Uisdean's Highland Mackay clansmen descendants to inherit the 'Gordon' title of Earl of Sutherland. Jane's marriage to Uisdean had brought great benefit to the Gordons by allying them with the powerful Mackay clan, but, despite his upbringing with the Earl of Caithness, Uisdean was sometimes too much of a Gael for the Gordons. He was still something apart – a Clan Chief, the head and symbol of a group of people who saw themselves as different, who could dress differently in plaids, who could speak Gaelic, and whose allegiance to the system of Earls and Crown could be questionable. Jane's brother Robert later said that Uisdean's 'one vice that overruled him ... was his extraordinary lust',[33] an indication, perhaps, of tension within Jane and Uisdean's marriage, which would influence how the Gordons saw him. 'Lust' in a sixteenth- or seventeenth-century context can mean an excess of energy – as when one of Mary, Queen of Scots' Four Maries was described as a 'lusty dancer' – but the implication is that Uisdean was a force of nature with energy in many directions. The Gordons needed his energy to bolster their standing in the north but perhaps they thought Uisdean – who was, of course, also slightly older and more experienced than Earl John – was taking over too much. Jane knew that loyalty to her husband was important in maintaining her family's powerbase, but that didn't mean she had to like it. Earl John wanted to clarify the family's legal position.

With the help of his new father-in-law, the Lord High Treasurer of Scotland, Earl John arranged to get a new investment of the whole Earldom of Sutherland. This legal proceeding confirmed the terms by which he held the lands, reinforcing the traditional rights of the Earl of Sutherland, but also including extra new details such as the making of Brora into a burgh of regality, and the declaration of other privileges. One of these other privileges was the confirmation that the Earl John held the heritable sheriffship of Sutherland and Strathnaver – a position which Wicked Earl George had occasionally wielded and very much wanted. Giving this position to Earl John, and making it hereditary, meant that Wicked Earl George lost both power and revenue.[34] The legal proceedings also stated that Strathnaver – the traditional Mackay lands – along with Edderachilis and Durness were all united into the Earldom of Sutherland. This meant that a large part of the Earldom was now made up of lands that had formerly been the independent possessions of the Clan Chiefs of Mackay – lands that could be legitimately claimed by the Gordon family partly through daughter Jane's marriage to the Mackay. However, Jane and her husband were the ones who suffered from the new deal: finally, and crucially, the rights of succession were outlined in detail. Earl John was to be succeeded by the 'heirs-male . . . lawfully begotten of his own body', and, if he did not have any sons, then the Earldom was to go to his brother Robert Gordon, and any sons of Robert, and, failing that, to his brother Alexander and any sons of Alexander – and if all of them died, then the Earldom of Sutherland was to go to Adam Gordon, the second son of Lord Huntly, and to any of Adam Gordon's sons.[35] This was not the usual method of succession, and was being deliberately designed and chosen to keep the Earldom of Sutherland in Gordon hands, and to make sure that Donald Mackay could never inherit. The Gordons had originally come into the title of the Earldom of Sutherland through marriage to a Sutherland daughter,[36] and by changing the rules of succession to keep out Jean's daughters and their heirs and passing the succession on instead to Jean's nephew purely to keep the Earldom in the family name of Gordon, the Earls of Sutherland created a situation that was "perhaps unique in the annals of the European peerage".[37] This was carrying the legal techniques that Jean and Alexander had used to keep the clans and Caithness in check to extremes.

James VI was happy to countenance it, as Earl John, with his European polish, fitted in with his court, and the plan of suppressing the Mackays fitted in well with James VI's aim of controlling the wilder Highland fringes of his kingdom. Since Donald's relegation to second-class citizen was later to cause friction with the Mackays, and personally to cause Donald much pain, it is possible that the full implications of the charter were not fully understood at the time – or were understood but thought to be something that could be tested. Earl John was making these arrangements, not Jean, so her feelings are hard to guess: true, she had fully convinced her children that her Gordon ancestry was the most important thing, and that the relationship with the Huntly Gordons must be maintained – but, on the other hand, her own Gordon descendants, her eldest child and her first grandchild, were being disinherited. Jean's childhood Huntly Gordon line was being given precedence over the Sutherland Gordon line she had created by marriage because of the union with the Clan Mackay. All this just as Jean herself had set aside the feelings of the

Gordons to follow her heart and finally marry Alex Ogilvie. Was the payoff that her son felt the need to reaffirm Gordon power by disinheriting half-Gordon half-clansman Donald Mackay? Did Jean unintentionally sacrifice her grandson's future for love?

The charter was also not calculated to improve relations between Caithness and Sutherland. Wicked Earl George, incensed at the greater power Earl John was receiving, revived his idea of going hunting on Sutherland territory. Wicked Earl George took a large party of men south and Earl John took a party of men north; the two armies met and camped facing each other at a place called Leayd-Reayfe.[38] There was an ancient prophecy that a battle would be fought at Leayd-Reayfe, 'that there shall be a battell foughten by the inhabitants of Sutherland, assisted by the Strathnaver, against the Caithness men, and that the victorie shall incline to Sutherland' – knowing this, it was with difficulty that Earl John held back his men. The prophecy also stated, however, that losses among the winning side would be greater than on the losing side. However, 'God prolongeth all things as pleaseth his divine majestie, vntill the appoynted tyme, which cannot be avoyded' – and Wicked Earl George chose to send messengers to Earl John rather than fight. Earl John's advisors were divided over whether or not to accept the peace envoy, but while they dithered, Wicked Earl George had sent some scouts, who took a good look at Earl John's forces and, feeling overwhelmed, encouraged their fellow 'hunters' to retreat – which they did in great disorder, 'fleeing and hurling together in such headlong haste, that everyone increased the fear of his fellow-companion'.[39] Wicked Earl George tried to save face by sending further messages saying he had only been making a point because he had been antagonised by Uisdean Mackay, not Earl John, and that he was happy for Earl John to enter into Caithness twice as far as the Caithness men had come into Sutherland. Earl John's men were left facing an empty field. They relieved their energy by collecting together lots of stones to build a giant cairn, which they called Carne-Teaghie, or The Flight Cairn.[40]

Although Earl John was allowed to continue to extend his power in the north, James VI was still aware that neither he nor Lord

Huntly had fully converted to the Protestant faith. Lord Huntly never returned to court on quite the same easy terms as he had once had with his king, remaining at home working on his project of rebuilding Huntly Castle. Earl John worked on the principle that if he did not draw too much attention to his faith, then he would be allowed to continue it. James VI might not tolerate Catholics – and especially Catholic plotting against him – but neither was he particularly fond of the strict Protestant ministers who continually told him that they had authority over Scotland and the Scots rather than the king. In 1602, the Protestant General Assembly decided that James VI was letting his Earls get away with too much, and appointed a minister to reside with Earl John and his family for three months at Dunrobin Castle, to instruct them in the reformed faith.[41] It made no noticeable long-term difference, and Earl John, like his mother Jean, continued to worship as a Catholic.

Jean's son Earl John continued to build his power in the north. Having seen the success of surrounding Caithness and making sure that Wicked Earl George always had to fight on several fronts – against both the Sutherland men and the Mackays – Earl John looked across the water from Caithness to the Orkney islands, and focused his next efforts of friendship on the Earl of Orkney. The Earls of Caithness had traditional links with Orkney, where, in the complicated history of their Earldom, the Sinclair family had roots. However, more recently the Earldom of Orkney had been given by Mary, Queen of Scots to another of her illegitimate half-brothers, Robert Stewart. Robert was not a pleasant man, and he has gone down in history for ruling Orkney – and, to a lesser extent Shetland – in a tyrannical way. His contemporaries at Mary, Queen of Scots' court had not been impressed with him, with the English ambassador Thomas Randolph describing him as "vain, worthless and full of evil".[42] Having only just managed to care about events as far north as Moray, Mary, Queen of Scots had shown even less interest in this more northern part of her kingdom until she had created Bothwell Duke of Orkney, but, following Bothwell's removal from the scene, Robert Stewart's son, Patrick, the 2nd Earl of Orkney, had taken over the Earldom again. Patrick seems to have taken after his unpleasant father, and is known in Orkney by the nickname 'Black Patie'. However he had spent time at the court in Edinburgh with James VI where he had not displeased the king – and Patrick had opportunity to meet Earl John in Edinburgh, where they could have compared notes on how they both disliked Wicked Earl George. In August 1602, Earl John, his brother Robert, and Uisdean Mackay 'and divers other gentlemen' went to Orkney to visit this Patrick Stewart.[43] Robert made little comment on Black Patie's personality, describing how he and his brother Earl John and their travelling companions set sail from Cromarty on Patrick's own warship, the *Dunkirk*, landing at Kirkwall, where they were 'honorablie received and heartelie enterteyned'. They stayed for just over a fortnight, and 'having concluded a band of freindship with Earle Patrick', embarked again and so returned home.[44]

Earl John was unusual in looking north. The focus of James VI and much of the rest of the country was to the south, where Elizabeth of England was an old, ailing woman, and the question of the succession of the throne of England was looming ever closer. There was little question in the mind of James VI that the source of power, revenue and – he was increasingly coming to believe – happiness lay in the south. The death of Elizabeth of England in 1603 and James VI's succession as King of England was a key turning point not only for the Sutherlands but for the whole of Scotland. The world of Jean's youth, and much of what she had known in her second marriage, was changed in a matter of years. A huge part of this was due to geography: for the people of the north of Scotland, the removal of the court from Edinburgh, already a long way distant, even further south to London had a massive effect on how they were able to interact with royalty, how their lands were managed and, crucially, on how the people who lived in the lands of the north were perceived.

James VI's key aim was always balance, in the pursuit of peace and the increase of his own power. His childhood experiences of being continually kidnapped had unsurprisingly given him a dislike for subjects who did not bow to his authority, and he also fought continual battles against a Protestant church that wanted to remind him that God was more important than kings. In the late sixteenth century he was interested in centralisation of government and control of the outlying Highlands and Border regions. He did not like the idea that the fringes of his kingdom could harbour malcontents and threats to his authority, and the Gaelic-speaking clansmen were a group who were obviously different and challenging. They did not fit with his ideas of a civilised European kingdom with a powerful king and a professional, centralised administration at its centre – the image of power he had seen in Scandinavia when he had collected his bride Anne of Denmark, or what he imagined went on at the court of Elizabeth of England. James VI saw Highlanders as wild, uncivilised men who did not even speak the language of government (i.e. they spoke Gaelic, not Scots).[45] Over the next decade James VI introduced a number of laws designed to control the Highlands, from trying to bring the clan system of land ownership in line with the feudal system in the rest of Scotland, to making a law that the eldest son of each Clan Chief must be educated in the Central Belt, in English (not Gaelic) before they were allowed to inherit their titles or land.[46] These were the same policies pursued in Sutherland and the north – the idea of educating the eldest son away from the family was one that James VI frequently employed for 'problem' subjects, including Catholics – and the policies all had the same aim of centralisation and control, with varying success rates. Highlanders needed special attention though, and were linked, too, on the west coast with the Gaelic-speaking Irish, who Elizabeth of England was in conflict with – the mercenary trade, where Scots went to Ireland to fight, was something that Elizabeth raised repeatedly and shrilly with James VI.[47] One of James VI's projects was the 'civilisation' of the Gaelic-speaking Highlanders of the Western Isles through the Lewis plantations, where he planned to import Lowlanders and put them in charge of the land and men of the west as a way of bringing that area under control and making it more profitable – people who failed to assimilate to Lowland culture were to be removed.[48] James had asked Lord Huntly to be involved in this project. Lord Huntly was of the north – but not a Highlandman. That was how the Earl John of Sutherland was seen as well. The Earls and the clan system were legally and socially distinct. The family links of the House of Gordon were not viewed the same way as the family links of the Clan Mackay. Jean, Earl John and their families likely spoke or at least understood Gaelic, but Scots was their native tongue and James VI was their overlord. Some confusion sometimes arises as those interested in clan history claim that 'Clan Sutherland' or 'Clan Gordon' were distinct entities, but in 1600 nothing could have been further from the truth. The Earls were not operating within the same system as the clans, and would have been horrified by that interpretation. The trouble was that the further south they went, the harder the distinction became to make: people in the south of Scotland and, later, in England, absorbed the idea that Highlanders and those from the north were barbarians. They did not distinguish between northern clansmen and northern Earls. To people in Edinburgh, for example, the Highlanders of the north and west could be conflated into one entity – with little distinction between the different cultures of the western Highlands, northern Highlands, the north-east and the Far North. The further south the royal court shifted, the easier it became to refer it all as 'the north' and all the people living there as 'Highlanders'. These later interpretations have both shaped modern thinking and muddied our understanding of 'north' and who belongs there and who the land of the north belongs to, and it is in the lives of Jean's children and grandchildren we see this shift begin.

When James VI received the news of Elizabeth of England's death, and decided to remove to London, Earl John did not follow him and the court. Like his father, Earl John later suffered ill health, and this "delicate constitution"[49] is given as the reason why he did not go to London – but his health problems were not yet a very serious matter. Instead, Earl John was concerned with the teeming life of the north, as his family chronicle shows, from vicious snowstorms[50] to clan feuds between the Macdonalds and Macleods,[51] the Macgregors[52] and later the Mackenzies,[53] to the excitement of beached whales (an ocean-gift for the Sutherland inhabitants)[54] or the tragedy (and gain) of shipwrecks,[55] as well as the interest of his growing family – especially as his children were of indifferent health. His wish to continue unobtrusively in the Catholic faith may also have influenced his decision to stay away from the king's court.

Another of Jean's children, however, had no wish to stay immured in Sutherland. Robert was Jean's second surviving son, and he is the child we know the most about because he was the family chronicler. His book *The Genealogical History of the Earldom of Sutherland* reveals him to be a man who was just as intelligent and competent as his mother – but also a man with a great sense of his own worth. He fully absorbed Jean's ideas of the importance of the Gordon family and the strength of the links between the Huntlys and the Sutherlands, and set them down as fact for future generations. He is assiduous in noting details of the wider Gordon network, and gives us much valuable information about cadet families, such as the Gordons of Golspitour, showing how much the networks of the House of Gordon were worth to him, and how they worked. He embraced, too, the idea that the Gordons were European, Scots with strong links to the continent, giving details of people who travelled widely. He saw Sutherland as linked to the wider world, not isolated in the north, and he wanted to travel and see that world for himself. When James VI succeeded to the English throne in 1603, Robert, along with his younger brother Alexander, had completed his studies in Edinburgh and had spent time at the Scottish court. Now he wanted to widen his experiences, and he applied to James VI for permission to go abroad. James VI had no problem in granting 'Robert and Alexander Gordon, brothers of John ... Earl of Sutherland, scholars ... special licence to pass forth of our realm ... for doing their lawful affairs ...' – with only the following caveats for the nephews of a well-known Jesuit and scions of a Catholic family: 'providing that the said persons do not attempt anything contrary to the religion as it is in our realm professed, nor prejudicial to our present estate, or hurtful to our crown ...'[56] Robert and Alexander, accompanied by suitable companions including tutor Mr

John Gray,[57] left on their journey in 1603, travelling down through England and then crossing to France.[58]

Robert and Alexander were to spend two years abroad, studying in various places, including the universities of Paris and Orléans, learning from and making contacts with the important people they met. They headed for places where there were many Scots already, including a Protestant academy at Saumur on the Loire, where Robert listened carefully to arguments about religion, logic and the philosophy of the Stoics. Another year was spent in Poitiers and then four months in Bourges and six months in Paris, where Robert studied law and 'employed himself in manly exercises'.[59]

The transition of James VI to being King of England as well of Scots was surprisingly peaceful. Robert noted that many outside commentators had thought that 'after Queen Elizabeth's decease', – particularly as she had always refused to officially name a successor – 'there must follow nothing in England but confusions and inter-reigns, and pertubations of estate, likelie far to exceed the ancient calamities of the civil wars between the house of Lancaster and York, but how much more mortal and bloody, when foreign competition should be added to domestic, and divisions for religion to matter of title to the crown ...'.[60] In the event, little of this feared calamity happened. Instead, Robert stated, 'the applause and joy' at James VI's succession 'was infinite ...'[61] Elizabeth, in her old age, had not been universally beloved (her transformation into a paragon of English royalty had not yet begun), and there was a desire for peace throughout England and Scotland. In Scotland itself, James VI's reign led to a period of "unprecedented tranquillity".[62]

Jean's life and surroundings in the north of Scotland were never wholly tranquil, but this period, when she was with Alex Ogilvie, was perhaps characterised by less major upheaval than any other time. As the court moved to London, the feuds in the north began to have less impact on the crown, and the country. Family and emotional life, in all their daily complexity, came to the fore, as Jean lived out the dreams of a young woman's romance.

CHAPTER SEVENTEEN

The Regulation of Noble Retinues:
1604/05–1610

In autumn 1605 Jean was expecting her two sons home from the continent. Robert and Alexander's last stop was Paris, and from there they journeyed home via England,[1] where James VI and I had by now established his court in London. When they finally reached their home in Sutherland, the autumn weather was closing in.

In Dornoch, there was a sudden and terrible storm, which caused massive damage to the cathedral. Dornoch Cathedral was partially ruined after being burnt down 35 years earlier by John the Stout and Aodh Mackay just after the poisoning of the Earl and Countess of Sutherland, but the tower and some fine Gothic arches were still standing. However, the gale force winds were so strong that this final part of Dornoch Cathedral fell: 'all the inner stone pillars of the north side of the body of the cathedral church ... were blown from the very roots and foundation ... clean over the outer walls'.[2] The pillars which had held up the roof were blown out – but to the astonishment of everyone in Dornoch the outer walls remained standing. It was as if the cathedral had been turned inside out by an explosion. Jean's family and the people around them in Dornoch were convinced that the storm in the Far North had been a sign to them that the Devil was at work, and bad things were brewing. In Scottish folklore, the Devil had long been associated with bad weather and strong winds. It was the night of 5th November 1605.

News travelled slowly to the north, but Jean's sons soon heard that as they had passed through England in October 1605 on their way north, they had missed Guy Fawkes' Gunpowder Plot by a matter of weeks. The people in Dornoch had known first that something bad was going to happen: the cathedral 'explosion' had been a premonition: 'As the devil was busy then to trouble the air, so was he busy, by these his firebrands [Guy Fawkes and the other plotters], to trouble the estate of Great Britain,' said Jean's son Robert.[3]

When James VI had acceded to the throne of England after the death of Elizabeth, English Catholics had thought that perhaps there might be a greater level of religious tolerance. In Scotland, Catholics and Protestants had been able to co-exist in some ways, with James VI maintaining personal friendship with Jean's nephew Lord Huntly, and Jesuits like Jean's brother Father James holding out hope that the Scottish crown might be open to debate – but when he reached England James VI did not make any major relaxation in the laws around religion.[4] Catholic plotting coalesced around what became known as the Gunpowder Plot. The plot horrified James VI for many reasons. Firstly, the idea that many people could be deliberately killed by one explosion was still relatively new and shocking, and was an idea that not only James VI but also Guy Fawkes and the other plotters wrestled with.[5] Secondly, James VI associated the horror of being blown up by gunpowder with the murder of his father Darnley, which brought back all sorts of associations. Finally, James VI had grown used to seeing England as a place where royalty was far more respected than in Scotland, and did not like having this idea challenged. The reprisals for those involved in the plot were fierce: after undergoing torture, Guy Fawkes was a broken man when he was finally led to the scaffold.

Jean's sons saw the Gunpowder Plot in different ways. At some point on their travels, the brothers Alexander and Robert had disagreed about religion. Robert had decided to become a Protestant but Alexander, like his mother Jean and older brother Earl John, remained a Catholic. All the universities in Scotland were, since the Reformation, Protestant, so from the moment they left home, the brothers had been exposed to new ideas on religion. Robert, the nephew of Father James the Jesuit, described the Gunpowder Plot as 'a monstrous and devilish plot, singular from all example, invented and devised by the Jesuits and their associates, against the king, queen, prince, and the whole state of Great Britain'.[6] Robert, who as a second son would inherit no guaranteed land or title, had already decided that he did not want to live permanently in Sutherland, but wanted to return to James VI's court in London. He had become committed to James VI's idea of a united England and Scotland and was horrified at the attack on the king's person. For Robert, religion was part of the state: "Be constant and sincere," he said, "without dissimulation in the religion that you professe, and which is now setled by the state of Great Britaigne."[7] Robert left Sutherland just a few months later and made his way back south, where he was to remain for many years. He was admitted to be one of the 'gentleman of the king's honourable privy chamber', or Gentleman of the Bedchamber, first temporarily, and then on a more permanent basis.[8] This meant he was in the king's inner circle of trusted noblemen at court. Robert was ambitious and wanted to advance in his 'career' as one of the king's nobles, and pursued his interest in the law, history, and the promotion of Gordon interests in London avidly.

Some commentators have suggested that the Gordon family simply decided that it would be good to have one foot in the other camp, but Robert's commitment to Protestantism was never questioned by his contemporaries. The religious convictions of all Jean's sons were strong, whether they converted to Protestantism or remained Catholic. In 1606, the same year that Robert left for London, Earl John's faith was questioned by the ministers of the reformed religion, and the idea was put forward that he and his family should be ordered to Inverness to receive religious instruction, although this never seems to have gone ahead.[9]

For the Earldom of Sutherland, it was certainly politic to have a member of the family so close to the king. It ensured that they were never forgotten, while their rivals – such as Wicked Earl George – were too far away from the southern court to consistently promote their interests. Robert was able to maintain good relations with his family, working on their behalf, despite their religious differences: "Keip God spairinglie in your mouth but aboundantlie in your heart," he said.[10] Jean, used to the tolerant days of Mary, Queen of Scots' court, seems to have encouraged this. In later letters Jean says she would not interfere with her servants' religion,[11] while Robert and, later, her grandson Donald's Protestant faith suggests that not only the Mackay clan but also cadet Gordon families such as the Golspitours may have been Protestant, meaning Jean was even happy to have her sons and grandson wet-nursed by people of different religion. Robert saw religious beliefs as private and if they would cause problems with his brothers, he would not speak about them even though his religious convictions were deeply held.[12] Robert always remained on excellent terms with his Catholic family. The true division between him and his brothers seems to have mainly been one of personality: his younger brother Alexander, who had travelled with him in France and been exposed to the same new philosophical ideas, never had any desire to leave the north of Scotland. Unlike his ambitious, self-aggrandising brother Robert, Alexander's main characteristic was his faithfulness to both his Catholic religion and to his family around him. Jean's sons were very different men.

Jean had now two of her sons, Alexander and Earl John, both living in Sutherland, as well as her two daughters, Jane (married to Uisdean Mackay and mother to a hopeful family) and Mary. Sadly, Jean's youngest daughter Mary died in 1605. Mary's marriage to Ross of Balnagowan had produced no children, and she was only 23 years old. Her brother Robert records her tribute, saying she was 'a virtuous and comely lady, of an excellent and quick wit'.[13] Along with her two sons who had died in infancy, Jean had now buried three of her children.

Jean also lost a grandchild in 1604: Patrick, the son of Earl John, who died shortly after his birth. Baby Patrick had been named after the Earl of Orkney, who Robert and his brother Earl John had recently visited. 'Black Patie' had been on a return visit to Dunrobin, where he had been 'honorablie entertained with comedies, and all other sports and recreations that Earl John could make him',[14] when the baby had been born. Earl John was still focusing on power relations in the north of Scotland, and was ready to stand as friend to Earl Patrick a couple of years later when Black Patie was summoned before Parliament in Edinburgh to answer a charge of treason. The proceedings against Earl Patrick were quashed by James VI as being 'frivolous'.[15]

Robert, meanwhile, was diligently doing all he could to promote his brother's – and his own – interests at court. Christian, King of Denmark and brother of Queen Anne, paid a state visit to James VI in 1606, and Robert was among James VI's retinue as they met Christian and his '8 great ships' at Gravesend.[16] Christian remained in England for around a month, and Robert would have been there as he was treated to the best entertainment that James VI could lay on: masques, hunting, sermons from the best preachers, feasting and lots of drinking.[17] While Earl John was preoccupied with local feuds and clan clashes, he always knew he could rely on Robert to keep him up to date with court events – and to continually present the Sutherland Gordon case to James VI. By contrast, Jean's nephew Lord Huntly, once so friendly with James VI, did not have a representative at court. Lord Huntly had remained in the north, and was struggling with the growing power of the Scottish kirk, which in 1605 had wanted to excommunicate him because of his continuing Catholic sympathies. Lord Huntly decided to travel to London – without leave from James VI – hoping that if he could only meet with the king in person he could sort things out. It was a long journey to make, and Lord Huntly found it was completely in vain. James VI refused to even see him, and Lord Huntly had to return home to the north. For Jean's nephew, once such a power in the land, it was humiliating.[18] James VI then asked Lord Huntly to send his eldest son (known as the Earl of Enzie) to London, to attend Henry, Prince of Wales – but Lord Huntly's son was never a representative of the Huntly Gordons at court: instead he was there so that he would be removed from the influence of his family and tutored up to be a loyal Protestant subject of James VI and the king's son Henry.[19]

James VI was still very keen to regulate his troublesome Scottish nobles, and to maintain his control over the north even though he was now based in London. Along with his plans to 'civilise' the Highland clans by ensuring their land ownership was in line with the system in place in the rest of Scotland and their use of Gaelic was curbed,[20] James VI was working to establish a professional, centralised administration, along the lines of the civil service in England.[21] Scotland had never had the same level of secretariat as England – for example, it did not have a regular system of taxation. These things had been in some ways unnecessary since Scotland was a cheaper country to run than England or France for several reasons including its geographical position: there was only one land border to police, and wars were less costly. The lack of regular taxation then theoretically made the nobles more loyal, and instead of bureaucratic efficiency Scotland and its rulers relied more on the obligation of kinship and personal lordship.[22] This was no longer going to work if James VI and his descendants were going to be king of a joint Scotland and England, so James VI wanted Scotland to fall in line with England. Other factors were also at play, including changing attitudes as strict Protestantism was adhered to by more of the population. James VI altered various laws, introducing new legislation on "gun control, curbing of duels[23] and private combat" and was later to add a new layer of administration into the justice system with the introduction of Justices of the Peace, who dealt with low-level offences such as vagrancy. Previously, nobles such as Lord Huntly would have dispensed justice, but now James VI was spreading out the responsibility among other layers of society.[24]

James VI also introduced new laws on "the regulation of noble retinues"[25]: the Earls of Sutherland or Huntly were used to travelling with a group of their friends and relatives at all times, a train of men who would clear the way for them, keep them company, and fight for them if need be – but these groups of young men and their imitators, as Jean had already seen, were getting out of control in the north-east. As the noble families in the north became less important in the scheme of Great Britain, cadet families were muscling in. In 1607,

Lord Huntly was asked to suppress a gang known as the 'Society and Company of Boys', who had banded together under the leadership of two younger brothers of two lairds: a cadet Gordon family leader, Gordon of Gight, and a John Forbes.[26] The Society and Company of Boys had formed with the idea of promoting "manly virtues and camaraderie" and had originally been tolerated by Lord Huntly because of their potential usefulness if a strongman was needed, but they rapidly degenerated.[27] They operated partly like a secret society: they had taken oaths of mutual defence and now swaggered around the countryside of the north-east, where Jean was living with Alex Ogilvie, disrupting the peace and committing "enormities" including robbery and murder, carrying dirks, pistols and large heavy claymore swords and demonstrated an "insolent contempt for the law".[28] They obtained a second nickname, the 'Knights of the Mortar', which did not really mean that they were knightly and chivalrous: "[the nickname was] a consciously obscene and humorous perversion of such ideals...", possibly referencing a contemporary play called "The Knight of the Burning Pestle", a farcical send-up of a romance, where a lowly grocer's apprentice thinks he is a knight, and puts a pestle on his shield. A 'pestle' was a well-known sexual slang term.[29] However, violence, not sex, may have been the Boys main preoccupation – or there may even have been a religious motivation: the Boys might have been seen as a particular threat by the Scottish state because their oaths were made under Catholic symbols and rites.[30] It took a good three years, but Lord Huntly, and his son Enzie, seem to have got the Society and Company of Boys under control eventually. John Forbes, one of the ringleaders was tried, convicted and executed for crimes including carrying arms and two murders fairly early on, but the Boys had gathered momentum, and others stepped up to lead the gang once he was gone.[31]

The society that Jean lived in had always seen a sharper delineation between men and women than our modern lives, but the saga of the Society and Company of Boys shows how this continued to evolve. A side-result of the move of the court to London, interacting with other factors such as the change in the royal household to a married family and the widespread changes in religion, was the shift that it encouraged in noblewomen's education and roles, which then spread out to other women in society. Jean's daughters, Jane and Mary, had not benefitted from the same level of education that Jean had, because of their earlier marriages, but they were part of a wider trend. Jean's own generation, including the well-educated Mary, Queen of Scots and Elizabeth of England, was turning out to have been a high point for women's education and participation in public life. Now that the court was in England, Scotsmen were having to travel for a fortnight to get to the centre of power – and that court looked very different to Elizabeth of England's regime. The King and Queen lived in separate households, while James VI worked and lived daily with a group of men – notoriously including his particular male 'favourites' – to decide on issues of state. When Scotsmen arrived there, they could find that they were unknowns – looking and sounding different to the English noblemen who were at court all the time. Sensitive to their status, Scotsmen were making sure that when they arrived at court they were educated: that they could read and write to the same standard as their English counterparts – without too much of an accent or too many foreign Scots words – or that, like Jean's sons Robert and Alexander, they had travelled on the continent and taken advantage of learning opportunities there. James VI was also eager to continue to have Scots nobles loyal to him, and, as he had done with Lord Huntly, encouraged anyone who was Catholic or otherwise suspect in their loyalty to send their sons away to school to learn more. While the sons, husbands, brothers and fathers were thus engaged, Scotswomen continued to run their estates. Jean, like her mother, had always been in charge of her husbands' lands and estates, working with land agents to arrange rent collection or projects such as the Brora salt mines. This had been an important and valued part of her life. However, it had never meant that she was cut off from joining in court life or the wider socialising of the nobility when the opportunity had presented itself. Now that was different: travelling long distances to London was expensive, and fewer and fewer Scots noblewomen made the journeys with their husbands.[32]

Indeed, it was important that they stayed behind, as the length of the journey would mean leaving the estate unmanaged for a long time. This had the effect of isolating many Scots noblewomen from the court: they were not ladies of fashion, they did not participate in court life and they were not close to the centre of power. No matter how important running the land was, if it was perceived as being far away from the centre of power, it gradually became perceived as being the less important role in a marriage. And, while noblemen's sons were travelling to court, going away to school or travelling on the continent, the daughters of Scots noble families were losing the benefit of living and working alongside their brothers. Scotswomen's education was changing – while, in addition, the new reformed religion was often now their main access to learning, with the result that many Scots noblewomen became deeply religious, with strong and strict Presbyterian convictions.[33] For Jean, dedicated to both her Catholic religion and used to running estates successfully, the gradual changes were no loss: they played to her strengths. Jean's sons and daughters all lived very different lives to the one Jean had experienced, but Jean's daughters and granddaughters had a loss of education, a restriction of travel and a loss of status that their male siblings did not fully share.

Jean's son Earl John never went to court in London for any length of time, leaving that to his brother Robert. Instead, Earl John was still concerned with the local problem of his neighbours, specifically Wicked Earl George, who was once again pushing the boundaries – quite literally, as he tried again to go 'hunting' in Sutherland without permission.[34] Lord Huntly intervened as peacemaker, and invited Earl John and Wicked Earl George to meet in Elgin in 1607 – but when Wicked Earl George made the journey he discovered it was less of a peaceful negotiation than a show of force: he found Earl John with a formidable array of his friends and supporters ranged behind him: Frasers, Dunbars, Mackenzies, Munros, Mackintoshes and others. Wicked Earl George was starting to realise that he was very much on the back foot, and refused to ever again hold any similar meetings with Earl John and Lord Huntly. Wicked Earl George then went on to express his resentment on Earl John's allies: Earl John had kept on good terms with Patrick, Earl of Orkney, and when some Orcadians were forced by 'a contrary wind and vehement storm of weather' to land in Caithness, Wicked Earl George saw his opportunity to make a point.[35] First, Wicked Earl George 'made' the stranded Orcadian sailors 'drunk, then in a mocking jest he caused shave the one side of their beards, and one side of their heads; last of all, he constrained them to take their vessel and to go to sea in that stormy tempest. The poor men, fearing his further cruelty, did choose rather to commit themselves to the mercy of the senseless elements and raging waves of the sea, than abide his fury, so they entered the stormy seas of [the] Pentland Firth (a fearful and dangerous arm of sea between Caithness and Orkney) . . .' The drunken, half-shaven sailors were either lucky or, as their friends insisted, benefitted from 'the providence and assistance of God, who had compassion on them in this lamentable and desperate case, and directed their course, so that they landed safely in Orkney'.[36]

Robert was outraged by the affront and indignity suffered by his Orcadian allies, who had not only been made to look ridiculous but had also genuinely been put in great danger by being forced to sail across a stretch of sea that could be treacherous in bad weather. Nonetheless, the image of the men staggering drunk across the deck of the ship with half their beards and hair shaved off is very funny – and a very childish sort of revenge tale. Along with stories of the Society and Company of Boys, the Earls of the north and north-east were not doing very much to challenge the perception of James VI and his court that everyone in the north of Scotland was a backwards savage living in a lawless land.

One of the ways that Earl John and Robert were pursuing the Sutherland Gordon interests at this time was through the official ranking of the nobility. This had been an ongoing process since Earl John had first made his appearance at James VI's court in Edinburgh. The noblemen of Scotland were, according to Robert the lawyer, 'enrolled according to the antiquity of their investments, grounded upon an act of council, ratified and confirmed by the king's commission' – there was a clear pecking order of who was more important, which was shown on state occasions by the order in which the Earls followed the king and the ceremonial duties they carried out.[37] Wicked Earl George had been most put out when Earl John, instead of him, was allowed to carry the sword of honour in front of King James VI. It was not just ceremonial duties though: if the Earl of Sutherland was ranked higher than the Earl of Caithness then he had more say in Parliament and more chance of favour from the king, be that financial, legal or land-based. Robert repeatedly insists in his family chronicle that the Earls of Sutherland had always been ranked higher in the lists of nobility than the Earls of Caithness – something which their relative power bases during Jean's lifetime did not always bear out. However, Robert, the debonair man at court, had managed to convince James VI that the Earls of Sutherland were definitely more important than the beard-cutting Wicked Earl George of Caithness and in 1606 a special commission had definitively ranked the Scottish nobles so they knew where to take their places in Parliament: Sutherland came sixth, and Caithness came fourteenth. Robert had then continued to push for this ranking to be consolidated through the legal courts, which the Earls of Sutherland were successful in doing.[38]

Jean's nephew, Lord Huntly, was also working to make sure that the Huntly Gordons were not completely left out or turned into savages in the mind of the king. He officially ended his feud with Moray in 1607, when a long-promised marriage alliance finally took place between Lord Huntly's eldest daughter, Anne Gordon, and the Earl of Moray. Meanwhile Lord Huntly's son, Enzie, was married to Lady Anne Campbell, the 13-year-old daughter of the 7th Earl of Argyll in an attempt to ally and heal the wounds between the two families who had fought against each other at the Battle of Glenlivet.[39] These marriage alliances did not solve all the Lord Huntly's problems, however, as his increasingly strong commitment to Catholicism inevitably brought him into conflict with Protestant ministers, and he was ordered several times into ward (effectively house arrest) or to attend church, and lost important administrative and legal position such as his role as lieutenant of the north. His old friend James VI may have had sympathy with him, and no real problem with him practising his religion if he did it discreetly, but the wider religious context meant James VI had to be seen to act against Catholics.[40] James VI was influenced not just by events in Scotland or England but also by happenings on the continent which were widely talked about, such as the 1610 assassination of King Henri IV of France, who had given up his Protestant faith to accede the French throne. This move had made Henri unpopular with both Protestants, who saw him as a traitor, and Catholics, who thought his conversion suspect. He had survived 23 assassination attempts but the 24th got him: he was stabbed to death by a Catholic fanatic as his coach was forced to stop in heavy Parisian traffic. The death of Henri IV was felt strongly in England, particularly by the heir to the throne, James VI's eldest son Henry.[41] Religious tolerance was very far from being a successful policy, and the fallout from the Reformation was to last for many years yet.

Jean's son Robert was doing well at court, and was knighted in 1609. Sir Robert Gordon also received a life pension from James VI, paid out of money from the English exchequer – money he could rely on for the rest of his life. Robert never became an overly prominent figure at James VI's court – which meant that although he did not reach dizzy heights, neither did he draw any unwelcome attention to himself. He perfected the art of being someone who was always there, always participating in court life (though perhaps never at the centre of it), a reliable, welcome presence – someone who knew exactly how things worked, and how that could benefit them.[42] James VI's court was an enthralling place to be for Robert: Jean's son met new people and discussed with them new ideas on history, philosophy, legal studies and religion. The cultural offerings were vastly different to those on offer in Sutherland, and Robert would have seen the original, premiere performances of Shakespeare's plays – Shakespeare's company were known as the King's Men, and his plays were given special performances in front of James VI. From 1606, when Robert first arrived in London, the new plays being performed were *King Lear, Antony and Cleopatra,* and *Macbeth.* Robert would have been one of the few people in the audience for *Macbeth* who knew exactly where Cawdor Castle was, who the Thane of Cawdor was – especially since his cousin Lord Huntly had been involved in killing the latest incumbent of that title[43] – and what the Highland landscape that Macbeth was fighting through was like. When Robert later turned author himself, writing the history of the Sutherland family, he made sure to include reference to the historical Macbeth, siding firmly with the Shakespearian interpretation that Macbeth was a traitorous villain who 'by force usurped the crown of Scotland', until the rightful King Malcolm was aided by friendly England to recover the kingdom of Scotland.[44] Robert cited the Scottish historian Boethius[45] as one of his sources; the same historian who influenced Holinshed, whose account Shakespeare relied on. Both historians had greatly maligned the real Macbeth in order to flatter the royal family who had taken his place: the ancestors of the current James VI and I. Robert was very firmly on the side of the Scots king and his project to unite the kingdoms of Scotland and England in his person, and had no interest in the interpretation of *Macbeth* which suggests that when Macbeth was killed, Celtic Britain, as epitomised by the Highlands, lost out in favour of a more southern, English-favouring attitude. Robert's account of the historical Macbeth concludes with a careful explanation of how one of Macbeth's victims was Robert's own ancestor Alan Sutherland, Thane of Sutherland, who 'abhorring and detesting [Macbeth]'s cruel tyranny, constantly remained faithful to his lawful sovereign, Malcom Canmore', even until death.[46] That image of the Sutherland family faithful to their king was the one that Robert was actively projecting at court.

Jean liked to hear about her son Robert's life in London in his regular letters to her, but, rather than being interested in cultural accounts, she had more pressing issues of illness and death in the family to deal with. Her son Earl John took after his father in having increasingly poor health as he grew older. As a young man, his brother Robert had described Earl John as being 'a well-disposed and able gentleman', coping with the continual simmering clan and family violence of his Earldom and dealing easily with the harsh weather conditions of Sutherland in winter. A description of a typically healthy young Earl John is told in the story of a violent snowstorm which overtook the Earl and his entourage as they travelled from Golspitour through the Glen of Loth. Some of the men drank whisky to warm them as the storm grew stronger, but it had the opposite of the desired effect. The journey ended in chaos, with some of Earl John's company sticking together and making it through the Glen, while stragglers had to be left behind. Some of the men were carried home on their friends' shoulders, to make a recovery at home, but three people perished and were found dead the next morning among the snow.[47] However, by June 1608, at the age of only 32, Earl John was sufficiently concerned to asked James for a licence to leave the country for three years, as he had been advised to go abroad for the sake of his health. In the end, Earl John decided not to go, but his worsening health continued to be a problem.[48] Like his father Alexander, we don't know just what Earl John's illness was, or why he was considered frail, but, as the story of the snowstorm shows, the Earls had to be in rude health to lead their men in the field, even in more peaceable times.

Another important person in Jean's life was also ailing. After only a few years, her idyllic romantic ending with Alex Ogilvie was coming to an end. They had lived quietly since their marriage in 1599, contained together as a couple with little impact on the world outside them and little to disturb them. It is the most private part of Jean's life; the only stage when she was able to make a choice for herself rather than directing her actions for the benefit of her family. We do not even know exactly when Alex Ogilvie died: several secondary sources make reference to him being alive in 1606,[49] but it could have been as early as 1601,[50] giving Jean only a couple of years with him. Certainly, they had less than a decade together, and by 1609 Alex Ogilvie was gone.

Alex Ogilvie probably died in the north-east, where his castle of Boyne was situated, as he seems to have been buried in a local churchyard there, Kirkton at Deskford; an Ogilvie family resting-place. He was laid to rest beside his first wife, Mary Beaton.[51] Alex Ogilvie and Mary Beaton had had children and Jean knew that they were the family unit: Alex Ogilvie was not to be buried in the Gordon or Sutherland family plots. His romance with Jean was private and nothing to do with family. They had overcome obstacles to be together but their romance had only been given its chance because of the early death of both their spouses: it was an extra, a lucky few years.

Now that Jean had been widowed again, she reverted to being wholly a Gordon. Her home and loyalty were once more with her children, in Sutherland.

CHAPTER EIGHTEEN

Plots and Mercenaries: 1611–1616/17

PART I: THE FALSE COINER

Widowed for the third time, Jean returned to Sutherland and her children and the Gordon family once more. Under the terms of her marriage contract with Alexander, which had been carefully preserved in the marriage contract with Alex Ogilvie, Jean was still entitled to her jointure lands in Sutherland; some property had been set aside for Jean from which she could draw an income. In wealthy families like Jean's, widows were usually also entitled to liferent of one of their husband's houses, which they could live in if they were widowed – a dower house. Jean had a house built, on the coast between Brora and Helmsdale – close to her salt and coal-mining operations – called Crakaig.[1]

Jean's son Robert had left for London, but the rest of her children were close by, and she was at the centre of a spreading family whose intermarriages and children were promoting Gordon interests and shaping the countryside around her. At Dunrobin, the Sutherland Gordon hub, Earl John and his wife Annas Elphinstone had a young family to raise but, tragically, Annas lost five of her children in infancy altogether. Jean saw, around this time, three baby grandsons and one baby granddaughter die.[2] Meanwhile, Jean's youngest son Alexander married a local girl, Margaret Macleod, daughter of the laird of Assynt, and granddaughter of Aodh Mackay.[3] This linked Alexander strongly to the north, and to his sister Jane and her husband Uisdean as Margaret's mother was Uisdean's sister. Although Earl John had made the legal arrangements to leave the Sutherland Gordon inheritance away from the Mackay clan and his sister Jane's in-laws, this was still an abstract concept that the rest of the Sutherland Gordons were not really following, as Alexander of Navidale linked them once again by marriage to the clans. In practice Jean and her children, especially Jane and Alexander, were very close to the Clan Mackay – or, at least, to the branch of it which was loyal to the Gordons. The Gordons were still balancing between the north and the law, their allegiances on the ground and their aims at court, and Uisdean Mackay still had an enormous amount of influence. When the Gordons went to court, they presented to James VI the appearance that the Earls were in complete control when in reality Uisdean, Chief of Mackay, was intimately involved in the running of the north.

There were particular changes at this time for Jean's eldest daughter Jane and for her grandson Donald Mackay. Jane and Uisdean had four children: two boys, Donald and John, and two girls, Anna and Mary. Jean's eldest grandson Donald Mackay was now in his early twenties and married in 1610. His new wife was Barbara Mackenzie, the daughter of the first Lord Kintail. Mackenzie of Kintail was a Highland Gael with interests in Ross-shire and further west,[4] who was loyal to the Scottish crown and James VI, and who had recently been raised to the peerage. Kintail was loyal to the Gordons, and linked to them already through his marriage to a daughter of the Rosses of Balnagowan – the same family that Jean's daughter Mary had been married into.[5] Over the last few years Jean's son Earl John of Sutherland, who had an old friendship with the Clan Mackenzie, had encouraged the Gordons of Golspitour to help Lord Kintail against his enemy Glengarry.[6] Donald and Barbara Mackenzie's marriage was an alliance that was designed to cement Gordon power in the north, and promote James VI's view of loyal Gaels and clans. Donald and his father-in-law were made Justices of the Peace for Inverness-shire and Cromarty.[7] Lord Kintail did not hold the position long before he died, but Donald was becoming established. His marriage to Barbara seemed to go well, as they started a family a year or so after their wedding with the birth of a son, John. Jean was now a great-grandmother.

Donald's father Uisdean Mackay started to take a back seat from about 1611, going into 'retirement' and leaving things to his son.[8] Uisdean was now 50 years old, and there are suggestions that his health was not so good, so he was happy to leave the more active part of being the clan or Gordon representative to Donald. Meanwhile, Uisdean held open house at his home in Tongue, where he fostered the cultural side of the Mackay clan: "he bred and brought up the young men still in his own company, that by daily conversing together familiarly, they might accustom themselves mutually to love one another".[9] It is unclear whether his wife Jane continued to live with him, but based on later references, Jane, like her mother before her, most likely split her time between her husband and their four children, and the childhood Gordon home of her parent and siblings. Jean's son Robert had said that Uisdean's 'one vice that overruled him ... was his extraordinary lust ...'[10] but his summing up of Uisdean's character was generally positive, and he added that towards the end of his life, as Uisdean took this 'retirement', he 'became exceeding penitent' for his lust, and that it was a vice 'which in great men (abounding in wealth and health), can hardly be avoided without the special grace of God'.[11] The wider family network was what Jean had taught her children to value, and Jane and Uisdean had clearly come to some sort of understanding over time.

Likewise, Uisdean's focus had turned in his retirement to the wider family of the clan of Mackay and their traditions: he brought into his house an important new person, Donald Mor MacCrimmon, the Isle of Skye piper. The MacCrimmons were legendary bagpipe players of great skill, and Donald Mor MacCrimmon had specialised in the pibroch, the difficult solo form of bagpipe playing called 'ceol mor' (or the 'great music'). Pibroch is also known as the classical music of the bagpipes and involves elaborate variations on a central theme, with difficult fingering and particularly unusual timings and groupings of notes, powerful and hypnotic when played well. MacCrimmon's notable tunes had already included a Salute to Macleod, "Faillte nan Leodach",[12] and "Cille Chriosd",[13] a song played while a party of enemies were burnt to death in a church – an incident which had apparently contributed to MacCrimmon leaving Skye and heading for Sutherland.[14] With Donald Mor MacCrimmon leading them, the Mackay clan now in turn became famous for their pibroch – helping to preserve the MacCrimmon genius in this difficult art form and meaning Uisdean promoted and left a legacy of music still played today.[15]

The Mackay clan and the Wicked Earl George of Caithness had never truly reconciled after Uisdean's marriage to Jane and defection to the Gordons, and one of Donald's cousins had been imprisoned by Wicked Earl George.[16] Donald visited Caithness frequently to ask for his release, and finally Wicked Earl George agreed – on the condition that Donald and Uisdean spent Christmas with him. Uisdean duly went along to spend time with his former childhood companion, and was 'well entertained for several days' at the refurbished Castle Sinclair-Girnigoe – but Uisdean took with him a different family member as Donald claimed he 'was prevented by some occurrence' from spending time with Wicked Earl George.[17] Donald's cousin was released and all seemed on the surface to have gone well, but Donald's non-appearance at the Christmas meal was not a good sign for future relations with Caithness. There might be an outward show of civility and reciprocal meals, but Jean's grandson was carrying on the Gordon Sutherland enmity to Caithness. Matters did not improve when Donald believed that Wicked Earl George mistreated a Mackay servant who had allegedly helped a member of the troublesome Clan Gunn to escape imprisonment in Castle Sinclair-Girnigoe.[18] Then, in 1612, Donald became involved in "an intricate and bizarre"[19] plot against Wicked Earl George, involving a false coiner called Arthur Smith.

The Arthur Smith plot was long and complex, and had started as far back as 1599 when blacksmith Arthur Smith and 'his man' were first discovered in Banff, in the north-east, making false coins – crafting currency so well-made that it could pass for the real thing.[20] Arthur Smith, using the established travelling routes, fled to Sutherland to escape the authorities. At this time, Jean had been in Sutherland, but had been well-attuned to events in the north-east as she was about to marry Alex Ogilvie, and she had given orders to have Smith arrested and handed over to the authorities. Arthur Smith was sent down to Edinburgh, where he was placed in captivity and condemned to death. His accomplice was in fact executed – 'burnt in ashes'.[21] However, Arthur Smith managed to obtain some tools in jail, and fashioned an extremely intricate lock: a stunning sample of his extraordinary ability that was 'of such exquisite invention and ingenious device that the like could not be found again'. The 'rare and curious' lock was taken to James VI, who was astonished at the high level of craftsmanship, and decided that a man as talented as Arthur Smith should not be killed.[22] With the advice and support of Lord Elphinstone, treasurer of Scotland and soon-to-be Jean's son Earl John's father-in-law, James VI pardoned Arthur Smith and he was set free. Smith then returned to the Far North.[23]

Wicked Earl George was always short of money, but in 1612 a suspicious amount of cash started appearing in Caithness, Sutherland and the surrounding area. When Jean's son Robert came home on a visit, he had no hesitation in tracing the source of the mysterious cash to the well-known false coiner Arthur Smith. Robert alleged to James VI that Arthur Smith was in the pay of Wicked Earl George and had a base set up under the rocks of Castle Sinclair-Girnigoe, connected by a secret passageway to Wicked Earl George's own bedchamber.[24] Receiving a commission from James VI to apprehend Arthur Smith and bring him again to trial in Edinburgh, Robert arranged for Donald Mackay and a band of Mackay and Gordon followers, including Donald's foster-brother and best friend Young Golspitour, to arrest the false coiner. Marching north in May 1612, Donald and Young Golspitour found Arthur Smith in Thurso, not in Castle Sinclair-Girnigoe, and discovered some gold and silver false coins in his house and in his pockets. This was enough for them to arrest Smith, who they mounted on horseback and sent, under guard, out of the town. However, the arrest had attracted a certain amount of attention so Young Golspitour stayed to try and placate the crowd that was gathering, showing them their written commission from James VI ordering Arthur Smith's arrest. This was not enough to calm the situation, and the town common bell was rung to sound an alarm. Various Sinclair men who happened to be in town with Wicked Earl George's daughter-in-law took exception to the idea of Donald and Young Golspitour coming into their territory and arresting a man who may have worked for George. A fight inevitably broke out between Young Golspitour and his men, and the Sinclairs. Hearing the noise, Donald and his companions turned back. The 'sharp skirmish' between Young Golspitour and the Sinclairs had ended with Young Golspitour's victory, and one Sinclair man dead – but it was too late for Arthur Smith. As Donald had returned to his foster-brother's aid, 'during the tumult, Arthur Smith was slain by the Strathnaver men, who had him in their hands at the town's end, when they first heard the noise, being loath that he should have been retaken'.[25] Robert claimed that the killings were done in self-defence – he carefully described how the dead men had condemned Wicked Earl George and proved his guilt with what they had said, but equally carefully made sure to point out that it was Mackay men and not Gordon men who had done the final acts of violence against Caithness.[26]

Robert's version of these events is slightly suspicious, and there are a number of unanswered questions. Why did Arthur Smith go to Caithness after he was released? In court documents it appears to say he used the alias 'Neill Nathnear':[27] was this a local name that showed he already had links and was a player in the north? Was Lord Elphinstone's involvement innocent? He was Jean's son Earl John's father-in-law, so had an interest in the north. Why did it take Robert's visit to the north to bring up Arthur Smith's crimes – why did his brother Alexander or his mother Jean not say anything before? Why was Arthur Smith in Thurso if he was in Wicked Earl George's pay – why not in Sinclair-Girnigoe Castle or Wick?[28] Reading between the lines of Robert's account, the extra details of Arthur

Smith's incredible craftsmanship, and the convoluted diversions into the iniquities of Clan Gunn, seem like a smokescreen to hide what the real plan was. Robert was trying to take circumstances that had been presented to him and use them to his advantage: his aim, as always, was to advance the house of Gordon and the Earldom of Sutherland. There was more than one plot going on here. First of all, Robert was making sure that Wicked Earl George's name was blackened as a man who had hired a false coiner to flood the Far North with fake coins – even after James VI had shown clemency to Arthur Smith before. But second, Robert knew that Wicked Earl George felt hostile to Uisdean and the Mackays and was trying to make sure that the enmity was primarily between Donald Mackay and Wicked Earl George rather than Wicked Earl George and the Earls of Sutherland. Poor, talented Arthur Smith was a casualty in a much grander plan which had been set in motion by Robert. Robert's account of events, written a few years afterwards with the benefit of some hindsight, tries to present him in the best light, emphasising that Donald Mackay killed Arthur Smith almost in cold blood. As a fairly recently appointed Justice of the Peace, Donald Mackay had thought that he was only doing his duty, and never suspected his uncle Robert of anything more devious. Donald's trusting nature where his Gordon relatives were concerned was starting to bring him problems, as Wicked Earl George was now his sworn enemy, and pursued Donald through the Edinburgh courts to try and obtain some sort of justice for the Caithness men who had been killed in the taking of Arthur Smith.

Robert was directing events because his brother Earl John's health had taken a decided turn for the worse. Earl John was subject to 'diverse diseases and infirmities of body' and 'for the recovery of his health he is advised to repair to foreign countries'.[29] Earl John applied again to James VI for leave to travel, and received a licence on 22nd January 1611 to go abroad. This time he went. James VI allowed him to 'pass forth of our realms and dominions to whatsoever parts beyond sea he pleases, and to remain forth thereof for seeking of ordinary remedies for his health, and doing of his other affairs, the space of three years'. Sutherland in January could be a cold, wet and grim place, with short hours of winter daylight so far north, and the warmer, drier air and light of the continent would certainly help a man in poor health. Earl John was reminded by James VI that 'during his absence furth of our realme [he should] behave himself as a dutiful and obedient subject to us, and do not attempt no thing in hurt nor prejudice of us, our realm and estate, nor the true religion presently professed within this our realm' and sent on his way, heading through England for France. Robert came up from London to take charge of the Earldom of Sutherland.

Robert felt that he was best suited to helping from a distance: he did not take part in the fight in Thurso as Arthur Smith was arrested because he had 'urgent and hasty business of law, appertaining to the house of Sutherland, to dispatch at Edinburgh, against the Earl of Caithness'.[30] After his years on the continent studying law, and his time at court in London, Robert believed that real power would come through legal means: he had learnt from the approach that Jean and Alexander had taken, and wanted to move that on further. Robert seems to have seen Donald Mackay as his strong man on the ground while he, Robert, would do the delicate legal work to shore up the House of Gordon and bring down their enemies. After Donald Mackay had done the dirty work, Robert's younger brother Alexander came down to Edinburgh to report.[31] Meanwhile, Wicked Earl George also sent his man to Edinburgh and both sides 'did cite and summon one another before the council and justice at Edinburgh'.[32] Robert and Donald Mackay argued that George and his cronies had resisted the king's commission to arrest Arthur Smith, while Wicked Earl George summoned Donald Mackay and Young Golspitour for the murder of the Sinclair man in Thurso, informing the Privy Council that the whole commission to arrest Arthur Smith had been a ploy and that the real plan all along had been the Sinclair murder – and, moreover, that Robert himself had lain in wait before at the Firth of Portnecouter to kill Wicked Earl George himself.

All the parties concerned came to Edinburgh for the hearing – bringing with them, of course, 'all their friends … sundry other gentlemen of good quality, too long [a list] to set down' to support them.[33] Wicked Earl George objected immediately that he was forced to face only 'seconds and children'[34] – where, he asked, were his equals in status? Where were Uisdean and Earl John?[35] Jean's approach had always been that the Gordons were one unit: the head of the family was fully supported by siblings, and siblings were of equal importance. But Wicked Earl George wanted to know why only Robert and Donald Mackay were there to face him? This was a severe underestimation of Robert's abilities – and an overestimation on Wicked Earl George's part of how important the Earldom of Caithness was now perceived to be. Wicked Earl George could bluster as much as he wanted, but Robert's approach was winning: the legal route was the way forward. At the council-day, all the evidence was heard, but the final judgement was reserved for James VI. Hearing this, Robert set out for London 'least the king should be sinistrouslie informed against him or his friends'.[36] Wicked Earl George sent a messenger south as well, but the energetic Robert – who had none of the sickly constitution of his brother Earl John – arrived first, and went straight to James VI to tell his side of the story, before returning to Edinburgh to await the outcome. During this whole process of complaint against Wicked Earl George, Robert stated that he rode from Scotland to the court of England at least six times in 15 months, 'to his great pains and extraordinary expenses'.[37]

James VI, distracted by the death of his son and heir Henry in 1612, still pursued his usual course of balance, aiming for reconciliation between Sutherland and Caithness. The two sides were persuaded to sign documents promising to try and be friends, and were told to stay in Edinburgh for the time being and be ready to discuss it all formally again in May 1613.

Shortly afterwards, Robert heard that his Gordon cousin, Enzie, the son of Lord Huntly, was passing through Edinburgh on his way home from England, where he had been allowed to visit James VI as part of his family's gradual rehabilitation.[38] Robert went to the Border to meet him.[39] Wicked Earl George was most put out by this, arguing that Robert was just recruiting more people to his cause, rather than truly trying to keep the peace. Late in the evening, Enzie, accompanied by various Sutherland men, happened to meet Wicked Earl George and his company on the High Street in Edinburgh between the cross and the Tron. The two groups jostled each other, trading insults, then swords started to be drawn. 'Freinds assembled speedily on all hands',[40] and Robert and Donald Mackay appeared on the scene. In the gathering darkness, Wicked Earl George perceived that he and his men were taking the worst of the hits, and decided on a strategic withdrawal home to his own lodging. Enzie pursued him and stood outside trying to get Wicked Earl George to come down and fight some more, but George stayed put. After a while, Enzie gave up and went home.

The next day, Wicked Earl George and Enzie were summoned before the Lords of the Privy Council and forced to once again officially reconcile, shake hands and make up.[41] When Robert and Wicked Earl George kept their appointment to return to Edinburgh to hear the final outcome of their cases, 'the matter was found so intricate and tedious' and time-consuming that it was decided that all the charges were formally dropped and both sides would sign a new submission to keep the peace.[42] Despite the street brawls and squabbles, it seemed that nothing more serious was going to happen, and the formal reconciliations were working well enough. Lord Huntly was once again asked to oversee reconciliations between Caithness and Sutherland. Earl John had also returned from his two years abroad in which he had travelled in France, Flanders and England, in May 1613, contributing to the idea that more stability was possible. However, Lord Huntly eventually decided that 'he would deal no further in the matter', and referred Caithness and Sutherland back to Edinburgh, 'for he knew well (as one who had tried them diverse times, and had often reconciled them) that to end a quarrel between two parties of such quality, deeply grounded and rooted in many other preceding particular debates, without disgrace or wrong to either side, was almost impossible, without extraordinary discretion and indifference; considering how the smallest circumstances were sufficient to put all out of frame and temper'.[43] Robert piously said that Wicked Earl George was the particularly problematic party. The enmity between Caithness and Sutherland was seemingly simply going to be a continuing problem that could be managed, but never fully resolved.

While Earl John had been away, his two brothers, Robert and Alexander, had done their best to manage the Sutherland lands for him, but had also thought about establishing themselves. Money seems to have been occasionally a problem for the Earldom of Sutherland, and Jean had established the salt and coal industries in Brora in order to improve cash flow, as the new London court necessitated more ready money and less exchange of goods and services.[44] As younger sons, neither Robert nor Alexander could count on inheriting any part of the Earldom, which according to the prevailing land laws was left only to the eldest, but both of them wanted to continue to live in a noble fashion. Robert had managed, in 1612, to obtain a gift of the living and lands of the lairdship of Balnagowan from James VI: this was the lands of the family that his sister Mary had married into.[45] Robert then worked some of his legal magic to resign the lands over to the Laird of Balnagowan, saying in his account of the affair that it was all to cement the friendship between Balnagowan and the Earls of Sutherland – but it is worth remembering that Balnagowan had previously been unhappy with the control Sutherland had over his land rights. In 1612 Robert also obtained, for the Earldom of Sutherland, a heritable gift of admiralty within the diocese of Caithness, which gave them rights over anything that landed on the seashore, from wrecks to whale meat, which could be a potential source of money.[46] Robert was continually thinking of new ways to raise funds and increase Sutherland power, working mainly through his influence at court or in Edinburgh. Robert also kept up with the Gordon cadet families, particularly the Gordons of Golspitour, who had fostered him and his siblings, and also Donald Mackay, and his family chronicle is full of their intermarriages, deaths, squabbles and general doings.

Alexander, too, was very involved in the management of the estates while Earl John was away, but soon Robert and Alexander's paths diverged. Alexander had obtained the use of some land from his brother before Earl John had gone abroad. Later, Earl John granted Alexander the use of more land in the north, including Auchindean near Dornoch, lands in Helmsdale and other parts of Kildonan, and finally Navidale – he became known by the title Alexander of Navidale.[47] Alexander became sheriff of Sutherland, and was concerned with maintaining order, usually through personal force at the head of a small group of retainers. His life was very firmly rooted in the north. In contrast, Robert continued his focus on the law and the more abstract pursuit of power through learning and the courts. Robert decided that his life was going to be at the king's side in London, and he would take a wife there. It was a different way of serving Gordon interests rather than any sort of break from his family, and Robert found a wife with impeccable Gordon connections: Louisa, known as Lucie. Lucie was the daughter of John Gordon, who could trace his family tree back directly to Jean's father, and who was now Dean of Salisbury and a Scottish churchman in the Church of England. Lucie's mother was a French heiress, and Robert's new wife had been educated on the continent, bringing to the marriage not only important French connections but also substantial French property and lands in Brittany, which Robert was now in control of.[48] Jean's sons had all established themselves well: John continued to run the Earldom of Sutherland and focus on his family now he had returned from the continent; Robert pursued his life in London; while her youngest son Alexander of Navidale remained close to his mother both physically, by settling near Dunrobin, but also spiritually, as he continued to embrace his Catholic faith. Jean may have been a widow again, but she was supported by all three of her fine sons.

PART 2: KRINGEN: VIKING METAL

The relative importance of her Gordon sons, however, was going to cause problems with Jean's daughter Jane, and particularly Jean's eldest grandchild, Donald Mackay. Donald Mackay did not go to the final hearing in Edinburgh about the Arthur Smith case, because he and his friend Young Golspitour, and Alexander of Navidale, were instead helping their ally Lord Huntly, and his son Enzie, against the Camerons of Lochiel.[49] The Clan Cameron had 'committed some depredations' which had 'put Lochaber in uproar',[50] and complaints had been made to the Privy Council of Scotland: the council had then ordered Enzie to deal with it. Clan Cameron had previously been allies of the Gordons, fighting on their side at Glenlivet for example,[51] but now the Gordons had to go against them. Enzie asked his Sutherland Gordon relatives for help a year before, and Donald Mackay and Young Golspitour had brought "300 choice men, well accoutred and furnished" to meet Enzie at Inverness on an appointed day – but then Enzie had decided that he would postpone the mission for one year. Now, in 1613, Enzie had asked Donald Mackay for his help again, and Donald again brought 300 men, along with 140 baggage-men to carry for the soldiers.[52] The expedition, however, did not go well: Allan Cameron of Lochiel lay secure on the south side of the river Spey, thinking that because heavy rain had made the river very swollen, he would be safe. Donald Mackay and Young Golspitour were not deterred, and managed to cross the river, surprising Cameron. But, when Donald was ready to attack Allan Cameron, Enzie suddenly stopped him, "pretending that he would bring Allan to reasonable terms in an amicable manner: at which Mackay and his friend Gordon [of Golspitour] were greatly offended".[53] Perhaps the Gordons' old alliance with Allan Cameron was in Enzie's mind, but the Privy Council, when they heard about it, were equally unimpressed with Enzie, and sent him, Donald Mackay, Young Golspitour and also Alexander of Navidale all back to deal with Cameron again for a third time. This time Allan Cameron yielded to Enzie and was imprisoned in Inverness – but Enzie again decided to liberate him once Cameron had promised to behave. In the words of the book of the History of the Mackay clan, "that business, which cost Mackay so much trouble and expense, ended in a mere farce".[54] Donald Mackay and his clansmen and the cadet family of Golspitour were being treated almost like mercenaries: they were the hired soldiers for the Gordon family, not only in the far north but also in the north-east. Donald had run around gathering men and arms together for Enzie every time he had been asked, leaving his own court case to one side to do so, but had gained little out of it for himself. Meanwhile, Enzie looked indecisive, and the power of the Gordons of Huntly looked less strong than it had for a long time.[55] The Gordon alliance between the Earls of Sutherland in the far north and Enzie and Lord Huntly in the north-east looked, for the first time since Jean had united the families by marrying Alexander, as though it might not be rock solid.

The idea of the men of the Far North becoming mercenaries, fighting for others' causes, was one that was starting to take a strong hold, and one that would become a developing theme, not just for the Mackays, but for the Sinclairs of Caithness as well.[56] The shift in power to the south of England, and the need for money, rather than exchange of goods and services – as seen with Jean's development of industry in Brora – was causing profound changes in society. Wicked Earl George and the Sinclairs of Caithness were continually short of money, but the Sinclair men's decision to work as mercenaries led to one of the most dramatic incidents of the time, which illustrated how precarious and undesirable this lifestyle could be.

Becoming a mercenary was becoming relatively common in Scotland, and around one-fifth of the adult male population experienced military service in Europe.[57] Money was a motivating factor – either the desire to earn more, or severe lack pushing people away from home. Famine times in Scotland in the late sixteenth/ early seventeenth century pushed men abroad, with even the government of Scotland encouraging the idea that young men could leave. Romantic ideas of chivalry and military heroism also played a part in encouraging men abroad, and strong religious beliefs also encouraged some to fight for their cause on the continent.

In 1611, a new king had taken over in Sweden, Gustavus Adolphus. When he first came to the throne, Gustavus Adolphus ruled a country that was fighting not only Denmark but also Russia and Poland. He needed men to fight, and Wicked Earl George and his Sinclair relatives were ready to supply those men. The primary battleground that the Scots were involved in was Norway, part of Denmark at the time. Theoretically, since James VI was married to Anne of Denmark, the Scots should have been on the side of the Danes – but in practice, mercenaries sold themselves to the highest bidder. A Scot who was in service in Sweden recruited a number of men for that country, made up of a group of Sinclair men from Caithness, including relatives of Wicked Earl George. The Sinclair group was thought to number around three hundred men – estimates of numbers vary depending on the source. They sailed in August 1612, taking four days of favourable weather to make the passage, with the aim of landing in and marching across Norway to join up with the main army in Sweden. Previous groups had taken this route with little trouble, but the Sinclair group ran into serious misfortune.[58]

The fate of Captain Sinclair, the red-bearded nephew of Wicked Earl George and leader of the expedition, has passed into Norwegian folklore.[59] Every part of their journey has been mythologised and put into story and song, starting with the mermaids who supposedly rose up from the depths of the ocean to warn the Scots as they travelled on their way from Caithness, and the discovery that Captain Sinclair's new wife had disguised herself as a man to accompany her husband as she could not bear to be parted from him. On arriving in Norway, at a place now called Skotshammer (Scots Craig) the Scots hailed a fisherman and his daughter to pilot them into safe harbour, gifting the daughter a pair of silver scissors and a silver thimble.[60] Robert Gordon described the superstitious Captain Sinclair as "running headlong to his own destruction".[61] The Norwegian peasantry had already suffered a lot from mercenary armies that had marched through their land, raping and pillaging as they went on their way, and it was the Scots' misfortune to arrive just as the Norwegians decided that they must make a stand. From the Norwegian perspective, it became about a nationalist heroic fightback by the peasantry against yet another armed and dangerous mercenary army that had the potential to maraud through their land on the way to fight for their enemy.

As the Scots travelled slowly across Norway, on Sunday 23rd

August a local magistrate received warning that they were approaching his village. Stopping only to grab his battle-axe, he ran to the church, where the villagers were gathered for their weekly worship, and interrupted the service, dashing to the pulpit and striking the floor three times with his axe, calling out that the enemy was upon them. The minister immediately dismissed the congregation, who gathered in the churchyard to plan. As Captain Sinclair and his band of Caithness men marched into the pass of Kringen, a narrow path that balanced precariously below cliffs and above a deep stream, they were already under observation by the local peasants, who were hiding among the rocks at the top of the cliff. A young girl, Pillar Guri, blew on a cowhorn to signal that the Scots had entered the pass. A small number of the Norwegians had guns and they started to fire upon the Caithness men, but the rest of the peasants were armed only with farmyard implements, so threw rocks and tree trunks down on them. "The slaughter was dreadful," said a later Caithness chronicler, naming Captain Sinclair as one of the first to fall – shot directly through the heart, said Norwegian legend, by a specially-fashioned silver bullet. "Many of the bodies of the killed tumbled into the river below, which was dyed with their blood . . . [others] were literally . . . crushed . . . to pieces" by the flying rocks and tree branches.[62] In contrast, only six of the Norwegians died. Robert Gordon said that the Sinclair mercenaries 'were all miserablie cut in pieces by the boors of that country [Norroway]',[63] but in fact the story got worse than that: about 130 (or maybe 170) of the Caithness men were in fact taken prisoner. They were put into a barn overnight, many of them lying wounded and in pain, while the Norwegian peasants decided what to do with them. Having previously suffered from the behaviour of other mercenary armies that had marched over their land, the Norwegians were delighted to have finally bested some of them, and spent the night in celebration. The following hungover morning, however, they were faced with a problem: they simply did not have enough food for all these extra dangerous enemy men – so they decided that they needed to be killed. The Scots were called out of the barn in pairs, and as each couple exited, blinking into the daylight, they were shot dead. Less than 20 were spared, some to stay and work as serfs or even mercenaries for the Norwegians – supposedly bequeathing both their Scottish names and their love of tartan to this part of Norway – while a very small number of officers were sent under guard to Oslo with an explanation of what had happened.[64]

The news gradually filtered back to Caithness and Wicked Earl George – tradition says via Captain Sinclair's wife, who had miraculously escaped death at Kringen to return to Scotland.[65] Meanwhile, in Norway, the Scots were either buried in a mass unconsecrated grave, or their remains left out on the hillside for the eagles (depending on the account) while the storytellers and songsmiths got to work praising the brave peasantry who had finally managed to stand up to an army of 1400 men: "Sinklar's Vísa", or Sinclair's Song, is still well known today. The words to the song as we know it today come mainly from the eighteenth-century Norwegian romantic nationalist tradition,[66] and the ballad was once banned in Norway in case it encouraged Norwegians to seek independence from the Danish kingdom. The Battle of Kringen has become a symbol of Norwegian nationalism, and the sentiments of the song have become important elsewhere. The somewhat dry, academic descriptions in contemporary Scottish histories include few details about the battle, but the Norwegian song, with its description of a group of brave locals standing up for themselves, includes vivid and elaborate imagery. The song also became well known in the Faroe Islands in its traditional form and is still popular today in some radically reworked contemporary versions.[67]

It may have been Jean and her family's actions that pushed the Sinclairs of Caithness out of the north to become mercenaries, but the Sinclairs' sorry fate and story has lasted and become one part of a symbolic song that means an enormous amount to many people. More recent commemorations of the Battle of Kringen have been a mixture of both Norwegian nationalism and a celebration of Scottish links, with the Caithness men who stayed in Scandinavia after the Battle of Kringen remembered, and efforts made to place the whole battle in its wider historical context. Jean and Wicked Earl George's people have cast a long historical shadow.

For the poorer men of Caithness and Sutherland, the Battle of Kringen illustrated the dangers of becoming a mercenary – but the rewards could equally be great, and for some the changing situation in the north resulted in the alternatives seeming more and more attractive. Jean's sons, on the other hand, were doing increasingly well. All of them were now married, with Alexander of Navidale and Earl John well settled in the north, while Robert still made regular trips up to see his family. In 1613, Robert was on one of his periodical trips to Scotland and set out with Earl John, Alexander of Navidale, Donald Mackay, Donald's younger brother John, and of course their usual entourage of young men and supporters, to visit Earl John's father-in-law Lord Elphinstone at the castle of Kildrummy in Mar. The purpose of the journey was to settle various Gordon land questions – Earl John's father-in-law was to arbitrate alongside the Gordons and Forbes to amicably sort out a few questions over land use and ownership. Earl John and Alexander of Navidale always got on well with their sister's children the Mackays, living together in the north in friendship, but Robert, fresh from court and full of southern ideas, introduced a note of dissension. The journey was thus marred by a dispute between the Gordons and Donald Mackay.

Donald Mackay was still only 23, but he had recently become a father for the first time, and was taking over more duties as Clan Chief Uisdean Mackay was failing fast. Donald was not much younger than his uncles and clearly saw himself as their equal. However, Robert had spent the last few years pushing for the ranking of the nobility and fixing the Sutherland position at court and had a keen lawyer's sense of his own importance and his own rights – and of where Earls and Clan Chiefs stood in relative importance to each other. Part of the land question that had come up, and which Earl John's father-in-law was supposed to sort out, was about land rights between the Mackays and the Gordons, and how grants that had been made by Jean and Alexander to Uisdean were to be interpreted now that Donald was taking over.[68] As they rode towards the castle of Kildrummy, Donald and his uncles fell to discussing the relative rights of the Mackays and the Gordons over land in the north. It was not a simple, straightforward discussion. "These questions having been agitated on their journey thither", Donald Mackay and his uncles appealed to Lord Elphinstone for help.[69] It seemed initially that Earl John's father-in-law Lord Elphinstone reached a good compromise, with Donald receiving the lands of Durness 'as a particular fie for his service to the house of Sutherland; and that the lands of Durness should always remain with the chief of the family of Mackay, and not to be given to any brother of that house',[70] but actually the Gordons remained very much the Mackays' superiors, with Donald Mackay convinced to give up the 'absolute warrandice' that he held over his lands. Warrandice is a complicated Scots legal term,[71] but by giving it up, Donald basically acknowledged that the Gordons were his superiors and in ultimate control of all his lands. Without absolute warrandice, there was a possibility, however slim, that a future Gordon could evict a Mackay from their land. Crucially, Robert Gordon was appointed to be the person in charge of any further disputes over this land. In some ways it made perfect sense for Robert to be in charge – a fine legal mind, with intimate knowledge of Gordon land and property – but, of course, it was ultimately unfair that a Gordon should be in charge of any dispute between Gordon and Mackay: obviously Robert would always favour the Gordon side.

Donald saw no reason not to trust his uncles – he had practically grown up alongside them, sharing the same foster-family, and was certainly on excellent terms with Earl John and Alexander of Navidale – but, ultimately, he trusted his uncles too much. They, especially Robert, saw themselves as Gordons and members of a noble family, and therefore above the Clan Mackay. Donald's position as their sister's son was hugely important to the Gordons, but there were still invisible divides between the true nobility and 'lesser' men.[72] The history of the Mackay clan offers this sad assessment: "Donald was second to none, where manhood, courage, and fortitude were called for; and he was possessed of a high spirit to a very singular degree ... but he was often rather incautious, some-what hasty in his calculations, and not sufficiently guarded against circumvention and fraud ... He was, in short, as to the management of legal, civil, or local transactions, an unequal match for his uncle [Robert], in whom, to his irreparable loss, he [Donald] placed every degree of confidence, until it was too late."[73] Donald had no legal training, and no real understanding of what Robert wanted to do. Robert, by contrast, saw the law as something of a game, a set of rules to be bent to his and his family's advantage, which he was trained to exercise. Donald "was cozened to give up the warrandice, which, though it appeared but of small importance, was preparative to the accomplishment of a deep and injurious scheme laid against him, as will shortly appear, whereby he was filched of a great portion of his lands".[74] At the time, however, Donald simply thought he was enjoying a short holiday at Lord Elphinstone's castle. Then, Donald, Earl John and Alexander of Navidale returned happily home to the north, while Robert took Donald's younger brother John Mackay (and some of his Gordon entourage) south to London for a further holiday. John Mackay then travelled on from England to France, where he stayed for just over two years.[75] John and Donald Mackay thought they were like the Gordons travelling abroad, but Robert saw it a little differently: 'Every time that Sir Robert returned from Sutherland to the court of England, he still took with him some young gentlemen of his own friends, that they might see that country, and to remark the court, thereby to serve the Earl of Sutherland, when it should please him to employ them again. By which means the chief gentlemen of the country of Sutherland became more civil than the rest of their neighbouring countries.'[76]

Back in the Far North of Scotland, things carried on as normal for Donald Mackay, and the full implications of the legal and land issues he had just agreed were not yet visible. He and his uncles received word that Wicked Earl George was once again considering another invasion of their territory, and Donald and his best friend Young Golspitour took up their by now traditional positions as leaders of a joint Gordon-Mackay army, accompanied by Alexander of

Navidale, to repulse Wicked Earl George and his Caithness men. It was easily done, as the Gordons and Mackays now drew on support from many families, including the Munros of Fowlis, the Rosses of Balnagowan (who were linked to the Gordons by marriage), Mackenzies of Cromarty, people from Kintail (the latter two being Donald's family through marriage), and several branches of the Clan Macleod. Despite the small cannon that Wicked Earl George had taken the precaution of bringing with him, when it was seen how formidable the Sutherland forces were, the Caithness men 'quickly yielded.. and so returned home', even 'in the extremity of a great storm and tempest of wind and rain, which was so vehement that they were in danger of drowning'.[77] Donald Mackay and Young Golspitour, along with Alexander of Navidale and with 200 men at their backs, followed them into Caithness, but the show of force was enough to stop any actual battle taking place.[78]

There was still no love lost between Caithness and Sutherland, and Wicked Earl George looked for new ways to bring down his enemies. Robert certainly blamed him for some of the troubles the Sutherland family experienced over the next while, saying that Wicked Earl George went to the archbishop of St Andrews and the clergy of Scotland 'to molest and trouble the Earl of Sutherland for his religion'.[79] Although Robert was Protestant, Earl John, Alexander of Navidale and Jean were all still practising Catholics. Wicked Earl George was at least nominally Protestant, though never seemed to have very strong religious convictions. James VI still had to be seen to take any Catholic 'threat' seriously, but Robert in London intervened on behalf of his brother and wider family as best as he could. Earl John was eventually ordered into ward in St Andrews: under house arrest, he had to attend church and do as the clergy said.

Meanwhile, Donald was effectively in charge of the Clan Mackay, because his father Uisdean was failing fast. On 11th September 1614, Uisdean died 'of a bloody flux and issue', at his retirement house in Tongue.[80] After Uisdean's death, his widow Jane does not seem to have stayed in Tongue, but instead came to Crakaig, her mother Jean's home. However, although she was still only 40 years old, Jane only outlived her husband by less than six months. Jean's eldest daughter died on 20th February 1615. It was a particularly cold winter, and conditions were bad and food scarce throughout Sutherland, though whether that contributed to her illness and death we do not know – her brother Robert gives no cause of death, saying only that Jane was 'exceedingly regretted by all that knew her. She was one of the comeliest and most beautiful women of her time in this kingdom,' he went on. 'These external gifts were accompanied with many rare virtues; she was no less modest and religious than fair and beautiful – a great ornament of the family and house of Sutherland'. Jean and her sons were certainly in mourning for Jane's death. Robert claimed that Jane and Uisdean had had such a happy marriage – despite Uisdean's faults and previous wife – that 'as they were happy in their mutual loves during their lives, so were they not less happy that their deaths were so near one another'. Donald was now an orphan. Robert sounded a warning note, though, when he added that Jane was 'most happy, that she did not see her eldest son's unkind dealings towards the house of Sutherland, from whence he had all his honour and being'.[81] As Jean and Alexander's marriage had been the tie between the House of Huntly and the House of Sutherland, so Jane and Uisdean's marriage had been the tie between the House of Sutherland and the Clan Mackay. With the ending of the marriages and the death of the spouses, the ties were weakened for the next generation. An official history of the Clan Mackay regretted that Jane was not buried beside Uisdean, but instead laid with the Gordon family.[82]

It was a long, cold winter in Sutherland in 1614/15, 'there fell out great abundance of snow (more than ordinarie) throughout all Scotland, which stormes continued all the spring, even until the month of May ... whereby the most part of all the horse, nolt [cattle], and sheep of the kingdom did perish; but chiefly in the north'.[83] These were the sort of conditions that were sending men abroad as mercenaries. Sutherland suffered greatly from the bad weather, and the deaths of Uisdean and Jane did not augur well for them, while Earl John was still in ward. Wicked Earl George had seemed, after his last ignominious retreat, to be a spent force, but he had still not given up completely. James VI still wanted balance, which meant the Earl of Sutherland could not have his own way in the north all the time. When Earl Patrick of Orkney, Black Patie, was finally brought to book for some of his less salubrious acts, James VI asked Wicked Earl George for help. Wicked Earl George had pushed hard to be asked to be the one to deal with Black Patie, not only because he had a long-standing family connection to Orkney, but also because he knew that Black Patie was the ally of the Gordons, and George wanted a way to go against the Gordons and improve his own standing with James VI.[84] Earl Patrick had been imprisoned in Edinburgh for his "crimes and acts of oppression" in Orkney,[85] but was still managing to collect rents and exercise power through the offices of his bastard son Robert Stuart. Wicked Earl George was sent to Orkney to deal with this, sailing from Leith in August 1614 with a number of soldiers and even allowed to take with him some cannon from Edinburgh Castle. The cannon were needed, as Earl Patrick's son barricaded himself into the family castle, but after "many hundreds of cannon-shot were spent", it was the treachery of one of the besieged 16 men inside that finally give Wicked Earl George victory.[86] It was not a bloodless victory, as several of George's men were killed during the cannon-attack on the castle, but Robert Stuart and his associates were all captured and taken by sea to Edinburgh, where they were executed. Earl John's former ally Earl Patrick of Orkney was also convicted and executed at the Mercat Cross of Edinburgh, on 6th February 1615.[87]

Wicked Earl George thought that after this success, and with Earl John still in ward for being a Catholic, he must surely now be riding high in favour with James VI. In January 1615 George made the long journey to England to ask for a reward. Robert got word of his coming, and hastened from his family home in Salisbury to court to keep an eye on him and 'to prevent the earle his machinations against him and his friends'.[88] Wicked Earl George drew on all the credit he had at court to try and stir up James VI against Earl John and the Sutherlands, but Robert was there at every turn, quietly reminding James VI that if he wanted to keep the peace in the Far North of Scotland, nothing prejudicial should be done against the Earl of Sutherland.[89] The best that Wicked Earl George could obtain was a general remission from James VI, absolving him of any previous crimes or offences; a yearly pension, 'upon condition that he should amend his life in time coming';[90] and a new position as a privy councillor of Scotland. With this, Wicked Earl George had to be content and, after two months in London, he travelled back to Edinburgh.

When Wicked Earl George arrived in the Scottish capital, he found Earl John there and 'began to brag, thinking now to astonish [Earl John] with his good success at court'.[91] Again, Robert had got there before him: Earl John had already received a letter from his brother telling him everything that had gone on in the south, and how Wicked Earl George had not succeeded in obtaining anything from James VI that would be overly prejudicial to the Sutherlands. The entourages of the two Earls fought it out, but Robert chooses not to give details – 'There happened some questions and debates between their servants and followers, during their stay then at Edinburgh, which I omit to relate,' Robert said primly – though Wicked Earl George claimed it went as far as an attempt on his life as he lay resting in his Edinburgh lodging.[92]

Earl John had convinced the clergy that, since he had to continue in ward, he should live in Edinburgh instead of St Andrews, where he felt he could be closer to his friends, and had moved, at his own expense, to Holyroodhouse.[93] His pregnant wife accompanied him there. Meanwhile, near London, Robert's wife was also pregnant. During his time in Edinburgh, Earl John wrote long letters to his brother: ridiculously, in the history of the House of Sutherland, these letters are labelled as being about the High Commission or the king – the letters are about these practical political things, but they are far more about the two brothers' families; an insight into the daily lives and thoughts of Jean's sons.[94] 'Loving brother,' Earl John begins in the first surviving letter, 'I received two letters of yours lately ... whereby I perceive your carefulness to attend the Earl of Caithness coming to court . . .' – but instead of discussing the details of Robert's actions against Wicked Earl George, Earl John is more concerned that Robert 'was absent from your lady [wife] in her greatest distress [that is, during her labour]; neither will I be glad until I hear of her recovery'. Robert and his wife Lucie had lost their baby. Earl John tries to offer words of comfort, 'You are both young enough, so if yourselves be in health, I hope in God you will have children anew, therefore be of good courage, for I know your melancolious humours have need to be expelled.' Earl John goes on to discuss Wicked Earl George's standing with James VI in more detail, before passing on to his religious troubles: he cannot pretend to his brother Robert that he has converted, but he states that he does 'daily haunt the preachings' and has done what the ministers desire.[95] Earl John hoped that Robert would be able to intercede with James VI on his behalf, promising that he would go to church if only he was allowed to return to Sutherland. He was particularly concerned that he was spending a great deal of money to stay in Edinburgh. He mentions too, that Donald had come to Edinburgh, and that Robert would need to put into practice what he had promised to do, and sort out land questions between the Mackays and the Earls of Sutherland. As always, Earl John talks of his 'sistersone' Donald as his friend, and suggests that Donald's younger brother John (still in France) might be a candidate for one of the new knighthoods that James VI was bestowing. The letter ends on a particularly poignant note: Earl John has been so sympathetic to Robert and Lucie about the loss of their child partly because Earl John and his wife had just lost their own newly born daughter. She had been born during their captivity in Edinburgh, and named Marie, but had only lived for about two months.[96]

Earl John obtained his wish to return home to the north for one brief spring. It was the spring after the harsh snowy winter, and he was shocked at the state of the people and land in the north, where Jean and her sick daughter Jane had been living through famine times. Earl John himself had little money after his forced sojourn in Edinburgh, and his time in the south had diverted much-needed money away from his estates at a time when they had needed it the most. Earl John pleaded with Robert to use what influence he could with James VI to help the Sutherland cause, and outlined his new plans that he and Donald Mackay would live in Dornoch over the coming winter, trying to improve that town and oversee the rebuilding of the damaged cathedral there. The letter ends with a postscript, asking Robert to send 'a pair of the finest double virginals you can get for money . . . seeing my bairns are learning to play and sing'.[97] Virginals were a type of harpsichord popular in Europe at the time; a double virginal was two instruments in one, which could be played together by two of Earl John's children at once. A family man to the end, Earl John did not make it through the next winter: even as the funeral obsequies for his sister Jane were just ending, Earl John himself then sickened and died on 11th September 1615, of 'a bloody flux and dysentery'. He was, according to his brother, much mourned in Sutherland, where he had been 'exceedingly beloved by the inhabitants of his country, especially by the common people, unto whom he had been a loving father and a careful master'. Robert assessed that Earl John was 'very religious and godly, not overruled by any notable or main vice, he was indued with divers good parts and qualities, both of mind and body, well disposed, and active in all manner of bodily exercises; of a comely countenance and personable body; for integrity and upright dealing, so just, that no man (yea not his greatest enemies) could touch his reputation with the least spot of dissimulation and deceit; being therein a right branch of the stock from the which he did spring'. The only criticisms Robert could make was that Earl John was sometimes too easy-going: 'He was loving, kind and courteous to all men, if not rather too familiar with his own . . .' – and that he had been forced to leave behind some debt, mostly because of the recent money he had been forced to spend on living in ward in Edinburgh. Earl John was only 39 years old when he died, and his son and heir was only six and a half. Alexander of Navidale sent a letter express to Robert in London and, despite the fact that his wife Lucie was pregnant again, Robert immediately travelled straight home, worried that the Sutherland's enemies would take advantage of the situation.[98]

Robert, as the next oldest Gordon brother, was officially the person who would be in charge of the Earldom of Sutherland until Earl John's son was old enough to take control himself – but in practice, once Earl John died the people on the ground in the Far North were Jean's youngest son Alexander of Navidale, Donald Mackay, Earl John's widow Annas, and Jean herself. Donald had been with Earl John in Edinburgh, and then had returned with him to make those plans for improving Dornoch and dealing with some of the Sutherland debts and needed improvements, but now that Earl John had died, Donald wanted to establish his own permanent home. He had been discussing with Earl John his claim over the lands of Golspitour, Kilcolmkil and Kinnauld, and Donald was keen to make his own home in Golspitour: the place where his foster-family had brought him up. Donald's foster-father, now established in Embo, was willing to sell him the land and house of Golspitour, within view of Dunrobin Castle.[99]

Meanwhile, in Dunrobin Castle itself, the family home of the Earl of Sutherland, where the new six-year-old Earl was actually based, the people in charge were Earl John's pregnant widow, Annas, and Jean Gordon. Annas gave birth to her final son in February 1616, and named him, with great literal-mindedness, George Posthumous Gordon, in recognition of his father's death.[100] As her daughter-in-law recovered, Jean, now aged 70 but as sharp as ever, was more than ready to take control now the House of Gordon needed her once more.

CHAPTER NINETEEN

Donald Duaghal and the Triumph of the House of Sutherland: 1616–1624

Immediately after her son Earl John's death, Jean encountered opposition, from both within and without the family. Her daughter-in-law Annas had different ideas about what was to happen on the Sutherland estates, and the two women had a serious quarrel which resulted in the closure of the coal mine at Brora.[1] The coal mines and salt pans were intrinsically linked as the coal was needed to light the fires to heat the water to extract the salt. We know that the salt pans were briefly reinvigorated around 1614, around the time Jean's son Earl John died and she took over managing the estates again: there are records of an Edinburgh merchant sailing to London in a hired ship to sell Brora salt.[2] The coal mines and salt pans had always been Jean's pet project, something she had specifically protected even in her marriage contract with Alex Ogilvie but now, as a result of the dispute with Annas, coal mining was halted. As Earl John's widow, Annas was entitled to control and manage a third of the Sutherland estates – but Jean was already the Dowager Countess of Sutherland, so perhaps there were clashes over the division of her and Jean's responsibilities; we have no details.

Jean's attention was rapidly taken elsewhere when, in April 1616, she was summoned to appear in Edinburgh before the High Commission to answer for 'her suspected religion'.[3] Despite her age, she was clearly still seen as someone who had the potential to be influential; someone powerful who needed to be controlled. Jean's son Robert answered for her to the High Commission, obtaining a three-month delay. Since Jean was a widow, Robert, as her eldest surviving son, was legally in some way responsible for her, as male head of household.[4] During the three months' grace, Robert convinced James VI that Jean should get 'an oversight and toleration of her religion during the rest of her days; and that from thenceforth she should be no more troubled for her conscience, providing that she would not harbour nor receipt any Jesuits'.[5] From Jean's point of view, when her son Earl John had been forced to give up his Catholicism, he had been sent away from the family home, his baby daughter had died, the deaths of his brother-in-law and sister had followed close behind, he had brought his family into debt, there had been a famine and extraordinarily severe winter, and then Earl John himself had died. Little wonder that Jean could still not be convinced that converting to Protestantism was a good idea. Although her brother Father James the Jesuit was now too old to travel, he was not sitting quietly but continued to write in Paris, spreading his ideas through his writings, which were published and disseminated across Europe. There was no way Jean was going to let her family down at this late stage, and that coda about not harbouring Jesuits was probably wise. Neither James VI nor the Scottish clergy stuck to their promises to leave Jean in peace as she continued to openly practise her religion.

Jean was now living between Dunrobin Castle again and Crakaig, the nearby dower house, with her daughter-in-law Annas Elphinstone and her grandchildren from Earl John: her grandson the new Earl (aged only seven), his brothers Adam and little George Posthumous, and her two granddaughters Anne and Elizabeth. Crakaig was a fairly large stone house of more than one storey, with big fireplaces and worked ironwork.[6] Jean was largely in control of the household of women and children, ensuring that Gordon ideas were always to the fore and clashing with her daughter-in-law Annas Elphinstone, who, after the argument about the coal mines, had gone on to suggest that removing her children to her own parents' home might be a good idea. Jean's son Robert had been appointed guardian to the new Earl, his nephew, and took the new title of the Tutor of Sutherland, but he continued to have his home in the south of England, administering the estates from there. He was kept up to date by letters from the north from Jean and his brother Alexander of Navidale, who carried out his instructions on the ground when Robert could not be there in person. Surviving documents from the time show both Alexander of Navidale and Robert signing off financial affairs – but within the papers, preserved by Robert, I found evidence of Jean signing and overseeing financial affairs as well, an unusual female name among the names of 'sundrie nother country gentlemen'. A 1623 document on "The rental of the Erldome of Suthirland" is drawn up 'in presence of My Lady Countess of Sutherland the elder' – i.e. Jean. It lists the rent of different parishes of the Sutherland lands, including the parish of 'Crakok' or Crakaig, where Jean was living: yearly, tenants in the parish had to hand over to the Earl measurements of grain, mutton, 18 geese, a side of lamb and so on.[7] Jean also continued to travel back and forth to the north-east, accompanying her granddaughter Anne, for example, when she went to Elgin to buy a riding dress, before going to Huntly Castle for an extended stay.[8] Meanwhile, over the next few years Robert racked up an enormous number of miles travelling from Salisbury to Dunrobin to oversee arrangements like this. On each of his journeys Robert's loving wife Lucie would write to him regularly, sending letters after him with news both national and familial: 'Dear heart,' she wrote as he travelled north again, 'this is the third letter that I have sent you since you left from London ... I received one letter from you from Morpeth [in the north of England] ... the plague still rages in London and this week 87 people have died ... many have fled from London and I wrote to [our friends] to ask they would like to come to stay at ours ... God have mercy on you, my mother sends her love and your children ask for your blessing ...'[9]

Robert focused his efforts on rebuilding the estates of the Earl of Sutherland, notably by pushing through Earl John's ideas for the rejuvenation of Dornoch by the rebuilding of Dornoch Cathedral, which he oversaw being re-roofed with slate from a providentially recently discovered local quarry.[10] He had grand plans for Dornoch Cathedral to be a Gordon showcase: a monument to his ancestors with a large tomb and paintings on the wall of all the Earls of Sutherland, along with descriptions of their lives.[11] Although this was never fully realised, his main and lasting contribution was to build the Gordon esteem and position in society, partly through the composition of what became his written history and chronicle of the Gordon family. Robert had already been working on a genealogy of his family for some time, writing to his brother Earl John about it in 1615,[12] and now he redoubled his efforts. He wanted the book to stand as a chronicle of the Gordons, showing their development as Earls of Sutherland, their long lineage and strong claim to rule over the north of Scotland. He also now thought it could be an instruction manual for his nephew, teaching the new child-Earl where he came from and what he needed to know to run the Sutherland estates effectively. Robert was concerned with leaving a lasting legacy, and thought his genealogy, "These dead papers", might be of use not only to the child-Earl as he grew up, but also to future generations: "Ther is a historie of your descent and genealogie written in Englishe by one that loueth and favours you and your house. I advyse you to preserwe and keip that historie saifflie . . . and whosoever advyses yow to the contrarie, trust him not . . . It is ane ornament to yow and your famelie to hawe your actions so truelie and lairglie descrywed."[13]

The seventeenth century saw a growth in family history chronicles like this. Previously, history had been written down and kept by the Catholic Church, but with the dismantling of the Catholic system and the destruction of both churches and church records, a new movement of historians grew up, spurred on too by Renaissance ideas.[14] At court and living in the south of England, Robert saw these new historians at work, and was taken with the idea of what it could do for his family: the new historians were not merely preserving ancient documents, but re-examining them. Robert's history of the Gordon family places heavy emphasis on the things he saw as important, such as the links with Moray and the Huntly Gordons of Aberdeenshire, and a reinterpretation of Jean's father and brother John's actions against Mary, Queen of Scots that would paint them in a good light. Robert's history of the Gordon family is of extraordinary importance to historians looking for information about the north of Scotland, as it is often the only source available, but it is also a family document, written by Jean's son and expressing the attitudes that Jean and his subsequent life had given him.

Robert had recently accompanied James VI to Cambridge, where Jean's son had been given an honorary MA,[15] and his *Genealogical History* is considered to be a well-written, thoughtful piece of extreme value, "his lasting contribution to the family's greatness".[16] It is certainly a great read, with no digression too small to be included, and the author's personality is stamped right through it. Robert took his duties as Tutor very seriously, working tirelessly not only on his writing but on any legal route he could pursue to bolster his young nephew's Earldom. Meanwhile, since Robert stayed in the south of England, either with his family or at court, the main man on the ground was Jean's youngest son Alexander of Navidale.

Portraits exist of both Robert and Alexander. They display a striking family resemblance, not only to one another, but to their father and mother as well. Both brothers have the same light brown hair and careful mouth. Both are dressed in fashionable black doublets, slashed to reveal bright white material, and with white lace frothing at Alexander's wrists. Both men wear starched ruffs. Clothes mattered to them: they signified their status. It was important to get clothes exactly right, Robert taught his nephew the child-Earl, 'Be not superfluous in your raiment like a debauched waster, not yet too base like a miserable wretch. Let [your clothes] be comely, honest, clean and proper'. It was better, Robert added, to spend a little less and not keep up with all the fashions: you should instead make sure your clothes were season- and age-appropriate – but at 'high times' and Parliament, 'spare not to be apparelled as your rank and quality requireth'.[17] Alexander once wrote to Robert to call on his tailor in Edinburgh to pick up 'a suit of black figured silk and a taffeta cloak' that the tailor had been altering, so he could wear it to a wedding:

and also, Alexander added, could Robert pick up some scarlet or fine grey London cloth, some silver lace and buttons, and some lining material to make a new riding coat, conforming to 'the best and newest fashion'.[18] There were five years between the brothers, but both portraits were painted when they were approximately the same age – around 40 years old, some years after Earl John had died, and their management of the Sutherland estates had become part of their daily lives.

Robert's painting is by a less sophisticated artist than Alexander's, and his features are less well-captured, but Robert stares challenging and confidently out of the painting. Robert took his duties as Tutor seriously, and was judged by his family to have discharged them "with great moderation, judgement and discretion". He was, in the final assessment, described as "a man indued with notable gifts of mind and body", but he could be a hard taskmaster, expecting others to live up to his high standards, and with complete confidence in his moral judgements. Even his friends said that he could be "too vehement", "a painfull and exact justiciary" and "a bitter enemie".[19] In his portrait, a black cloak or other material covers one arm, and he wears around his neck a chain with a silver-coloured ring and some other ornament on it. In Robert's preserved papers there are letters to a London goldsmith concerning delivery of a gold chain to Robert Gordon: these were fashionable at court, ostentatiously displaying wealth and status.[20] Robert looks like a courtier.

Alexander's portrait is larger, and it is attributed in the Dunrobin records to artist Adam de Colone, a Dutch painter active in Scotland during the reign of James VI, who painted the king himself as well as many other nobles.[21] Both brothers were men of status who were able to advertise that through the commissioning of costly portraits. In Alexander's picture, he is posed almost awkwardly, with one hand on a table, touching a set of keys,[22] while his other hand is holding his white gloves. Because his gloves are off and his hands bare, we can see that he wears an expensive-looking ring on his long, thin, white fingers. An elaborate silver belt buckle is also visible to set off his austere black and white costume. Not only Alexander's features, but also his expression, are reminiscent of his father's portrait: although still clearly a wealthy, strong man, he seems more hesitant, less challenging than his brother – there is a small suggestion of diffidence or reserve, though he is just as haughty as Robert.

In their surviving letters to one another, too, we get a sense of the brothers' different priorities in life. Alexander wrote regularly to Robert to update him on what was happening in the north, with much minutiae and detail of local squabbles and names, and very little interest in Robert's life at the glamourous royal court. Alexander always spoke highly of his sister's son Donald Mackay, not placing so much distinction on who was a clansman and who a nobleman, but considering who lived and worked together in the north. He was, in fact, closer to Donald than he was to be to his nephew, the child-Earl, even supporting Donald's son in a marriage alliance with the Earl of Caithness.[23] Further, Alexander remained, like Jean, a committed Catholic. Meanwhile, Robert pursued his court and legal life, living as a Protestant, very aware of appearances and the position of the Gordons in relation to other nobles. For all their differences, however, the two brothers worked well together and were both committed to the House of Sutherland. They must have known each other very well, after spending their childhood and schooldays, then their time at university together, and in France and then Edinburgh as young men: they had watched each other grow up and were happy not to challenge each other's choices in life, but to respect their differences – especially when living with enough distance between each other that their differences did not cause daily clashes. Throughout Robert Gordon's genealogy is his strong philosophical belief that family is the important thing: any Gordon 'faults' can ultimately be excused simply because that person is a Gordon.[24] Alexander, when he wrote to Robert, signed himself "wishing you all happiness, I rest, youris worschips most affectionate brother to serw yow to death, A Gordonne".[25]

Wicked Earl George may have been initially thought to be a potential threat to the child-Earl of Sutherland by Alexander of Navidale and Robert, but in fact after his brief moment of favour with James

VI after his work in Orkney, George managed to sabotage his own success once more – with a little help from Robert. The remission for his crimes which Wicked Earl George had received in London was revoked in Edinburgh after George was accused of causing arson.[26] Arson, in this time when wood was used for building homes, was a very serious crime: it was one of the four 'pleas of the Crown', along with murder, rape and robbery – crimes so serious that they had to be tried by the royal courts rather than the burgh or local courts.[27] Like the Arthur Smith false coiner plot, this arson trial became very complicated – the more so because the most comprehensive source we have for it is Robert's genealogy, which is obviously biased towards telling what Robert wants to tell. It began when some corn stacks belonging to some tenants of Lord Forbes were burnt at Sansett (Sandside), in the Far North near Thurso and Dounreay, close to the border between Caithness and the Mackay land of Strathnaver. Wicked Earl George was blamed for the fire, which was considered exceptionally serious given how scarce food had been in the north with recent bad winters. His motivation was supposedly that the land that the corn was on had originally belonged to his Sinclair family and that he resented this Forbes, who had moved to his wife's property.[28] The dispossessed and landless Clan Gunn were supposed to be the men who had actually committed the fire, partly at their own instigation, but with George's blessing.[29] However, when challenged, George refused to take responsibility and retaliated by blaming the Mackays: Donald's men were the ones who had caused the fire, he said. Complaints were made to the Privy Council, but the witnesses to the fire disappeared. Rumour said that Wicked Earl George had caused the witnesses to be drowned so that no proof could be found against him.[30]

Wicked Earl George wrote to Lord Huntly, who was supposed to be the neutral party in any quarrel between Caithness and Sutherland, complaining that Robert and Donald Mackay 'went now about by all means to get him within the compass of treason, and to extinguish the memory of his house, by slandering him with the burning of the corns of Sansett . . .' He also accused them of setting him up with the

Arthur Smith trial, and killing his relatives, and many other things –
but when Robert and Donald Mackay travelled into Aberdeenshire
on other business, Lord Huntly simply told them everything Wicked
Earl George had said, and they denied it.[31] All the parties involved
were summoned to Edinburgh, where Robert managed to stop the
previous remission that Wicked Earl George had received from
James VI from being fully passed, various unfortunate scapegoat
Gunns were imprisoned – but ultimately the outcome was that
Wicked Earl George was the loser in the court case. He was not only
declared a rebel but, in a neat turning of the tables for what Robert
saw as Earl John's unjust warding in his final years, even had his
religion questioned.[32] Wicked Earl George only managed to remove
the weight of the court case for arson from his head by resigning
his sheriffdom of Caithness, meaning he was no longer responsible
for justice in the county – and by forfeiting the yearly pension he
had just been awarded by James VI, money that he could ill-afford
to lose. Wicked Earl George's son and heir had been imprisoned in
Edinburgh while the corn-burning court case was completed, but the
moment that court case was settled and George's son released, he
was immediately imprisoned again for the family's debts. He was
to languish in jail for five years. George himself only escaped the
debtor's prison by returning rapidly to the Far North where he was
out of reach.[33] It was all a neat piece of manoeuvring by Robert, who
was working towards successfully neutralising Wicked Earl George
as well as actively juggling all the different competing interests in
Sutherland, including the smaller clans and cadet families. However,
Robert's biggest problem and challenge was not to be Wicked Earl
George at all, but instead his 'sistersone': his own relative, Jean's
grandson, Donald Mackay.

Donald Mackay had been on excellent terms with Earl John
before his death. In Robert's own words Donald, 'in the later end of
his uncle Earl John his days, swayed almost the affairs of the whole
country of Sutherland'.[34] Donald was on good terms with Alexander
of Navidale as well and, as far as Donald was concerned, they were
all one big happy Gordon-Mackay family. However, Donald was

interested in making some land purchases, choosing a place where he could establish himself in the north separately from his family at Dunrobin. Donald had bought the lands and house of Golspitour from his best friend Young Golspitour's family, his own foster-family: it was Donald's childhood home, within sight of Dunrobin, and the Golspitours were now settled in Embo so were happy to sell.[35] He also set in motion plans to buy other land. Donald talked to Earl John's widow Annas Elphinstone, and they had started to come to an agreement. Importantly, this included taking over some land, and the rights over that land (which brought in money),[36] which Annas Elphinstone had been left.[37] Donald made an arrangement with Annas Elphinstone to take over her whole estate and jointure; in exchange 'for payment of a certain yearly silver duty unto her'.[38] Essentially, what Donald had been aiming to do was to have a home and base in the north that was his, rather than part of the Earldom of Sutherland. Given that Annas had already expressed a wish to take her children to her own Elphinstone family to be raised, it seems that she too was interested in disassociating herself from the House of Sutherland. Theoretically, as Earl John's widow, Annas Elphinstone was entitled to terce, the liferent of a third of her husband's her-itable estate, which she could then dispose of as she wished[39] – so Donald Mackay could potentially run one-third of the estate of the Earldom of Sutherland. The House of the Gordons of Sutherland did not like the idea of Annas Elphinstone and Donald Mackay doing deals about what they considered to be Gordon Sutherland land, without Gordon Sutherland consent – and they most certainly did not want the child-Earl of Sutherland removed from Sutherland and the Gordon sphere of influence.[40]

Jean, a Gordon married to another Gordon, did not recognise Annas' wish to return to her own family. For Jean, the Gordons must always be everything. Likewise, Robert – another Gordon married to a Gordon[41] – did not see Donald as part of one big happy Mackay-Gordon family. He thought rather that Donald and his best friend Young Golspitour had too much power, and could be setting them-selves up as a potential threat to the new child-Earl. Robert believed that the Golspitour lands were ones that should have belonged to the Earldom of Sutherland: they had once been part of their lands before being 'given away', he said, and the Earldom of Sutherland 'could hardly be without them, they lying so nigh his chief dwelling, and being so convenient for him'.[42] Robert started to bring a lot of pressure onto Donald to comply with what he, as the Tutor of the House of Sutherland and representative of the child-Earl of Sutherland, wanted to happen. Robert kept pushing for Donald to give up his land claims, and, by talking up Donald's place in the House of Sutherland, eventually succeeded in getting Donald to give up not only Golspitour, but also his arrangement over land with Earl John's widow.[43] 'I was forced to buy Golspitour,' Robert explained later, 'to put ane enemie to the door.'[44] Donald did not at first realise the magnitude of what Robert had done, especially as Robert's next action was the seemingly friendly invitation of an equal to accompany him to visit James VI. In April 1616, Robert decided to return to court in London, and invited Donald Mackay to travel down with him. The trip was to be a huge turning point for Donald.

When Donald travelled down to London, he thought that he was Robert's equal. Donald was introduced to James VI and Prince Charles, and knighted, one of many young men to receive this honour as James rewarded those who had pleased him. However, the newly-created Sir Donald Mackay soon realised that he was a curiosity at court: Robert was not bringing a member of his family forward, he was showing off a tame clansman. Donald was one in a long line of minor Gordon henchmen that Robert took pride in showing around the court. Robert had shown Donald's foster-brother Young Golspitour around five years before, for example, and had also taken Donald's younger brother to London as well,[45] showing them what they were missing and what they could aspire to – and how far they really were from true power. Robert was the one who was comfortable here, who had status in the south, and he was not sharing that status with Donald; he was showing Donald how far beneath the court he really was. Donald, 'comely and firm',[46] with his dark hair and swarthy complexion, his north of Scotland accent and his knowledge of Gaelic and the Highlands, was an exotic. For a trip to court, Donald would have dressed in formal clothes, much like the slashed black and white doublets of Robert and Alexander's painted portraits,[47] but people at court knew that Highlanders and clansmen often wore the outlandish and strange kilt or plaid. People looked at Donald and saw, not a knight who could achieve anything, but a savage Highlander who had been tamed by the Gordons and was now amply rewarded. Someone who should be grateful for any attention he got.

This time at court was an epiphany for Donald. He realised that his uncle Robert had never seen him as an equal and would never treat him the same as someone of full Gordon blood. In Robert's description of the event, he says that the king 'graciously used' Donald Mackay, and 'withall desired him to do his duty to the house of Sutherland, seeing that by them he had the honour to appertain to his majesty'.[48] But Robert was clear that he saw Donald as inferior: the Clan Mackay is the vassal of the House of Sutherland, said Robert, 'and because they [the Mackays] are usually proud and arrogant, let them know that you are their superior'.[49] Away from the north and influenced by the court, Robert's attitudes hardened, and he crystallised them into writing: he wanted the Earls of Sutherland to 'take away the relics of the Irish [Highland/Gaelic] barbarity which as yet remains in [Sutherland], to wit, the Irish language [Gaelic], and the habit [Highland dress]. Purge your country piece and piece from that uncivil kind of clothes, such as plaids, mantels, trews and blue bonnets. Make severe acts against those that shall wear them. Cause the inhabitants of the country to clothe themselves as the most civil provinces of the kingdom do, with doublet, hose, cloaks and hats'.[50] Robert wrote this a few years after Donald's visit to London, but it is clear these attitudes were already forming, presaging later Sutherland attitudes to the clans even though Donald was Robert's nephew. The hurt ran deep. Donald stayed at court for about a month, then returned to Edinburgh 'in the later end of the year 1616'.[51] It is from his actions in Edinburgh onwards that Donald gained his Gaelic by-name of Donald Duaghal, or Donald of the Troubles:[52] from this point on he embarked on a series of actions that can be understood by seeing his time at court as causing a total reassessment of his entire life.

When Donald returned to Edinburgh, his mind was in turmoil from everything he had seen at court. He was in Edinburgh to finish sorting out the court case with Wicked Earl George about the burning of the corn stacks. To Donald, in the grips of his new understanding of his relationship with Robert, it must have looked as though every part of his life was about the Gordons: he really was their tame Highlander. Here he was in Edinburgh, fighting for his reputation because he had been defending their land against their enemy. Everything in his life had been organised for Gordon interests, down to his marriage to someone the Gordons wanted to ally with.

Donald had left his wife, Barbara Mackenzie, at home in the north, pregnant and ready to deliver their child. At this, the worst time, Donald heard a rumour that Barbara's child was not his. We do not know where this rumour started although we do know Donald and Barbara's marriage had not been as happy as it could have been for some time. Now, armed with this belief that Barbara was carrying another man's child, and feeling like his entire marriage had been a sham arranged for Gordon gain anyway, Donald fell into a scandalous affair with Mary Lindsay, the daughter of the 11th Earl of Crawford. Mary's reputation was already in ruins after she had supposedly been "ravischeit and away took" by a servant six years previously.[53] The Earl of Crawford's family attracted attention for their spendthrift way with money, and their unconventional affairs. "Dissipation had, in fact, become the family occupation" it was later said,[54] with another Earl known as the 'Prodigal' when he returned home after years of excess, and womenfolk who had run away with – or been taken away by – their social inferiors. Clearly there were no strong brothers guarding Mary Lindsay, and she and Donald came together in Edinburgh before setting sail for Strathnaver together from Leith in August 1616.

Donald's erratic behaviour was not what his family and friends in the north had expected. They had been waiting for a new knight to arrive with stories of the court in London, but instead Robert started to receive several letters from his correspondents in the north, detailing their shock and disappointment at what Donald and his new mistress were up to. The first letter preserved in the Sutherland family archives is to Robert from George Gray, who was writing to discuss some land management issues about a month after Donald had returned to the north. George Gray had been speaking to Robert about the vacant bishopric of Caithness and who should be appointed to that post – but the letter-writer is soon side-tracked from this official business onto gossip: 'I doubt not but you have heard of the misfortune trouble renewed and falling forth again between [Donald] Mackay and his wife,' he begins. Barbara Mackenzie was 'delivered of a son, which Mackay refuses to be his own'.[55] In fact, Donald had gone a little further than simply refusing the child: when Donald and Mary Lindsay had returned to Strathnaver from Edinburgh, they had found Barbara resting in her house in Durness after giving birth only a few days earlier. Donald had marched in and questioned the paternity of the child, and had then had Barbara and the new born child thrown out of the house: he had "caused lift [Barbara] out of the bed where she lay, transported her out of the chamber where she lay to another house without a roof, where he has made her a close prisoner".[56]

'Our whole friends here heavily regret this unhappy enterprise,' said Robert's correspondent circumspectly, particularly lamenting the fact that Donald had brought 'with him to Strathnaver the Earl of Crawford his sister [Mary Lindsay], in doing whereof he has lost many friends, and in special the kirk of Scotland cries out terrible on him'.[57] Donald, unrepentant, had installed Mary Lindsay in his house in place of his wife. Barbara's family were up in arms, and even Wicked Earl George was reportedly shocked.

The next letter Robert received was from his mother, Jean herself. Jean, like his last correspondent, was concerned with the desirability of appointing John Gray to be Bishop of Caithness, but she was soon drawn into other family affairs: 'One thing I write with grief of heart, your sister's son [Donald] Mackay, his home bringing [of] a sister of the earl of Crawford to his great disgrace...'[58] Even if Donald had been able to prove his allegations against his wife, Jean writes – though she doubts he could have – his actions have made him in the wrong, and he has lost many of his friends. She complains too that Donald has not been to see her, or anyone in the family, since he came home from England, and that he has not been in touch with either his grandmother Jean or with Alexander of Navidale apart from when he first told them he had made it back safely.

Jean's letter is written in a stronger Scots 'accent' than other letters Robert was receiving at the time. She had neat, well-formed handwriting, but there is a sense that these are letters from an older lady, from someone who speaks the Scots of her Aberdeenshire youth, unchanged by the court in England and contact with people from further south. The spelling is different and the sense sometimes harder to get at – but there is absolutely no diminishment of personality. Jean is very much a woman in control. The bulk of her family letter to Robert is actually about the Bishop of Caithness, but she has a very specific reason for wanting Mr John Gray to be appointed to this position: Jean had arranged for her grandson, the child-Earl of Sutherland, to be educated by this John Gray, because she felt that his education was lacking without some outside input, and she not only thought highly of Gray, but wanted him rewarded.[59] However, the boy's mother, Earl John's widow, disagreed: she wanted to educate her son herself, and to increase the influence of her family over him. Jean was again clashing with her daughter-in-law Annas Elphinstone over the raising of the Earl of Sutherland, and Earl John's father-in-law, Lord Elphinstone, had been drawn into the argument as well. Jean's aim, as always, was to further the House of Sutherland. She saw the child-Earl as a Gordon who must be educated into his position in the way that she knew best. She did not want to recognise the claim of her daughter-in-law's family over him.[60] Jean added that she herself was 'not well in health presently, which makes me that I cannot write many things to you that I would' – but actually she seems to be doing very well at imposing her will on the family around her. The child-Earl and his younger brother were eventually sent to school in Dornoch as she wished, boarding out in the town.[61]

The next to write to Robert was his brother, Alexander of Navidale. He had been speaking to his sister-in-law and her father too and, despite saying that he will not reply to any 'daft letters'[62] from Lord Elphinstone, asserts that he is on good terms at the moment with Earl John's widow Annas Elphinstone. We learn, though, that it is not just the child-Earl's schooling, but also some land questions that have arisen between Annas Elphinstone and her in-laws. There are various different issues, in fact, as well as a shortage of ready cash, which Alexander of Navidale finds difficult to deal with – and he hopes that the rumour they have heard of James VI coming to Scotland the following March is true, as that will mean that Robert is able to come home for a time too. Alexander lets slip that Donald has been helping him with the land questions, and clearly Donald and Alexander are still good friends and Donald is still actively involved in managing the Gordon estates.[63] But having covered all these topics, Alexander turns lightly to Donald's troubles: 'I doubt not but you have heard by now how [Donald] Mackay took away with him a sister of the Earl of Crawford. I am sorry he should have lost such good fame as he had for so wild a cause.' Can you tell me how his actions are seen by people in the south? asks Alexander – has James VI heard of it? He tries to make light of the Mary Lindsay situation, saying that Donald 'thinks to put her away shortly' – but follows this up with the revelation that Mary Lindsay is now 'great with child and remains as yet in the "Iyll off Lochtryoll" [isle of Loch Loyal?]', and that not only are Donald's wife Barbara's family furious, but Donald still wants a divorce from Barbara whether or not he stays with Mary Lindsay.[64] Robert was very harsh – he believed adultery and 'lechery' was wrong; that it brought 'a curse to your posterity and a deadly hatred among them where you converse, besides perpetual damnation in the life to come'.[65] He did overlook this stern advice for some friends but for Donald, Robert would accept no excuses.[66]

Even though Donald had clearly managed to reopen

communication with Dunrobin Castle, and he and Alexander were still managing to be friendly, Donald's relationship with his mother's Gordon family was at an all-time low. It was not just the divorce from Barbara – there was also ongoing rancour over those questions of land ownership, not only his previously attempted purchase of Golspitour, but also his arrangements with Jean's increasingly unpopular daughter-in-law Annas Elphinstone, who kept trying to remind people that the new child-Earl was, like Donald, only half a Gordon. When Donald did finally write to his uncle Robert himself, he claimed that previous letters had gone astray, but was clear to him that: 'About my wife: she has had a baby boy who by all reason and likelihood I have nothing to do with.'[67] Donald also wanted to have his say on John Gray and the Bishopric of Caithness: he wanted to be part of any decision-making in the north. Donald's letters to Robert are partly defensive, as he speaks of his wife and visits he has not made, but partly still show the ambiguities of his relationship with Robert and the Gordons, who were still his family: "P.S.", he finishes, "Remember my boots."[68]

Although Robert spoke to people whenever he was up north, and directed events as best as he could, particularly when pursuing land deals and other matters through the courts and institutions of London and Edinburgh, it was actually Jean and Alexander of Navidale who were on the ground in Sutherland. They kept Robert updated as best they could by mail, but getting letters from Sutherland in the far north of Scotland down to London or Robert's family home in Salisbury relied on a network of Gordon friends and travellers. Jean is assiduous in pointing out in her letters when notes have arrived and how they were delivered. The next surviving letter from her is actually a reply to a much-earlier, much-delayed letter from Robert: Jean writes that only now, on 25th November 1616, has she received a letter that he wrote from Salisbury on 27th June, asking for linen cloth. 'Truly if I had got it in time, I would have sent some, but at this time of year it is not in my power to get it,' she laments. Linen cloth was often in particular demand when giving birth,[69] so Robert had probably wanted it for his wife Lucie – it was a request with much behind it, so it is easy to understand why Jean was particularly annoyed that the letter had gone astray and begged Lucie's forgiveness: 'Herefore blame me not, for I would be very loath to have disappointed her father's daughter...'.[70] She urged Robert to 'let me know of your health', and added the traditional greeting of the elderly mother who wishes to guilt her children into writing more often, 'you know not how long you will have me to write to, and perhaps may wish to have me when you will not get me... your loving mother, Jane C. Sutherland'.[71] Robert could not keep up with everything, as much as he tried.

Donald thought that Robert was interfering far too much, however – particularly as he heard that Robert had been intercepting his letters. Robert was open to his (Gordon) family but he recommended spying on Mackay – the House of Sutherland should always have a "trustie secret friend" and "secreit pensioner" in Strathnaver, Mackay country.[72] On 5th May 1617, Donald finally wrote directly to his grandmother Jean, trying to give his side of the story, and asking her to speak to Robert on his behalf. 'My very honourable good lady and loving mother,' he began, '...it is no little grief to me to hear the reports that your ladyship's son, Sir Robert, has been speaking about me in every place when he was last in Moray, of my unnatural dealing to the Earl of Sutherland...' Donald hoped that Jean could act as intermediary between her grandson and her son, and promised that he was willing to co-operate if only Robert would too. Donald did not want to do anything that might hinder the child-Earl of Sutherland, he said, and did not think he should be blamed if anything did go wrong because he was doing his best. He appealed to Jean to remember how much work she had already done to bring together the Mackays and the House of Sutherland, and begged her to work to see that friendship continue: 'We [Donald and Robert] have all the honour as to be descended of your ladyship, therefore none should be so careful to see things settled as your ladyship... the world knows that I am an imp of that same stock that himself [Robert] is of... So, madame, it is best that it [the quarrel between Robert and Donald] is settled in time, before we both repent too late'.[73] He ended by telling his grandmother that he was seeking peace, and hoped that he still had Jean's trust: 'I rest and shall ever remain, your ladyship's loving son to serve you, S. Donald MacKie.'[74]

Donald was realising now that he had really been left with very little, and that Robert's actions in persuading him to give up Golspitour and the other land he had wanted had left him a dependant on the House of Sutherland, rather than an equal part of the family. Still, however badly Donald was treated, he did not always help himself with his actions. His wife Barbara Mackenzie had not disappeared quietly, but was complaining to the Privy Council of Scotland with details of her ill-treatment at Donald's hands, and asking for compensation. Rather than dealing with this in any sort of effective way, Donald and his best friend Young Golspitour instead got themselves involved in a particularly unpleasant contretemps with another young woman who lived locally. Jean wrote about it to Robert – 'I don't want to trouble you with country affairs,' she said, but 'something in particular I think good to let you know.' It was just weeks since Donald Mackay had written to Jean asking her to intervene between him and Robert, and presumably Jean had not acted as Donald had wanted because Donald had now gone to both Annas Elphinstone, and to his best friend and foster-brother Young Golspitour for help instead. Donald was still interested in purchasing the house and lands of Golspitour, the place he had grown up with his foster-brother and family, the place that Robert had persuaded him to give up before. Now, Young Golspitour and Annas Elphinstone were again trying to help him. Young Golspitour had remembered some of the legal deals that Robert had been involved in surrounding Golspitour lands, and had tried to make them more public in a way that would be to Robert's detriment, declaring them in the kirk of Dornoch. Jean's letter then suddenly seems to veer off topic by starting to talk about a new act that was passed in Parliament which said that anyone 'who ravished a damsel without her parents' consent (albeit she would say it was with her own will), it should be treason'[75] – but she is leading up to something important, something that Robert could use against Young Golspitour and might aid him in any land dispute.

The previous February, Jean explains, Young Golspitour and his entourage – she names at least ten men and says that, including servants etc., there were more present – had all gone to the village of Culmaliemoir at about ten o'clock in the evening. Approaching and entering the house of Alastair Chisholm, the group of young men forcibly took away Alastair's daughter Janet. They carried her off to Golspitour house, where she was 'kept two nights and ravished' by one of Young Golspitour's friends. Jean tried to intervene, but she did not have strong enough backup – her son Alexander of Navidale was in the south, and, as a woman of over 70, there was little she could do herself against a group of young men like this. Of all people, Jean had to turn to Wicked Earl George for help: he came to Skibo, 'at what time I threatened if they would not put the damsel to liberty I should take him [Wicked Earl George] by the hand to revenge it'. Faced with this formidable, combined force of Jean and Wicked Earl George, Janet Chisholm was finally set free, and brought to Jean. Janet told Jean that 'what was done was against her will; and to give proof thereof she remains ... with her father and mother, and will never hear to marry that man albeit there has been fair offers made to her'.[76]

Rape was no less of a serious crime in the seventeenth century than it is now, one of the four crimes which had to be judged by the crown court, but there were some differences in the way it was viewed. As with the case of Mary, Queen of Scots and Bothwell, if the woman who was raped later agreed to marry her rapist, then charges could be dropped. Janet had been offered marriage by her abductor, but she would not accept. Jean's implication was that Robert could use Janet's horrific experience as a tool to take Young Golspitour to court, have him tried as a rapist, and in this way stop any land grab by either Young Golspitour – or his friend Donald Mackay.

There was more to the story as well. Annas Elphinstone, Jean's daughter-in-law, was supporting the supposed abductor Young Golspitour: 'Your gudsistir [goodsister or sister-in-law] is altogether guided by her father, and that at her father's desire'. Annas was still refusing to be completely a Gordon, and was automatically supporting people who were against the Gordons, promising land to Young Golspitour and his family.[77]

Having told Robert all this, Jean left it in her son's hands: 'Take what course you please herein; but I see no course taken here by these men but that which is little for the Earl of Sutherland's profit or yours.'[78] Jean showed some concern for Janet, doing her best to have her released from her captors, but ultimately she is more worried about the implications for the House of Sutherland. Jean wanted Young Golspitour punished for his actions in colluding in the abduction and rape of Janet Chisholm, not solely because she wanted justice for a poor girl but because she saw the bigger picture and wanted to remove a group of young men who were not only threatening the damsels of the neighbourhood but might also start to threaten the Sutherland Gordons.

It was a violent time and disputes between family and neighbours might start with bad words but escalate quickly to violence. However, Jean still had to live with all of these people. Donald was still her grandson; Young Golspitour was still her grandson's best friend; Annas Elphinstone was still her daughter-in-law. No matter what she thought of their actions, they were in a small community and everyone had to work together somehow. Jean might be writing to Robert and thinking of nefarious ways to deal with Young Golspitour, but she added a little extra to the letter showing that she and Annas Elphinstone were still living together and dealing with the practicalities of life: Annas had not managed to get some smart clothes that she had promised for her son and Jean wonders if Robert could send them up something. 'My guddochtir [daughter-in-law] is disappointed of clothes she promised to her son, therefore my bairn wants, and I have no ready silver, therefore I will desire you to cause bring home a stand of holiday clothes to him with the furnishing, cloak, doublet, coat, breeks and shanks [i.e. leg-coverings – trousers or perhaps long socks to go under the breeches/breeks].'[79]

Jean's letter to Robert shows her good understanding of the law, and how it could perhaps be manipulated in the Gordons' favour – the method she and her husband Alexander had used so effectively when developing the House of Sutherland. Jean had developed this method over time. As so clearly shown by the Golspitour episode, it was one method of power that was open to a female in charge of land, as she certainly could not ride out in armour to fight young men. She briefly mentions some feu lands and warrandice issues, which she says she will elaborate on later when she can send word with Alexander of Navidale – but at least the coldness in her manner of dealing with things in this way is tempered by her fight to have Janet Chisholm released, even to the extent of involving her old enemy Wicked Earl George, as well as working with Annas for the good of Annas' children. However, Robert's response to Jean's letter about Janet Chisholm and Young Golspitour takes his disassociation from the people and the land of the north, and his now automatic legal response to events, to new levels. Robert had learnt from Jean both the importance of Gordon assets, and that the law was the way to maintain these assets – but he took things in a new direction.

The next letter that we have about the incident is from Lord Huntly to Robert. Robert's instinct had been to go to his Gordon ally in the north-east. From the reply that we have, we can see that Robert took a completely different tack than the one Jean had suggested: neutralising Young Golspitour and any potential threat he could cause to Sutherland land by taking him to court for rape. This would have seen some measure of justice for Janet Chisholm. Robert, however, clearly did not think this would have worked – perhaps the offer of marriage that Janet had received would have made things complicated, or perhaps it was the fact that it was allegedly another man, not Young Golspitour himself, who had raped Janet. The letter from Lord Huntly makes it clear that what Robert thought to do was involve an allegation of witchcraft.

Witchcraft was a very serious allegation. Belief in witchcraft was popular and widespread, and in 1563 the first Witchcraft Act was passed in Scotland.[80] Robert knew from his brothers' letters that there had been 'abuses of witchcraft' in Sutherland, that had been taken seriously by the clergy and brought to trial in Dornoch, within the last couple of years.[81] It was very much a current topic in the Scotland of James VI, whose own fascination with witches is well known, but it was common through all levels of society. The Witchcraft Act was first passed in a Parliament held by Mary, Queen of Scots, and set out a sentence of death for those who dealt in witchcraft. It was probably written by a minister rather than a legal expert as part of the wider idea to reform the Church, and the act contained some ambiguities.[82] "In essence . . . [the witchcraft act] criminalized the residual manifestation of paganism and some aspects of traditional culture . . . in an endeavour to inculcate a Protestant orthodoxy".[83] As people questioned their religious beliefs and the safety net of the old religion fell away, they saw dangers on all sides. Practically, witchcraft accusations fed not only on the grand questions of good and evil raised by church reform, but also on suspicion between neighbours, and the daily fears and anxieties people lived through. In the north of Scotland, there were fewer witch hunts than in other parts of the country, but accusations were still present: there were 14 people accused of the crime of witchcraft between 1560 and 1740. Meanwhile, in the north-east, in Aberdeen there were 78 people accused in 1597 alone, but this was not a typical year – there tended to be panics about witches that caused spikes in the number of accusations.[84] Robert, however, living in the south of England and travelling regularly, was well aware of witchcraft accusations, and also aware of the legal position. The seventeenth-century *Mackenzie's Criminals*, one of the standard legal textbooks we have remaining from around this time, is surprisingly measured when talking about witchcraft: the author points out that, even if witchcraft does exist, those in the legal system should be very wary when dealing with accusations, as it was often poor, uneducated, credulous people who were involved in the cases.

Robert was neither poor, nor uneducated, nor credulous. His suggestion to Lord Huntly was that Golspitour had been bewitched by Janet Chisholm.[85] Robert's aim was to discredit Golspitour and make everyone think that he had been bespelled, which would have made people mistrust and even fear and shun him. The less power he and Donald Mackay had, the easier it would be for Robert to gain control of Golspitour's land. Janet Chisholm would be collateral damage: not only abducted and raped but also brought to trial for a crime that Robert probably never believed she had committed. Robert was cynically exploiting what he saw as an interesting legal tool in order to bring down his enemy.

In this shameful episode, Robert reveals the extent to which he has broken from the north of Scotland. His interests are still Gordon interests, he still wants to protect and extend Gordon land – but he no longer seems to see the people of the north of Scotland as his people. Jean helped and protected Janet Chisholm as best as she could, even while she hoped to turn the situation to her advantage. For Jean, Donald was still her nephew, and he and Golspitour were men she saw every day. For Robert, they were becoming an abstract problem he tried to solve from a distance, far less important than the men he saw around him at court and in the south of England. Robert was swayed by contemporary theories of neo-Stoicism at court, which emphasised the ideals of self-control and morality. Although in some ways this dovetailed with James VI's ideas of the middle ground and compromise, it was a theory that could lead to a high-handed and high-minded fanaticism. Public duties were carried out with impartiality, even if they involved something distasteful.[86] For Jean, Janet Chisholm was a woman in distress – certainly a woman of lower birth than herself, but a woman living on Gordon lands and under Gordon protection who deserved help. For Robert, a poor woman like Janet Chisholm was nobody to him; she could be sacrificed for the greater good.

It is hard enough, at a distance of 500 years, to find out what Jean did and thought, but finding out about someone like Janet Chisholm is almost impossible.[87] We only know about her from this brief reference in Jean's letter: she was obviously from a well-known local family, and had enough standing, beauty or character to attract the attention of various young men of good birth, but that is all we know about her. What we do know, however, is that her name does not appear in the Survey of Scottish Witchcraft, the comprehensive list drawn up by the University of Edinburgh which collects together the names of all people brought to trial in Scotland for witchcraft.[88] Robert did not pursue his plan any further, Golspitour was not publicly accused of being under Janet's spell and Janet was not publicly accused of being a witch. She fades out of history and back into obscurity.

Robert became busy with other things. In summer 1617, James VI made a trip back to Scotland. Robert wanted to return to Sutherland anyway, to 'advance the Earl his nephew's affairs', so he tacked on to James' retinue, or 'took occasion to accompany his majesty', as he puts it.[89] James VI headed for Edinburgh, where he held Parliament, and Robert went with him. Robert's brother Alexander and a party of Sutherland men travelled down to meet Robert and see the king. Jean, too, accompanied her son Alexander of Navidale: mother and son had been in contact with Robert for some time in advance to plan the journey, getting Robert to send them details of his and the king's itinerary so that Jean could arrange accommodation before everything in Edinburgh got booked up for the royal visit.[90] During the Parliament, Robert 'was very careful least any thing should then pass at that convention in prejudice of the Earl of Sutherland'.[91] The Sutherland men made an excellent showing at Holyroodhouse, and, as well as Robert's manoeuvrings on behalf of his nephew and estate, Jean saw her son Alexander of Navidale and several other men from the Far North knighted.

It was the first time James VI had returned to Scotland since taking up the throne of England, and he had brought with him many English noblemen who wanted to see the northern country. James VI was anxious to put on a good show for them, and there were all sorts of entertainments devised. In the garden of the king's residence of Holyroodhouse, an exercise in 'praise of archery' was held – since archery was a sport in which 'the English nation do much delight and excel'. The best and most skilful archers in Scotland were invited to show off their prowess, and a silver arrow was awarded to 'the best deserver'. Sutherland archers always had a good reputation, and Robert proudly tells us that: 'At which time Sir Robert Gordon, tutor of Sutherland, did win and bear away the prize and silver arrow, in presence of the English and Scottish nobility. The Englishmen did exceedingly like their entertainment in Scotland.'[92]

Following this triumph of entertainment, James VI returned to England, while Robert journeyed north to Sutherland and Jean, where he was to stay for the next few years.[93] There, Robert says, he 'was received with the general joy of all the inhabitants', before setting about doing what he could to settle his nephew's affairs.

Debts and relations with neighbours were the most pressing issues for the Earldom of Sutherland. The child-Earl of Sutherland had inherited his father's debts and, although the rents for the estate looked good on paper, in practice Jean was arranging the collection of rent in kind. She received things as varied as grain, tallow, lambs and poultry.[94] This was of no use for paying off legal debts in Inverness or Edinburgh – and these sort of rents in kind also suffered in times of scarcity, such as in 1615, when there had been famine in parts of Sutherland. The salt pans, the money-generating industry started by Jean some years previously, had only had a short-lived period of real success. Although Jean had tried to reinvigorate them around 1614, after the closure of the coal mines the salt pans would necessarily suffer as the two were linked. It seems the salt pans were sold off completely in 1617. The sale of the assets, i.e. the iron from the salt pans, gave a much-needed though one-off boost to the Sutherland coffers of £666-13s 4d.[95] Robert also met with Donald to settle some questions over land ownership, which they managed to do amicably, with the mediation of Alexander of Navidale and various other men.[96] Jean, for all that she was on the spot and managing the day-to-day running of the estate, was not mentioned in any negotiation like this – and neither were any other women. These sorts of negotiations over land were meetings where men talked and signed documents, but there was still always the sense that land disputes could end up like the disputes between Caithness and Sutherland – things to be settled by violence, on the battlefield.

Women's rights over land, however, were very real, and Robert spent some time setting up a meeting with his brother's widow to discuss and negotiate with her over her rights over Sutherland land.

However, here he was overtaken by events. Earl John's widow Annas Elphinstone had not had an easy time since her husband's death. She had, understandably, thought about returning to her own family and taking her children with her, but Jean and the rest of the Gordon family had refused to let the child-Earl heir be taken away from Sutherland. Jean had assumed control over the child-Earl's education, ensuring that it was in the north of Scotland. Backed by Robert, who was the child's official Tutor, Jean was charged with teaching him what he needed to know to run the Sutherland estate. Then Annas Elphinstone had tried to come to an arrangement about selling the land and property which she had inherited on her husband's death – not unreasonably, she had thought that making a land deal with her husband's nephew and close companion Donald Mackay would be acceptable, but again, this had been blocked by Jean, Robert and the rest of the Gordon family. It was these lands which Robert was anxious to negotiate with her over. Faced with this situation, Annas Elphinstone had retired to the house of Crakaig, where she had invested her own money in making repairs to this property. There is an implication that Annas was living in the dower house, and Jean was in control in Dunrobin Castle. Annas continued to spend the money from her estate on her children. Since she had to stay in the north to be close to her three sons and two daughters, and could not travel home to see her family, her brother, Lewis Elphinstone, made the journey up to see her instead. Lewis was 'a young gentleman of good expectation' and the Elphinstone siblings passed a pleasant visit together, but disaster struck on Lewis' journey home: when Lewis reached the river Deveron on his journey home he discovered the waters had risen and it was overflowing. He rashly attempted to cross the swollen river on horseback, but the force of the water was too much and he was swept away and drowned.[97] There were great lamentations when news of his fate was relayed back to Crakaig.

Poor Annas died unexpectedly a few months later, in the autumn of the following year, 18th September 1617, at Crakaig. She had been a loyal wife to Earl John, and had given him ten children, five of whom had survived infancy. She was buried in Dornoch, next to her husband. Despite the fact that he had been worried by her plans for selling her land, her brother-in-law Robert praised her for always putting her children first. She was only 36 when she died.[98]

Because Annas Elphinstone died without leaving a will, Robert was appointed as administrator, charged with dealing with her property, money and dependants. This effectively solved his problem over the sale of Golspitour and meant the child-Earl was indisputably in his control. Since Robert was only temporarily based in the north, it was Jean who was effectively now in control at Dunrobin once again, in charge of her grandson. Jean's influence had been steady now for three generations, as she worked with her husband Alexander, when she ran the estates for her son Earl John in his minority, and now as she took the reins again for her grandson. Her policy of friendship with the Huntly Gordons was the guiding light throughout all this time, and her influence on the House of Sutherland cannot be underestimated. However, as shown by the incident with Janet Chisholm, Jean was still in a woman's place: when faced with violence as the means of establishing control, she could not ride into battle as her husband and son had. Instead, she had fostered the use of legal methods of challenge, and this, too, was hugely influential on the course of the House of Sutherland which, unlike Caithness, adapted well to the newly bureaucratic court, written legal code, and relatively peaceful times of James VI.

The cause of Annas Elphinstone's death is not recorded, but it may have been a time of sickness as Robert lists a series of other deaths which took place around the same time, including the death of Donald Mackay's eldest son and heir. Donald had truly entered the time when his by-name 'Donald of the Troubles' was to prove its truth. His son had been fostered with the Gordons of Golspitour, as Donald had been himself, so the grief was felt strongly in the whole wider Gordon family. Donald's son was only six when he died. However, as some consolation, the child was buried in the sepulchre of the Earls of Sutherland at Dornoch, indicating that Donald was reconciled in some way with Robert, Jean and the Gordons of Sutherland, and received some comfort from them at this time.

The tense situation between Robert Gordon and Donald Mackay had only temporarily been put aside, however. In 1618, Robert bought Golspitour, the land and property that Donald had so desperately wanted. Robert also made overtures to various of Donald's friends and dependants, such as the Matheson family, encouraging them to pay allegiance direct to the House of Sutherland and not to Clan Mackay. With Robert's brother Alexander now knighted and made sheriff of Sutherland, Alexander was taking on practical outdoor management of the Sutherland estates, while Jean dealt with the domestic side of raising the child-Earl. Donald was hardly involved in Sutherland affairs at all any more – a sharp contrast to the trust that Earl John had had in him. Donald decided that, in the face of his treatment from the Sutherlands, he was going to go over to the other side: he began talking to Wicked Earl George.[99]

Donald and Wicked Earl George met at Dounreay. Their talk was wide-ranging and productive, covering the alliances in the district and the ways that Mackay and Caithness could be allied and work together. As had happened before, the unfortunate Clan Gunn became the proxies for the enmity between Caithness and Sutherland: Mackay and Wicked Earl George decided that they would work together to get rid of the Gunns from Caithness and Mackay territory, on the grounds that the Gunns had been working as Sutherland agents. Wicked Earl George was still smarting from the burning of corn stacks by Gunn tenants of Mackay, which had resulted in Caithness paying a large sum in compensation money – Wicked Earl George, short of cash as usual, hoped that a new alliance with Mackay might improve his fortunes. As an incentive for Donald, Wicked Earl George also intimated that he might be able to find documents that would prove that Mackay owed allegiance to Caithness, not Sutherland: this would free Donald from any legal obligation to his mother's family.[100] They also discussed marriage alliances between various Sinclair relatives of Wicked Earl George, and Donald's sisters and brother.[101]

Donald had two sisters, Mary and Anna. Mary was married in 1618 to the brother of prominent landowner Hector Munro of Foulis from Easter Ross, between Dunrobin and Inverness. This was fairly unremarkable, but the Sutherlands were disconcerted to hear that Donald's other sister Anna was to marry a Caithness Sinclair.[102] For Robert, it only confirmed his suspicions, and made him more determined to exclude Donald Mackay.

Robert set to work in his usual Machiavellian way. If Caithness was to become a threat through alliance with Mackay, then Wicked Earl George must be neutralised. Robert did this by, once again, appealing to George that Earls must stick together against clans: Robert proposed that Caithness and Sutherland should be friends again, and that George should act as arbitrator in the dispute between Sutherland and Donald Mackay. Wicked Earl George was in a rather dire situation by this point, mainly because of debt. He could not leave his home in the Far North to travel anywhere because of his lack of money and the creditors who were after him. This meant he was becoming more and more isolated, unable to go to Edinburgh, and certainly unable to travel to London to have any influence whatsoever with the king. Maybe the weight of his debts was too heavy; maybe Wicked Earl George's Gordon wife's influence was strong; or maybe his ties to Donald were simply not strong enough, but for whatever reason, Caithness made his choice: once more, Wicked Earl George let down the Mackays and accepted the hand of friendship held out by the powerful and influential Sutherlands. George wrote to Robert, "Right truest and my most assured Cousin...," in his careful, elegant handwriting, saying that his amity to the House of Sutherland was everything it could be, and he would support them and ensure that Mackay's relations to the Gordons were as those of a vassal to a superior. 'Remember me to your mother [Jean]', Wicked Earl George signed off.[103] George believed in Robert's good intentions and the idea, however unlikely, that the three neighbours, the Sutherland, Caithness and Mackay (not the Gunns of course) could finally all be friends. He wrote Donald cheerful, positive letters about the situation.

Donald of the Troubles knew better; he knew now that his uncle Robert would stop at nothing to consolidate Sutherland power, and that the Mackays were once again left isolated in the game of the north.[104] Donald wrote a bitter letter to his grandmother Jean in reply to a note that she sent him: 'My very honourable good lady and loving mother', he began, and protested that he had always been friendly to the House of Sutherland, 'I was and shall be ever willing to serve that House', and that this would naturally continue as the child-Earl came of age. Donald pleaded that he had not meant the quarrel over Golspitour to be taken as him encroaching on Sutherland lands: 'For I protest to God that I never craved nor crave not a foot of ground that pertains to the Earl of Sutherland'. All Donald had wanted, he said, was to establish himself securely. Jean had asked Donald to speak to Robert and Caithness, and he promised to do so, 'to give your Ladyship satisfaction'. Donald then asked Jean if she could help ensure that the others also kept their word, and to write to him to arrange for everyone to meet and discuss. 'I rest and shall ever remain, your Ladyship's Loving Son to serve you', Donald signed off.[105]

Donald Mackay's tangled private life was also continuing to occupy him. His wife Barbara Mackenzie had continued to pursue Donald, furious at her treatment while Donald continued to live with his mistress Mary Lindsay. Barbara had taken her case to the Privy Council of Scotland, who had briefly imprisoned Donald in the Tolbooth, before in 1620 finally processing the case completely and fining Mackay 2000 merks for his adultery.[106]

Robert was continuing to scheme but, distracted by the death of his father-in-law, the saga of the Gunns and the burnt corn stacks petered out.[107] Robert also had other interests, closely following the scheme for a colony in Nova Scotia.[108] He was eventually awarded a baronetcy there, though this was mainly a paper title in exchange for providing finance. However, Robert's groundwork in setting people against Wicked Earl George, coupled with Caithness' own debts, were starting to close in: in 1621, James VI told his Scottish Privy Council that Wicked Earl George had engaged in "Godless and beastly behaviour" and that his territory of Caithness was "so evil disordered as no part of the Highlands, or most remote islands of that our kingdom, were ever more barbarous". James VI asked Robert to take up fire and sword against Wicked Earl George.[109]

Without Donald Mackay's backing, Sutherland was still not strong enough to take on Caithness. Donald now refused to have anything more to do with Robert.[110] However, Wicked Earl George was finally brought down by his debt. He had always struggled with money, ever since he had inherited his title but not the monies to go with it. Now he could not show his face in Edinburgh for fear of creditors, and his son and heir was still in prison in the Scottish capital because of those same debts. Denounced by the crown as a rebel, Wicked Earl George ran away to Orkney.

Knowing that Caithness was without a leader, Robert finally took up the commission of fire and sword. He made sure, too, to take every precaution: Robert was not really a man of action but a cautious man of letters, and he asked for as much help as possible. Robert took with him extra weaponry from Edinburgh, as well as asking for Wicked Earl George's son to be released and allowed to travel with him so that he could be used as a bargaining tool. It is also notable that the Privy Council ordered Donald Mackay by name to support Robert as the official vassal of Sutherland. Mackay was not informed of this directly, however, and wrote several letters to Robert trying to establish what was going on. Robert, arriving in Caithness to find it undefended, its people deliberately disarmed by order of the crown, ordered Donald not to intervene. Backed by his army and unopposed, Robert easily took over Wicked Earl George's castles.

All of the Caithness paperwork was destroyed. The titles to land that they owned, historical documents, correspondence, and any documents that showed that the Mackays owed allegiance to them (rather than to Sutherland) no longer exist. It cannot be proved that this was the action of Robert Gordon at this time, but it looks suspiciously like his handiwork; a wanton act of destruction that ensured that Caithness had nothing to fall back on, no documents to prove which land he owned or who owed him money or allegiance. Robert the historian would have known exactly how important these documents were. "From the Saga period to the seventeenth century the history of Caithness is virtually a blank," said one later analysis, "and this blank is perhaps the most formidable achievement of Sir Robert Gordon's destructive genius."[111] Robert himself, raised to lyricism by his dislike of Caithness, wrote: "I wish I might, if it were possible, imitate the fact of the Ephesians, who made a law, that the name of Herostratus should never be recorded in the books of any of their historiographers..."[112] Robert wanted to wipe Caithness from history – and he almost succeeded. Wicked Earl George was finally allowed back from his self-imposed exile in Orkney, but he was stripped of all responsibilities and retained only his title. Robert and the Sutherlands had finally neutralised Caithness.[113]

Of course, the Far North of Scotland did not suddenly become a peaceful place. As Wicked Earl George struggled with Robert and with his debts, the strife was carried over to other members of the Sinclair family, and their friends and networks, stretching from the far north of Scotland all the way to the south. Sinclair family members fought duels in Leith as the House of Caithness descended into debt and different branches of the family tried to take power. Smaller lairds who owned territory in Caithness and Sutherland tried to turn the situation to their advantage. Among it all Robert sat, trying to guide events so that they would fall out in favour of the House of Gordon.[114]

Robert's eye was still on Donald Mackay. The laird of Duffus was a friend of Donald's, but had become embroiled in a dispute with Donald Mackay's other friend Young Golspitour: Duffus and Golspitour met up in an attempt to sort out their differences but both men turned up to the meeting with their respective entourages. "Matters running high in the course of the debate, and some provoking language having passed", Young Golspitour was suddenly attacked and severely wounded.[115] Many Gordons then pursued Duffus, and the whole affair ended up in front of the courts. Donald was torn between his two friends, Duffus and Young Golspitour, both of whom "confided in his friendship", and he did his best to reconcile them – but ultimately he supported his foster-brother Young

Golspitour.[116] Meanwhile, Robert, alongside William Sinclair of Mey, had originally supported Duffus. Affairs and loyalties were hopelessly tangled.

Duffus only had a small part of his property in Sutherland, so felt he could hold himself aloof from the Gordons, and did not need their approval. Young Golspitour, however, with his land in Sutherland territory, realised that the friendship of the Gordons was indispensable. Faced with Robert's opposition, Young Golspitour decided to buy land in Caithness and Strathnaver, and left his home in Sutherland. Meanwhile, Robert managed to persuade Young Golspitour that Donald Mackay had secretly been supporting Duffus all along. The final result was that Donald Mackay fell out with his foster-brother and long-time friend and ally Young Golspitour. Robert had once again succeeded in manoeuvring Donald into a position where he was more isolated. Donald did not lose all status, being made a Justice of the Peace in 1623 for example, and managing to negotiate new land purchases in territory that was not controlled by the Sutherlands.[117] But by reducing the number of allies Donald could count on, Robert had effectively neutralised him as well. Despite the fact that the Earl of Sutherland was still a child, the House of Sutherland, taking advantage of circumstance and led by Jean and her sons Robert and Alexander of Navidale, had finally triumphed over Wicked Earl George and Caithness, and over the Mackay clan, establishing themselves as the main power in the north.

CHAPTER TWENTY

The Practical Juliet: 1625–1629 and After

Jean was the last of the Gordon siblings, the last of the children of the King of the North. The oldest brother and sister Alexander and Elizabeth had died before Corrichie; dashing John had been executed in front of Mary, Queen of Scots; careful George had collapsed on the football pitch. Jean's sister Margaret had died in exile in Ghent, Belgium, where she had gone to live with her two sons William and John, the friars. Margaret was written about in Catholic sources as a wronged saint:[1] her ex-husband had wanted to stop William and John inheriting, especially after he had children with his second wife, but in the end both Margaret's sons died young. Margaret herself died in January 1606, and her last son John just a few months later,[2] contracting the plague after nursing plague victims. The title of Lord Forbes went to the eldest son of Margaret's ex-husband's second marriage.[3] Of Jean's remaining siblings, William, Jean's other religious brother, died in Paris. Warlike Adam had died near Perth in 1580, after seeing one last revival and resolution of the Forbes-Gordon feud,[4] leaving only an illegitimate son who bore his name and lived and fought and died in France, as one of the king's bodyguard.[5] Patrick had died at the Battle of Glenlivet; Robert had been killed in the firearms accident – and younger brother Thomas had faded from history so we do not know his fate. Jean's brother James the Jesuit had died in Paris in 1620, aged 77,[6] becoming more cautious – "an auld feartie" – in his old age.[7] Jean was the last of her

Gordon generation, outliving all her brothers and sisters, all three of her husbands, four of her children, two queens (Mary and Elizabeth), and one king, as James VI died in 1625.

There is a portrait still hanging in Dunrobin Castle of Jean in her old age. The fresh-faced young woman from the wedding portrait with Bothwell is gone, but the outlines of her high, arched eyebrows and defined nose remain, though her face is wrinkled, her jawline softer and her lips thin with age. The artist has captured her face clearly, showing a woman in her seventies or eighties with probably only some flattery, but the half-length portrait mainly shows her clothes and the rosary she is holding, signifiers of her status and beliefs. She is wearing mostly black, swathed in copious folds of materials, with a peaked widow's headdress covering most of her hair. The hair that is shown is tinted the reddish-brown of the earlier portrait, and her eyes gaze out of slightly hooded lids with a hint of sadness, but in a challenging, direct gaze. A white collar frames her face. In her hands she holds a black rosary, with a metal cross clearly visible as the beads twine around her long, delicate fingers. As the only object she holds, it is a clear sign that her Catholic religion remained extremely important to her.[8] Jean's painting is attributed in the Dunrobin records to 'Scottish School c 1620', and is framed with a plaque with her date of death. However, the frame and plaque are of later date than the painting, and at least one historian has no hesitation in ascribing the portrait to "Scotland's Van Dyke", the eminent portrait painter George Jameson himself.[9]

In the castle today, Jean's portrait is hung in the Duke's Study, next to the painting of her son Robert. Although they do not seem to be by the same artist – the features in Robert's painting are less well-captured – they seem designed to be companion pieces. Robert's painting has an inscription on it saying he was 41 when it was painted, placing it around 1621.[10] At this time Robert was in Scotland, moving between Edinburgh and the north as he launched his final, decisive campaign against Caithness. He may have had his painting done in order to leave it at his family home for his mother and nephew to remember him while he went back home to the south of England. Having seen Robert's painting, perhaps Jean wanted the same, in order to emphasise her own status.[11] There are no further records of Jean leaving the north, so it is likely the painter came to her. Jean expected people to pay court to her, and in her portrait her pose and her clothes show how important she is.[12]

Jean was still very active, and surviving letters from her to Robert give a glimpse into her domestic life. An undated letter from Jean to Robert talks about her servants – she is worried that one girl, Barbara Low, might leave her – 'honest and faithful servants are hard to be found', she says. Jean also passes on information about her other son Alexander of Navidale's movements, journeying up to Caithness, and mentions that Wicked Earl George had not been seen by another friend – these details may have been domestic, but they also gave Robert valuable information to help him make decisions for the Sutherland estates.[13] Jean's life was always this mixture of domestic and dynastic: that was how she, as a woman, exercised control. When her house was the centre of power, the domestic details of where her sons were, and who they spoke to, were also political details that shaped the lives of many people around her.

Another letter, dated 1623, also discusses servants: Jean writes, 'Loving son, your brother has told me that you are minded to come to this country, whereof I am most glad.' Robert was in constant contact with his brother Alexander of Navidale by letter, corresponding about the Sutherland estates, and Jean heard all of Alexander's news. Robert was evidently planning on going to Huntly Castle first, and Jean asks him to bring 'Annie' with him, and perhaps also Annie's nephew[14] – it is unclear who Annie is, but as Jean also mentions an Elspeth Leslie these seem to be women who work with the Gordon family – some of the many retainers who lived in the castle alongside the main family members. Jean maintained the lifestyle she had grown up in, managing a large clan-like family around her. Jean adds some advice to Robert, saying that 'horse meat is very scarce in their parts [that is, around Huntly Castle], therefore you shall do well to come from Moray by sea'; Robert would have trouble finding horses to ride for the journey. Jean adds a further explanation, saying that she has been trying to get Annie and her nephew to come to Dunrobin for a while but that Annie's brother-in-law had been concerned about Jean's religion. 'He need not fear matters of religion,' Jean says, 'for the bairn is not capable of that, and when he is, he shall be at his own command'. Jean continued to practice as a Catholic while exercising the sort of tolerance fashionable at Mary, Queen of Scots' court when she was young: Jean expected to be able to worship in her own way but did not demand that others followed her. She wanted to be left to her own devices and would in turn leave others to theirs.[15]

This had become an unfashionable viewpoint. Times had moved on, and the religious debate had become hardened as both sides became more entrenched. The ferment of ideas in the Reformation of the sixteenth century had been about the possibilities and excitement of the new, whereas the seventeenth century was the long, slow, painful exploration of what these new ideas meant, the adjustment to a new reality, the testing of the extremes of where these new ideas could take people. Jean was the product of an earlier era, and was now living under the third monarch of her life – James VI died in 1625, and had been succeeded by his son Charles I.

Charles had become the heir apparent after the early death of his older brother, but unlike the solidly Protestant Henry,[16] Charles had been influenced by his mother, Anne of Denmark, who had secretly converted to Catholicism. He was also married to a Roman Catholic, the French Henrietta Maria. His religious sympathies were suspect to Protestants – and one effect of that was that Catholics were pursued with renewed vigour as Protestants showed how they would be prepared to stand up for their beliefs.[17] Jean's holding to the old religion was well known and, despite her age, still seen as dangerous. Not only was her own soul in danger but, because of her position of power, she could bring others into danger as well: it was widely known that she had supported and housed her persuasive brother, the Jesuit James, who had once even preached to royalty. With a new king now on the throne who might be sympathetic to Catholic ideas, Jean must be controlled. The minister at Golspie[18] spoke against Jean from the pulpit in 1627, publicly excommunicating the 82-year-old.[19] Jean's son Alexander of Navidale and his wife were also excommunicated, and Alexander was called before the Privy Council to explain himself – but he and his family simply ignored the summons and carried on as if nothing had happened.[20] Jean's relative Lord Huntly was also excommunicated in 1629, and the current Earl of Moray was once again given the lieutenancy of the north. Over the next few years Lord Huntly also lost his sheriffships of Inverness and Aberdeen along with the income these positions brought.

The Gordons lost power and influence due to their religion but were devout enough to continue to refuse to convert.[21] For Jean, there was no question now of changing her beliefs. She had explored her feelings towards Protestantism during her early marriage to Bothwell, but after the shambolic end to that period of her life it was Catholicism and the beliefs of her childhood which had provided her with strength and security with her family and in her later marriages. Religion and family were the central tenets of Jean's life, and they were completely interlinked.

However, Jean's relationship with one member of her family, her grandson Donald Mackay, remained difficult. Donald was her eldest daughter's son; he had been her first grandson. Through Jean's daughter's marriage the House of Sutherland and Clan Mackay had briefly united. But now Jean's own son Robert continued to emphasise Donald's difference as a half-Mackay, half-clansman. In 1626 Donald Mackay decided that there was no place for him in the north of Scotland any more, and he applied to the new king, Charles I, for permission to raise an army to fight as mercenaries on the continent. What has become known as the Thirty Years War had begun in 1618, and showed no signs of abating, as Protestant and Catholic forces across Europe clashed. Mercenaries were in high demand and, despite the sad example of the Sinclairs at the Battle of Kringen, Donald felt that this was his best way forward. Being a mercenary, or paid soldier, was seen as a valid and common career choice and had been for some time, but it became even more common as the Thirty Years War took hold. Men were used to fighting, and it was almost a rite of passage to join the army, while being an army officer was a prestige position. It was a way out of poverty, with food and clothing supposedly guaranteed for soldiers, and the possibility of plunder – and it played to young boys' desire for excitement and adventure, while others believed deeply in the religious causes they were fighting for. Many Scots had already joined the fighting, and around one-fifth of the adult male population of Scotland experienced military service in Europe during the brutal Thirty Years War – percentagewise, this is more men than went to fight from Britain in the First World War.[22] The Thirty Years War had begun as a religious war between various Protestant and Catholic states, but had become a wider battle between rival powers as states fought for political dominance. Mercenaries were employed by all sides and the general devastation as entire areas of croplands were ruined and soldiers and civilians slaughtered made it one of the deadliest conflicts in history.

As a Clan Chief, Donald Mackay could raise an army of loyal followers, many of whom were used to fighting in the local skirmishes of the north, which gave them huge advantages over the untried recruits and conscripts who could make up other regiments. Mackay was allowed by the king to raise up to 5,000 men; by August 1626 he had gathered 3,600, who embarked on ship at Cromarty, to set sail for Europe, and the service of King Christian IV of Denmark, Protestant uncle of Charles I.[23] Donald was not fighting on the side of the Catholic religion of his grandmother Jean. Although Donald was initially prevented by illness from sailing with the rest of his men, he soon joined them on the continent. Mackay's Regiment, dressed in their distinctive clothing of plaids or kilts, soon gained a fearsome reputation.[24]

Donald came home to Scotland to recruit more men in 1628, but was based primarily in Edinburgh rather than the far north. He remained on cordial terms with Alexander of Navidale and some of the Gordons who remained in Sutherland, including his grandmother Jean, but he never forged a friendly relationship with new child-Earl of Sutherland, and he never forgave Robert. On hearing that Robert had asked for his mail to be intercepted, he wrote sorrowfully to Alexander of Navidale saying that, although he felt something for Alexander and Alexander's son, he could not be their true ally but must now stick to his own clansmen and the army he was raising. 'I am sorry there is too much evidence thereof [of Robert's treachery]', he wrote to Alexander of Navidale, 'I am but one, and let never the earth bear me, but I would do for your son as for my own, but I pray you, uncle, excuse me that I must now follow part of the advice of them that thinks to die for my defence, and in defence of their fathers' lands. I am sorry that I know not in whom to trust, my own uncle [Robert] betraying me. The world would not make me believe it, if I had not seen his hand.'[25] Donald did continue to maintain some sort of relationship with Robert, and letters between the two exist from later dates, but although Donald continues to formally address Robert as 'my very honourable and dear uncle', one memorable phrase from a 1635 letter, where Donald is touching on debts owed, has Donald describe Robert as 'arch in his own particulars': "a vivid rendering of the Gaelic word 'Eolach', generally used to denote the person who is knowing in his own business".[26] Donald, the Highland clansman, was wary of Robert the smooth man at court.

On his return to his regiment, Donald moved his eldest sons out to Europe with him. His sons were not initially there to fight, but to continue their education in Denmark. Soon the entire Mackay family followed them over from Scotland: not just Donald's children, but also his wife, servants and retinue.[27] Donald's first wife Barbara Mackenzie died in the 1640s, but Donald had long continued his marital 'Troubles', discarding Mary Lindsay (and their child), and taking up with a woman called Rachel, who later claimed that he had married her bigamously, before abandoning her and the child they had together. Donald went on to marry a fourth woman, Elizabeth Thomson, with whom he also had a daughter to add to his now numerous family.[28] After Elizabeth died, Donald married a Caithness woman, Mary Sinclair. Donald received elevation to the peerage and the reward of the title of Lord Reay for his military service, but the claims of the women he abandoned added to his

'Troubles', damaged his reputation and cost him financially: by the 1640s he was insolvent, and he had to sell some of his northern lands. A treason case that Donald brought to King Charles I further confused his reputation. Mackay's Highland soldiers were gradually absorbed into the larger European army, but the military Mackays were well known for generations, and were the forerunners of a proud history of Scottish regiments.

Although based in Europe, Donald and the Mackays maintained their connection to the north. The Mackays remained, however, allied to Wicked Earl George, and Donald's eldest son married one of the Earl of Caithness' daughters.[29] Although Jean's son Alexander of Navidale attended this wedding – writing to Robert for that black figured silk suit and taffeta cloak from Edinburgh – when Donald was forced to sell land, the Earls of Sutherland eagerly snapped it up, and pushed to acquire more. The Sutherland-Mackay connection that Jean and her daughter Jane had established was no longer working.

As Donald continued to fight in Denmark, Jean's other grandson, the child-Earl, was sent to continue his studies in 1628, first in Edinburgh and then in St Andrews.[30] This grandson, son of Jean's son John, had the same name as his father. In St Andrews he acquired the nickname 'John Glas', *glas* being Gaelic for the blue-grey colour of his eyes. The extraordinary thing was that an Earl of Sutherland became happy to acquire a Gaelic nickname. John Glas was proud of his northern connection and happy to emphasise it to his schoolmates, but he was probably not a native Gaelic speaker. His uncle Robert Gordon advised him to learn some Gaelic in order to converse with his tenants who spoke that language, but John Glas was no hybrid clansman-Earl. When Robert advised John Glas to learn Gaelic, this was the first time learning the language was mentioned: in Jean's youth, being multi-lingual was the default setting and unremarkable. Only when language becomes a barrier is it mentioned. John Glas definitely thought himself a class above Donald of the Troubles. Donald Mackay himself was no longer seen as any sort of threat. The Clan Mackay were a spent force, and Gaelic was becoming a signifier of John Glas' northern roots, the source of a nickname to entertain his new schoolfriends – not the language of a people who could seriously challenge the Earls' authority. John Glas' move to St Andrews was part of a radical break with the land, and even the people, of the north.

Both James VI and then his son Charles I encouraged the education of sons away from home.[31] The sons of Catholic families, such as Jean's grandson John Glas, were to be educated in Protestant places. The Statutes of Iona, passed in 1609, meant that heirs of Western Isles clan chieftains were not allowed to take up their titles unless they spent a certain amount of time educated away.[32] It was a policy that worked in the way that it was intended – encouraging the young men of noble families to become Protestant – but which also had many unintended consequences. Two crucial differences were that it changed women's education, and it caused a break with the land that was most radical for those in the Highlands who were furthest from the centre of power.[33] Jean's granddaughters would have rarely seen their brother after he went away to school – their physical world reached only as far as their shopping trips with Jean to Elgin and the north-east. The gap between their experiences and their brother's might have made it hard for them to forge the same sort of bond that Jean and her siblings had. Meanwhile, John Glas, like other young noblemen, was off to university. John Glas was learning that being Earl of Sutherland meant mixing with other people of his rank in places like the university town of St Andrews, the capital cities of Edinburgh and London, and the court. It did not mean living among and leading the people of Sutherland and the north of Scotland as his father had done. Unlike Jean, John Glas' world stretched southwards. Jean had spent her life riding, walking and sailing around the coast of the Moray Firth. John Glas did not have this learned, intimate, repeated knowledge of the land that gave him his title and power. Even Robert and Alexander of Navidale had already completed much of their education in Dornoch before Robert had petitioned Jean to be allowed to go to university – their link with the north, especially Alexander of

Navidale's, was strong. John Glas' split with his northern heritage was far deeper. The money to pay for his university education came, according to Robert, from a voluntary contribution from John Glas' people, including his cousin Donald Mackay, with every gentleman in Sutherland willingly giving 'a general contribution (every one according to his estate and ability)' because: 'So much did they value and regard the good breeding and education of him who was to govern and command them, knowing how much it doth concern every state and country to have well bred and wise superiors.'[34] The Sutherland gentlemen might soon have questioned the return on their money; Sutherland became, for John Glas, the place where he was born, the place where his title came from, and the place where his revenue came from. The disassociation between landowner and tenant meant both sides were no longer working towards a common goal: there had been little practical difference between the 'House' of Gordon and 'Clan' of Mackay in their common family feeling in Jean's youth but now the 'clan' feeling of wider family was diminishing even more rapidly, replaced by a gulf between rich Earl and poor vassals who served him.

Jean's son Robert continued to push the Sutherland Gordon cause at court, and Charles I made the town of Dornoch a Royal Burgh in 1628. To be a Royal Burgh gave a town privileged status, allowing it to exercise a monopoly on trade, and thrive as a trading centre and seat of justice.[35] Robert had big plans for Dornoch, aiming to make it the centre of the Sutherland earls' territory, with a library, schools and market.[36] Meanwhile, as the energetic man on the scene, Jean's youngest son Alexander of Navidale was still interpreting Robert and John Glas' wishes in Sutherland. Robert might have helped Dornoch's elevation to Royal Burgh status, but it was Alexander of Navidale who met with the relevant townspeople to arrange Dornoch's new market days, making sure they fell on days that would be good for trade and did not clash with the established markets in nearby Tain.[37] Alexander of Navidale journeyed from Sutherland to Aberdeenshire, and down to John Glas' university in St Andrews when the need arose.[38] He communicated with Robert by letter, but the reliability of the mail from the north of Scotland to Robert's home in the south of England was a constant problem: "I received two letters from you the last week," Alexander wrote to Robert, "one dated at London the 28th day of May, the other the 20th day of June, whereby I perceive that you have received none of my letters since February last, whereof I marvel, for I wrote to you both in March and in the beginning of April ... Since Wednesday I wrote twice to you, once from Aberdeen and one from Dundee ... and I daily expect the answer ..."[39] Alexander of Navidale was constantly problem-solving in Sutherland and elsewhere on behalf of his nephew and brother, and, as one of Jean's sons who had remained firmly in the north, he did not agree with John Glas remaining so long in St Andrews. The problems with mail showed clearly that governing from afar could have limitations. Alexander of Navidale visited his nephew and urged him to come home, but John Glas refused.[40] Robert was more sympathetic to his nephew's viewpoint that he could improve his prospects by remaining away from home and continuing at university – after all, this was what Robert himself had done – and Robert told John Glas not to stir from St Andrews, unless his mother's family sent for him. Jean's two sons, Robert and Alexander of Navidale, disagreed here; it was one of the fundamental splits between their personalities. Robert believed in the benefits of leaving the north; Alexander in the benefits of staying in the north. Jean's grandson John Glas sided with Robert, and was delighted to receive permission to stay in St Andrews, where he was enjoying himself – though he does not appear to have been as keen a student as his uncle Robert. Robert kept encouraging him, but also spent a lot of time cautioning against the myriad distractions of sport, hunting, cards, dice and gambling. Sport could be necessary training for war, but football was 'a dangerous and unprofitable exercise'.[41]

Earlier remaining records of John Glas' schooling in Dornoch focus on money spent on bows and arrows, golf clubs and balls and saddle and horse furnishings, or mention his hunting expeditions, and John Glas seems to have continued to apply himself in a similar manner – taking advantage of his uncle Alexander of Navidale's visit, for example, to buy a new horse.[42] He was particularly friendly with his contemporary the Earl (later Marquis) of Montrose, and they invited each other to breakfast and other festivities.[43] In a letter reporting on his progress it was remarked dryly that 'if [John Glas] would take pains [he] would do reasonably'. His brother Adam was judged 'not sufficient', but there were higher hopes for youngest brother George Posthumous: 'George (God willing) will be the scholar'.[44] John Glas stayed at university until 1630, when he was 21, before making his way very slowly back to Sutherland.[45]

In Sutherland, Alexander of Navidale continued to run the estates – and care for his mother Jean. By 1628 Jean was weakening, in body at least. Alexander of Navidale wrote to Robert in summer 1628, describing how Jean had been particularly ill for the last six weeks, 'And nothing expected of her ladyship daily but death.' However ill she was in body, though, Jean was not giving up yet. She had dedicated her life to the Gordons, and she wanted to know that they appreciated her and would give her the final respects that she thought she deserved. Alexander says to his brother, 'It has been proposed to me by some, that it will be necessary, whenever God calls her [Jean], to give her an honourable burial, and have some of her ladyships most honourable friends there.' I don't know if this idea came from Jean herself, Alexander continues, and she certainly did not say it openly to me, but it would be very expensive and 'against the custom of our house'. Not only that, but Jean's illness was becoming very expensive as well. What should I do? Alexander of Navidale plaintively asks his older brother. I do not want to spend any more money, but if it is 'her ladyship's special commandment on her death bed' he would have to obey. Of course, Alexander admits, Jean has not asked him outright to arrange an enormously lavish funeral; all she has said is that he is to be sure and pass on her best wishes to Robert, his wife and children – but it is really clear that Jean is telling everyone that, after all her hard work, she thinks her sons should take care of her to their best abilities and give her the best send-off possible.[46]

Jean did not die that summer, but hung on tenaciously until the following spring. She sent for Robert, and he travelled north in time to see her before she died. Of the six children she had borne to her second husband Alexander, Robert and Alexander of Navidale were the only two surviving. Jean had outlived her other sons and daughters, her three husbands and most of her contemporaries. Both her sons were with her when she died, and Robert "wes so happie as to receave her last blissing befor her death".[47]

Jean named Robert as the executor of her will, and he and Alexander of Navidale did carry out her last wishes: she was buried in the newly refurbished Dornoch Cathedral, laid to rest alongside her second husband Alexander. Jean, who had led the House of Sutherland during the lifetimes of her husband, her son and her grandson, was laid to rest in the place reserved for the Earls of Sutherland, with the full honours usually given only to a male head of household. Any analysis of the Sutherland line which focuses solely on the male line and ignores her contribution is flawed and misses the enormous influence she had in shaping the way that the House of Sutherland acted, their loyalty to the throne, loyalty to Catholicism and strong connections with the Aberdeenshire House of Huntly. Her positive legacy was to her family: she had put aside her love for Alex Ogilvie of Boyne and committed herself entirely to the Gordon cause. Robert said that "in this [she was] much to be commended, that dureing the continuall changes and particular factions of the court in the raigne of Quein Mary, and in the minoritie of King James the Sixt … shoe alwise managed her effairs with so great prudence and forsight, that the enemies of her familie culd never prevaile against her".[48] She made it through "the troublesome stormes" of the reign of Mary, Queen of Scots and the drama with Bothwell, to forge a new life with Alexander Earl of Sutherland, not only becoming his Countess but "Further, shoe hath by her great care and diligence brought to a prosperous end many hard and difficult bussines, of great consequence, apperteyning to the house of Sutherland … shoe … tak vpon her the managing of all the effairs of that house a good whyle, which shoe did performe with great care, to her owne credet, and the weill of the familie." The House of Sutherland, as an extension of the House of Gordon, Jean treated with "singular affection". Robert memorialised his mother in his family genealogy as a woman "of great vnderstanding above the capacitie of her sex".[49]

Jean had provided a remarkable continuity for the House of Sutherland during her lifetime, but after her death her grandson John Glas seemed to be almost wilfully destroying what she had built. He was a modern individual, returning from university with his own ideas ready to put his stamp on things, throwing out the ideas of the previous generation in favour of his own wishes. It was a marked contrast to the way that Jean's brother George, for example, had run Huntly Castle and the House of Huntly. Instead of returning to take his place among his ancestors, John Glas wanted to move forward alone, using the Sutherland estates as a financial asset to fund his life. Unlike Jean's brother George, who had happily taken in Jean, his brother-in-law Alexander Earl of Sutherland, and many of Alexander's followers, John Glas did not want his family around him in the same way at all. The image of Jean's brother George happily sorting out the quarrels of his retainers before calling all his men around him to play football contrasts sharply with the approach taken in the early 1600s: Robert advised his nephew to make lists of names of all his retainers and men and reward each of them in turn.[50] It was as though Jean's son Robert wanted to follow the example of his ancestors, but needed to codify it, whereas for Jean's brother George it had come naturally. In among Robert's papers are various lists of names supporting his own use of this administrative approach.[51]

Jean and Alexander of Navidale had done much together to maintain the Sutherland estates for the child-Earl but, when he came of age, John Glas did not seem particularly grateful. He took his time about coming home from university, and, when he arrived, did not return the support that he had been given, ignoring both Jean's religious beliefs and her devotion to family. Alexander of Navidale had stayed true to the old religion like Jean, and he was experiencing more and more problems. Catholics were no longer welcome in Scotland, and it became apparent that, like Robert, John Glas had found it prudent to become Protestant. Alexander of Navidale decided that the safest course of action for him was to go into exile, and take himself and his family off to Ireland. Alexander wanted to give his Navidale lands into his nephew's safekeeping, but, as Alexander wrote angrily to Robert, "I culd get nothing done with my brother sone, the earll ... I think I mey say it without offence that thair was never any man so onnaturallie delt withall for goode serwice ... God grantme patiens, seing I hawe no recowrs now bot only to God, for I sie it is not to man to lean to mortall men ..."[52] I am not the first cadet, or younger son of the house, to be cast out of their homeland in this way, Alexander continued sadly, but I must be the first so ungratefully used. Robert tried to encourage John Glas to be respectful, but with little change for Alexander.[53] Alexander and his family made their way to Ireland in the hope of practising their religion more freely and, although he came back to visit Sutherland a couple of times, his movements become hazy after that. Alexander, full of his religious scruples, considered a pilgrimage to Jerusalem, but, burdened by debt, he only made it as far as Italy where he spoke to people about Scottish Catholic alliances with Spain, but also found time to wait upon 'the braiv Julia, who is the most teaking courtesan that evir I sau in my lyf tym'.[54] His brother Robert disapproved, specifically warning John Glas that he should: 'Suffer not your sons willinglie to pass the Alpes ...' as they would learn bad habits on the continent, mentioning Italy and the dangers of the Catholic religion.[55] Perhaps, as the Thirty Years War progressed, religion came before family for Robert in the end. Meanwhile, Alexander of Navidale travelled on in France and Belgium, before returning to Ireland. He did not return again to his home in the north.

At least two of Alexander of Navidale's sons, like the Mackays, went to fight on the continent as mercenary leaders, one with Colonel Hepburn in Sweden. Although Scot Colonel Hepburn was a Protestant, he fought on the side of the Catholics: religious loyalties were sometimes confused or forgotten for professional soldiers in the clamour of war, but ultimately Alexander and his sons ended up on the opposite side to Donald Mackay, as Donald had sadly predicted would happen. Alexander's sons later fought with the Royalists for Charles I.[56]

Meanwhile, as Alexander of Navidale was left to fend for himself, John Glas showed a similar disregard for the strong links that Jean had fostered with the Huntly Gordons. Lord Huntly was of an older generation, and even his heir, Enzie, was 19 years older than John Glas. The Huntlys clung to Catholicism and, although they remained more and more at home and less and less at court, their powerbase in the north was weakening even as John Glas turned to Protestantism and looked outwards. The direction the two Houses were heading in was diverging and, more importantly, the personal links between the two Houses were getting weaker. Everything came to a head at the tragic fire of Frendraught in 1630.

There was an ongoing feud between the families of James Crichton of Frendraught and William Gordon of Rothiemay, who lived in the Huntly Gordon territory in the north-east: the dispute had its roots in a disagreement over fishing rights, but, as is the way with these feuds, had escalated and dragged more and more other people into the argument, while the complicated family networks of the north-east ensured that everyone was picking a side. Events got out of hand with skirmishes, shooting and slaughter. The feud had been ongoing for some years, since before Jean died, and, because of her family connections to it, Jean was probably well aware of it – Alexander of Navidale had been writing to Robert about the feud as early as 1628.[57] The Gordons were not only related to Rothiemay, but Jean's involvement was even more personal as her granddaughter, John Glas' sister Elizabeth, had married Frendraught. The marriage had taken place some years earlier, in 1619, arranged by Jean's son Robert.[58] Elizabeth was the little girl whose father Earl John had bought her a 'double virginal' harpsichord to play with her sister.[59] After the death of her father and mother, Elizabeth, now Lady Frendraught, had been brought up partly by Jean.

Just as the Frendraught-Rothiemay situation escalated, Jean's son Robert returned to the north for a visit. His visits north were as frequent as ever, but now that he was no longer managing the Sutherland estates for his nephew, Robert was looking to purchase land of his own. Unlike his brother Alexander, Robert had further sources of income from his wife's lands and his pension from court. For Robert, Jean's son, there was no question that Moray and the north-east was his home as much as the Far North ever was, and he was eventually to retire there, with his extended family, in 1643 – though the troubled religion of those times made it a less than peaceful retirement.[60] Meanwhile, Robert, as certain as ever of his own importance and ability, busied himself in becoming involved in the local feuds, attempting to stage-manage Gordon affairs in the north-east as he had done for so long in the minority of John Glas. Robert spoke to his cousin Lord Huntly, and in an attempt to calm the escalating Frendraught situation down and effect a reconciliation, Lord Huntly invited Frendraught to stay at Huntly Castle. After what seemed like a very successful couple of days, negotiations were sealed with a handshake between all parties in the orchard at Huntly Castle.[61] The peace did not last, however, and soon Frendraught was back with Lord Huntly for more negotiations. Once again Lord Huntly was hopeful that a lasting truce had been reached, and this time he sent Frendraught home, accompanied both by the new heir to Rothiemay and by an escort of Gordon men, including one of Lord Huntly's younger sons, Aboyne.[62] They were hopeful that this could be the end to the feud. When they reached Frendraught's home, Frendraught invited Rothiemay and the Gordon men, including Aboyne, to enjoy a return of hospitality and stay the night. Rothiemay and Aboyne were lodged together in the same room in the tower, just a little distance from Frendraught's main residence. However, during the night, disaster struck: Frendraught's tower caught fire. The fire burnt fiercely round the base of the tower, stopping the men inside from escaping. As Frendraught's people gathered outside, they could see Rothiemay and Aboyne at the window – but the windows were barred and they could not jump to safety. The people crowded at the foot of the tower heard the screams as Rothiemay and Aboyne – and four of their men – were burnt to death. The story of the gruesome burning was turned into a ballad, full of lurid details: Aboyne presses against the "wire-window", shouting to the crowd below, and, taking the rings from his long white fingers, throws them down with instructions that they are to be taken to his wife. "I cannot leap, I cannot come," Aboyne laments, "I cannot win to thee. My head's fast in the wire-window, my feet are burning from me. My eyes are seething in my head, My flesh roasting also, My bowels are boiling with my blood . . ."[63]

With emotive language like that, and the bad blood of the ongoing feud, it was no wonder that the ballad soon finds someone to blame for the fire: Elizabeth Lady Frendraught, Jean's granddaughter. The Lady Frendraught, it was said, stood at the foot of the tower gloating as the fire took hold – 'I'll mourn you, Aboyne,' she said, 'but I will never mourn my family's enemy Rothiemay'. Rothiemay called out to her to have shame – the feud had taken his father, and now he was to die, and his mother would be twice bereaved. The ballad shows Lady Frendraught, unrepentant, throwing the keys to the tower in the "deep draw-well".[64]

Immediately after the fire, the Lady Frendraught did what she could in the way of damage limitation: wearing a white plaid, riding on a broken-down horse, and accompanied only by a page-boy, she went humbly to her cousin Lord Huntly, weeping and mourning. At the gate of Huntly Castle she desired entry, wishing to explain and grieve the deaths. Lord Huntly refused to let her in. It was the first time Huntly Castle had refused entry to one of Jean's family. The Lady Frendraught had to return home, riding the way she had come.

The cause of the fire was never fully determined, with servants interrogated and suggestions of a third party being involved – but the Lady Rothiemay had no hesitation in blaming the Lady Frendraught, and Lord Huntly, distraught at the loss of his son Aboyne, sided with her. Frendraught was brought to trial – but exonerated. This, however, did not stop Lord Huntly, and many others, believing in his guilt, and the north of Scotland "descended into chaos and disorder as bands of Highlanders and Gordon adherents proceeded to conduct a series of raids on Frendraught's lands".[65]

John Glas could not condemn his sister Elizabeth and his

brother-in-law Frendraught for the fire. In 1632 John Glas too came to Huntly Castle, but, like his sister before him, he was not welcomed there. For the first time since Alexander had escaped the Earl of Caithness and come to the Gordons for help, for the first time since a Huntly Gordon had married the daughter of the Earl of Sutherland in 1500,[66] the doors of Huntly Castle were not open to a Gordon of Sutherland. And crucially, for the first time, a Sutherland Gordon did not submit to a Huntly Gordon. The Huntlys had always been the senior branch of the House, and had expected the Sutherland Gordons to follow them. But now John Glas would not support Lord Huntly – and he did not really suffer for it. The Huntly Gordons were no longer the power they had been when Jean's father was Cock o' the North, and the Sutherland Gordons could manage well enough without them. The House of Gordon began to split definitively in two: the House of Huntly and the House of Sutherland. The House of Huntly's story become one of ever-declining power and influence, as their Catholicism isolated them, and they failed to establish a strong presence either at court or in the towns, or even to realise the commercial potential of their land.[67] Meanwhile, the Earls of Sutherland forged onwards; Protestant, government-supporters, major landowners.[68]

For the strongest legacy that Jean left John Glas, so strong that not only did he never break it but he never even thought to question it, was that the Earls of Sutherlands were the major power in the north of Scotland. Jean's actions with her husband Alexander, then her stewardship in the minority of her son and grandson, the battles but also the patient, torturous legal actions, had completely annihilated the threats posed by the Earls of Caithness and the Clan Mackay. There was no real competition any more: the Earls of Sutherland ruled supreme in the Far North.

Robert left his nephew John Glas valuable advice on how to manage his land, though it is unclear how much of it John Glas read or followed. "One thing I would wish yow to do, which is, that yow never height nor augment the rentall of your land," Robert cautioned, with words that could have been better heeded by later Sutherlands:

do not be careless enough to ask your tenants for more than they can afford or provide from the lands they have: "How can they pay the dewtie when the ground will not yield it? A poore tennant maks a poore maister, and a rich tennant a rich maister."[69] Robert, although he was living in the south, knew that the land in Sutherland was not rich: it was not possible to ask from it more than it could give – it would never be as fertile as farmland in the south of England. Here, Robert foresaw one of the future dangers of the Earls of Sutherland being dislocated from their lands: if they did not understand the land itself, and the people on it, there would be problems.

Other northern lords faced similar problems of dislocation from the north brought on by their education elsewhere: John Glas' kinsman Enzie, the son of Lord Huntly, spent many years at court, and, like John Glas, was more of a Protestant than a Catholic like the rest of his family. Enzie was sometimes seen by his contemporaries as having 'English' manners, embracing the Stoical, unemotional stance that James VI had promoted at court.[70] But each August, Enzie would return to his northern estates with his friends to go on extended hunting trips – wearing tartan hose, kilts and plaids. The north was a playground, a temporary return, a place to dress up; the court, and court dress, was real life.

Robert tried to predict the future for John Glas, to see how things would work out for him. One thing that Robert saw clearly was that James VI's project to unite 'Great Britain' would have a massive, long-running impact, and that this could affect the power of the nobility in Scotland.[71] After Charles I took over from his father, Robert saw too the changing current political situation and by 1643 had decided that it was time for him to retire from the court. Robert bought lands in Morayshire, at what became known as Gordonstoun, and moved his wife, elderly mother-in-law and children up to the north-east.[72] Like his mother Jean, Robert was long-lived, dying in his mid-seventies, in 1656.[73]

The Earls of Sutherland continued and thrived. The current Earl of Sutherland traces his ancestry directly back to John Glas, to Earl John, to Jean and Alexander.[74] The policy that Jean had encouraged, of maintaining and expanding their land in the Far North, was pursued – though with very different outcomes to those that Jean could ever have imagined. One of the most significant and distinctive aspects of Scottish history is the continuity and lack of change in ownership of land: the Sutherland estates are still currently among the top ten largest landholdings in Scotland, at 87,898 acres.[75] The current Earl of Sutherland succeeded to the title in December 2019: prior to that his title was Lord Strathnaver, the Mackay lands of Strathnaver have been, for generations now, Sutherland land.

Jean was remembered by her family as virtuous, beautiful, judicious and intelligent; a woman who had a strong memory of her own family's past, and a strong belief in what was due to her family. Her running of the Sutherland estates was warmly and effusively praised. Jean's son Robert stressed that she had been 'forced'[76] into taking a leading role in managing the Sutherland estates and protecting them from enemies, something that women did not always do and which he felt had to be explained, but there is every evidence that Jean was not only good at it, but relished being in command, as she returned several times to take over the running of the estates for her husband, her son and then her grandson. Her marriage contracts show her desire to own and run her own lands and affairs, and to keep control over these even when she remarried. Jean had come through 'variable courses of fortune' through the reigns of Mary, Queen of Scots and the regencies in the minority of James VI, through James VI's reign and into that of Charles I, while maintaining her own grip on power.[77] Jean's place in history is assured through her association with the Earl of Bothwell and Mary, Queen of Scots, but after the humiliation of the collapse of her marriage to Bothwell she had built a new life. She found happiness in her relationships with her siblings and dedication to the wider Gordon family, and then in her second marriage to Alexander, Earl of Sutherland. Jean lived within the strictures of her time, yet was lucky to live long enough to defy fortune and convention to finally marry the man she loved, Alex Ogilvie. Her time with Alex Ogilvie was brief, but she found later happiness and purpose again in her children and grandchildren, as she returned to the place she had made her home, Sutherland.

Jean created around herself the same sort of family she had enjoyed when she was younger; siblings who were close, who "loved one another intirlie; which mutuall love wes a comfort to themselues, a crose to their enemies, and a great joy to all that favored them; the more notable in that it is extraordinarie, far exceeding the brotherly love of these our tymes, and without any nighbouring example".[78] 'Family' meant not only Jean's brothers and sisters and sons and daughters, but also the wider House of Gordon: everyone with her surname was family in a way that was almost clan-like.[79] 'Let there be still a strict friendship and inviolable union between you and your surname . . . otherwise it may undo you all. For your surname is envied in this area for its greatness and prosperity, which (doubtless) will increase so long as you serve God truly . . . Your family had ever that good property to keep a perpetual love and friendship among themselves.'[80]

Jean's son Robert wrote that: 'The rising, decay and continuance of all estates and families is in the hand of the Almighty everliving God. He raiseth and exalteth men from the very dust to be princes, and throws down principalities even below the earth, as he in his divine wisdom thinketh expedient.'[81] She undoubtedly believed something similar: that she and her Gordon family should be in charge, because God meant them to be, but she was closer than Robert to the times when power was gained by the sword rather than by the law, and she knew from her father's downfall how easy it was to lose it all. 'Although we should rather strive to be citizens in heaven than for precedence on earth, yet my advice is . . . to seek your due, and that rank whereunto God hath called you . . .'[82] Jean fought as hard as she could, using the tools she had access to, to continue to promote Gordon interests, talking to her extended family, supporting their choices and pursuing their claims through the courts. Jean's God was Catholic: when she turned away from her religion, she saw her family falter, as in her marriage to Bothwell or when her son Earl John was kept in ward and saw his child die, and so for Jean Catholicism was something she was prepared to fight for as well. Through her encouragement of her brother James the Jesuit, in particular, Jean was seen as a threat to the king of Scots: even though she was a woman, it was understood that she was a major player in the north and north-east of Scotland. Because Jean was a woman and unable to fight in battle, she, and through her the House of Sutherland, embraced the law over the sword. This made an impression on Jean's children, and Robert, the lawyer, in particular.[83]

Jean's two younger sons, Robert and Alexander of Navidale, seem like two parts of her own personality: strait-laced Robert was the cool, rational part of her, devoted to the Gordon cause and anxious to improve their social standing at court, the rational woman who had been able to reconcile the idea of living at court with Mary, Queen of Scots even though Mary had been responsible for the death of her father and brother. Alexander, Knight of Navidale, living in the north with his wife and children and extended family – extending even to Donald and the Clan Mackay – and embracing his Catholic faith to the point of exile, was the passionate part of Jean, the part that loved her unruly sibling Adam, that dressed in mourning black on her honeymoon, or who held on for years to her love for Alex Ogilvie.

Jean was, like all of us, a mixture of rational and emotional, a mixture of her own choices and the vagaries of fate, the practical and pragmatic Juliet who both lost and gained her heart's desire several times over.

"Now, to conclude, I advyse yow to liwe wertuouslie that yow may dye patientlie, for he who lives most honestlie will dye most willinglie; that so, liwing a good man, yow may dye in peace, lamented of your countrey men, admired by your neighbours, and leaving a good fame behind yow on earth, yow may obteyne the crowne of eternall felicitie in heavin."[84]

" ...the Lord by his providence, had brought me thither, with a number of my friends to follow, and obey him, as they were bound by oath to obey me. And then I thought with my selfe, after I had awaked from sleepe, going on to march, that my life was much like a tale, and that we should not care how long this life of ours should last, but that wee should bee carefull, how well our life should bee acted, for it is no matter, where wee end, if wee end well; and we should not aske, when, or where, but we ought to bee ever mindfull, how wee are prepared going to fight. Nature did beget us miserable, we live over-burthened with cares, and like a flower, wee vanish soone away, and dye. Our hunting then here, and our care should bee onely for a perpetuall good name to leave behind us, that so being absent wee are present, and being dead, wee live".[85]

Endnotes

1. See my first book, *Josephine Tey: A Life*. While 'truth is the daughter of time' is a phrase I learnt from Tey's wonderful detective novel of that title, it actually dates back to a time period that is more appropriate for this book: Tey may have got it from Francis Bacon (1561–1626), and it was also used as a motto by Bloody Mary I of England.
2. Lucie Gordon to Robert Gordon, NLS Dep 175/79 /4792. My translation / paraphrasing (original in French).
3. "bring that to light, which heirtofore hath bien so long obscured, and too much neglected" (Robert, xi).
4. Sutherland book, vol 2, 366; NLS Dep 175 Acc 10824 Box 2, Robert's final letter of advice to his nephew.
5. Mary, Queen of Scots was three years older than Jean.

Part One: The Marian Years

CHAPTER ONE: The King of the North's Daughter: 1545–1561

1. 1545 is the date of Jean's birth. See note 12 below for the probable date of Mary of Guise's visit to Huntly.
2. Huntly Castle has also been known as Strathbogie; the name was changed by act of Parliament in 1544. Robert, 110.
3. Population statistics from Porter, 256.
4. Tabraham (Huntly), 1996.
5. Forbes, 10.
6. ODNB.
7. CSP, Henry VIII, 9th January 1543; Aboyne, 447.

8. Tabraham (Huntly), 1996; Goodman, 3; Thomas, 32.

9. 'Servants' in the 1500s were not the same as servants in the eighteenth or nineteenth century, but had a much closer relationship with their masters and mistresses – while 'serving' a noble family was something often done by people of a younger age, rather than people who were perceived to be of lower class. Goodman, 3, 117–18.

10. Sanderson, 1987: 36; reference to the Leather Chamber in Aboyne, 498. Quotes are altered from the original Scots if there is any potential for misunderstanding.

11. It was later used by Mary, Queen of Scots at Lochleven.

12. Aboyne, 454. Mary of Guise made two tours of the north of Scotland, following almost exactly the same route, holding justice ayres in Inverness, Elgin, Banff and Aberdeen. The first, in summer 1552, was with Arran when he was Regent, and Mary of Guise took every opportunity to undermine him. The second was in 1555. On the second tour she was particularly looking for money, punishing offences with fines (Marshall, 2017). It's not wholly clear on which visit this story of 'the Cock o' the North' happened. The second tour seems likely: because she was looking for money, Huntly's opulence would have really stood out. At Huntly Castle itself, information panels say it was the second trip. However, one secondary source specifically says it was the first trip (Huntly, 27) – because this is written by a Huntly descendant, their access to primary sources is excellent, but as the book is not fully referenced it cannot be checked.

13. George married Anne Hamilton in 1557.

14. Williams, 26.

15. Robert, 130; Aboyne, 447–8; ODNB.

16. Kirk in Inverness Field Club, 25.

17. Which can be partially understood by the concept of 'dùthchas', where the chief of the clan had an obligation of kindness to the people of the clan, which included a guarantee of secure access to territory. The responsibility of the landowner to the tenant was as important as the rights of the landowner over the tenant.

18. Wightman, 7, 71. Difference in clan use of land included the system of tanistry, where property and title did not automatically pass from father to son. This, along with dùthchas, was an evolving, living system, just as feudalism was.

19. Arguably, the start of the decline of the clan system is the end of the Lordship of the Isles in 1493. The last claimant to the title of the Macdonald Lordship died the year Jean was born.

---

20. Guise Correspondence, 381 (my translation).
21. Dating events in the sixteenth and seventeenth century can be difficult as the Julian calendar changed to the Gregorian calendar at different points in different countries in Europe – so the date could differ from place to place. The Gregorian calendar was first introduced in 1582 to try to match the calendar year more closely to the equinoxes and solstices: this was important because it had an impact on when religious festivals such as Easter were celebrated. Scotland and England operated different calendars after 1600. The New Year was celebrated in March in the Julian calendar and January in the Gregorian. So there is often confusion both in contemporary documents and in later analyses. Mary of Guise became Regent of Scotland on 19th February 1553, or 1554, depending on whether the new year is counted as starting in January or March.
22. For all of Jean's life, feuding in the Highlands was particularly severe. Huntly and the Scottish crown were engaged in a constant low-level battle of violence with the clans, partly caused by the collapse of the Lordship of the Isles.
23. *A Satire of the Three Estates* was a morality play by David Lyndsay first performed in 1552, and of lasting influence. It is an attack on the three estates represented in the Scottish Parliament: the clergy, lords and burgh representatives. 'Estates' can be understood (loosely) as 'social classes'. While there was a lot of crossover, as we will see, between the clans and the nobles, this changed over Jean's lifetime as they became more distinct. The distinction between clans and nobles is also very useful for anyone reading popular history, as 'clans' and 'nobles' tend to be treated differently in different books: for example, the History of the Mackay clan [Mackay book] gives a very different interpretation of events to that given by Robert, Jean's son.
24. They were both married by 1547, when Huntly was a prisoner of the English.
25. Grant Simpson, 11–12. There are no figures for literacy in Scotland, but based on English figures around 40 per cent of the population could read to some extent by 1530. See also Goodman, 2016: 109.
26. Several of Jean's handwritten letters in Scots survive, and will be discussed in later chapters. A book of saints' lives in Latin, *Legenda Aurea*, is listed as having belonged to Jean's library in later life. (Graham, 1908: 56; Laing, 359). Some have commented that owning a book did not mean Jean could read it (Stuart, 33), but this seems unlikely in the face of the evidence of her well-written letters and educated family.

27. "It is also requisite that yow learne to speak the vulgar langage of the countrey", Jean's son advised the future heir to their Earldom, meaning that he should learn to speak Gaelic. (Sutherland book, vol 2, 357.)

28. The writings of James Fraser of Kirkhill in the later sixteenth and early seventeenth centuries are a brilliant example of the range of languages known in Scotland, as this Gaelic speaker describes his travels on the continent, where he converses happily in English, Scots, Latin, Hebrew, Greek, French, Spanish, Italian, German and Hungarian.

29. An Englishman commenting on a letter from Catholic priests trying to get printed books into Scotland in the sixteenth century said that, "Our language is common to both us and the Scots" (Forbes-Leith, 1889: 173–4). However, Mary, Queen of Scots, who spoke Scots and French, had to learn English when she was in captivity in England (Fraser, 1994: 172; Fraser, 2015: 296). There is a letter from Mary to Knollys, who she was lodged with in England, where she talks about her 'evil writing this first time' as she writes 'in this language', i.e. in English. It was, and is, possible for an English speaker to read Scots with no extra training – but it is probably easier for a Scot to do this (than an English person) because you need familiarity with many different words.

30. Languages weren't any easier to learn though, despite their importance: Jesuits were some of the most highly educated people, but there are records of one who "spoke reasonable French, albeit with a broad Scots accent" (Yellowlees, 50) and another who "expressed a desire to learn the local language [German] as quickly as possible [but] never fully mastered it" (Yellowlees, 56).

31. "my wyiffe schawis me that the quyenis grace hes ane ewyll opponzeone of my serwice touerts hyr grace" (Guise Correspondence, 395).

32. An English version of the name 'Aodh' could be 'Hugh'. It is the same element that is in the name 'Mackay', i.e. Mackay or Mac-Aodh means 'son of Aodh'. It was a difficult name to pronounce for Aodh's non-Gaelic speaking contemporaries, and he is represented in documents under various spellings, including 'Iye' and, my personal favourite, the enigmatic 'Y' (as in the cipher-like 'Y McY'). 'dh' in Gaelic is pronounced something like the 'ch' in 'loch' and a representation of the pronunciation of the name could be something close to 'ooo – ich'. For Aodh's refusal to attend the circuit court, see Grimble, 1993: 31.

33. See Grimble (22–5, 27). Supporting the English were other "assured Scots" in the Rough Wooing period – mainly Protestants – see Wormald, 63. It might seem strange that Highland clans supported England, but there are other similar stories from the same time. For example, descendants of

the Lords of the Isles saw themselves in opposition to the Scottish crown, so looked to Scotland's enemy England for help to restore their power – Huntly then worked for the Scottish crown to stop them, showing how the earl and clan systems could interact (Huntly, 21–4).

34. Sutherland book, vol 2, 3–4.
35. The Scottish Parliament made the offer of the crown matrimonial, but the Hamiltons and Protestants opposed the move. The offer was never revoked, but was not actually fulfilled (Guy, 93).
36. Fraser, 1994: 95–6.
37. According to Potter (2002: 58) Huntly was in his late forties in 1561. Figure for average life expectancy from Fraser (2009: 102).
38. James Stewart's mother was Margaret Erskine, Lady Douglas.
39. CSP, Elizabeth, Randolph to Cecil, 24th October 1561, footnote.
40. Forbes, 17. Potter (2002: 52) says that items were taken to Huntly Castle in 1559.
41. Wormald, 91: "the effective rulers of the two countries [France and Scotland] were now, after all, the two Guise brothers in France and their sister the regent in Scotland".
42. Marshall, 2017: 94.
43. Treaty of Leith 6th July 1560. See Steer (Petworth map).
44. Forbes-Leith, 72–3.
45. ODNB; Marshall, 2017: 99. Mary of Guise was buried in Normandy, at the church where her sister was an abbess. A splendid monument was erected, but destroyed in the French Revolution.
46. Aboyne, 459.

CHAPTER TWO: They Would Go to Aberdeen: 1562

1. Elizabeth's descendants eventually numbered "the Earl of Atholl, the Lords Seton, Lovat and Ochiltrie" – all notable Gordon supporters (Robert, 143).
2. The feud between the Forbes and the Gordons probably had its roots in changes that Jean's father had made to land rights: the Forbes had been farming tenants of church lands, but Huntly took these lands over and placed cadet Gordon families in charge, and even replaced some Forbes with Gordons (Forbes, 9).
3. Spalding Misc, 150. My translation.
4. Forbes, 108.
5. Balfour Paul, 59. Margaret's first child was a son, William. She then had three girls, and a second son (Forbes, 111).

6. Though Huntly never had the title of Duke, the Gordons were eventually given a Dukedom, and there is reference to an earlier version of the song being 'the Lord o' Gordon': the title has been changed as time went on. The song has been linked to Jean by many commentators.

7. Gardner, 1893: 548; Buchan, 1985: 161.

8. Since there is to be more than one important person in Jean's life called Alexander, I have decided to use the shortened version of Alex Ogilvie's name to distinguish him – and to indicate the longstanding, informal relationship he had with Jean. Alex Ogilvie's age is unclear: different sources place him as being born between 1530 and 1540.

9. Alex Ogilvie's father was Walter Ogilvie. Walter had married Christian Keith, a daughter of the 3rd Earl Marischal Keith. Christian Keith was Jean's mother's aunt. The Keiths were linked by marriage to the Gordons more than once.

10. Alex Ogilvie's father, Sir Walter Ogilvie, 3rd of Boyne, died c. 1561 (Taylor).

11. Gardner, 1893: 548; Buchan, 1985: 161.

12. All the branches of the Ogilvie family were linked, and saw themselves as linked. See for example Douglas Peerage, 262. This is an older peerage; newer versions are usually used, but there are some interesting details, and links to charters which can be followed up and verified.

13. Alexander Ogilvie of Deskford and Findlater. There are a lot of Alexanders, so I omit his first name for clarity.

14. Guise Correspondence: Alexander Gordon to the Queen Dowager c. Sept 1549, my translation/paraphrasing.

15. She was also related to Young Golspitour: see later chapters (Robert, 104).

16. Sometimes known as 'James Ogilvie of Cardell'.

17. Aboyne, 461.

18. Aboyne, 461.

19. CSPS, 656. It's not clear what happens to Elizabeth after she's locked up, but Forbes (35) thinks she is the Elizabeth Gordon named on a tomb in St Mary's Kirk, Old Cullen, meaning she survived until 1606, and was buried alongside her Ogilvie husband.

20. Potter, 2002: 61.

21. Potter, 2002: 60.

22. CSP, Randolph to Cecil, 24th September 1561: "The Earl of Huntly and Lord James greatly discord..."

23. Marshall, 2017.

24. Robert, 140.

25. Lord Ogilvie of Airlie's first name was James. So both Lord James Ogilvie of Cardell, who had been disinherited, and Lord James Ogilvie of Airlie, his friend, cousin and supporter, were out fighting together on the streets of Edinburgh. Many reports say that 'Lord Ogilvie' or 'James Ogilvie' was wounded, and understandably this causes confusion: a lot of sources say that James Ogilvie of Cardell received the injury to his arm, when in fact it seems to have been his cousin, James Ogilvie of Airlie. This is confirmed by checking Peerages – and by the severity of the injury: Airlie perhaps even lost his arm, but Cardell is seen later accompanying Mary, Queen of Scots, with no mention of any injury. See Sharpe, 502.

26. Knox, 275.

27. Potter, 2002: 61; Forbes-Leith,1889: 84; Marwick, 28th June 1562; Knox, 275.

28. If he bleeds again it will kill him. Marwick, 28th June 1562.

29. Forbes-Leith, 1889: 84.

30. Aboyne, 468. His title came from the new lands he owned: Sir John Ogilvie of Deskford.

31. CSP, Randolph to Cecil, 24th October 1561: "[Agnes Keith] is lately come to this town. They look shortly to see what will become of the long love between Lord James and her." Lord James' intended bride had been Christine Stewart of Buchan. Christine was three years old when Lord James was 19. If he had married Christine he would have been Earl of Buchan (Bennet et al, 33).

32. Marshall, 2006: 127. From now on, Lord James Stewart will be known by his title, Moray.

33. Gatherer, 19–21. It's a practical diary, noting where they stopped and ate, rather than a journal discussing his feelings.

34. Aboyne, 462 (my translation: "Her gr/ journey is cumbersome paynful and mervilous longe, the weather extreame fowle and colde, all victuall mervilous dere, and the corne that never lyke to come to ripeness.") There was a mini ice age in Europe at that time, so the weather was particularly bad: recent research suggests that the climate was altered by the colonisation of the Americas. Disease brought by European settlers killed so many native Americans that it radically changed land use: cultivated land was abandoned to forest and vegetation, which pulled down so much carbon dioxide from the atmosphere that the temperature across the world dropped (Amos, BBC).

35. Probably Jean was there: Marshall, 2006: 127; Sanderson, 36.

36. Potter, 2002: 62; Aboyne, 462; Forbes-Leith, 85.

37. Potter, 2002: 63; Aboyne, 463; Huntly, 30.
38. The roof at Darnaway Castle is the oldest surviving example of ham-merbeam construction in Britain. The hall is popularly said to be able to hold 1,000 armed men – based on a remark made by Randolph at the time of Mary, Queen of Scots' visit. Dendrochronological analysis has shown that the oak trees used to make the roof were felled in 1387 – and that some of the trees were at least 418 years old. (Smout, 71, 80). This means the trees were saplings at the time of the Vikings.
39. Potter, 2002: 65; Aboyne, 463.
40. One historian argues that the refusal to allow Mary entry was "merely a mistake in administration rather than an act of rebellion" (Potter, 2002: 64).
41. Mackay book, 130; Aboyne, 463; Forbes-Leith, 1889: 86; Potter, 2002: 65.
42. Mackay book, 130.
43. Wardlaw, 148. This was Hugh Fraser (Uisdean Ruadh, or Red Hugh), the 5th Lord Lovat (for historical context, the Old Fox is the 11th Lord Lovat). Hugh Fraser 5th Lord Lovat later married Jean's niece (her sister Elizabeth's daughter).
44. Some historians mistakenly say that the commander of the castle, Captain Alexander Gordon, was Jean's brother of the same name but he was too young to be there. The captain was Alexander Gordon of Bothrom (Robert, 140).
45. Mackay book, 130 quotes John Knox as saying some of them escaped. CSP, Elizabeth, Randolph to Cecil, 18th September 1562.
46. Fraser, 1994: 240.
47. Wardlaw, 149. Actually, some of the Frasers joined the Huntly-Gordon side.
48. Lewis and Pringle, 4.
49. Taylor, 12–13
50. Taylor, 12–13.
51. Potter, 2002: 67; Aboyne, 463–4; CSP, Elizabeth, Randolph to Cecil, 23rd September 1562.
52. Tears were more socially acceptable from men in the sixteenth century: John Knox, for example, was noted as a weeper.
53. CSP, Elizabeth, Randolph to Cecil, 23rd September 1562.
54. Kirkcaldy of Grange is important to the story later (Aboyne, 465; Sanderson, 36).
55. Aboyne, 466; Fraser, 1994: 242.
56. Aboyne, 466; Fraser, 1994: 242.

57. Forbes-Leith, 1889: 86. Some of the besieging soldiers were killed (Forbes, 28).
58. Being 'put to the horn' literally meant that a horn was sounded before a public announcement was made: people put to the horn were not supposed to be helped by anyone, even family, and could be captured on sight and brought to a local magistrate for execution.
59. Aboyne, 466.
60. CSP, 846, The Queen to Queen Mary, 15th October 1562.
61. The 'boy' was the younger brother of Sir Thomas Kerr of Fernihurst, Huntly's chief counsellor. So Mary, Queen of Scots was being slightly disingenuous to call him a 'stable lad' (Forbes, 28).
62. Potter, 2002: 67.
63. Herries, 66.
64. Potter, 2002: 69–71.
65. Potter, 2002: 70.
66. Diurnal, 74 ("he bristit and swelt, sua that he spak not one word, bot deceissit"); CSP, Randolph 28th October.

CHAPTER THREE: The Downfall of the House of Huntly: 1562–1564

1. The chief witch was named as 'Janet' or 'Jonet'. Knox, 1880: 279.
2. Knox, 280.
3. Knox, 280.
4. Knox, 280.
5. CSP, Randolph to Cecil, 2nd November 1562.
6. CSP, Randolph to Cecil, 2nd November 1562.
7. Apparently after an appeal by one of the Queen's Four Maries, Mary Fleming (Forbes, 91).
8. Robert, 142. Robert, Jean's son, is obviously a very pro-Gordon source, and, writing with the benefit of hindsight and the intervening decades, he said that Moray had prevented Mary, Queen of Scots from speaking to the Countess even though Mary, Queen of Scots had been very anxious to have a conversation. Robert relied on written sources when writing his history, but he also asked his family for memories of events, so, although he is certainly biased, many of his accounts of the Gordon family's doings are vivid and immediate.
9. Robert Gordon names one of the other executed men as George Gordon of Coclarachie (Robert, 142).
10. Herries, 66.

11. Diurnal, 74; Potter, 2002: 71; Fraser, 1994: 245. Historian Potter states that John was beheaded by the Maiden, a precursor of the guillotine, but this doesn't seem to match with the records in the National Museum of Scotland, where the Maiden is preserved. The NMS says that the Maiden was first constructed in Edinburgh two years after John's death, in 1564.

12. CSP, Elizabeth, Randolph to Cecil, 12th December 1562. Flu as a new disease: see Fraser, 1994: 247.

13. Darnley's bed and Bothwell's doublet. Fraser, 1994:245.

14. Grimble, 1993: 33.

15. Sutherland book, 120. Helenor Stewart, his second wife and mother of Alexander, his heir.

16. After his father's death, George would have inherited his title 'Huntly' – but I will continue to refer to him as George to avoid confusion, his given name showing his closeness to his sister Jean.

17. Yellowlees, 37.

18. They were forfeited of their lands and titles after Corrichie, which leads some to say that they were at the battle, e.g. Huntly, 34, who says James, Patrick, Robert and Thomas (but not the elder William) were all there – but for the most part, the younger brothers are not mentioned.

19. Marshall, 2017.

20. ODNB.

21. Aboyne, 470; Diurnal, 75.

22. Robert, 143; ODNB.

23. Knox, 281.

24. CSP, Randolph to Cecil, 16th December 1562.

25. See, for example, Marwick, S. on the history of Huntly House/the Museum of Edinburgh.

26. Marshall, 2006: 128.

27. Knox, 287. "The lady Huntly craftily protested, and asked the support of a man of law."

28. CSP, Randolph to Cecil, 3rd June 1563.

29. Knox, 288.

30. Forbes, 133.

31. Potter, 2002: 73.

32. 'The coffin was sette upright, as if the Earle stoode upon his feet, and upon it a pece of good black cloth with his armes fast pynned…' 'His accusation beinge read his proctor answeringe for him, as if himself

had been alive, the inquest was impanellede. The verdict was given that he was found guilty and judgement given thereupon as by the law is accustomed. Immediatelie hereupon the good cloth that hung over the coffin was taken away, and in its place a worse hanged on, the armes torn in pieces in sight of the people, and likewise stroken oute of the herald's booke.' Aboyne, 468. Some spelling standardised for ease of reading.

33. Mackay book, 132.
34. Potter, 2002: 74.
35. CSP, Randolph to Cecil, 13th June 1563.
36. Knox, 288. By which he means the large number of women.
37. Knox, 288–9.
38. CSP, Elizabeth to Thomas Randolph, 5th June 1563; CSP, Randolph to Cecil, 13th June 1563.
39. Knox, 284.
40. Potter (2002: 74) argues that Huntly's eldest son was traumatised by the experience of the trial, and by the threats to his own life – which seems like a fair assessment.
41. ODNB.
42. Forbes-Leith, 1889: 58–65; ODNB. Forbes (157) states that James left with de Gouda, before Corrichie, but Yellowlees (33) thinks James made his own way to the continent a little later, after the defeat.
43. Yellowlees (39) says that Thomas' name appears briefly in the Jesuit records and then disappears. We have records of Thomas later in the north-east so he must have decided that the life of a Jesuit was not for him for whatever reason, although he seems to have remained Catholic.

CHAPTER FOUR: The Royal Court: 1565–1566

1. Although most commentators state that Jean and her mother became instantly integrated into Mary's circle, it was more likely to have been a gradual process, starting slowly when they first arrived in Edinburgh after Corrichie and the trial in 1562/3.
2. Marshall, 2006: 128.
3. Carpets were so expensive that most people hung them on the walls: only royalty could walk on them. Grant, 98.
4. Grant, 98.
5. Dalyell, 9.

6. Gore-Brown, 220.
7. Balfour Paul, 56; Taylor, 13.
8. *The Biographical Dictionary of Scottish Women*; Duncan, 366.
9. Hamilton, 34.
10. Charles, Archduke of Austria.
11. A polite way to describe Mad Arran. The book was written by a Hamilton descendant.
12. The Prince of Condé.
13. Erik, King of Sweden.
14. Weir, 58.
15. This was Darnley's first meeting with Mary as adults in Scotland, but they had actually met before, in France.
16. Mary, Queen of Scots was already aware of Darnley as a potential suitor, having been introduced to representatives from his family as far back as 1561, through the Earl of Sutherland, who was married to Darnley's father's sister (Ring, 161).
17. Darnley's mother was a niece of Henry VIII; his grandmother was Margaret Tudor, widow of Scotland's King James IV; and Darnley was Mary, Queen of Scots' half-cousin.
18. "He was of a comely stature, and none was like unto him within this island. He died under the age of one and twenty years; prompt and ready for all games and sports, much given to hawking and hunting, and running of horses, and likewise to playing on the lute, and also to Venus' chamber. He was liberal enough: he could write and dictate well; but he was somewhat given to wine, and much feeding, and likewise to inconstancy; and proud beyond measure, and therefore contemned all others. He had learned to dissemble well enough, being from his youth misled up in popery." Knox, 352.
19. Ring thought it may have been contracted on his trip north to meet Mary, which doesn't improve readings of Darnley's character (193); Weir thought it may have been contracted on an earlier trip to France (191) – both agree that it was probably contracted on an occasion when he was out from under the watchful eye of his ambitious parents.
20. Lord Robert Stewart.
21. Weir, 60.
22. Weir, 65.
23. Forbes-Leith, 98. Of course, since this is a Catholic document it is obviously biased against Moray, but it doesn't seem unlikely that, as

Moray saw the potential for his influence waning, he made a final, desperate plea to have some sort of official recognition.

24. ODNB.
25. Diurnal, 80.
26. Diurnal, 80.
27. Aboyne, 471.
28. Diurnal, 80.
29. CSP, Randolph to Cecil, 4th October 1565.
30. CSP, Randolph to Cecil, 8th October 1565.
31. Diurnal, 81.
32. CSP, Randolph to Cecil, 4th September 1565; Gore-Brown, 215.
33. See CSP, Randolph to Cecil, 1st September 1565: "Does not see how they [Moray's forces] are able to withstand her [Mary's] force, for neither are there so many as she has, nor yet have they any arquebusiers."
34. Weir, 80.
35. Weir, 81.
36. ODNB.
37. The Earl of Sutherland's second wife, Helenor Stewart, who died around this time, was Darnley's aunt.
38. CSP, Randolph to Cecil, 19th/20th September 1565.
39. CSP, Randolph to Cecil, 4th October 1565. Jesuits, who also had no reason to love Protestant Bothwell, were more generous in their assessment, calling him "a courageous man" (Yellowlees, 55).
40. Gore-Brown, 1937: 162.
41. ODNB.
42. Wormald, 155.
43. Marshall 2013: 278, 301.
44. Marshall, 2013; Dawson. The Geneva Bible that Knox used had annotations – James VI's dislike of the annotations that were critical of royalty led in part to his commissioning of a new translation of the Bible, the King James Version (Dawson, 270).
45. CSP, Randolph to Leicester, 18th October 1565.
46. Bothwell returned to Scotland in September 1565; his marriage was in February 1566.
47. Unfortunately, like another Stuart many years later, Mary, Queen of Scots only realised the power of the Highlands and outlying areas when her power was on the decline.
48. CSP, Randolph to Cecil, 24th October 1561.
49. CSPS, 290.

50. A contemporary nickname or byname, used here to aid the reader in distinguishing between different 'Johns'.
51. See Marshall, 2017: 80.
52. Simpson, 1973: 17–18.
53. Gore-Brown, 1937: 225.
54. Gore-Brown, 1937: 225.
55. Sanderson, 38; Stuart, 94–100.
56. Stuart, 95.
57. Jean's mother's own marriage contract had made special note of the necessity of obtaining dispensations from Rome before marriage (Parker, 20).
58. ODNB.
59. A holograph is a manuscript handwritten by the person named as its author – a document written wholly in the handwriting of the person whose signature it bears. See Guise correspondence, e.g. pxxii.
60. Aboyne, 469; Spalding Misc, 150–2. The latter contains the text of the marriage contract.
61. Knox, 279.
62. Which is another argument against Elizabeth needing her hand held because she was ill: why would Jean make a point of distinguishing her signature in this way, if Elizabeth only needed help to sign because she was weak?
63. Thomas, 99.
64. Gore-Brown, 224.
65. Not in Canongate Kirk, as some sources say, as the Kirk was not yet built – it replaced the Abbey of Holyrood later.
66. ODNB.
67. Gore-Brown, 224; quote from Diurnal, 88.
68. Gore-Brown, 224.
69. Lindsay, 186.
70. The story of Jean in mourning appears in several secondary sources. In the (disputed) sonnets written by Bothwell's mistress (see next chapter), there is particular reference to Jean's poor choice of dress after her marriage: "In her dress, she showed without a doubt..." (Bell, 47).
71. Gore-Brown, 252. Gore-Brown makes the compelling argument that some of the notorious Casket Letters, used at Mary, Queen of Scots' trial, were forged out of letters sent to Bothwell by both Anna and Jean, meaning these letters give intimate details about Bothwell's relationships with both these women.

CHAPTER FIVE: Jean and Bothwell: 1566

1. Weir (102) states that Bothwell came back to Edinburgh alone after a week because the honeymoon was such a disaster. Most other people simply don't mention where Jean was.

2. Note in Boduel about Darnley's murder states that Bothwell shared a bedroom with Jean at Holyrood.

3. Fraser, 1994: 286.

4. The four families were the Bruces, the Comyns, the Stewarts and the Douglases. See Thomson, 2003.

5. Ruthven account.

6. Gore-Brown, 232; Ruthven account.

7. Knox, 285.

8. Ruthven account.

9. Andrew Kerr of Fawdonside, who held his pistol to Mary, Queen of Scots' pregnant belly, later married John Knox's daughter Margaret.

10. Ruthven account.

11. Much of this description comes from Gore-Brown, 233–6 and Fraser, 1994: 303, as well as Aboyne, 473. Quote from Mary's letter in Labanoff, 346.

12. Nau, 5. In Nau's account of the Rizzio murder, written some time after the event but with information given to him by Mary, he includes the detail about Lady Huntly's whereabouts. Fraser goes along with this and says that Lady Huntly took the initiative in thinking of plans and bringing them to Bothwell, but Gore-Brown seems to be under the impression that Bothwell was able to speak to Lady Huntly and give her ideas on how Mary might escape. Nau's account is a little vague, but it seems that Lady Huntly was in the palace, spoke to Mary, left to go somewhere (possibly still within the palace), then returned the following day having managed to get word to George and Bothwell somehow.

13. Nau, 10.

14. Gore-Brown, 241.

15. Gore-Brown, 242; Nau, 23. The Ruthven family waited out their exile until Protestantism was in favour again in Scotland, then Ruthven's son returned to Scotland, where he was given the position of Lord Treasurer of Scotland for life (Miller, 39).

16. ODNB.

17. Likewise, the earlier gift of marriage to Mar was also ignored. Alex Ogilvie's intended Forbes bride, Elizabeth, married Henry, Lord

Sinclair, instead (Balfour Paul, 56; Taylor, 13). See DSL for 'double avail' – the amount of money Alex Ogilvie may have had to pay could have been considerable.

18. Taylor, 13.

19. Forbes, 157.

20. It was a mirror of Mary Fleming and Lethington's courtship, with a similar age difference.

21. Macdonald; CSP, Randolph to Cecil, 1st April 1563. This is Randolph's own description of the woman he loved, prior to her marriage. The quote is often given as "hardest and wisest", but the original seems to read "hardieste and wyseste" (Taylor, 15) and I believe 'hardiest' is a better translation: to be hardy – brave or valiant – was a compliment. 'Hardiest' would fit in with the context of the original quote in the CSP, and is an adjective more often used at the time than 'hardest' to describe a woman.

22. Mary Beaton was called 'The Duenna' by Mary, Queen of Scots, as the oldest of the Four Maries (Taylor, insert). Beaton was the eldest daughter of Robert Beaton of Creich and Jeanne Gresoner. She had three siblings (Taylor, insert).

23. Robertson, Scotland Magazine. There are no portraits that can definitively be said to be of Mary Beaton, so we do not know exactly what she looked like. One portrait which is often labelled as being her shows a woman in full court dress, with an elaborately stitched dress with lace at the sleeves and neck, topped off with a hat and expensive jewellery. Blonde curls frame a slightly plump, soft face – she looks nothing like the more angular Jean. (National Portrait Gallery of Scotland accessed via Art UK (artuk.org)). However, the fashions shown in this portrait are not consistent with Mary Beaton's dates, and the portrait is on canvas, not wood, which also suggests a later date. There are also questions over whether Mary Beaton would have had access to a portraitist. (ref: Rosalind Marshall, private emails to Jennifer Morag Henderson). There is another portrait from an English collection which is sometimes described as being Mary Beaton, but it is clearly a different woman to the portrait in the NPG in Scotland, and again there are questions over dates, provenance etc. A portrait described in the past as being held in Cullen House shows a woman with dark-brown hair (Taylor, insert).

24. Mary, Queen of Scots once wrote a will – not used – that left French, English and Italian books to Beaton (Duncan, 370).

25. The similarity in their handwriting is noted during discussions over whether or not the Casket Letters were forged (Corporaal, 151–63).

26. £100 a year. 'Livres' is French for pounds. 'Livre tournais' was an accounting term; originally referring to 'Tours pound' it became used to refer to a standard amount. Lang, 349.

27. Marshall, 2017:54 – Bothwell's father was supposed to be less attractive than Mary of Guise's other suitor, Lennox (Darnley's father).

28. Tabraham (Crichton).

29. Gore-Brown, 144. John Stewart, along with Mary's other half-brother Robert, had accompanied her to France in her childhood (Marshall, 2017: 69).

30. I have primarily followed the conjecture of Gore-Brown, 412–17. While most historians have focused on whether or not the letters were written by Mary, Queen of Scots, Gore-Brown's compelling biography of Bothwell approaches the letters from the standpoint of trying to see how they fit Bothwell's life, affording him different perspective and insights. Fraser (1994: 469) agrees with the analysis that: "It becomes apparent that some letter... written by Mary herself, has been loosely and not particularly skilfully run together with a love letter written to Bothwell by some other woman..." Weir agrees that the Casket Letters are partial forgeries, but did not agree with Gore-Brown's analysis that some were written by Anna, as she did not believe that Anna could write good enough French or was in Scotland at the correct times (2004: 472). Anna met Bothwell in France, so her French *was* probably good enough (particularly at a time when language learning was commonplace). Her visits to Scotland were handled with such discretion by Bothwell that it is hard to prove when she was here: the belief in Norway that she was strongly linked with Scotland suggests that she did make several visits to which she ascribed great importance.

31. Agnes Sinclair mentions Bothwell's son William in her will. This is all we know about him.

32. Fraser (1994: 477) agrees that these sonnets are definitely not written by Mary, quoting the refutation of contemporary poets who knew Mary's writing. Weir is more cautious, believing they could have been representative of Mary's early, immature style and quoting others in support of this, but eventually concluding that they were probably at least tampered with, if not wholly written by someone else (362). Guy (2004: 399) says that, "Very few literary experts believe them to be genuine. They are extremely clumsy and would pass only with the greatest difficulty as the work of a native French speaker" – something worth bearing in mind in conjunction with Weir's analysis of Anna's French abilities (see note 30). Another theory is that some of the poems

were written by Mary Beaton, whose handwriting was so similar to that of Mary, Queen of Scots that it is conjectured that her work was used to help forge the Casket Letters – but, as with most things about the Casket Letters, others disagree. See Duncan, 370; Corporaal.

33. Gore-Brown, 413. See also Bell, 54–5 – Bell presents the sonnets as being written by Mary, Queen of Scots.
34. Bell, 35.
35. Bell, 34–5. Even Bell, identifying the author of the sonnet as Mary, Queen of Scots, identifies 'the dolt' as Alex Ogilvie. 'dolt' is Bell's translation. Fâcheux is used contemporarily as an adjective, meaning 'annoying'.
36. Bell, 39.
37. Bell, 45.
38. Bell, 46–7.
39. Gore-Brown numbers this as letter 3, Fraser and Weir as letter IV.
40. Gore-Brown, 415.
41. Gore-Brown, 414.
42. Weir, 2004: 147.
43. Gore-Brown, 224.
44. Bell, 47.
45. Gore-Brown, 254.

CHAPTER SIX: The Death of Darnley: 1566–1567

1. Mary made a will before James VI was born: George, his wife and Jean's mother were all beneficiaries (Forbes, 57).
2. Melville, 158.
3. Lynch, 1–2.
4. Sanderson, 40. Jean is not mentioned as attending, but her non-attendance would surely have drawn comment, so she was most likely there.
5. Thomas, 194.
6. Lynch, 2.
7. See portrait in Thomas, 195.
8. Gore-Brown, 257.
9. Gore-Brown, 270; Graham, 230.
10. Gore-Brown, 271.
11. Graham, 231.
12. Thomson, 194; Amos; Historic Scotland. It was once thought that Prince James' baptism was the first time fireworks had been seen in

Scotland, but recent research has discovered that fireworks were used as early as 1507. Fireworks were used again in celebrations to mark James V's first marriage, and also at the coronation of his second wife Mary of Guise. Mary, Queen of Scots also incorporated fireworks into the celebrations for her marriage to Darnley. They were hugely expensive, and still very uncommon.

13. Lynch, 6.
14. Or he may not. Syphilis sufferers can live for many years with the disease, and it is unclear from the historical evidence how advanced Darnley's disease was, if it actually was syphilis. See Weir, 191.
15. Weir, 252.
16. Gore-Brown, 315; Fraser, 1994: 365.
17. "This was the first gunpowder conspiracy against a European prince" (Weir, 265). Elizabeth of England immediately ordered all the doors to her apartments to be locked and the keys removed, leaving only one heavily guarded entrance (Graham, 244).
18. Gore-Brown, 302.
19. Weir, 250.
20. Dunn, 354. Darnley was of course related to Elizabeth.
21. Les Affaires du Comte de Boduel, 13: "Tesmoinguage du lieu ou j'estois quand le Roy fut trahy... [in bed with] ma premiere Princesse, seur du Comte Huntly." [Testimony of where I was when the King was killed... in bed with my first Countess [wife], the sister of the Earl of Huntly [i.e. Jean]].
22. Guy, 309. Mary, Queen of Scots had ordered him to investigate from the start.
23. Weir, 242.
24. Bennett et al, 35.
25. There are many, many descriptions of the night of Darnley's murder and conjectures about how exactly events proceeded. It is possible to read Mary, Queen of Scots' letters describing the event, Bothwell's own description in his autobiography, to see the contemporary drawings made of the crime scene and to read other contemporary descriptions, as well as the later 'confessions'. Secondary sources I have used include Dunn, Fraser (1994), Gore-Brown, Graham, Guy and Weir.
26. CSP, Sir William Drury to Cecil, 29th March 1567.
27. Fraser, 1994: 368.
28. Gore-Brown, 328.
29. Aboyne, 474.

30. CSP, Sir William Drury to Cecil, 28th February 1567.
31. CSP, Sir William Drury to Cecil, 28th February 1567.
32. In *The Records of Aboyne*, a Gordon-sympathetic piece of writing published in the nineteenth century collating history from earlier times.
33. Confession of French Paris, 9th August 1569: "Bothwell came where I was, and rounded unto me, saying Paris, I find me not well of my sickness, the bloody fluxes..." Paris' 'confession' is highly suspect, however, extracted, as it was, through cruel torture.
34. Gore-Brown, 225.
35. Fraser, 1994: 374.
36. Gore-Brown, 333.
37. Gore-Brown, 336; CSP, Sir William Drury to Cecil, 15th April 1567.
38. Dunn, 350.
39. Dunn, 359.
40. Lord John Hamilton, second son of Chatelherault, the brother of George's wife, and John, Master of Forbes, George's sister Margaret's husband (Weir, 338).
41. Gore-Brown, 334; Taylor, 17.
42. Weir, 344; Fraser, 1994: 375. Guy (326) agrees that there is some confusion over some signatories: specifically highlighting the fact that Cecil was misinformed and Cecil's mistakes are sometimes repeated: for example, Cecil believed Maitland of Lethington signed, but actually Lethington had declined to attend the dinner. "Lord Ogilvy" is listed as a signatory in Weir.
43. Guy, 316.

CHAPTER SEVEN: Divorce: 1567

1. CSP, Sir William Drury to Cecil, 29th March 1567.
2. CSP, April 1567 (ref 1091).
3. CSP, 24th April 1567 (ref 1127).
4. CSP, 25th April 1567 (ref 1128).
5. CSP, Sir William Drury to Cecil, 30th April 1567. This is after Bothwell abducted Mary, Queen of Scots, and the particular objection seems to be to Janet Beaton.
6. Weir (353) says they all had their swords drawn. They probably at least all had swords.
7. Fraser, 1994: 376.
8. Gore-Brown, 361; Weir, 364.
9. Gore-Brown, 348.

10. Not everyone agrees: Guy (329) thinks Mary was too strong-willed and conscious of her position as queen to have married Bothwell if he had raped her, and argues that they had separate suites of rooms and that Mary could have barricaded her door.

11. In a letter to the Bishop of Dunblane, a Catholic, who went on to be involved in Bothwell and Jean's divorce. Quoted in Fraser, 1994: 379.

12. Gore-Brown, 348. There is some confusion over whether the argument was between Lethington and George, or Lethington and Bothwell, see Weir, 362.

13. Gore-Brown, 345; CSP, Sir William Drury to Cecil, 30th April 1567; CSP, Sir William Drury to Cecil, 6th May 1567.

14. Gore-Brown, 347.

15. Guy, 330.

16. Gore-Brown, 357; Marshall, 1983.

17. Marshall, 2006: 132. Williams, 188, states that Jean filed for divorce before Mary, Queen of Scots was abducted, on 21st March. This contradicts every other source (e.g. Stuart, 16; Guy, 330) and appears to be an error.

18. Marshall, 1983.

19. Marshall, 2006: 133.

20. Marshall, 2006: 133.

21. It is impossible to know whether Mary was aware of the dispensation, but Stuart (1874: 32) considers that she did, given how involved she was in arranging Bothwell and Jean's marriage.

22. The same advocate, Edmund Hay, represented Bothwell at both his trial for the murder of Darnley and in his subsequent divorce: the cases made his name. Edmund Hay was the brother of John Hay, who became a Jesuit and part of the Scottish mission in 1578–79 (Yellowlees, 69).

23. CSP, Sir William Drury to Cecil, 13th May 1567: "The Lady Bothwell remaining at Crighton is much misliked of the Queen."

24. Marshall, 2006: 134.

25. Gore-Brown, 361.

26. CSP, Sir William Drury to Cecil, 13th May 1567.

27. Weir, 374.

28. Gore-Brown, 366. Rape was still one of the four most serious crimes in the eyes of the law, but consent after the fact stopped capital punishment – though not all punishment (Mackenzie's Criminals).

29. Gore-Brown, 369; Weir, 375.

30. Diurnal, 112: "At this marriage thair wes nathir plesour nor pastyme vsit as vse wes wont to be vsit quhen princes wes marijt."

31. Forbes, 139.
32. Forbes, 136. Jean's brother Adam now took the title 'Adam of Auchindoun'.
33. Hardly the actions of someone crazed for power. BBC MQS documents article; Capital Collections online (50642).
34. Fraser, 1994: 390.
35. Guy, 338.
36. CSP, Act of the Secret Council of Scotland, ref 1287, 12th June; CSP Foreign, Proclamation against the Earl of Bothwell, 30th June.
37. Dunn, 339; Guy, 340.
38. Fraser, 1994: 393; Guy, 342; Weir, 388; Potter, 2002: 87.
39. CSP, ref 1300, 15th June.
40. "The Queen's apparel in the field was after the fashion of the women of Edinburgh, in a red petticoat, sleeves tied with points a 'partlyte', a velvet hat and muffler", CSP, Sir William Drury to Cecil, 18th June 1567; Guy, 343.
41. Dunn, 371.
42. Guy, 345.
43. Guy, 346. The rebel lords put forward several suggestions: Gore-Brown says one proposal was one James Murray of Purdovis; Guy also mentions Sir William Murray of Tullibardine; see also Graham, 260.
44. Guy, 345.
45. There are differing accounts of what happened on the battlefield. I have primarily followed Gore-Brown's account, which is very sympathetic to Bothwell but which also draws on the lords' account of the day. Guy has a slightly different version, which does not mention Kirkcaldy of Grange advancing.
46. Mary did have the comfort of two of her Four Maries: Mary Livingstone and Mary Seton were both with her – even though Mary Livingstone's father was on the opposite side at Carberry Hill (Marshall 2006: 146).
47. Gore-Brown, 391–2.
48. For example, Moray was ostentatiously not there when both Rizzio and Darnley were murdered.
49. CSP, Sir Nicholas Throckmorton to the Queen, 25th July 1567: "The Countess of Murray is with the Queen at Lochleven."
50. "The Earl of Murray was received into Edinburgh with great joy of all the people", CSP, Sir Nicholas Throckmorton to the Queen, 12th August.
51. Sanderson, 41; Gore-Brown, 398.

52. Sanderson, 41; Stuart, 47.
53. CSP, Sir Nicholas Throckmorton to the Queen, 22nd August.

CHAPTER EIGHT: North: 1567–1572

1. Forbes-Leith, 121–2.
2. Aboyne, 475.
3. CSP, Sir Nicholas Throckmorton to the Queen, 16th July 1567.
4. CSP, Sir Nicholas Throckmorton to Cecil, 12th July 1567.
5. CSP, Answer of the Lords of Scotland to Throckmorton, 21st July 1567: "this quarrel, which was only intended against Bothwell's person..."
6. CSP, Sir Nicholas Throckmorton to Cecil, 18th July 1567.
7. CSP, Instructions for Sir Nicholas Throckmorton sent to the Queen of Scots, 30th June 1567.
8. See for example CSP, Bedford to Cecil, 19th and 20th July 1567: "The Borders have grown rather to further disorders..." "The troubles and disorders upon the Borders grow and increase..."
9. CSP, Sir William Drury to Cecil, 18th June 1567.
10. CSP, Sir William Drury to Cecil, 1st July 1567.
11. CSP, Sir Nicholas Throckmorton to the Queen, 31st July 1567. The whole Rokesby incident is very convoluted. Behind it all there probably lies a plot by Cecil which had gone wrong. After acting suspiciously in Edinburgh, Rokesby had been arrested and imprisoned on Bothwell's orders. Rokesby was first held in the Bishop's Edinburgh residence before being moved up north. Meanwhile, the Bishop's sons' full motivation is also unclear.
12. CSP, Sir Nicholas Throckmorton to the Queen, 31st July 1567; Gore-Brown, 401.
13. Bothwell seems to have sent at least one ship first to the south, to collect more provisions by calling into Eyemouth near Dunbar. This ship may not have made it back. Gore-Brown, 399.
14. Gore-Brown, 399; Lewis and Pringle, 9.
15. See next chapter.
16. Brill, 1996. Merchants from Bremen were not uncommon in Scotland, and Gerdt Hemelingk had been given trading rights in the Sumburgh area. He was a Hanseatic merchant: the Hanseatic League was a commercial and defensive confederation of merchant guilds and market towns – basically a whole group of city states in what are now modern northern Germany and Poland which worked together. Hemelingk spent a considerable amount of time in Shetland.

17. Gore-Brown, 404; CSP, Sir Nicholas Throckmorton to the Queen, 9th August 1567; CSP, Kirkcaldy of Grange to the Earl of Bedford, 10th August 1567. The abbreviated version of the CSP available online does not have the full quote; this comes from Gore-Brown.
18. Gore-Brown, 405.
19. Brill, 1996.
20. Christian Aalborg.
21. "On being asked for his passport he answered 'disdainfully, and enquired from whom he should get passport or letter, being himself the supreme ruler in the country'" – Beveridge, 1904.
22. Brill, 1996; Gore-Brown, 408.
23. Gore-Brown, 406.
24. If Gore-Brown's analysis of the Casket Letters is correct, then Anna was in Scotland during Bothwell's marriage to Jean and afterwards. Gore-Brown places Anna in Scotland until summer 1567.
25. Beveridge, 1904: 384.
26. Beveridge, 1904: 385.
27. Potter, 2002: 88.
28. Aboyne, 477.
29. ODNB.
30. Potter, 2002: 90.
31. Potter, 2002: 90. The Earl of Argyll was a good friend to Mary, Queen of Scots, and married to her half-sister.
32. Potter, 2002: 91.
33. Duncan, 370; Malden, 25; Marshall 2006: 146.
34. Herries, 102, 104, 105.
35. Taylor, 18.
36. Forbes, 113. The date of Lady Huntly's death is difficult to ascertain. Forbes cites an unpublished source.
37. Potter, 2002: 91.
38. Aboyne, 478.
39. Potter, 2002: 92.
40. Aboyne, 485.
41. Aboyne, 479.
42. Aboyne, 483–5.
43. ODNB.
44. ODNB.
45. Ring, 225.
46. Potter, 2002: 94.
47. ODNB.

48. Because of the change in calendars, the assassination date is often written as January 1569/70. January can either be counted as 1570 if the year is considered to start on the 1st of that month, or 1569 if the calendar is counted as starting in March.

49. Ring, 299. The guns of the time were, in comparison to today, cumbersome. See Miller, 26.

50. Diurnal, 156.

51. Marshall, 2013; Dawson, 283. Although Moray was buried at St Giles Cathedral in Edinburgh, there is another strange memento of the Good Regent: at Darnaway Castle, the seat of the Earls of Moray, there is a section of his skull. This was cut from his embalmed body after his death, and is now displayed in a sealed glass case just outside the main Hall, not far from Moray's portrait.

52. Bennett et al, 35.

53. Williams, 270.

54. Stuart, 24.

55. Potter, 2002: 97.

56. Potter, 2002: 97.

57. Potter, 2002: 98.

58. Or possibly stabbed in the back (ODNB; Gore-Brown, 448).

59. Robert, 165.

60. Potter, 2002: 99.

61. Diurnal, 255; Robert, 165 – see also Chapter 9.

62. Lewis and Pringle, 5.

63. Margaret was supposedly involved with one of the Bishop's sons called Patrick, parson of Kinnoir. It's not clear if this was one of the sons involved in the spy Rokesby incident (see note 11) or not, especially since the Bishop had more than one illegitimate son called Patrick (after himself) (Balfour Paul, 59). 'Parson of Kinnoir' was a term that was 'merely titular' and gave the holder access to land rent (Forbes, 118).

64. Potter, 2002: 100; Balfour Paul, 59–60.

65. Aboyne, 489.

66. Potter, 2002: 100; Aboyne, 489, Diurnal, 255.

67. "Adam Gordone, who playis king Herot in the north, vpoun the kingis freindis and guid subjectis; bot in speciall vpoun the Forbesses..." Bannatyne, 197.

68. Scottish Catholics, 164.

69. Aboyne, 490.

70. Aboyne, 490; Diurnal, 305: quote given is from Aboyne, in Diurnal it reads: "My freinds and brethren, haue in remembrance how God hes

grantit to me victorie and our hand in yow, grantand me the same vand and sching to puneiss yow, quhairwith my vmquhile [late] father and brother wer puniest at the Bank of Fair; and since syne, of the great slaughter maid on the quenis grace trew subjectis, and maist filthilie of the hanging of my fuddartis heir be the rele of Lennow; and since syne, be the hanging of ten men in Leith, with vther wnlawfull actis done contrair the lawis of armes; and douts nocht gif I wer vnder their dominioun, as ye ar vnder myne, that I sould die the deith maist crewallie. Yit notwith-standing, my good brethren and cuntriemen, be nocht affrayit, nor feir nocht, for at this present ye sall incure na danger of your bodies, bot salbe treatit as brethrine; and sall doe to yow efter the commandment of God, in doing yow good for evill, forgetting the crewaltie done to the queen and hir faithfull subjectis, and ressavand yow as hir faithfull fubiectis in tymecuming..."

71. Diurnal, 305. "Efter the quhilk the regent past haistile out of Striueling to Dundie, chargeand all maner of men to follow him with xx dayes victuallis, on the said Adam Gordoun. Bot their wald neuer ane man in thaj pairtis obey the charge, be ressoun of the band maid of befoir, and of the great gentilnes of the said Adame."

72. Miller, 46.

CHAPTER NINE: Further North and Further Back: 1567–1573

1. ODNB.

2. Elizabeth, 10th Countess of Sutherland (1470–1535) married Adam Gordon of Aboyne, younger son of the 2nd Earl of Huntly. Elizabeth then deposed her brother, who was supposedly mad, and she and Adam ruled Sutherland. They were succeeded by their grandson John, as their son Alexander predeceased them. The numbering of the Earls of Sutherland is sometimes confusing: some people count Elizabeth as the 10th Countess, meaning her grandson was the 11th Earl; others choose to count her grandson as the 10th Earl, not giving Elizabeth a number at all. I have followed the current members of the family in choosing to number Elizabeth as the 10th, her grandson as the 11th, and so on.

3. Sutherland book, 129.

4. ODNB. In 1563 he was ordered into custody in Edinburgh for murder-ing the servants of the Earl Marischal, that is, servants of the Keith family – the Keiths, of course, being Jean's mother's family, and the family of Agnes Keith, wife of the Earl of Moray.

5. Robert, 145; Calder, 118. There is some dispute over when exactly Caithness was granted this role; Robert Gordon argues that it was a reward from Bothwell for participating in Darnley's murder, but this is probably Gordon propaganda against Caithness – it was a position the Earls of Caithness had held before, as Calder explains.

6. ODNB. Caithness switched back to the Queen's party before Langside, and remained for the Queen's party while she was in exile, but in this brief moment he was with the confederate lords, against Bothwell.

7. Isobel Sinclair was the wife of Gilbert Gordon of Garty, the Earl of Sutherland's uncle (Gilbert was brother to the Master of Sutherland). She was also related to William Sinclair, Laird of Dunbeath – a contemporary account (Robert Gordon) says that she was Dunbeath's sister; a later account by Calder seems to make a mistake in saying that she was his daughter. William Sinclair was also the Earl's uncle, as he had married Beatrix Gordon his aunt: i.e. brother and sister William and Isobel had married brother and sister Gilbert and Beatrix. Isobel was also the cousin of the Earl of Caithness. There are several slightly conflicting variations of Isobel's place in the family tree, but this is the most accurate picture I can draw.

8. Isobel's claim for her son to be next in line to the Sutherland title (which would probably not have been undisputed) comes through her husband's descent from the Huntly and Sutherland Gordons and her brother's marriage into the Gordon line, but her high status in the Caithness family also contributed.

9. Who was also called John Gordon.

10. Calder, Chapter 7; Sutherland book, 128; Robert, 147. When reading Robert Gordon's account of the Isobel Sinclair poisoning, biases against the Sinclairs and in favour of the Gordons must always be kept in mind – as must the fact that he was writing some years later, but, in favour of his accuracy must be the fact that Robert is Alexander's son: when Robert writes that the Earl of Sutherland dragged the tablecloth off the table and ordered Alexander to Dunrobin for his own safety, he is writing about his father and grandfather, repeating stories that have been told to him directly.

11. Calder, Chapter 7.

12. While the Earl of Sutherland was in exile, his estates had been managed by his father's brothers and sisters and their spouses, i.e. by his aunts and uncles. Isobel and William Sinclair were his aunt (married to his uncle Gilbert) and uncle (married to his aunt Beatrix). Sutherland book, 128; Robert, 148.

13. Calder, Chapter 7. Recently there has been renewed focus on this story, including a claim, repeated in BBC articles and originating from Timespan museum, that this poisoning was the inspiration for Shakespeare's *Hamlet*. The idea that Isobel Sinclair was the direct inspiration for Shakespeare's *Hamlet* is dubious. *Hamlet* was written between approximately 1599 and 1602 – but since the story of the 1567 events in Helmsdale do not seem to have penetrated even to the south of Scotland it seems very unlikely that they were being retold as far south as London. There is a possibility that Shakespeare may have visited Scotland around 1601 – there are records of a troupe of actors including men Shakespeare knew being brought to Edinburgh and Aberdeen by James VI (see Hannan; Anderson, 242–3) – but the evidence is pretty slim, and the story of Isobel Sinclair and the poisoning was not necessarily even being told in Aberdeen at that time. Isobel's story certainly does not appear in any of the historical sources that Shakespeare was known to have used. My own research has found no contemporary account of the trial until that of Robert Gordon (written about 1630, and privately circulated only among the Gordon family). There were numerous other places that Shakespeare could have found inspiration: scholars have attributed the inspiration for *Hamlet* to either a previous Elizabethan play on the same theme, or even traced it back, via medieval Latin texts, to a pre-thirteenth-century Icelandic saga. One other case local to the north of Scotland with some parallels is the trial for witchcraft of Katharine Lady Fowlis, who was accused of attempting to use a drink laced with rat poison to kill a relative in order to advance the cause of her own close family. The story of Lady Fowlis – who was distantly related to the Earls of Sutherland – is far more widely known, included in Pitcairn's Criminals for example, and later disseminated by Walter Scott. If nothing else, it shows that Shakespeare's story in *Hamlet* was not a uniquely imaginative plot: feuds between family members are all too common, and poison was a method available in the sixteenth century.
14. Alexander was legally not the Earl of Sutherland until he reached his majority: see Murray, 237.
15. Robert, 150.
16. Robert, 150.
17. Robert, 150; ODNB.
18. Sutherland book, 131: Alexander was born in Darnaway Castle and fostered by the Dunbars of Grangehill in Moray, who were linked to the Sutherlands by marriage.

19. Robert, 150.
20. Mackay book, 138; Robert, 150.
21. Girnigoe Castle was extended by the addition of Sinclair Castle around 1600 (Sutherland "Sinclair..."). Skibo Castle too, where Alexander had been staying, was described a couple of years before as 'very ruinous' (Sutherland book, 131), see also Grimble, 36. See also National Record of the Historic Environment, Castle Sinclair Girnigoe record. The suffix 'goe' is another word for a natural inlet (from the Old Norse 'gjá').
22. Kirk in Inverness Field Club, 31. Elizabeth Graham's father was a Catholic who did not convert to Protestantism and consistently acted alongside other Catholic noblemen during the reign of Mary, Queen of Scots. See Potter 2002: 59, 68, 90.
23. ODNB.
24. Not much is definitively known of Francis' early life, but in later life he sought refuge among his Caithness relatives, so must have been familiar with them. As the nephew of Bothwell and heir to Bothwell's title, the Scottish court may not have been the most welcoming place for him after Carberry Hill, so it would make sense if Janet had kept him with her and they had both retreated to the Far North.
25. See his son's assessment of Alexander's character (Robert, 233) – discussed in more detail in Chapter 10.
26. Robert, 154: Alexander's son described him later as having been "perpetually attended by the Earle of Catteynes his servants, and his libertie then much restrained".
27. ODNB.
28. Murray, 238.
29. "by which meanes the Earle of Catteynes maid himself strong and potent in freindship and alliance within this dyocie", Robert, 151.
30. Calder, Chapter 7.
31. Grant (Golspitour). Some also went further north, to Orkney (Mackay book, 140).
32. See for example Sutherland book, 132; Robert, 151.
33. Grimble, 36.
34. Mackay book, 138.
35. Grant (Golspitour); Bulloch, 1907.
36. Robert, 153.
37. Robert, 154.
38. Alexander Gordon of Sidderay.
39. Robert, 154; Calder, Chapter 7.

40. Robert, 154; Sutherland book, 134. The ferry routes were essential to the Highlands: see Worthington, History Scotland.
41. Mackay book, 139.
42. Robert, 156.
43. Mackay book, 140; Simpson, 1989.
44. Mackay book, 139–40; Robert, 157.
45. Mackay book, 140; Calder, Chapter 7.
46. Mackay book, 141.
47. Mackay book, 141; Grimble, 37: Legally, Mackay had to be loyal to the Earl of Sutherland. But now, Mackay's loyalty to Huntly could not be automatically transferred to Alexander, without Mackay's own consent, even when Alexander came of age.
48. Calder, Chapter 7.
49. Calder, Chapter 7.
50. Mackay book, 142; Calder, Chapter 7.
51. Robert, 166.
52. Robert, 167.
53. Potter, 2001: 101.
54. My interpretation, but see Marshall, 2013: 211.
55. Potter, 2003: 111–12.
56. Grant, 115. The Earl of Argyll and his wife divorced after the castle siege ended: the divorce made Scottish legal history by being the first in Scotland to be granted on grounds of separation, and required an Act of Parliament as well as a decision in both the civil and church courts. The couple had not got on for years, and Mary, Queen of Scots had even at one point worked with the unlikely partner of John Knox (since the Earl was a Protestant) to try and reconcile the couple (Dawson [Futurelearn]).
57. Potter, 2003: 139. Potter's book focuses mainly on the military decisions around the siege and does not look at what must have been the fascinating personal relationships among the besieged. It was quite difficult to find out, since he doesn't dwell on it, which women were actually in the castle.
58. Potter, 2006 (2); Potter, 2003: 98.
59. Potter, 2006 (2).
60. Wormald, 190.
61. There was particular bad blood between Kirkcaldy of Grange and Morton because Morton had treated Kirkcaldy's sister, Helen, badly – see Aboyne, 491.
62. Duncan, 367.

63. Miller, 46.
64. Aboyne, 492.

CHAPTER TEN: The House of Gordon: 1573–1575

1. Quote from Aboyne, 469; Balfour Paul, 539; Bannatyne, 232.
2. Bannatyne, 232: "The ffryday preceiding, which was the 25 day, Mr Robert Gordon, Huntlies brother, was slaine be a man of his owin, rackleslie, as he was clengene his dag." A dag was a short gun or pistol. Double 'f' in old handwriting is a capital 'F'; quoted as printed.
3. Bannatyne, 232: "Sua can the Lord, when he pleasis, cause the wicked ilk ane to destroy vther; whairof this may be a begyning of their farther destructione!"
4. Forbes, 121.
5. The second thing was to make arrangements for the divorce from Jean's sister Margaret on the grounds of her adultery with Patrick Hepburn, parson of Kinnoir (Forbes, 87, 119).
6. Aboyne, 494; Diurnal, 327: "grit slauchter of baith sydis".
7. Robert, 170.
8. Forbes, 88.
9. Forbes, 92.
10. Robert, 170: "Adam Gordoun… travelled into France, pairtlie for his recreation [!], and pairtlie to eschew exhorbitant authoritie of his enemies, the Earle of Mortoun (then regent), who mortallie hated him and all the Gordouns. Adam was verie kyndlie and honorablie interteyned at Paris, by King Charles the Nynth of France." Charles was of course Mary, Queen of Scots' former brother-in-law, son of Catherine de Medici and brother to the late Francis.
11. Lang, 348. Of course, this money might not have reached the north-east.
12. See Malden, e.g., 30 for links between the Beatons and Huntly.
13. Banffshire Reporter.
14. MacGibbon and Ross.
15. Taylor, insert.
16. See also Canmore (Boyne Castle) and Scottish Castles Association.
17. Boyne Castle was inhabited until the early eighteenth century – there were still people living there in 1723 (Coventry, 2006). It was still owned by a branch of the Ogilvie family until 1731, when it was purchased by the Earl of Findlater. However, by the end of the 1700s it was noted as dilapidated. Not too much is known of the history of the building and why it fell into ruin, but the 1700s were the period of Jacobite unrest,

and a time when many Scottish families lost power and felt the full effects of the shift of power to the south of England.

18. Douglas Peerage, 262. There is another possible, and very interesting, idea mentioned in the Douglas Peerage: it states that James Ogilvie of Cardell (the one who had argued with Jean's brother John) married, as his second wife, one of the Four Maries, Mary Livingstone (Douglas Peerage, 262). Mary Livingstone had been the first of the Four Maries to marry, but was widowed. If this was true, it would have meant that two of the Four Maries were now living close together in the north-east. However, it does not fit in with the date of Mary Livingstone's first husband's death (1579). The Douglas Peerage then goes on to say that Mary Livingstone gave birth to Ogilvie's heir. However, Balfour Paul's *The Scots Peerage* (p25), which supersedes Douglas, states that "Marioun" Livingstone married James Ogilvie of Cardell. 'Marion' is sometimes written in place of 'Mary', however, repetition of similar (or the same) names in families was not uncommon, so 'Mary' and 'Marioun' could also have been sisters, i.e. the younger sister of one of the Four Maries married into the Ogilvie family. At least Mary Beaton would have had familiar faces around her.

19. Many secondary sources say that there was a ten-year age difference, and that Jean was 28 to Alexander's 18. According to the Sutherland book (131) Alexander was born at midsummer in 1552, which would make a seven-year age gap, with Jean 28 and Alexander 21. Alexander being 21 would make sense, as that would mean he had legally come of age. Neither of their birth dates are known exactly, but it seems likely that their age difference was rounded up to a decade to emphasise the gap – or that people forgot 21 was the legal age of majority rather than 18, and this was then repeated without context.

20. Sir Colin Campbell, brother to the 5th Earl of Argyll, Archibald, who had no children. Agnes had probably known Colin for years, as he was a friend of her first husband Moray.

21. Robert, 232–33: "Earle Alexander wes... verie liberall... he wes verie vpright in all his actions, vnfitt for these our dayes, wherein integreitie lyeth speechless, and vpright dealling is readie to give up the ghost."

22. There are some historians, notably Ian Grimble, who argue that the idea that Barbara was Aodh's mistress is a Gordon fiction created after the fact to help Alexander obtain an easy divorce, saying that Aodh

was in the last months of his life, and that his adultery with Barbara was a "falsehood" only believable if the Gordons had "possessed astonishing knowledge of the secrets of Girnigoe Castle" (Grimble, 38). However, I would argue that the Gordons did have that knowledge: the Gordon chronicler who made the assertions was Alexander's son, and Alexander had the most intimate knowledge of Barbara's home life.

23. Sutherland book, 137.
24. See Grimble – but he argues for a ten-year age gap, when in fact it was seven years (see note 19).
25. Sutherland book, vol 2, 342. Robert learnt from the example of his parents, and had a happy marriage himself, and this was the sum of his advice to his nephew. In the preceding pages of his letter of advice he discusses respect for one's parents; his advice on marriage would seem likely to be drawn from his own upbringing.
26. Sutherland book, 136.
27. Sutherland book, 507. Janet had previously been married to Alexander, laird of Innes, but he died in 1576, and Janet remarried to Thomas after that.
28. Robert, 168.
29. Bennett et al, 36.
30. Blakeway in Reid and Kerr-Paterson, 14.
31. ODNB.
32. Donnachie in Inverness Field Club, 52.
33. Robert, 1–8. Matthew (168) notes: "Rural prosperity is equated with beauty [in the description of Sutherland by Jean's son] and the countryside is seen beneath the light of a northern summer."
34. Robert, 5. They would hunt sandeels, on horseback. Robert has a very vivid description of the men and horses swimming out to sandbanks exposed by spring or summer low tides, where the men would then leap on their horses and gallop to be the first to arrive at the fishing place, where they could take enough fish to see them through Lent, and for a large part of the year.
35. Robert, 10. Strictly speaking in Mackay country, not Earl of Sutherland territory. There was a gold rush in the north of Scotland in the 1860s. See also Clarke.
36. Fraser, 2009: 47.
37. Licence, 205.
38. Licence, 166.
39. Watson, 20.

40. Old Lady Huntly had probably died around the time of the battle of Langside, as previously mentioned, although the date of her death is not wholly clear.

41. Worthington, 2016. There is plenty of evidence to show that people travelled by boat. See also Fraser-Mackintosh, 88, a 1669 letter also demonstrating that people travelling south from Sutherland and Caithness crossed the Moray Firth rather than going by Inverness.

42. Arguably Jean Gordon created, rather than strengthened, the connection between Sutherland and the Huntly territory. The link between the two coasts is geographic, with tides being a strong link, and the theories of coastal history emphasise this, but the human link is primarily maintained by the Gordon family, and specifically by Jean Gordon's marriage.

43. In her study of women's lives in the early modern period, Antonia Fraser (2009) uses concrete examples such as letters to show how men and women of this period thought about their children: for example, the birth of a healthy baby was greeted with delight whether they were a boy or girl; stillborn children were no less mourned even if infant mortality rates were higher.

44. Fraser, 2009: 93; Ewan and Meikle, Chapter 18.

45. Weir, 138: Sir Henry Killigrew reported that he was sent a message by the queen saying that: "I was welcome and should have audience as soon as she might have any ease of the pain in her breasts" but that Mary was "in a good state for a woman in her case". See also Fraser, 321 and Guy, 267. Lady Reres was the wet-nurse.

46. Jean's son Robert describes this in his family memoir – it seems to have been an arrangement of long-standing and the Gordons of Embo are frequently mentioned in Robert's account, so I am assuming that all of Jean's children were sent to the same family. It is possible that someone else nursed Jane, but it would have caused great comment if Jean had done it herself.

47. Mackay book, 144–5.

48. Robert, 170: "pacified the countrey of Southerland, and the clannes therof, with such admirable and happie dexteritie, that ther wes not one drop of blood shed; which he so wyslie performed, and with so great forsight, that he procured the love of all his cuntrey-men, eaven of such as had been formerlie most eager against him."

49. Sanderson, 43.

50. Mackay book, 145.

51. Stuart, 53.

52. Sanderson, 44.
53. Taylor, inserts.
54. Taylor, 18–19. The later marriage certificate of Alex Ogilvie and Jean Gordon in 1599 (NLS Dep 175/63/1) also reveals some of these financial difficulties: Sir George Ogilvie of Dunlugas had taken over Boyne Castle and some of Alex Ogilvie's lands because of Alex's debt. Boyne Castle became associated with Sir George to the point where some guide books list it as being built by him (Coventry, 2006).
55. Robert, 164 – Robert Gordon argued that Aodh died "pairtlie through greiff" after John's capture "and pairtlie through the torment and truble of conscience which he had conceaved for his bypast actions". Given Robert's dislike of Aodh and his actions the latter statement should probably be taken with a pinch of salt.
56. Uisdean's name is sometimes represented as 'Hugh' (see Mackay book) or 'Houcheon' (Robert) – like his father 'Aodh' the Gaelic pronunciation and spelling was difficult for Scots speakers. I have tried to choose the version of Gaelic names that are closest to the original Gaelic.
57. Grimble, 40–1. Caithness also abducted Uisdean's younger brother William, bringing him to Girnigoe as well (Robert, 179).
58. Sutherland (469) says Janet divorced John on grounds of "adulterous connection with several women". There were limited grounds for divorce; divorcing because your father-in-law kept your husband chained in the basement while you had to be polite to him over the dinner table upstairs was not common.
59. Calder, Chapter 7.
60. The exact time is not clear. Robert (164) says seven years, but one source (Sutherland, 470) says other contemporary documents show it was shorter: two and a half years.
61. Calder, Chapter 7. Another version of the story says that John was given instead only brandy, and he drank so much he became mad and then died.
62. Calder, Chapter 7.
63. Robert, 173.
64. Mackay book, 144.
65. Mackay book, 144.
66. Mackay book, 145. The author of the Mackay book thinks the idea that the killing of Little John was authorised by the Earl of Caithness is a Gordon slur, portraying it instead as an accident in the heat of battle which Caithness then took advantage of.
67. Grimble, 41.

Interlude: The Living Tomb, Mummification and Transcendental Peace

1. Miller, 37.
2. Gore-Brown, 448.
3. Gore-Brown, 456.
4. Gore-Brown, 459.
5. Other people have been attracted to Bothwell by their common name: actress Audrey Hepburn's father changed his surname to Hepburn-Ruston, saying that he was descended from James Hepburn, Earl of Bothwell (Crawford-Smith) – there was more to the story as well, but actually he wasn't related to Bothwell in any direct way.
6. Including a letter from Scottish novelist George Macdonald Fraser, best known for his Flashman series but also the author of books on Borders history: he did not think that Bothwell's body should be repatriated, but supported the idea of commemorating Bothwell in Scotland.

Part Two: The Gordon Years

CHAPTER ELEVEN: Death and Land: 1576–1581

1. Aboyne, 496.
2. Kirk in Inverness Field Club, 31.
3. Robert, 170; Balfour Paul, 56.
4. Robert, 170–1. Enfants de la Mat: I haven't found any other reference to this group, or a definitive translation. I would suggest 'Children of the Night' – mat as in 'matt black' – although this is more commonly used as an adjective. Alternatively it could mean 'mast' – perhaps a group of ex-sailors? – or 'mat' translating as 'mate', as in 'checkmate' – game, set and match to the gang.
5. Gold chains were a fashion statement that signified wealth – and could be used as instant cash or credit if needed (Wode, 13).
6. Robert, 170–1 (my updating of spelling and language in quotes). Note that Robert is clearly anti-Forbes and the note tucked into the hat is very convenient.
7. NLS Dep 313/487. I was amazed when I first went to see Jean's letters some years ago that they were stuffed into a cardboard A4 folder with other miscellaneous items, and that I was allowed to handle them relatively freely, without even wearing gloves. Of course, most researchers now rely on the transcriptions of Jean's letters, which were published in the Sutherland book many years ago.

8. Sutherland book, 131. Uncle Alexander died in Elgin.

9. See also Sutherland book, 142 for another example, as Alexander pursued feu-lands originally granted to his father.

10. Other letters from the same time period show the same thing: e.g. the Breadalbane letters, which show Katherine Ruthven, wife of Colin Campbell the 6th laird of Glenorchy, dealing with business and working as a team with her husband. She was particularly friendly with Maitland of Lethington. Likewise, later letters from Jean's son Robert show him writing to Duncan Forbes, 1st of Culloden – and, when Duncan is out of town, to Duncan's wife Christian, who Robert knows will pass on the relevant information (e.g. NLS Dep 175/65/79 and 81).

11. My translation. Original reads: "doutis nocht bot your ladischip will seill and subscrywe the said precept of clare constat wyth plessour and gude will, and siklyke will causs my lord, your husband, do the sammyn…"

12. Sutherland book, vol 2, 112. Jean's name occasionally appears under different spellings as Jean, Jeane, Jehanne or Jane. I first encountered her as 'Jean', and think this would be closest to how her name was pronounced in a Scots accent.

13. Sutherland book, 141.

14. Aboyne, 497.

15. Bannatyne 333-334.

16. Shaw in Inverness Field Club, 10.

17. Bannatyne 333-334.

18. Bannatyne 333-334.

19. Bannatyne 333-334.

20. Bannatyne, 333-334.

21. Robert, 171.

22. Robert Douglas, Earl of Buchan and the Cranstons of Mureton were engaged in "various transactions" to do with the new Earl of Huntly's lands. Aboyne, 499.

23. George's son had the same name as his father and grandfather, George Gordon Earl of Huntly. To distinguish him from Huntly and George, I have called him 'Lord Huntly'.

24. Potter, 2002: 124.

25. Aboyne, 499: "some contentious words between George Gordon of Gight and Alexander Forbes, younger of Towie, in the presence of the king". The two men killed each other shortly after (Forbes, 102).

26. Robert, 172. This was in 1577.

27. Forbes, 147.

28. Sutherland book, 143.
29. Robert, as discussed in the Sutherland book, 143.
30. Sutherland book, 143.
31. This version of events is not wholly unchallenged: as the Earldom of Sutherland gained its own power and autonomy through the years, the idea that they were a subsidiary of the House of Huntly was robustly refuted.
32. Grimble, 43.
33. Elizabeth Sinclair.
34. John Robson.
35. Robert, 173.
36. The name Creagh-drumi-doun only appears in Robert Gordon's history of the Earldom of Sutherland. It doesn't correspond to any placename, and seems to be a Scots description of the battle. A 'creagh' or 'creach' was a Highland foray or plundering raid, or the booty gathered on such a raid – the word seems to be originally Gaelic, but is found in Scots as well. 'Drumi' is probably 'drums', and 'doun' is 'down' (probably with a connotation of 'going down-hill'). Altogether perhaps we're being given an image of the noise of a fierce raid as drums were beaten and men charged downhill.
37. See previous chapter for more on Little John's death. Also Mackay book, 146.
38. For an interesting discussion on James VI's precise relationship with his male favourites, see Young, 2016.
39. Esmé's aunt was Alexander's mother.
40. Robert, 175.
41. Robert, 172.
42. Robert, 173.
43. We only have that much because one of Jean's sons later wrote a family history, consulting Jean as he wrote. This suggests Jean thought it important to record these lost sons' names and talk about them to some extent with her remaining family.
44. See, for example, Fraser, 2009: 87–9.
45. Forbes, 103, 147.
46. Robert, 175.
47. Forbes, 121.
48. Sanderson, 43.
49. Including Culmaily, a property near Golspie, granted to Alexander's father by the Earl of Caithness. Sanderson, 43.
50. Robert, 104.

51. Bulloch, 1907: 8–9. John Gordon of Drummoy's sister was Elizabeth of Findlater, the discarded wife or mistress of Jean's dashing and doomed elder brother John.
52. Alexander of Sidderay.
53. Robert, 104.
54. Forbes-Leith, 166–7. Letter from Fr. Robert Persons to Fr. Aquaviva, General of the Society of Jesus, 26th September 1581.
55. Reid and Kerr-Paterson, 4.
56. Blakeway in Reid and Kerr-Paterson, 12–14.
57. Robert, 175–6. No one ever calls Darnley King Henry – even Mary, Queen of Scots only did for a few weeks.
58. Robert, 175. The title of Earl of Lennox, held by Darnley's father (who was Esmé's father's brother) had passed to Darnley's brother, who had died in 1577 and had not had any sons, and then had gone to Esmé; the creation of the title 'Duke of Lennox' came from James VI.

CHAPTER TWELVE: Neighbours: Two Companies of Pretty Men: 1582–1585

1. The ODNB says he died at the beginning of September 1582; Robert (177) says he died at the end of August 1583. The Mackay book also says that he died in 1583 (147) but based on the actions that are described as happening either side of his death, the ODNB seems to have the correct date.
2. ODNB.
3. Mackay book, 147; Robert, 177. Robert goes on to describe Caithness as being "the instrument of civill dissention and shedding of much blood; the vnnaturall destroyer and scourge of his owne children; a memorable example to posteritie, that God doth often punish the children of this world by themselves and ther owne practices". He also said he was "a worldlie-wyse man, politique, craftie, and provident".
4. Calder, Chapter 8. Not everyone agrees that old Caithness was quite so bad, e.g. Sutherland, 468, but they do have to rather tie themselves in knots to argue that there are "extenuating points". Most people agree that "The Earls were able, but... unscrupulous and tyrannical" (Fraser-Mackintosh, 5).
5. Robert, 178: "So that all these riches are quyt vanished away, and were never imployed to any good or profitable use". Robert thought riches should only be used to maintain family estates.

---

6. Robert, 180.
7. Calder, Chapter 8.
8. Calder, Chapter 8 and Robert Gordon (180) give slightly different versions of the story. Calder says that David was killed first, before the wedding. Robert adds that one of Wicked Earl George's motivations for the killings was that Ingram and David supported the Earl of Sutherland. This doesn't seem very likely (as Calder points out), and is probably added after the fact: Robert is busy at this time pointing out all the reasons why George is so Wicked and Terrible.
9. Sutherland book, 137.
10. ODNB.
11. Sutherland book, 146. Mohammed Al-Fayed owns this land now.
12. A merk was two-thirds of a pound or 13 shillings and fourpence. A Scots pound was worth less than an English pound; something like one-twelfth (Futurelearn).
13. Sutherland book, 147.
14. Sutherland book, 138.
15. Shaw in Inverness Field Club, 15.
16. Sutherland book, 145.
17. Sutherland book, 146.
18. Grant in Reid and Kerr-Paterson, 58; Young, 2016.
19. Potter, 2002: 126.
20. Yellowlees, 58.
21. Yellowlees, 97, 142.
22. Yellowlees, 142.
23. The 'Parson of Clatt' (Forbes, 169).
24. Potter, 2002: 126.
25. Forbes-Leith, 197–8; ODNB.
26. Forbes-Leith, 201–2.
27. Sutherland book, 129.
28. Yellowlees, 115.
29. Mackay book, 147–9.
30. Potter, 2002: 132.
31. Mackay book, 149.
32. Grimble, 44. Pro-clan historian Ian Grimble argues that, from as early as 1582, the Gunns' fate was sealed.
33. "they wer judged to be the principall authors of these troubles and commotions which wer liklie to ensue in that dyacie [diocese]", Robert, 181–2.

34. Robert, 92.
35. Robert, 182. The modern Clan Gunn makes something of a virtue of this sense of difference, emphasising their Viking roots. Most of their history though is either traced back to Robert, whose account is very biased, or to the sagas, which are not accurate historical documents. Alternatively there is also a persistent idea that the Gunns could be descended from the original Picts who lived in Caithness (who were superseded by the Gaelic clans). Writers Neil Gunn and, in more modern times, George Gunn, both of whom have an interest because of their own names, promote this idea (Gunn, 125).
36. Mackay book, 150; Robert, 182.
37. Wardlaw, 202.
38. Robert, 184.
39. Robert, 184.
40. Robert, 185.
41. Mackay book, 151.
42. Mackay book, 152.
43. Wardlaw, 204.
44. Robert, 185. Caithness didn't gain much by releasing the prisoner either, as apparently he immediately swore loyalty to the Earl of Sutherland.
45. Edmund Hay and John Durie (Yellowlees, 108).
46. ODNB; Forbes-Leith, 207–10.

CHAPTER THIRTEEN: Creachlarn: The Great Spoil and the Three Weddings: 1585–1590

1. Stuart, 54.
2. Sutherland book, vol 2, 363.
3. Potter 2002: 142.
4. James Stewart was the son of a minor baron, but related to Agnes Keith's second husband Colin Campbell, Earl of Argyll.
5. Potter, 2002: 117–22, 129; Bennett et al, 35.
6. Potter, 2002: 135.
7. Potter, 2002: 136.
8. Wormald, 197; Watson, 54.
9. Robert, 192.
10. Robert, 192.

11. Marle was the name of his village. Since there are so many George Gordons, I've chosen to use that as his name here to avoid confusion. George Gordon of Marle was the bastard son of Gilbert Gordon of Garty, whose wife Isobel Sinclair had poisoned Alexander's parents. Sutherland book, 149; Mackay book, 158.
12. Mackay book, 158.
13. I have heard stories of horses' tails being cut off in other clan disputes in the north of Scotland – it seems to have been a standard way to make the enemy lose face.
14. Robert, 193.
15. Robert, 194–5.
16. Robert, 195.
17. Sutherland book, 150.
18. Sutherland book, 151.
19. Robert, 197; Grimble, 44. Robert Gordon's chronology at this point is a little confusing, understandably since so many people are swapping sides.
20. Robert, 196.
21. Robert, 197.
22. Sutherland book, 151.
23. Gunn, 138. Gunn argues that Wick was made a Royal Burgh in the same year of 1589 because James VI realised that the Sutherlands had gone too far. James VI continually tried to balance the power of his noblemen, never letting one get too much stronger than any other. However, the Sutherlands had won a decisive victory this time.
24. Sutherland book, 154.
25. Robert, 198–9.
26. Forbes-Leith, 203.
27. Forbes-Leith, 203.
28. Yellowlees, 115.
29. Forbes-Leith, 204.
30. The fellow Jesuit was Crichton. Yellowlees, 105.
31. The Master of Forbes had remarried to Janet, daughter of James Seton of Touch (Aboyne, 469). ODNB; Balfour Paul, 58–60; Forbes 123–5.
32. Aboyne, 506.
33. Aboyne, 506.
34. A large Spanish boat with 300 men on board crashed into Fair Isle. Since the population of Fair Isle at that time was only 115, even the captain's offer to pay for food could not help them much. The bad weather meant it was seven weeks before help could be sent for, and

during that time 50 Spaniards died. Eventually the survivors were shipped to Shetland, and then down to Anstruther in Fife.

35. Angus Calder, 2003: 16, 139.
36. Aboyne, 507.
37. Aboyne, 507.
38. Potter, 2002: 128. The young woman was the daughter of Sir Thomas Kerr of Fernihurst, but she doesn't come into this story at all.
39. See Young, 2016, for discussion of the nature of James VI's relationships with his favourites. Modern understandings of relationships between men are not always applicable to the sixteenth century, when there were different societal mores. See also Zuvich, xi and Chapter 21.
40. Grant in Reid and Kerr-Paterson, 69.
41. Aboyne, 506; Potter, 2002: 138.
42. Robert, 208.
43. See Grant in Reid and Kerr-Paterson, 59.
44. Potter, 2002: 139.
45. Aboyne, 507.
46. Aboyne, 508.
47. Forbes, 178.
48. James IV got as far as Tain. After James VI, it was a long time before any other member of the royal family went north: Charles II landed at Garmouth at the mouth of the river Spey in 1650, but the royal family were comprehensively England- and London-based after James VI. It is not until much more modern times, with Queen Victoria, that royalty returns to the Highlands. Ironically, Jean's home of Dunrobin Castle, as the home of the wealthy Earls of Sutherland, became a place for noblemen and women to visit and relax on holiday. Much, much later, the Queen Mother took over the Castle of Mey, which was one of the minor homes of the Earls of Caithness; Mey was the title given to the old Earl of Caithness' second son – the branch that got the money, while Wicked Earl George got the title of Earl.
49. Robert, 200.
50. Robert, 200.
51. This was a much more significant age difference than between Jean and Alexander. I have read a number of historians' comments on the age difference between Jean and Alexander: few on the difference between Jane and Uisdean. One key difference is that in Jean and Alexander's marriage, the woman was older. At the time, an age difference in marriage would not have caused comment.
52. Sutherland book, 158–9.

53. Mackay book, 157.
54. Grimble, 44.
55. There was Castle Varrich, known as a traditional Mackay stronghold, but that was probably held by the Abrach Mackays, a different branch of the family to Uisdean (Cheape).
56. Jean did not use the word 'race' as we do, but there are many indications that she and her family saw the clans as different to themselves, including the recent battles Alexander had fought with the Clan Gunn. This feeling of 'difference' between the clans and earls was one that intensified over the course of Jean's life, as we will see. However, there was a tendency to see every family or House as a separate unit, whether it was the House of Caithness or the Clan Mackay – intermarriages between any would be carefully considered. Jean's son Robert specifically uses the word 'race' to describe the Clan Gunn, as well as to describe other clans (Robert, 277, 327, 357). He associates it with the words 'tribe' and 'clan' and gives it a negative connotation. He also describes the House of Caithness as a 'race' (435, 441).
57. Sutherland book, vol 2, 344.
58. Sutherland book, 161–5.
59. Robert, 200.

CHAPTER FOURTEEN: Jean's Two Nephews: 1589/90–1594

Part 1: A Grandson and a Nephew

1. See Marshall 2016: 136.
2. In the Dunrobin records, this portrait is recorded as being 'Alexander 12th Earl of Sutherland, from the circle of George Jameson' (email from Castle Managing Director Scott Morrison to Jennifer Morag Henderson, 31st August 2016), which is problematic. Jameson was Scotland's first eminent portrait painter, born in Aberdeen and trained on the continent (possibly under Rubens). However, the date of Jameson's birth is given as 1589 (Nat Gall online): this would mean Jameson was too young to have painted a portrait from life of Alexander, as it would have to have been completed before 1594 – so either the labelling is wrong because it is not by Jameson, or because it is not Alexander. This is a very accomplished painting, which must have been completed by an expert: it is very lifelike, the fashion details are consistent with it being Alexander, and the man bears a strong resemblance to paintings of Alexander's children, so I would argue that it is unlikely to have been completed after Alexander's death. My

conclusion is that the Dunrobin labelling is wrong in one respect: it is definitely Alexander, but it is not by Jameson. There is the possibility it could have been done by Jameson from an earlier sketch, but artist and expert Kathryn Emily Henderson suggests instead that the painting has certain details that could suggest it was done by a Dutch or Flemish artist. Either Arnold von Bronckorst or Adrian Vanson, court painters in Scotland, could be possibilities (see e.g. Goldring, 178). The Dunrobin labelling of their paintings is incomplete, and finding out more about the painting would require both detailed examination of the painting itself by experts, as well as a search within the Dunrobin archives (which are not fully indexed) for any accompanying paperwork.

3. Robert, 201.
4. Robert, 201.
5. Robert, 202.
6. Robert, 203.
7. Robert, 202.
8. Robert, 202–3; Sutherland book, 155. Robert said there were "weill neir 1500" archers, but this might have been an exaggeration.
9. Sutherland book, 155.
10. Robert, 374. Robert also mentions that Wicked Earl George's brother was fostered with the Clan Gunn and chose to be loyal to the Gunns over his brother.
11. Robert, 104.
12. See Bulloch, 1907, for the fiendishly complicated family tree of this cadet branch of the Gordons, who were linked by blood not only to Jean, and also Alexander, but even to George Gordon of Marle (the man who had cut off the horses' tails), Jean's brother John's discarded wife or mistress Elizabeth of Findlater, the Earl of Huntly, Isobel Sinclair (the poisoner of Alexander's parents) and several other branches of the family. They are a good illustration of how Scottish families of the time inter-married, and how widely spaced large families cause confusion amongst the generations when devising family trees.
13. Grimble, 47.
14. See Sutherland book, 164–6 for some of the legal cases Alexander was simultaneously pursuing at this time.
15. Watson, 65.
16. McLaughlin in Reid and Kerr-Paterson, 138. Although they were both perhaps unlikely guardians in some ways, they were also both Stewarts, so of royal blood.

17. ODNB. His wife was Margaret Douglas, a relative of his mother Janet's third husband – Janet remarried shortly after Francis' wedding. Margaret Douglas was a widow and a little older than Francis. She seems to have been very forbearing, considering what Francis was to put her through. They had eight children, four sons and four daughters, in the 11 years between 1584 and 1595. Margaret seems to have mainly taken control of their home life, rather than being involved on the national stage, as she is rarely mentioned.
18. Tabraham (Crichton), 9.
19. Tabraham (Crichton), 10.
20. Tabraham, (Crichton), 20.
21. Hercules is associated with Hailes Castle; beyond that there isn't much information about him.
22. ODNB.
23. Watson, 67.
24. Of course, Jean's husband Alexander also had Stewart blood.
25. See Fraser, 1977: 47. There is plenty of literature discussing exactly when James VI became interested in witches, and to what extent.
26. Watson, 134.
27. Fraser, 1977: 47. The witch's name was Agnes Sampson.
28. ODNB.
29. Watson, 78, 186. Ross of Balnagowan being the family who Jean and Alexander had tried to unite their youngest daughter Mary in marriage with, who had switched sides to being friends with Caithness. In 1592 the Privy Council reprimanded them for aiding Francis again, which they had apparently also done in the past as well. The Rosses of Balnagowan later continued Francis' interest in witchcraft, in the person of Lady Foulis, Catherine Ross of Balnagowan, who was notoriously brought to trial in 1590 (Watson, 87).
30. Francis became a family name for the Sinclair Earls of Caithness (D1189/1/1).
31. Watson, 75–6.

Part 2: Another Nephew and Glenlivet
32. Potter, 2002: 178–9. Forbes (185) says the Bonnie Earl's face was slashed by John Gordon of Buchie, and the fatal blow that killed him came from Lord Huntly. The story I tell here of the face-slashing, and many of the details of the portrait, were told to me in Darnaway Castle by the Bonnie Earl's descendants as we stood in front of the Bonnie Earl's death portrait.

33. Margaret.
34. Potter, 2002: 179.
35. See Potter, 2002, especially Chapters 13 and 14, for an extremely comprehensive account of the feud between Huntly and Moray, including the involvement of other families such as the Forbes (once again enemies of Huntly, who later carried the Bonnie Earl's bloody shirt as a banner into battle) and Cawdors (supporters of Moray, conveniently killed at around the same time) in the north. John Maitland, the Lord Chancellor, and brother of William Maitland of Lethington, was also heavily involved – he had supported his brother, and been in Edinburgh Castle during the siege there, but had eventually come back into favour with James VI. Like William Maitland, John Maitland had also married a Fleming girl: Mary Fleming's niece Jean.
36. There is more than one version of the ballad, and some of them draw on other similar works, but they are generally agreed to be contemporary with the event. Some of the lyrics are not historically accurate – Moray would never have been king, and certainly didn't have an affair with the queen – but, like the Edom o' Gordon ballad, the song had a huge impact on how Moray and Huntly were remembered by history. Propaganda at its finest.
37. Grant in Reid and Kerr-Paterson, 68.
38. Patrick Gordon was currently holding the position of sheriff depute of Aberdeen. The other signatories were the Earls of Angus and Errol (Yellowlees, 126).
39. Potter, 2002: 205–6; ODNB.
40. Yellowlees, 130.
41. Yellowlees, 119, 124.
42. Potter, 2002: 210; Forbes-Leith, 223.
43. Yellowlees, 130, 134.
44. ODNB.
45. ODNB.
46. Potter, 2002: 211.
47. Yellowlees, 134.
48. Yellowlees, 134.
49. Forbes-Leith, 223.
50. ODNB.
51. Bennet et al, 35.
52. Aboyne, 520.
53. Forbes-Leith, 224.

54. Forbes-Leith, 224.
55. Forbes-Leith, 225. Praying on the battlefield was not uncommon: John Knox had also done this.
56. Potter, 2002: 217. The warrior was Neil Macnares.
57. Historic Environment Scotland Battlefield Inventory.
58. Potter, 2002: 214.
59. Historic Environment Scotland Battlefield Inventory; Potter, 2002: 218.
60. Potter, 219.
61. friendsofbenrinnes.org.uk/Ballad.html accessed via Historic Environment Scotland Battlefield Inventory.
62. Paul Macdonald, Macdonald Armouries, Facebook post 20th October 2016.
63. Potter, 2002: 218.
64. Potter, 2002: 220. A 'gowk' is a cuckoo; a gowk's storm is when snow falls in spring, at the time when the first cuckoos are heard – i.e. it is a storm that doesn't last long. 'Gowk's Day' is April Fool's day: the association is with something foolish.
65. Aboyne, 521; Potter, 2002: 221.
66. Potter, 2002: 222; Forbes, 209.
67. Yellowlees, 138. The Jesuit was William Murdoch who also visited Jean's brother Patrick's widow, Agnes Beaton, to offer her comfort.
68. John Colville.
69. ODNB.
70. Watson, 175.
71. Watson, 175.
72. ODNB. Watson, 175, says the ships were got with the help of an Edinburgh merchant, Francis Tennant.
73. Miller, 61.
74. ODNB.
75. ODNB; Robert, 233.
76. Alexander was probably 42 – as previously mentioned, his date of birth is recorded as midsummer 1552, although the reports that say there is a decade between his and Jean's ages would make him aged only 39 when he died.
77. Robert, 232.
78. Robert, 232.
79. Robert, 232.

CHAPTER FIFTEEN: Salt: 1595–1598

1. Or more (half) if there were no children. Ewan and Meikle, Chapter 15.
2. Marshall, 1983: 129.
3. Sutherland book, vol 2, 9.
4. Lord Huntly's wife Henrietta, daughter of James VI's favourite Esmé and by now a favourite of Queen Anne and established at court, certainly did not suffer too much for her husband's actions. Even Francis' wife had been helped numerous times – though Francis and his family were some of the few that James VI never truly forgave.
5. In October, indicating that the remission was probably granted within three months – unless the old calendar was being used, in which case it was within six months.
6. Sutherland book, vol 2, 9, my translation.
7. 'skaith' – Scots word meaning damage, hurt, injury, harm or mischief. Like 'scathe'.
8. Sutherland book, vol 2, 9, my translation.
9. In the Sutherland book (171) he is listed as the 12th Earl – this is the alternate numbering, which does not count the Countess of Sutherland who married a Gordon. The current Sutherland family use the same numbering I do (see Strathnaver, 50). See note 2 in Chapter 9.
10. Sutherland book, 171.
11. Sutherland book, 168.
12. Sanderson, 44.
13. Sutherland book, 168.
14. Sutherland book, 168.
15. Lord Huntly did not actually go into exile until mid-May 1595 (ODNB) so Earl John had not rushed over to Aberdeen but had waited until a few months after his father's death.
16. Ludovick was Lord Huntly's wife Henrietta's brother. He was a Stewart, as Earl John's paternal grandmother had been.
17. Robert, 233.
18. Sutherland book, 171.
19. Robert, 234.
20. Although William Pape was a good scholar, he and his brothers became unpopular when they began to speculate in property, raising the rents for their tenants. Eventually, a fight led to the notorious 'Pape riots', where one Pape brother was killed by William Murray the Gobha Gorm ('the blue blacksmith' – perhaps named for a scar

or birthmark on his face). The Gobha Gorm and his associates had to flee, to Lewis, and some to Holland. Robert (256–7); Rogart Historical Society.

21. Grant in Reid and Kerr-Paterson, 72; Robert, 208.
22. Sarah Fraser, 34.
23. Aboyne, 521.
24. And his accomplice at Glenlivet the Earl of Errol.
25. Aboyne, 522.
26. Aboyne, 522.
27. Sarah Fraser, 53.
28. Robertson, 31.
29. Tabraham (Huntly), 10, 21–3.
30. Forbes-Leith, 226.
31. Forbes-Leith, 226–7.
32. Forbes-Leith, 232.
33. Forbes-Leith, 234.
34. Forbes-Leith, 234.
35. Forbes, 212.
36. Forbes-Leith, 234.
37. Brochard, (The Integration of the Elite), 2015: 3.
38. The Jesuits were generally ill-informed about Scotland, and what little they did know about was from the court (see Yellowlees, 18).
39. Forbes-Leith, 238.
40. Forbes-Leith, 241.
41. Forbes-Leith, 245.
42. Forbes-Leith, 250.
43. Forbes-Leith, 260; Forbes, 214.
44. ODNB.
45. Sanderson, 51.
46. Sutherland book, 172.
47. Sutherland book, 172.
48. Robert, 236.
49. Sutherland book, 173–4; Robert, 236.
50. Robert, 314.
51. Robert, 314–5.
52. Robert, 315.
53. Sutherland book, 184–5.
54. Forbes, 149; Sutherland book, 174.
55. Robert, 237.

56. BBC, St Monan's Salt Mine; Donaldson, 246–7 and 258.
57. Ongoing information on the Brora salt pans is given on the Brora Salt Pans Research Group Facebook page.
58. Sanderson, 45.
59. See for example *The Telegraph* article on Salt mining in India, Nair.
60. Shorewatch, Brora Survey Report, 2004.
61. Crawford in Reid and Kerr-Paterson, 117.
62. Kirk in Inverness Field Club, 45.
63. Brochard, 2014: 210.
64. Worthington, 2012.

CHAPTER SIXTEEN: Alex Ogilvie: Family and Clan: 1599–1603

1. Mackay book, 162; Robert, 240.
2. Robertson, 17.
3. Peerage online.
4. Robert, 169.
5. Marshall, 2006: 147.
6. Alex Ogilvie and Mary Beaton had at least three sons: James, Andrew and Robert (Spence, 1873). There is no record of any daughters (Taylor).
7. Fraser, 2009: 93. A young average age does not mean most people were around that age.
8. Stuart, 53–4; NLS Dep 175/63/1. A particular thank-you to Rosalind K. Marshall for her help in transcribing and translating Jean and Alex Ogilvie's marriage contract. Any errors of interpretation are my responsibility.
9. Taylor, 20–1. Sir George Ogilvie of Dunlugas is mentioned by Coventry (2006) as the owner of Boyne Castle. MacGibbon and Ross say that Sir George Ogilvie "acquired" the castle and estate from the elder branch of the family. Sir George Ogilvie of Dunlugas' name appears in the marriage certificate, though the precise nature and extent of Alex Ogilvie's debts are not clearly spelled out.
10. It seems that Alex Ogilvie had made over the liferent of the lands of Boyne to Sir George Ogilvie of Dunlugas, but was supposed to reclaim it so that he could arrange a new infeftment. Alex Ogilvie's second son Andrew is named in the contract – not his eldest son James – and it may have been that this was to prevent problems with the inheritance of what was left of the Ogilvie estates, and the Ogilvie of Boyne title.

11. Sanderson (45) says that Earl John returned to Scotland in 1600 but the marriage contract is dated December 1599. Earl John is named in the contract as one of the parties involved but is not one of the signatories – James Drummond, his "servitor" signs in his absence. Earl John had to be involved because of his greater rank as an Earl, and his position as head of the Sutherland Gordon family. This is the contract, drawn up before the wedding, and the wedding was supposed to take place before 10th January 1600, so Jean's son Earl John could have come back to Scotland in time for the wedding.

12. Most aristocratic widows kept their titles. Jean does seem to have been referred to as Lady Boyne (causing confusion over when Mary Beaton died as people thought she was referred to by this title), but generally she was still the Countess of Sutherland.

13. Around 25 per cent of the population married twice, around 5 per cent (like Jean) married three times. Fraser, 2009: 102.

14. NLS Dep 175/89/4. My translation/transcription. Original reads: "A collection of the names/ of herbes baith in latein and/ Inglis copylit and gadrit to/gyddir oute of syndry author/ wrytand of the vertues of her/bes/ and now collected in this/ litill volume be alex[ande]r ogilvy/ ane verye studious and ay desir[and]/ to knaw of the wertues of the/ forsundis herbis/ 1587 yeris".

15. I was interested to remember that Alex Ogilvie's first wife was a Beaton: the Beaton medical herbals and notes are some of the most important survivals of the Scottish Gaelic medical tradition. However, Mary Beaton's family were not linked to the medical Beatons – the surname is a coincidence.

16. Mary, Queen of Scots had proposed leaving her French, Italian and English books to Mary Beaton in her will.

17. Robert, 8.

18. Jean's right to a home and land in Sutherland even after her husband the Earl Alexander's death was one of the things that would have been written into her Sutherland marriage contract, and which was then preserved in her marriage contract with Alex Ogilvie.

19. Sutherland book, 172.

20. ODNB. Jean's nephew is generally known to history books as the Marquis of Huntly – 'Marquis' was the Scottish spelling, reflecting the French influence in the country. Marquess is used in England, and can also correctly be used in Scotland.

21. Shorewatch, Brora Survey Report 2004: 5.

22. Sutherland, 'Sinclair and Girnigoe Castles'. The castle is usually now referred to as Castle Sinclair-Girnigoe.
23. Confusingly also called Jean or Jane Gordon.
24. Brochard (The Integration of the Elite), 2015: 4.
25. Brochard (The Integration of the Elite), 2015: 4–6.
26. Canmore (Sinclair-Girnigoe).
27. Brochard (The Integration of the Elite), 2015: 4.
28. 'Annas' is the version of her name which she used to sign her letters (NLS 175/65). She is also recorded as 'Agnes' or 'Anna', but since other people with these names are already part of the story I have used 'Annas'.
29. Annas' younger sister was also called Jean.
30. Sutherland book, 174.
31. Sutherland book, 190.
32. Robert, 240; Sutherland book, 190: five of their nine children died young.
33. Robert, 302.
34. Sutherland book, 176.
35. Robert, 243.
36. When Elizabeth Sutherland married Adam Gordon in the early sixteenth century (see note 2 in Chapter 9).
37. Grimble, 49.
38. Leayd-Reayfe (Leathad Riabhach) is at Greamachary, by Bein Ghrim in Kildonan in Sutherland. It is sometimes also called Inis Chomraig (Field of Contest) (Canmore).
39. Robert, 241–2.
40. Sutherland book, 177; Robert, 242. The charter was granted in April and Caithness invaded in July. Robert rather sneakily puts the two incidents in the opposite order, making it seem that Caithness invaded without provocation. The cairn, also written as Carn-teicheadh (the Cairn of the Flight, or the cairn of retreat), is supposed to still be located there, though archaeological surveys question both the date of the cairn, and its continued existence (Canmore; Highland Historic Environment Record).
41. Sutherland book, 186.
42. Grimble, 50.
43. Robert, 248; Grimble, 50; Sutherland book, 179.
44. Robert, 248. 'Dunkirk' could mean 'church in the dunes'; it probably has nothing to do with the French town of the same name.

45. See Brochard (The Integration of the Elite), 2015: 1; Robertson, 37.
46. Wightman, 43, 46.
47. Crawford in Kerr-Paterson and Reid, 118.
48. Fraser, 1977: 63; Kirk in Inverness Field Club, 45–6.
49. Sutherland book, 174.
50. Robert, 246.
51. Robert, 244.
52. Robert, 247.
53. Robert, 248.
54. Robert, 239.
55. Robert, 239.
56. Sutherland book, vol 2, 11.
57. Later dean of Caithness.
58. Sutherland book, 192; Allan, 26.
59. Quote is from Sutherland book, 193, paraphrasing Robert, 249: "imploying his tyme not onlie in the studie of civill lawes, and in trawelling through that cuntrie, bot lykwise in all exercises fit for a gentleman of his birth and qualitie'.
60. Robert, 250.
61. Robert, 251.
62. Antonia Fraser, in her short biography of James VI and I, quotes an (unnamed) historian who argued that from 17th December 1596 to 23rd July 1637 – the dates of two riots in Edinburgh – there was relative calm throughout the country (Fraser, 1977: 63).

CHAPTER SEVENTEEN: The Regulation of Noble Retinues: 1604/05–1610

1. Sutherland book, 193.
2. Robert, 255.
3. Robert, 255. See Jennifer Morag Henderson 'How God gave a small Scottish town advance notice of the Gunpowder Plot' in *The National* newspaper, 4th November 2017.
4. Fraser, 1977: 84.
5. Shapiro, 198.
6. Robert, 255.
7. Sutherland book, vol 2, 337.
8. Robert, 255; Allan, 27.
9. Sutherland book, 186.
10. Sutherland book, vol 2, 337.

11. e.g. NLS Dep 175/79/4773.
12. Robert's later descendants included prominent Quakers.
13. Robert, 252.
14. Robert, 252.
15. Sutherland book, 179.
16. Robert, 255.
17. Shapiro, Chapter 13.
18. ODNB.
19. ODNB.
20. Wightman, 43, 46.
21. Robertson, 37.
22. Wormald, 27.
23. Duelling and fencing had become something of a fashionable craze. In London there were many fencing schools and teachers and the well-dressed young man about town wore a rapier at his side. Shakespeare could fence, and there are plenty of sword-fights in his plays – think Mercutio, or even Hamlet: these are the sort of young men James VI is legislating against (Cohen, 34–9).
24. Robertson, 52.
25. Robertson, 52.
26. Stevenson, 182.
27. Potter, 2002: 134.
28. Robertson, 52; Aboyne, 527.
29. Stevenson, 183. "Pestle was a well-known slang term for penis," a historian explains laboriously, "hence, in popular terminology, the word 'mortar' came to be a euphemism for vagina". The secretive nature of the Boys, and their incredible activities, have attracted a fair amount of attention from fascinated historians, who have put forward varying sexual interpretations of their nickname. Another five pages are dedicated to the same topic in a later edition of *The Scottish Historical Review* (Roberts).
30. Roberts, 84.
31. Aboyne, 527; Stevenson, 182.
32. Being constantly pregnant, as many noblewomen were, could also limit the amount they travelled.
33. See Rosalind K. Marshall's interesting and valuable analysis of women's education in the seventeenth century in *Virgins and Viragos* 1983: 127.
34. Sutherland book, 178.
35. Robert, 258.
36. Robert, 258.

37. Robert, 235.
38. Sutherland book, 173.
39. Aboyne, 527; Potter, 2002: 231–2.
40. ODNB; Robertson, 55.
41. Sarah Fraser, 169.
42. Allan, 27.
43. See Chapter 14. Potter, 2002, Chapter 13: 181.
44. 'In this mean-time Macbeth,' explained Robert, 'being pinched by the worm of a guilty conscience, was troubled in spirit: yet nevertheless he exercised all kinds of tyranny against such of the nobility of the realm, as either he was afraid of for their constancy to Malcolm, or were falsely accused before him of treason, til he became daily more and more odious, and being transported with the fury of cruelty, he ceased not still to slay his nobles and to confiscate their goods for most frivolous causes… Macbeth thought the profit so sweet which came to him by the slaughter of his nobles, that he could not desist from it…'Robert, 23.
45. Hector Boece.
46. Robert, 23.
47. Robert, 246.
48. Sutherland book, 180.
49. See for example Spence, 1873. Secondary sources sometimes also assert that Mary Beaton was also alive in 1606, but I think this must be because an original source refers to "Lady Boyne" – which by this time would be Jean's official title – or because something at Alex Ogilvie's joint burial place with Mary Beaton references 1606. However, it is also difficult to ascertain exactly where Alex Ogilvie and Mary Beaton are buried, as there is more than one kirkyard with an Ogilvie resting place, who have found the link with Beaton and Mary, Queen of Scots interesting enough to highlight.
50. Taylor, 22.
51. There are some conflicting reports over where Mary Beaton was buried (see note 49 above). One other suggestion is Boyndie church, but see Taylor (inserts), who disagree with this.

CHAPTER EIGHTEEN: Plots and Mercenaries: 1611–1616/17

Part 1: The False Coiner

1. Sanderson, 48; Robert, 345. Original spelling 'Cracock'.
2. The Sutherland book (190) does not give details of the birth dates of daughters, so it is difficult to establish the exact time line.

3. Margaret's parents were Donald Bane Macleod (alias Neilson), Laird of Assynt, and Moir Mackay. Moir was the daughter of Aodh Mackay and Christine Sinclair of Dun – she was Uisdean's sister. So Alexander married his brother-in-law's sister's daughter (see Robert, 262–5 for more about Assynt and its complicated history). Alexander married Margaret in 1610, and they went on to have five sons and two daughters.
4. Especially Lewis.
5. Peerage online.
6. Robert, 248.
7. ODNB; Grimble, 59.
8. Grimble, 54.
9. Grimble, 54; Robert, 302.
10. Robert, 302.
11. Robert, 302. After listing Uisdean's four children with Jane, Robert also mentions his child (a daughter, Christian) with his first wife. No other children are mentioned, however, which does bring into question what Robert means by 'lust'. Perhaps Robert would not have mentioned illegitimate children – though in his eyes, Christian would have been thought to be illegitimate also, since the Gordons had insisted at the time of his wedding to Jane that Uisdean's first marriage was a forced marriage. Perhaps Uisdean recognised Christian but not any other children that he had – we do not know. Alternatively, by 'lust' Robert might just mean that Uisdean was, in his eyes, overly active: that Uisdean was too much involved in what should have been Gordon affairs.
12. Tobar an Dualchais, 51332 'MacLeod's Salute'.
13. Tobar an Dualchais, 75819/1 'Cille Chriosd'.
14. However, this story about the pibroch 'Cillechriost' or "Cill Chriosd" is one that is repeated elsewhere and attributed to other pipers as well: for example, it is sometimes called 'Glengarry's March' and is reputed to have been played by a Macdonnell of Glengarry as he marched round a burning church full of his enemies after a battle with Donald's in-laws the Mackenzies of Kintail.
15. Grimble, 55.
16. Mackay book, 169–70. The cousin was called John Sutherland. He had apparently 'been much harassed' by Wicked Earl George and resolved to retaliate. George summoned him to appear before council in Edinburgh, but John refused to go. John was declared rebel and had to hide. George took his lands and goods. John then took lots

of George's cattle. George sent a lot of men to search for John. John was advised that they were coming and ambushed and killed many of them. George then summoned both John and Uisdean to Edinburgh to appear before council. Uisdean went to Edinburgh and met Robert there, and was advised to meet George to try and sort things out that way. Uisdean and George met and George promised that if John was given up to him he would imprison him for 12 months only then call it quits. Uisdean agreed. Donald was not impressed and started to ask for John to be released. These are the sort of long and convoluted stories that take up pages and pages of the official family and clan chronicles.

17. Mackay book, 170.
18. Robert, 280; Calder, 141. The Clan Gunn man, William Macangus Gunn, was a servant of Wicked Earl George, who had allegedly stolen from his master. He was imprisoned in Castle Sinclair-Girnigoe, but escaped by jumping from a window. However, William Macangus Gunn broke his leg in his jump to escape and so was recaptured. Once his leg healed, he again jumped from the castle into the sea, and swam ashore. The Mackay servant, Angus Herriagh was supposed to have aided these escapes, and was then imprisoned in turn in Castle Sinclair-Girnigoe. Donald's intervention saw Angus Herriagh eventually declared innocent and released. Angus Herriagh is also named in trial documents as Angus McWilliame, alias 'Herrach', while in the Mackay book (170) he is named as Angus or Andrew Henderson – there are several versions of the story, but all the names refer to one person.
19. Grimble, 55.
20. Mackay book, 170.
21. Robert, 279.
22. Robert, 279.
23. Grimble, 56.
24. Mackay book, 171; Robert, 279.
25. Robert, 283.
26. Robert's full and somewhat involved version of these events (279–87) is the nearest to a complete contemporary source for the Arthur Smith plot. Some contemporary legal documents are available in Pitcairn. Calder attempts to put a Sinclair spin on the story (136–41), with a few added details for which he does not give sources. The Sutherland book (181) summarises the story briefly. The Mackay book (172) emphasises the importance of the previous incident with the Clan Gunn servant, and questions some of Robert Gordon's motives. Grimble (56–7) continues this questioning of Robert's motivation.

27. The legal document says Wicked Earl George and his son and others are being charged to appear before the Justice to answer to the law 'for the slauchter of Neill Nathnear, vmqle Airthour Smyth, taking captiue and prisoner of Angus McWilliame, alias Herrach, but Commission; and dyuerse vtheris crymes specifeit in the faidis Letteris' (Pitcairn, 231). 'vmqle' is short for 'umquile': this can mean late or deceased, but this meaning wasn't settled until after 1700 (DSL): prior to that, i.e. at the time this was written, it could also mean 'sometimes' – i.e. 'Neill Nathnear, alias or sometimes Arthur Smith'. I can find no other reference to a Neill Nathnear, and cannot identify a specific incident linked to this case where a different man was slaughtered.

28. Grimble, 56, brings up the last of these questions; the rest are mine.

29. Sutherland book, vol 2, 12: licence by King James VI and the Privy Council to John 12th Earl of Sutherland, to go abroad for three years, 22nd January 1611.

30. Robert, 282.

31. Robert, 284.

32. Robert, 284.

33. Robert, 284–5.

34. Robert, 285; Grimble, 57.

35. Both were too sick to travel.

36. Robert, 285.

37. Robert, 318.

38. ODNB. Lord Huntly had been allowed to leave his house arrest and visit the king at Whitehall 'an act that marked the gradual reinstatement of Huntly in the king's favour'.

39. Mackay book, 175.

40. Robert, 287.

41. Robert, 287.

42. ODNB (Donald Mackay); Robert, 294.

43. Robert, 295.

44. Sutherland book, 185.

45. Robert, 278.

46. Robert, 279; Sutherland book, 185.

47. Sutherland book, 206.

48. Allan, 28–9.

Part 2: Kringen: Viking Metal

49. Sutherland book, 206 for Alexander's involvement; Mackay book, 174–6; Robertson, Chapter 2.

50. Mackay book, 175.
51. See Chapter 14.
52. Mackay book, 175.
53. Mackay book, 176.
54. Mackay book, 176.
55. See Robertson, Chapter 2; Reid and Kerr-Paterson, 3 mentions "a noticeable rise in the prominence and importance of cadet branches, lairds and lesser nobles in Scottish society", as well as a decline in the making of bonds of manrent (see also Wormald).
56. Strictly speaking the word 'mercenary' wasn't in common use yet, but that is what they were. Contemporary documents call them things like 'waged men of war'.
57. Miller, 10–12. See also Worthington, Chapter 3.
58. See Calder, Chapter 9. Note also that although Gustavus Adolphus was the great Protestant champion, it's still often said that the Sinclairs were Catholic. They were mercenaries, not men fighting for a cause.
59. There is some debate over whether Captain Sinclair was in fact the leader of the expedition: he seems to have been one of the leaders, but his family connections increased his importance in retellings of the story.
60. Beveridge.
61. Robert, 289.
62. Calder, Chapter 9.
63. Robert, 289.
64. Beveridge.
65. Calder, Chapter 9.
66. From the poem by Edvard Storm.
67. For example, the version by Pól Arni Holm and his group Hamradun. One reason the incident retains its fame is because of the Faroe Islands' vibrant, internationally renowned heavy metal music scene.
68. Mackay book, 180.
69. Mackay book, 180–1.
70. Robert, 269.
71. From The Chambers Concise Scots Dictionary: 'warrandice: *law* the undertaking by a granter or seller to indemnify a grantee or buyer of *esp* HERITABLE property threatened with eviction through defect of title'.
72. Meikle, 1992.
73. Mackay book, 181.
74. Mackay book, 181.

75. Mackay book, 182.
76. Robert, 320.
77. Robert, 297.
78. Mackay book, 182.
79. Robert, 298.
80. Robert, 301.
81. Robert, 311.
82. Mackay book, 187. Robert says Jane was buried 'in the sepulchre of her fathers', but this complaint is typical of the Mackay book's attitude to Jane: the author also complains that Robert refers to her as 'Jane Gordon' not 'Jane Mackay': strictly speaking, although the Mackays deserve sympathy for the way they were treated, this complaint over names is completely wrong, as Scottish noblewomen did not take their husband's names when they married.
83. Robert, 309.
84. Robert, 299.
85. Mackay book, 184.
86. Mackay book, 185.
87. Robert, 300. There was a story that Black Patie was so wicked that his execution had to be delayed for several days as he needed time to learn the Lord's Prayer, to say before he died – since he had never bothered to learn it before.
88. Robert, 310.
89. Sutherland book, vol 2, 113–14.
90. Robert, 310.
91. Robert, 310.
92. Robert, 311.
93. Sutherland book, 187.
94. Sutherland book, vol 2, 113–21.
95. Sutherland book, vol 2, 114; Grimble, 61.
96. Sutherland book, 187.
97. Sutherland book, vol 2, 121. "Ane pair of the finest dowle virginal-lis". Double virginals could be played by one or two people. Robert sometimes sent other gifts, including a spyglass, and tobacco – the latter being apparently much appreciated (Forbes, 150).
98. Robert, 313.
99. Grant (Golspitour).
100. Robert, 329.

CHAPTER NINETEEN: Donald Duaghal and the Triumph of the House of Sutherland: 1616–1624

1. Sutherland book, vol 2, 363.
2. Aitken, 5.
3. Robert, 320.
4. Husbands legally had to pay fines for their wives' 'ecclesiastical misdemeanours' (Forbes, 152).
5. Robert, 321.
6. There are records of repairs to the house, including 'lofting and lathing' (i.e. fixing the boarding between one floor and the next (indicating that there is more than one storey), and fixing leaks in the roof), expensive payments to smiths for ironworks, and payments to a master mason called Andrew Thomson, who fixed the chimneys and some cracks in the walls (Sanderson, 49). There is still an old private house at the site of Crackaig.
7. NLS Dep 175/85/1 papers of Sir Robert Gordon, accounts. My transcription/translations.
8. Forbes, 153.
9. NLS Dep 175/79/4792 and 4793: letters from Lucie Gordon to Robert Gordon. My translation (originals in French).
10. Rev Simpson, 1989: 4.
11. Sutherland book, vol 2, 339.
12. Sutherland book, vol 2, 115: Earl John wrote, "As concerning suche thingis as ye wreit wnto me to send yow anent our genelogie, ye knaw I can do lytill in that matter, being still heir [Edinburgh]. I sent all your informations to our brother Alexander, and mervellis he hath not send me ansuer bak again. Ye knaw it wilbe hard to try the particular dayis and yeiris of suche affaires, and if I wer at home I knaw there is amagst the wreittis that wer in Kynnairdis custodie that wald do yow goode. Bot ye must haue pacience whill my hame-going..."
13. Sutherland book, vol 2, 365–6.
14. See for example Carson, 345, talking about where information for history comes from.
15. Allan, 29.
16. Allan, 29.
17. Sutherland book, vol 2, 365. I have modernised some spelling for ease of reading.
18. Bulloch, 1925: 16; Sutherland book, vol 2, 168.

19. Robert, 443. The assessment of Robert's character is done by Gilbert Gordon of Sallach, who added a postscript to Robert's genealogy, bringing it from 1630 to 1651. Gilbert knew Robert, and was related to him.
20. Dep 175/65/2: letters 1608–1638. 1608, London: John Toshie (Mackintosh) to Mr Francis Hueson, goldsmith – concerning delivery of a gold chain etc. to Mr Robert Gordon.
21. Nat Gall online.
22. Since Alexander was effectively in charge of Dunrobin for his nephew, perhaps the keys are for Dunrobin? Alternatively perhaps they are for one of the properties he lived in, such as the now destroyed Helmsdale Castle, which he had renovated.
23. This was the marriage for which Alexander wanted Robert to find him the black figured silk suit and taffeta cloak. Donald's eldest son married Lady Isabel Sinclair (Bulloch, 1925: 16; Sutherland book, vol 2, 168–9).
24. See Brochard, 2010, on Robert and his affinity with emergent neo-Stoic philosophical thought, which "endorsed the Tacitean aspiration for a reconfiguration of political morality along pragmatic lines, however disturbing these were. The defence of kinship thus became paramount over the immorality of the actual acts(s) and justified it/them. This philosophy peppered Sir Robert's genealogical work in the defence of the House of Sutherland and was carried out in actions and legal deeds in the defence of the comital House sometimes at the expense of morality".
25. Sutherland book, vol 2, 169. From the letter asking for the wedding suit.
26. Robert, 310; Grimble 63–4.
27. Inverness Burgh Court book 1602–21; Robertson, 14.
28. Grimble, 63.
29. Robert, 332; Grimble, 64.
30. ODNB.
31. Robert, 333.
32. Robert, 336; ODNB.
33. ODNB; Robert, 339.
34. Robert, 322.
35. Robert, 323.
36. The lands were Kinnauld, Golspitour and Kilcalmkil. See Mackay book, 167.

37. See Robert, 323. Places change names, and Robert is also very partisan in his descriptions of what happened. Other lands Robert mentioned that Donald had an interest in are an area in Strathfleet, and the lands of Over Skibo, as well as a house in Dornoch. He also talks about Mackay encouraging his clansmen to pasture Mackay cattle near Lairg, very close to some land whose ownership was disputed between the Mackays and Gordons.
38. Robert, 323.
39. Ewan and Meikle, Chapter 15.
40. Robert, 325.
41. Lucie Gordon, Robert's wife, was the daughter of John Gordon, the Dean of Salisbury. John Gordon was an illegitimate son of Alexander Gordon, the bishop of Galloway. Alexander Gordon was the brother of Jean's father; the clergyman who had married Jean and Bothwell. So Lucie was descended from Robert's great-uncle.
42. Robert, 480.
43. Robert, 326.
44. Sutherland book, vol 2, 347. Robert bought the Golspitour lands in his name, but later gifted them to the Earl of Sutherland (his nephew) (Robert, 480).
45. Robert, 316. See Chapter 18.
46. Grimble, 65.
47. See Brochard (The Integration of the Elite), 2015: 10: when discussing a later appearance by Donald at court Brochard points out the absence of comment on his dress: "The English commentators... did not report on an ethnic or regional appearance."
48. Robert, 335.
49. Sutherland book, vol 2, 351. I have standardised the spelling for ease of reading.
50. Sutherland book, vol 2, 359.
51. Robert, 335.
52. Ceol Sean, Piobaireachd, 5; Mackay book, 328.
53. Bulloch, 1925.
54. Grimble, 65.
55. Sutherland book, vol 2, 122.
56. Grimble, 66.
57. Sutherland book, vol 2, 122.
58. Sutherland book, vol 2, 124.
59. He seems to be the same John Gray who accompanied Robert and Alexander of Navidale to the continent – or at least from the same family.
60. Sutherland book, vol 2, 123.

61. Sutherland book, 213.
62. Sutherland book, vol 2, 125.
63. Grimble, 67.
64. Sutherland book, vol 2, 128.
65. Sutherland book, vol 2, 338.
66. Grimble (1993: 68) claims that Donald and Barbara got back together and they had six more children after this point – but that does not seem to fit. They had already been married for six years, so their children had already been born while, as later events show, Donald definitely remarried and Barbara pursued legal action against him.
67. "Anent my wyff, schow is becoum to bed of ane boy qlk be all resoune & liklyhoud I haiff nothinge ado wt." (Fraser-Mackintosh, 3).
68. Fraser-Mackintosh, 4.
69. See Amy Licence.
70. Sutherland book, vol 2, 124–5.
71. i.e. Jane Countess of Sutherland.
72. Robert gave his nephew the child-Earl the advice to always have a spy in both Caithness (to spy on Wicked Earl George, the Earl of Caithness) and Strathnaver, home of the Mackays (Sutherland book, vol 2, 349).
73. Sutherland book, vol 2, 129–30.
74. Signing off with his still-new title, as Sir Donald Mackay.
75. Sutherland book, vol 2, 131–2.
76. Sutherland book, vol 2, 131–2.
77. Sutherland book, vol 2, 131.
78. Sutherland book, vol 2, 132.
79. Sutherland book, vol 2, 132.
80. Margaret MacDougall collection (REF D390/5/2 Archive Centre).
81. Sutherland book, vol 2, 113.
82. Margaret MacDougall collection (REF D390/5/2 Archive Centre).
83. Brochard (Scottish Witchcraft), 2015: 45.
84. Survey of Scottish Witchcraft.
85. Huntly's reply states that he 'has sent to the Gudeman of Buckie, my cousin, and have willed him to do justice on the witch which you wrote to me has bewitched Golspitour's son. Therefore you may advertise Buckie whensoever he comes to Inverness for that effect'. However, this is only a mention in a short letter, the rest of which is concerned with a 'white hound' that Robert has asked for but which Lord Huntly cannot send to him as he will be using the hound in a wolf hunt: this seems to suggest where Huntly's priorities lay. (Sutherland book, vol 2, 132; Fraser-Mackintosh, 4–5).

---

86. See Fraser, 2017: 119 for a good summary of the theory and how it was applied by Prince Henry.
87. Sanderson (48) says Janet was a relative of Jean's – but if so (and I can't find the connection) she was a distant and relatively poor relation.
88. Survey of Scottish Witchcraft.
89. Robert, 343.
90. Forbes, 157.
91. Robert, 343.
92. Robert, 344.
93. Forbes, 151.
94. Sanderson, 44–5.
95. Aitken, 5.
96. Robert, 344.
97. In 1616. Robert, 338. The river is named as the 'Doverne', which is the old form of 'Deveron'.
98. Sutherland book, 190; Robert, 345.
99. Mackay book, 196.
100. Grimble, 71.
101. Mackay book, 203.
102. Grimble, 69.
103. Earl of Caithness to Robert Gordon, 6th October 1619, NLS Dep 175/65/68: my transcription/translation.
104. Grimble, 72, 74.
105. Donald Mackay letter to Jean, 2nd July 1619, NLS Dep 175/65/90. N.B. this letter was written before the one from Wicked Earl George quoted above (see note 103), but the entire correspondence is not extant, so I have selected relevant parts out of order to make the feelings of the participants clear.
106. Grimble, 68 for Tolbooth, ODNB for date of fine. The ODNB conflates the two events but the date of the fine is clear so there must have been a delay, i.e. he was imprisoned first, then fined later, in 1620. A merk is two-thirds of a (Scots) pound.
107. Grimble, 75.
108. ODNB; Lenman in Inverness Field Club, 175.
109. Grimble, 75–6.
110. Grimble, 76.
111. Grimble, 78.
112. Robert, 179. The quote continues "...becaus he brunt the famous temple of Diana at Ephesus. For although the trueth requireth that they should be registrat (being so notoriously known through the

kingdome), yit reasone and Christianitie wold have the memorie of such dangerous exemples to be buried in oblivion; and therefor I will be as sparing as I can". He then goes on to talk about Caithness for pages and pages.

113. Historian Ian Grimble thought that Robert's ultimate aim may have been to take over the Earldom of Caithness, in the way that the Huntly Gordons took over Sutherland (78), perhaps with a view to expanding Robert's own personal estates – however, I think neutralising the threat Caithness posed to Sutherland was Robert's main aim. Taking over Caithness completely would have been a large undertaking – and at this point, Robert was settled in London and Salisbury. Robert did eventually move back north, but he was able to afford to buy himself good farming land in Moray, better than Caithness. Matters were also complicated by the fact that Robert's cousin, from the Huntly Gordon family, was married to Wicked Earl George.

114. Mackay book (206) tells the story of a duel fought in Leith between Sir William Sinclair of Mey (possibly Wicked Earl George's cousin) and a bastard son of Wicked Earl George, called Francis Sinclair: the cause is unclear, but the bastard Francis was the victor: he drove his sword right through William's body, and fled, leaving William for dead. William was discovered in time to be helped and recovered, while Francis remained in hiding in Berwick. Robert then intervened in the quarrel, and obtained a remission for Francis. The Mackay book (206) says this was not just because he wished to support Francis, but because this meant he was against both William and William's current ally the laird of Duffus, but this seems obtuse, as at this time Robert was supporting Duffus in his quarrel with Golspitour. We are hampered, as always, by the lack of Caithness documents. The ultimate problem still seems to be that one branch of the family inherited the title, and the other the money: it all stems back to John the Stout's quarrel with his father.

115. Mackay book, 206.

116. Mackay book, 212.

117. ODNB.

CHAPTER TWENTY: The Practical Juliet: 1625–1629 and After

1. Forbes, 108.

2. August 1606.

3. Arthur Forbes.

4. Aboyne, 500.
5. Robert, 175.
6. Forbes, 155.
7. Yellowlees, 157. James the Jesuit's Scottish mission had failed in its aim to reconvert King James VI and his country. One reason for lack of progress in Scotland was arguably the failure to treat it as a separate country to England. Knowledge of Scotland amongst the Jesuits was limited, and focused primarily on the Lowlands and the rich nobles at court. There were different responses to things in Scotland and England, e.g. in England non-attendance at Protestant services was punishable by a fine, whereas in Scotland non-attendance could result in excommunication, which had serious social, legal and financial ramifications. James the Jesuit had always argued that Scotland must be treated the same as England, and was not in favour of Scottish Catholics attending Protestant services, no matter what the consequences. In this he was influenced by his own experience as a wealthy, high-ranking man (Yellowlees, 153, 159, 18).
8. Brochard (The Integration of the Elite), 2015: 8. Brochard says that her hair is silver, but in the portrait in Dunrobin it is clearly not. I have seen copies of this portrait for sale online; perhaps in a reproduction the hair was silver – or perhaps the painting in Dunrobin has been retouched. See also Cooper, 2012 for discussion of portraits.
9. John Bulloch, 1885. In Bulloch's description he clearly states that the portrait has silver hair – as Brochard does (see note 8 above). Brochard may have copied Bulloch, but Bulloch seems to have viewed the painting himself. One possibility is that the portrait of Jean had been restored and touched up at a later date, and her hair had been repainted to match the colour of her hair in the early portrait of her. This seems to be supported by what Bulloch says, as he describes the painting he has seen as having "lost tone and become very brown from successive varnishings, applied with the mistaken view of refreshing it". Bulloch also thinks that what I have interpreted as a high pointed widow's hood is in fact a chair back: he thinks that she is sitting on a chair and that it is merging into her clothes. If he saw an earlier, untouched portrait, he may have been able to perceive details that we no longer can see. In the Dunrobin records, this painting says that it was painted c.1620, and that Jean is 84. She was 84 in 1629 – in 1620, she would have been 75.
10. In the Dunrobin records it is attributed to a follower of George Jameson.

---

11. The inscription on Robert's painting saying his age is a common device in Tudor and Jacobean portraits, but one well-known painter who used this distinctive lettering was Adam de Colone. The portrait of Robert's brother Alexander of Navidale is attributed to Colone, but could Robert's painting be an early Colone? It is not as sophisticated in its depiction of features as the portrait of Alexander of Navidale, but it is done on a different medium (wood not canvas) so the difference could be explained by that, and by it being an early work.

12. Others have also tried to describe Jean's personality from looking at this portrait. Forbes (153) thinks she looks "wise, knowing, practical and intelligent – an example of a self-possessed woman of character". For my part, I think Jean mainly looks rich.

13. Stuart, 60; NLS Dep 175/79/4773.

14. The son of Any's gudbrothir, in the letter, would be her nephew. Gudbrothir being her brother-in-law.

15. Sutherland book, vol 2, 142.

16. Sarah Fraser, 2017.

17. Robertson.

18. Alexander Duff.

19. Sanderson, 52.

20. Bulloch, 1925: 8.

21. Robertson.

22. Miller, 10.

23. ODNB; Grimble 80.

24. Monro's Expedition gives a contemporary source for the Mackays' experiences abroad. See also Scott (2011) *The Best Soldier*: this life of Sir John Hepburn has more information on the Thirty Years War – and has an interesting Bothwell connection, as author Elizabeth Scott is the sister of Sir Alistair Buchan-Hepburn (see Interlude) and a descendant of Bothwell.

25. Sutherland book, vol 2, 152–3.

26. Letter dated 1635 addressed: "To my very Honobill and Deir Unkill Sir Robert Gordoun, Knytt and Baronett, one of His Maty. Privie Consellors off Scotland, at Court, or at Robert Carall's Hous in King Street, at Brudrs. Yard, ye 6… I know you ar arche in yor owin perticouler, yit in this I hop yors sall coum off wit creditt. I end, and sall ever reman to daithe, your loving Nephew to serf you." Fraser-Mackintosh, 34–5.

27. ODNB. For some reason the ODNB says his mother came with him, but of course by this time Jane was dead. Perhaps it was his mother-in-law?

28. ODNB.
29. Lady Isabel Sinclair. Bulloch, 1925: 16; Sutherland book, vol 2, 168–9.
30. Sutherland book, 215. He was in Edinburgh for a short time only and there is no record of his time there.
31. Robertson, 68.
32. Withrington in Inverness Field Club book, 60.
33. See Brochard, 2010 and Marshall, 1983: 127. This split affected the clan system perhaps most dramatically, but I would argue it applies to everyone in the north – and can be extrapolated to understand all small communities located far from the centre of power. The change in women's education is discussed earlier (see Chapter 17).
34. Sutherland book, 215; Robert, 382.
35. Brora Survey Report, 2004. This moved the focus of trading from Brora to Dornoch.
36. Sutherland book, vol 2, 361.
37. Sutherland book, vol 2, 150. Dr David Worthington of the UHI argues that Dornoch and Tain are interesting coastal towns, as they are not orientated to maritime pursuits – perhaps because Robert artificially built them up?
38. Sutherland book, vol 2, 147: letter from Alexander of Navidale to Robert.
39. Sutherland book, vol 2, 147, 150: letter from Alexander of Navidale to Robert, quote from letter from Alexander to Robert 21st July 1628.
40. Sutherland book, vol 2, 149.
41. Sutherland book, vol 2, 359, 363–5.
42. Sutherland book, 213, 216.
43. Sutherland book, 215.
44. Sutherland book, vol 2, 149.
45. See Sutherland book, 217; Robert, 389.
46. Sutherland book, vol 2, 151.
47. Robert, 409.
48. Robert, 168.
49. Robert, 168.
50. Sutherland book, vol 2, 341: "Keip a wryten scrolle of all your servants and folowers, and still reward them by turns."
51. NLS Dep 175; see also Acc 10824, Box 3.
52. Sutherland book, vol 2, 154.
53. Robert said, "Be thankfull to those that hawe bred yow, for they ar your second parents..." Sutherland book, vol 2, 341.
54. Bulloch, 1925: 13–14.

55. Sutherland book, vol 2, 344.
56. Sutherland book, 207.
57. Sutherland book, vol 2, 147.
58. Robert, 360.
59. Sutherland book, vol 2, 121. See Chapter 18.
60. Sutherland book, 202.
61. Robert, 419.
62. His full name and title was John Gordon Viscount Melgum; the Aboyne lands were part of the Huntly estates and given to him by his father, and he was usually known by the title 'Aboyne' (though is occasionally found under the title 'Melgum') (Robertson, Chapter 2; ODNB).
63. Buchan, 1985: 124.
64. Buchan, 1985:123.
65. Robertson, 77. Lady Rothiemay was a Forbes, and her marriage to Rothiemay (a Gordon) had been meant to promote peace in the old Forbes-Gordon blood feud. So that worked well. (ODNB).
66. Elizabeth, Countess of Sutherland's marriage to Adam Gordon of Aboyne, son of the 2nd Earl of Huntly took place in c1500; this was the marriage that had made the Sutherlands Gordons.
67. Robertson.
68. They even eventually changed their surname from 'Gordon' to 'Sutherland'.
69. Sutherland book, vol 2, 354.
70. Robertson, 93–4.
71. Sutherland book, vol 2, 357.
72. Robert, 510.
73. Allan, 30.
74. The Countess of Sutherland in the eighteenth century – the one who was involved in the Clearances – was made a Duchess of Sutherland, and her husband Duke, in addition to their titles of Earl and Countess. The English titles of Duke and Duchess are only passed on from father to son, while the Scottish titles of Earl and Countess can be passed through the female line. Because at one point there was only a daughter in the family, the two titles became separated in the 1960s – the titles of Duke of Sutherland and the Earl of Sutherland are not given to the same person any more. The land in Sutherland remains with the Earl. The current Duke of Sutherland is Francis Egerton, who lives in England and has little to do with Dunrobin and Sutherland. The current Earl of Sutherland succeeded to his title in December 2019, when Elizabeth Millicent Sutherland, the Countess of Sutherland,

died at the age of 98 (Northern Times). This branch of the family own Dunrobin Castle (Strathnaver, 48).

75. Wightman, 115.
76. Robert, 169.
77. Robert, 168–9.
78. Robert, 169.
79. Robert, despite his professed anti-clan mentality, said, "Let a Gordones querrell be your own, so farr as he heth right and equitie on his syde. Preferre your surname… to your nearest allyance" (Sutherland book, vol 2, 358).
80. Sutherland book, vol 2, 354.
81. Sutherland book, vol 2, 337.
82. This was Robert's advice to Jean's grandson, John Glas (Sutherland book, vol 2, 348): Robert was the product of his upbringing.
83. Always keep a good agent in Edinburgh, and have a good lawyer, Robert advised John Glas (Sutherland book, vol 2, 355).
84. Robert, 366.
85. Monro's Expedition, Part 2, 63.

Selected Bibliography

Including all titles referenced in endnotes. Does not include all titles read or consulted. Arranged by type, i.e. book, article, primary source, etc., then alphabetical by author.

Referencing style: Author Last Name, First Name *Title* (place: publisher, date), page number. [abbreviation for endnotes, if different from normal referencing].

URLS last accessed June 2021.

Books

Bell, Robin (transl. & ed.) *Bittersweet Within My Heart: The Collected Poems of Mary, Queen of Scots* (London: Pavilion Books, 1992)

Bennett, Susan et al (eds) *Women of Moray* (Edinburgh: Luath, 2012)

Earl of Bothwell (ed by Thorleifr Repp) *Les Affaires du Comte de Boduel* (Edinburgh: Bannatyne Club, 1829) [Les Affaires du Comte de Boduel]

Buchan, David *A Book of Scottish Ballads* (London: Routledge & Kegan Paul, 1985)

Bulloch, John *George Jameson, The Scottish van Dyck* (Edinburgh: David Douglas Ltd, 1885) [John Bulloch]

Bulloch, John Malcolm *The Gay Adventures of Sir Alexander Gordon, Knight of Navidale* (Dingwall: Ross-shire Printing & Publishing Co, 1925)

———. *The Gordons in Sutherland, including the Embo family* (Dingwall: Ross-shire Journal, 1907), accessed via nls.uk

Calder, Angus *Gods, Mongrels and Demons* (London: Bloomsbury, 2003) [Angus Calder]

Calder, J.T. *History of Caithness* (Wick: Caithness Reprints, 1973)

Carson, Annette *Richard III: The Maligned King* (Stroud: The History Press, 2013)

The Chambers Concise Scots Dictionary (Aberdeen: Aberdeen University Press, 1985) [Chambers Concise Scots Dictionary]

Cohen, Richard *By the Sword* (London: Pocket Books, 2010)

Cooper, Tarnya *A Guide to Tudor & Jacobean Portraits* (National Portrait Gallery, 2012)

Coventry, Martin *Castles of Scotland* (Edinburgh: Birlinn, 2006)

Dawson, Jane *John Knox* (London: Yale University Press, 2016)

Donaldson, Gordon *Scotland: James V–James VII, The Edinburgh History of Scotland Vol 3* (Edinburgh: Oliver & Boyd, 1978)

Dunn, Jane *Elizabeth and Mary: Cousins, Rivals, Queens* (London: Harper Perennial, 2004)

Ewan, Elizabeth and Maureen M. Meikle (eds) *Women in Scotland c.1100– c.1750* (East Linton: Tuckwell, 1998) [Ewan and Meikle]

Ewan, Elizabeth et al *The Biographical Dictionary of Scottish Women* (Edinburgh: Edinburgh University Press, 2006)

Forbes, Anne L. *Trials and Triumphs: The Gordons of Huntly in Sixteenth -Century Scotland* (Edinburgh: John Donald, 2012)

Forbes-Leith S.J., William (ed) *Narratives of Scottish Catholics under Mary Stuart and James VI: Now first printed from the original manuscripts in the secret archives of the Vatican and other collections (New Edition)* (London: Baker, 1889) [Forbes-Leith]

Fraser, Antonia *King James VI of Scotland and I of England* (London: Sphere, 1977)

———. *Mary Queen of Scots* (London: Mandarin, 1994)

———. *The Weaker Vessel: Women's Lot in Seventeenth-Century England* (London: Phoenix, 2009)

———. *My History: A Memoir of Growing Up* (London: Weidenfeld & Nicolson, 2015)

Fraser, Sarah *The Prince Who Would be King* (London: Collins, 2017)

Fraser, Sir William (ed) *The Sutherland Book, Volume I – Memoirs* (Edinburgh: 1892) [Sutherland book]

———. (ed) *The Sutherland Book, Volume II – Correspondence* (Edinburgh: 1892) [Sutherland book, vol 2]

Fraser-Mackintosh, Charles (ed) *Letters of Two Centuries: Chiefly connected with Inverness and the Highlands, from 1616 to 1815* (Inverness: A & W Mackenzie, 1890)

Gardner, Alexander (ed) *The Ballad Minstrelsy of Scotland* (London: 1893)

Goldring, Elizabeth *Nicholas Hilliard: Life of an Artist* (London: Yale University Press, 2019)

Goodman, Ruth *How To Be A Tudor* (Penguin, 2016)

Gordon, Robert *A Genealogical History of the Earldom of Sutherland, from its origin to the year 1630, with a continuation to the year 1651* (London: Forgotten Books, 2017). Also consulted: Glasgow University edition; online edition via Google Books. [Robert]

Gore-Brown, Robert *Lord Bothwell* (Glasgow: Collins, 1937)

Graham, Roderick *An Accidental Tragedy: The Life of Mary, Queen of Scots* (Edinburgh: Birlinn, 2008)

Grant, M.W. 'Golspitour: a forgotten house in Sutherland' in *Golspie: miscellaneous material* (Sutherland: 1979) (Highland Libraries notes) [Grant (Golspitour)]

Grimble, Ian *Chief of Mackay* (Edinburgh: Saltire Society, 1993)

Gunn, George *The Province of the Cat* (Isle of Lewis: The Islands Book Trust, 2015)

Guy, John *My Heart is my Own: The Life of Mary Queen of Scots* (London: Harper Perennial, 2004)

The Duke of Hamilton *Maria R: Mary Queen of Scots: The crucial years* (Edinburgh: Mainstream, 1991)

The Marquess of Huntly *The Cock o' the North: The Story of the Gordons* (London: Butterworth, 1935)

Inverness Field Club *The Seventeenth Century in the Highlands* (Inverness: Inverness Field Club, 1986)

Lewis, John and Denys Pringle *Spynie Palace and the Bishops of Moray, History, Architecture and Archaeology* (Edinburgh: Society of Antiquaries, 2002)

Licence, Amy *In Bed With the Tudors* (Stroud: Amberley, 2013)

Mackenzie, George of Rosehaugh *The Laws and Customs of Scotland in Matters Criminal, 1678* (facsimile copy) (New Jersey: The Lawbook Exchange, 2005) [Mackenzie's Criminals]

Marshall, Rosalind K. *Virgins and Viragos: A History of Women in Scotland from 1080 to 1980* (Chicago: Academy Chicago, 1983)

———. *Queen Mary's Women* (Edinburgh: John Donald, 2006)

———. *St Giles: The Dramatic Story of a Great Church and its People* (Edinburgh: St Andrews Press, 2009)

———. *John Knox* (Edinburgh: Birlinn, 2013)

———. *Mary of Guise: Queen of Scots* (Edinburgh: NMS Enterprises, 2017)

Matthew, David *Scotland Under Charles I* (London: 1955)

Miller, James *Swords for Hire* (Edinburgh: Birlinn, 2007)

Monro *His Expedition with the Worthy Scots Regiment (called Mac-Keyes Regiment) levied in August 1626* (London: William Jones, 1637) [Monro's Expedition]

Porter, Linda *Crown of Thistles* (London: Macmillan, 2013)

Potter, Harry *Bloodfeud: The Stewarts and Gordons at War in the age of Mary Queen of Scots* (Stroud: Tempus, 2002)

————. *Edinburgh Under Siege 1571–1573* (Stroud: Tempus, 2003)

Reid, Steven and Miles Kerr-Paterson *James VI and Noble Power in Scotland 1578–1603* (London: Routledge, 2017)

Ring, Morgan *So High a Blood: The Life of Margaret, Countess of Lennox* (London: Bloomsbury, 2018)

Robertson, Barry *Lordship and Power in the North of Scotland: The Noble House of Huntly, 1603–1690* (Edinburgh: Birlinn, 2011)

Sanderson, Margaret *Mary Stewart's People: Life in Mary Stewart's Scotland* (Edinburgh: The Mercat Press, 1987)

Scott, Elizabeth *The Best Soldier* (Hawick: Buchan-Hepburn Publishers, 2011)

Shapiro, James *1606: Shakespeare and the Year of Lear* (London: Faber & Faber, 2015)

Simpson, Grant *Scottish Handwriting 1150–1650: An Introduction to the Reading of Documents* (Edinburgh: Bratton, 1973)

Smout, T.C. (ed) *People and Woods in Scotland: A History* (Edinburgh: EUP, 2003)

Stuart, John *A Lost Chapter in the History of Mary Queen of Scots Recovered* (Edinburgh: Edmonston and Douglas, 1874)

Taylor, Alasdair and Hetty *The Ogilvies of Boyne* (Aberdeen: AUP, 1933)

Thomas, Andrea *Glory and Honour: The Renaissance in Scotland* (Edinburgh: Birlinn, 2013)

Thomson, Oliver *From the Bloody Heart: The Stewarts and the Douglases* (Gloucester: Sutton Publishing, 2003)

Watson, Godfrey *Bothwell & the Witches* (London: Robert Hale, 1975)

Weir, Alison *Mary Queen of Scots and the Murder of Lord Darnley* (London: Pimlico, 2004)

Wightman, Andy *The Poor Had No Lawyers: Who Owns Scotland (And How They Got It)* (Edinburgh: Birlinn, 2011)

Williams, Kate *Rival Queens: The Betrayal of Mary, Queen of Scots* (London: Arrow, 2019)

Wormald, Jenny *Mary Queen of Scots: A Study in Failure* (Edinburgh: John Donald, 2017)

Worthington, David *British and Irish Experiences in Central Europe, c.1560–1688* (Surrey: Ashgate, 2012)

Yellowlees, Michael *'So strange a monster as a Jesuiste': The Society of Jesus in Sixteenth-Century Scotland* (Argyll: House of Lochar, 2003)

Young, Michael B. *King James and the History of Homosexuality* (Fonthill, 2016)

Zuvich, Andrea *Sex and Sexuality in Stuart Britain* (Yorkshire: Pen & Sword, 2020)

Primary sources
NLS = National Library of Scotland

Sutherland Papers
Household and Personal Papers to 1703:
NLS Dep 313/487 Jean Gordon letters

Gordon Cumming of Altyre and Gordonstoun Papers
Marriage Settlements and Wills:
NLS Dep 175/63/1 Marriage certificate of Alexander Ogilvie of Boyne and Jean Gordon Countess of Sutherland, 1599.
Correspondence – NLS Dep 175/65 – Letters, 1608–1638:
NLS Dep 175/65/2 Letter concerning delivery of gold chain to Robert Gordon
NLS Dep 175/65/68 Letter from Earl of Caithness to Robert Gordon
NLS Dep 175/65/79 Letter from Robert to the Forbes
NLS Dep 175/65/81 Letter from Robert to the Forbes
NLS Dep 175/65/90 Letter from Donald Mackay to Jean Gordon Countess of Sutherland
Correspondence – NLS Dep 175/79 – Letters, no date:
NLS Dep 175/79/4773 Letter from Jean Gordon to Robert Gordon
NLS Dep 175/79/4792 Letter from Lucie Gordon to Robert Gordon
NLS Dep 175/79/4793 Letter from Lucie Gordon to Robert Gordon
Papers of Sir Robert Gordon:
NLS Dep 175/85/1 accounts: "The Rentall of the Erldome of Sutherland"
Literary papers:
NLS Dep 175/89/4 Alex Ogilvie's herbal – "A collection of the names of herbes..."
NLS Dep 175 Acc 10824, Box 2 – 'Robert's final letter of advice'
NLS Dep 175 Acc 10824, Box 3
NLS, MS 3804.1743–1825 Catalogue of books belonging to Sir Robert Gordon of Gordonstoun, Baronet, 1743

Selected Bibliography

Inverness Burgh Court books 1576–1578, 1602–1621, Highland Archive Centre

Margaret MacDougall collection, REF D390/5/2, Highland Archive Centre

Case of Sir James Sinclair of Mey Baronet, Asserting His Right to the Title & Dignity of the Earl of Caithness (family tree), D1189/1/1, Highland Archive Centre

Guide books, pamphlets etc.

Aitken, Jacqueline E. *Salt Pans, Brora Back Beach, Clyne, Sutherland: A Report on the History of the Salt Pans and Summarised Survey Report – June 2004* (Clyne Heritage Society/Shorewatch, 2005)

Simpson, Rev. James A. *Dornoch Cathedral: Glory of the North* (Derby: Pilgrim Press, 1989) [Rev Simpson]

Lord Strathnaver (ed) *Dunrobin Castle: Jewel in the Crown of the Highlands*, (Derby: Dunrobin Castle, 2003)

Sutherland, Iain *Sinclair & Girnigoe Castles* (Wick: Signal Enterprises) [Sutherland "Sinclair ..."]

Tabraham, Chris (ed) *Crichton Castle* (Hawick: Historic Scotland, 1996) [Tabraham, Crichton]

———. (ed) *Huntly Castle* (Historic Scotland, 1996) [Tabraham, Huntly]

"Singing the Reformation: Celebrating Thomas Wode and his Partbooks 1562–92" (Edinburgh: Wode Psalter Project Team, 2011) – booklet to accompany exhibition in the Main Library, University of Edinburgh 6 August–28 October 2011. [Wode]

Essays/Articles

Allan, David '"Ane Ornament to Yow and Your Famelie": Sir Robert Gordon of Gordonstoun and the "Genealogical History of the Earldom of Sutherland"' in *The Scottish Historical Review*, Vol 80, no 209, Part 1 (April 2001), pp24–44, Edinburgh University Press

Anderson, John 'On the Site of Macbeth's Castle at Inverness' in *Archaeological Scotia: or Transactions of the Society of Antiquaries of Scotland*, Vol III, Edinburgh, 1831, pp234–44

Beveridge, John 'Lady Anne Bothwell: The Scottish Lady' in *The Scottish Historical Review*, Vol 1, No $ (Jul 1904), pp379–88, Edinburgh University Press. Accessed via jstor.org [Beveridge, 1904]

———. 'The Scottish Expedition in Norway IX 1612', accessed via https://www.electricscotland.com/history/articles/norway1612.htm [Beveridge]

Brill, E.V.K. 'Bothwell, Hemelingk and the Pelikan' in *Shetland Life*, March 1996, accessed via Yahoo group

Brochard, Thomas 'Exile and Return from the Far North of Scotland from the Reformation to the Revolution' pp19–39, Études Écossaises 13, 2010, accessed via https://etudesecossaises.revues.org/215 [Brochard, 2010]

——. 'Scottish Witchcraft in a Regional and Northern European Context: The Northern Highlands, 1563–1660' in *Magic, Ritual and Witchcraft*, Vol 10, No 1, Summer 2015, pp41–74, University of Pennsylvania Press, accessed via http://www.academia.edu [Brochard (Scottish Witchcraft), 2015]

——. 'The Integration of the Elite and Wider Communities of the Northern Highlands, 1500–1700: Evidence from Visual Culture' in *Northern Scotland 6*, 2015, pp1–23. [Brochard (The Integration of the Elite), 2015]

——. 'The socio-economic relations between Scotland's northern territories and Scandinavia and the Baltic in the sixteenth and seventeenth centuries' in *The International Journal of Maritime History*, 2014, Vol 26 (2) 210–34. [Brochard, 2014]

Cheape, Hugh 'Caisteal Bharraich, Dun Varrich and the Wider Tradition' in *Northern Studies* Vol 30, 1993, pp53–62, accessed via https://www.ssns.org.uk

Clarke, Dr Neil 'An expert guide to gold mining in Scotland' in *History Scotland*, 21st March 2014, accessed via https://www.historyscotland.com

Corporaal, Marguerite 'Mary Stewart and Mary Beaton: The Construction of a Female Poetic Voice' in Alasdair A. Macdonald and Kees Dekker (eds) *Rhetoric, Royalty and Reality: Essays on the Literary Culture of Medieval and Modern Scotland* (Paris: Peeters, 2006)

Crawford-Smith, James 'Audrey Hepburn at 90: A Cinderella narrative' in *The Lady* magazine, 19th April 2019, pp10–14

Dawson, Jane 'The Fifth Earl of Argyll and Mary, Queen of Scots', accessed via Futurelearn/University of Glasgow *Early Modern Scottish Palaeography*. [Dawson, Futurelearn]

Duncan, Thomas 'The Queen's Maries' in *The Scottish Historical Review*, Vol 2, No 8 (July 1905), pp363–71, Edinburgh University Press, accessed via jstor.org

Gatherer, W.A. 'Queen Mary's Journey from Aberdeen to Inverness 1562' in *The Scottish Historical Review* XXXIII: 19–21, 1954

Henderson, Jennifer Morag 'How God gave a small Scottish town advance notice of the Gunpowder Plot' in *The National* newspaper, 4th November 2017

Lang, A. 'The Household of Mary Queen of Scots in 1573' in *The Scottish Historical Review*, Vol 2, no 8 (July 1905), pp345–55, Edinburgh University Press, accessed via jstor.org

Lynch, Michael 'Queen Mary's Triumph: The Baptismal Celebrations at Stirling in December 1566' in *The Scottish Historical Review*, Vol 69, no 187, Part 1 (April 1990), pp1–21, Edinburgh University Press, accessed via jstor.org

Malden, Henry Elliot 'Notes on the Family of Betoun in Connection with some royal Letters of James VI' in *Transactions of the Royal Historical Society*, New Series, Vol 7 (1893), pp21–36, Cambridge University Press on behalf of the Royal Historical Society, accessed via jstor.org

Marwick, Sandra *History of the Museum of Edinburgh*, accessed via City Art Centre, Edinburgh

Meikle, Maureen M. 'The Invisible Divide: The Greater Lairds and the Nobility of Jacobean Scotland' in *The Scottish Historical Review*, Vol 71, no 191/192, Parts 1&2 (April–October 1992), pp70–87, Edinburgh University Press, accessed via jstor.org

Murray, Athol 'The Marriage of the Earl of Sutherland, 1567' in *The Scottish Historical Review*, Vol 51, no 152, Part 2 (October 1972), pp237–41, accessed via jstor.org

'"Devoted" countess dies', *Northern Times* newspaper, Friday 3rd December 2019, p1. [Northern Times]

Parker, Heather 'Family, Finance and Free Will: Marriage Contracts in Scotland, c.1380–1500' in *Scottish Archives* 2012, Vol 18, pp10–24, The Scottish Records Association

Potter, Harry 'The Douglas Wars' in *History Scotland*, Vol 6, no 1, January /February 2006, pp27–33

———. 'The Siege of Edinburgh Castle, 1573' in *History Scotland*, Vol 6, no 3, May/June 2006, pp26–34 [Potter, 2006 (2)]

Roberts, Alasdair 'The Knights of the Mortar: An Alternative Suggestion' in *The Scottish Historical Review*, Vol 79, no 207, Part 1 (April 2000), pp82–6, Edinburgh University Press, accessed via jstor.org

Steer, Francis W. 'A Map Illustrating the Siege of Leith, 1560', accessed via Museum of Edinburgh

Stevenson, David 'What was the Quest of the Knights of the Mortar? An indelicate Suggestion' in *The Scottish Historical Review*, Vol 68, no 186, Part 2 (October 1989), pp182–4, Edinburgh University Press, accessed via jstor.org

Sutherland, George M. 'George, Fourth Earl of Caithness of the Sinclair Line' in Alexander MacBain (ed) *The Celtic Magazine*, Vol XII (1889), pp465–470, A & W Mackenzie, Inverness

Worthington, David 'Ferries in the Firthlands: Communications, Society and Culture along a Northern Scottish Rural Coast, c.1600 to c. 1809' in *Rural History* (2016) 27, 2, Cambridge University Press

Online resources (including books, articles, websites etc.)
Charles, XI Marquis of Huntly etc. (ed) *The Records of Aboyne* (Aberdeen: New Spalding Club, 1894), accessed via the National Library of Scotland, www.nls.uk [Aboyne]
Amos, Ilona 'Scottish skies lit with fireworks over 500 years ago', Monday 31st August 2015, *The Scotsman* website [Amos]
Bannatyne, Robert *Memoriales of Transactions in Scotland* (Edinburgh: Bannatyne Club, 1836), accessed via Google Books. [Bannatyne] inc. 'The maner of the Erle of Huntlies Death' p333
Banffshire Reporter 26th August 1903, on http://toonloon.bizland.com/ppap/?page_id=1112 [Banffshire Reporter]
BBC website – article on St Monan's Salt Mill, Fife [BBC, St Monan's Salt Mine]
BBC News website 'America colonisation "cooled Earth's climate"', Jonathan Amos, 31st January 2019 [Amos, BBC]
BBC News website 'Mary Queen of Scots documents found at Museum of Edinburgh' [BBC MQS documents article]
Repp (ed) *Les Affaires du Comte de Boduel* (Edinburgh: Bannatyne Club, 1829) [Boduel]
The Breadalbane Collection, School of Divinity, University of Edinburgh https://www.ed.ac.uk/divinity/research/resources/breadalbane
Calendar of State Papers (Foreign), accessed via British History Online, www.british-history.ac.uk [CSP]
Joseph Bain (ed) *Calendar of the State Papers relating to Scotland and Mary, Queen of Scots 1547–1603*, Vol 1 1547–1563 (Edinburgh: HM General Register House, 1898) [CSPS]
Balfour Paul, Sir James (ed) *The Scots Peerage, founded on Wood's Edition of Sir Robert Douglas's Peerage of Scotland, Vol IV* (Edinburgh: David Douglas, 1907) [Balfour Paul]
Cameron, Annie I. (ed) *The Scottish Correspondence of Mary of Lorraine* (Edinburgh: Scottish History Society, third series, Vol x, 1927) [Guise correspondence]
Capital Collections online, the image library for the collections of Edinburgh Libraries and Museums and Galleries, Mary Queen of Scots documents from the Museum of Edinburgh. Item no 50642, Accession number HH163: document signed by Mary and Bothwell

Ceol Sean: Online Bagpipe Music: https://ceolsean.net/home.html

————. 'Historical and Traditional Notes on the Piobaireachds, no III (Donald Duaghal Mackay's Lament) p5

The Diary of Robert Birrel, burges of Edinburgh, 1532–1605 in Dalyell, John Graham (ed) *Fragments of Scottish History* (Edinburgh: Archibald Constable, 1798), accessed via NLS [Dalyell]

Dictionaries of the Scots Language online https://dsl.ac.uk/ [DSL]

A Diurnal of Remarkable Occurents that have passed within the country of Scotland since the death of King James the Fourth till the year MDLXXV (Edinburgh: The Bannatyne Club, 1833), accessed via archive.org [Diurnal]

Douglas, Robert *The Peerage of Scotland* (Edinburgh: R Fleming, 1764) [Douglas Peerage]

Futurelearn Course: University of Glasgow *Early Modern Scottish Palaeography: Reading Scotland's Records*. Course leader Dr Scott Spurlock

Graham, Harry *A Group of Scottish Women* (New York: Duffield & Co, 1908), accessed via www.electricscotland.com

Grant, James *Memorials of the Castle of Edinburgh* (Edinburgh: William Blackwood, 1850), accessed via archive.org

Hannan, Martin 'Celebrating the other Bard: Did Shakespeare visit Scotland?', 15th October 2016, *The National* [Hannan]

Lord Herries *Historical Memoirs of the Reign of Mary Queen of Scots, and a portion of the reign of King James the Sixth* (Edinburgh: 1836) [accessed via NLS] [Herries]

Highland Historic Environment Record https://her.highland.gov.uk/Monument/MHG9420 (The Flight Cairn, Carn-Teicheadh)

Historic Environment Scotland Battlefield Inventory http://portal.historic-environment.scot/designation/BTL33 (Glenlivet)

Weir, Dalton 'The Original Rocketmen of Scotland', 1st November 2019 https://blog.historicenvironment.scot/2019/11/original-rocketmen-scotland/ [Historic Scotland]

The Internet Archive – https://archive.org – online versions of *The Sutherland Book*, etc.

Knox, John *The History of the Reformation of Religion in Scotland* (Glasgow: Blackie, Fullarton & co, 1831), accessed via archive.org

Labanoff, Alexandre *Lettres, instructions et memoires de Marie Stuart, reine d'Ecosse* (London: Charles Dolman, 1844), accessed via archive.org

Laing, Malcolm *The History of Scotland from the Union of the Crowns on the Accession of James VI to the Throne of England to the Union of the*

Kingdoms in the Reign of Queen Anne with a Preliminary Dissertation on the Participation of Mary, Queen of Scots, in the Murder of Darnley, Vol 1 (London: Mawman, 1819), accessed via Google Books

Mackay, A.E. (ed) *Robert Lindsay's The History and Chronicles of Scotland* (Edinburgh: Blackwood & sons, 1899) [Lindsay]

Macdonald, Mary A. 'Bits and Pieces about Portsoy', 1962 (booklet), quoted on http://toonloon.bizland.com [Macdonald]

MacGibbon, D. and T. Ross *The Castellated and Domestic Architecture of Scotland from the Twelfth to the Eighteenth Century* (1887), quoted on http://www.walkhighlands.co.uk/Forum/viewtopic.php?f=9&t=25079

Mackay, Robert *The History of the House and Clan of Mackay* (Edinburgh: 1829), accessed via archive.org [Mackay book]

Marwick, J.D. (ed) *Extracts from the Records of the Burgh of Edinburgh 1557–1571* (Edinburgh: Scottish Burgh Records Society, 1875)

Melville, Sir James *Memoirs of his Own Life* (Edinburgh: Bannatyne Club, 1827)

National Galleries of Scotland – pages on Adam de Colone and George Jamesone www.nationalgalleries.org [Nat Gall online]

National Portrait Gallery of Scotland, accessed via artuk.org

National Record of the Historic Environment, Castle Sinclair Girnigoe, Boyne Castle, Greamachary [Canmore]

Nau, Claude *The History of Mary Stewart: From the Murder of Riccio Until Her Flight into England* (Edinburgh: William Paterson, 1883), accessed via archive.org

Oxford Dictionary of National Biography, accessed via the National Library of Scotland, NLS [ODNB]

Confession of French Paris, accessed via private email group. [Confession of French Paris]

The Peerage website www.thepeerage.com [Peerage online]

Pitcairn, Robert (compiled by) *Ancient Criminal Trials in Scotland: 1488–1542,* Vol III, Part 1, (Edinburgh: Bannatyne Club, 1833)

Portsoy Past and Present website http://toonloon.bizland.com/ppap

Robertson, James Irvine 'The Four Marys' in *Scotland Magazine,* Issue 63 www.scotlandmag.com/magazine/issue63/12010371.html [Robertson, Scotland Magazine].

Rogart Historical Society Facebook page post, 'Rogart Minister Involved in Riot' 27th September 2018, quoting also 'The Gobha Gorm and the Pape Riots' in North Tolsta Historical Society newsletter. [Rogart Historical Society]

Lord Ruthven *The Rizzio Murder: Account by Lord Ruthven One of the Chief Culprits*, accessed via www.marie-stuart.co.uk [Ruthven account]

Scottish Castles Association website https://www.scottishcastlesassociation.com/

'Did William Shakespeare visit Scotland to win over James VI', 22nd September 2017, *The Scotsman*, https://www.scotsman.com/whats-on/did-william-shakespeare-visit-scotland-win-over-james-vi-1439127 [Scotsman]

Sharpe's Peerage of the British Empire, Vol 2 (London: John Sharpe, 1830), accessed via Google Books. [Sharpe]

Shorewatch website: Recording the eroding archaeology of Scotland's coasts – The Brora Saltpans www.shorewatch.co.uk/brora [Shorewatch] including 2004 report (revised 2005) on the History of the Salt Pans by Jacqueline E. Aitken. [Brora Survey Report]

Miscellany of the Spalding Club Vol 4 (Aberdeen: William Bennet, 1849), accessed via the NLS [Spalding Misc]

Spence, James *Ruined Castles in the Vicinity of Banff* (1873) quoted on http://toonloon.bizland.com/ppap/?page_id=1112 [Spence]

The Survey of Scottish Witchcraft, 1563–1736. By Julian Goodare, Lauren Martin, Joyce Miller and Louise Yeoman, Edinburgh University, January 2003 [Survey of Scottish Witchcraft]

Fraser, Sir William *The Sutherland Book Vol I: Memoirs* (Edinburgh: 1892) [Sutherland book] [accessed via archive.org, also consulted in Highland Archive Centre and NLS]

———. *The Sutherland Book Vol II: Correspondence* (Edinburgh: 1892) [Sutherland book, vol 2] [accessed via archive.org, also consulted in Highland Archive Centre and NLS]

Nair, Rupam Jain 'Salt mining leaves bitter taste for Indian workers' *The Telegraph* 24th February 2010

Tobar an Dualchais/Kist o Riches website tobarandualchais.co.uk

Walk Highlands website www.walkhighlands.co.uk

Fraser, James *Chronicles of the Frasers: The Wardlaw Manuscript entitled 'Polichronicon seu Policratica Temporum, or, the True Genealogy of the Frasers'* (Edinburgh: Scottish History Society, 1905), accessed via archive.org [Wardlaw]

Other

Worthington, David, History Scotland lecture on Coastal History, September 2018, Highland Archive Centre

Index

Note: Page numbers followed by 'n' refer to endnotes.

Index

nobles 134
Reformation 19, 304–5
Regents 177
St Bartholomew's Eve Massacre 158

Randolph, Thomas 25, 37, 38, 49, 51, 57,
58, 66, 68, 70, 71, 72, 73, 88, 177,
297, 410n38, 418n21
Reay, Lord *see* Mackay, Donald
Reformation 1, 26, 78, 127–28, 159, 173,
189, 203, 215, 250, 314
Regent Moray – *see* Stewart, James, Lord
(1st Earl of Moray)
Renaissance 20, 74, 98, 348
Rizzio, David 81–84, 87, 89, 109
ambassador of Savoy 81
attracted Mary's attention 81
and Darnley 81–82
death/murder of 5, 80, 85, 103, 108,
134, 145, 146, 159, 417n12
Robert (ship) 130
Robert the Bruce 26
Rokesby, Christopher 128, 425n11
Romeo and Juliet (Shakespeare) 287
Ross, David, of Balnagowan 207, 208,
281, 293, 306, 319, 448n29
Ross, George, Laird of Balnagowan 207,
208, 229, 251, 280–81,
Caithness and Sutherland and 246, 281
unhappy with Alexander 241
and Wicked Earl George 281
Ross-shire 207, 319
Rothiemay 394, 395, 396
Rough Wooing period 16, 23, 24, 78,
406n33
Royal Mile 34, 78, 267
Ruthven, Katherine 439n10
Ruthven, Lord 82, 83, 84, 85, 417n15
fled to England 87
Ruthven Raid, of August 1582 203, 204,
210

salt pans 282–85
A Satire of the Three Estates (play) 405n23
Scott, Elizabeth 471n24
Scott, Walter 16
'Rough Wooing' 16
Seton, George, 7th Lord Seton 79, 98–99,
104
Seton, Marion 147, 149–50
Seton, Mary 89, 424n46

Seymour, Jane 173
Sinclair, Agnes 89, 92, 419n31
Sinclair, Barbara 152, 153, 155, 238,
434n22
Alexander divorce to 168–69
death of 169
Sinclair, David 205
Sinclair, Elizabeth 238, 246
Sinclair, George, 4th Earl of Caithness 84,
108, 145, 146–47, 149, 155, 161
Alexander's wardship 152, 156
buried at Roslin 204
claimed chieftainship of Mackay 180
death of favourite son 180
in Far North 52
informed Alexander about marriage
152
left Dunrobin 170
quarrel with son 155, 157, 179
Sinclair, George, 5th Earl of Caithness
3–4, 179, 208, 210, 213–20, 223,
226–30, 238, 239, 241, 286, 291, 292,
297, 298, 305–6, 313, 321–28, 334,
337–42, 351–52, 357, 364, 374–77,
381, 386, 442n8, 459n16, 461n27,
469n114
and Alexander 243
allies of 227–28
and Arthur Smith 321–24
assembled force to enter Sutherland
243–44
and Caithness and Sutherland 338
Castle Sinclair-Girnigoe 291–92, 322
and Clan Gunn 219
clan troubles 220
debts 376, 377
and Donald Mackay 321, 324, 325, 326,
337–38, 373
and Earl John 296, 311–12
exile in Orkney, self-imposed 376
and Francis 251
and grandfather of 204–5
and James VI 340, 341, 342
lack of money 331, 373
last ignominious retreat 339–40
lost power and revenue 294
and Mackay clan 321
remission from James VI 353
and Robert 324, 326, 374, 375
Ross of Balnagowan and 281
and Sinclair relatives 331–32

500